The Case for Palestine

An International Law Perspective

John Quigley

Duke University Press

Durham & London

2005

© 1990 Duke University Press
All rights reserved
Printed in the United States of America
on acid-free paper ∞
Library of Congress Cataloging-in-
Publication Data appear on the last
printed page of this book.
Revised and expanded edition © 2005

To my parents
John and Ruth Quigley

Contents

Acknowledgments

I am indebted to many persons for intellectual stimulation and factual information that were critical to the writing of this book. A number of Palestinian and Israeli lawyers and political analysts have provided encouragement and source material. My colleagues at the College of Law, Ohio State University, engaged me in productive dialogue. Law students in my international law seminars provided me with new perspectives on points I thought I had solved. The College of Law provided research support and invaluable assistance with computing. Its Law Library staff located publications in libraries around the world.

I profited greatly from the reading of an early draft by Professor Isaak Dore of St. Louis University, Professor Nasila Rembe of the National University of Lesotho, attorney Abdeen Jabara, Rabbi Elmer Berger, Ernest G. Nassar, attorney (and my wife) S. Adele Shank, and my mother Ruth Quigley. Duke University Press's readers saved me from factual errors and pointed me in important new directions. I thank Duke University Press Editor Reynolds Smith for his steadfast support and encouragement, and his help in transforming my original manuscript into a book.

The years following the publication in 1990 of the first edition of this book have witnessed monumental developments in the Israeli-Palestinian conflict. Israel and the PLO agreed to negotiate. They identified issues to be resolved: a division of territory, the status of Jerusalem, Israel's settlements in Gaza and the West Bank, the repatriation of the Palestine Arabs dispersed in 1948 to other countries. Each side formally recognized the other, and a Palestinian authority entered into limited administration of the Gaza Strip and West Bank.

The negotiation process broke down in 2000, however, leading to a disastrous period of lethal violence that brought new suffering and hardship. This tragedy lent new urgency to the attainment of a negotiated peace. To understand the validity of the positions asserted at the negotiation table, one must understand how the conflict developed and how the legal rights of the parties were affected by events. That history, as recounted in the first edition, is retained in this second edition.

I have added an analysis of the legal considerations underlying the issues the parties have identified to be resolved. The impasse in negotiations may be broken sooner if informed opinion from other sources, from governments and from the world public, is brought to bear on the parties. The positions of each side need to be tested in the public arena. It is my hope that this new edition will promote such a process.

Violence at the international level since September 2001 has set the Israeli-Palestinian conflict in a new context of regional, and even worldwide, conflict. The Israeli-Palestinian conflict has become a critical piece in a larger puzzle. Although this book limits itself to the Israeli-Palestinian conflict, these wider ramifications lend an added urgency to the quest for a durable settlement.

In writing this book, I have been acutely aware of the passion that is felt on each side of the Israeli-Palestinian divide. The difference is not confined to what each side sees as desirable outcomes to the conflict but extends to factual disagreements over what has occurred at critical historical junctures. This difference in perception of facts makes it difficult to describe events in a way that will not give rise to objection. I have made every effort to recite only reliably attested facts. Extensive notes allow an interested reader to explore the sources on which the text is based.

The project of presenting a factually accurate picture is not limited to deciding whose facts are correct. Out of all the facts that relate to the conflict, a writer necessarily includes some and omits others. I have attempted to focus on those facts that are most relevant to an assessment of the conflict from the standpoint of legal entitlement.

The issue of legal entitlement is at the heart of the analysis presented in this book. That emphasis is not merely a manifestation of my own professional background. The conflict needs to be resolved, in my estimation, in a manner consistent with the legitimate expectations of the two populations as regards rights of residency, of property, of fair treatment. Those expectations are found in the rules that the world community has developed for the treatment of individuals, for control over territory, and the like. It is a thesis of this book that the rights of the individuals who make up the two populations must be respected in a settlement. My fear is that a settlement that does not respect those rights will not be accepted and may only perpetuate the conflict.

I understand that most writers on the Israeli-Palestinian conflict find an emphasis on legal entitlement to be unrealistic, even counterproductive. They point out that politics has played a decisive role in shaping the conflict and say that if settlement proposals are confined to propositions based in international law, no agreement will be reached. I acknowledge the difficulty of bringing about a settlement based on legal entitlement. At the same time, I remain convinced that a peace not based on justice may turn out to be no peace at all.

Part One

Origins of the Zionist-Arab

Conflict in Palestine

1

Zionist Settlement in Palestine:

The British Connection

... to a good and broad land, a land flowing with milk and honey.—*Holy Bible*, Exodus 3:8

A movement formed in the late nineteenth century among Jews in Europe to establish a Jewish state in Palestine, a land that during the first millenium B.C. had been the site of a Hebrew kingdom. The movement took its name—Zionism—from Mount Zion in Jerusalem, and its purpose was to escape discrimination in Europe. Mass killings of Jews had erupted from time to time going back to the eleventh century during the time of the Crusades when Jews had been forcibly converted to Christianity. In the fourteenth century Jews were held responsible for the Black Death, and large numbers were executed. Jews were frequently expelled from their places of residence, and in many places they were forced to reside in designated sectors.

The French Revolution improved the situation of Jews in Western Europe, but not in Eastern Europe. Most Eastern European Jews lived in Russia or Poland, which was ruled by Russia at the time, and in Russia Jews were by law restricted to residence in a so-called pale, as well as limited in the professions they could pursue. After several decades in which these restrictions were relaxed, in 1881 reactionary Alexander III became tsar and the situation of Jews worsened. Alexander III excluded Jews from the legal profession and from the right to vote in local government assemblies. He reduced the area of the pale and forbade Jews to settle in rural areas, even within the pale. By law he forbade Jews to take Christian given names.[1] Ultimately, serious mob attacks against Jews (pogroms) occurred in Russia and Poland in the late nineteenth century and, as a result of Alexander III's policies, Jews left Russia in large numbers. Most went to the United States, but some went to Palestine.

In 1897 Zionism emerged as a European-wide political movement with the first World Zionist Congress held in Basle, Switzerland, where Theodor Herzl, an editor of the influential Viennese paper, *Neue Freie Presse*, had emerged as a leader. Herzl's 1896 pamphlet *Der Judenstaat* (The State of the Jews) had called for a Jewish state in Palestine, and its publication in Vienna made a great impact. Not surprisingly, Zionism had its strongest following in Russia, but even there it was only one of several nationalist currents in Jewry.[2] Despite the difficult circumstances of life, most Jews remained in Eastern Europe and of those leaving most still preferred the United States.[3]

In Palestine, an Arab-populated country under the Ottoman (Turkish) Empire, Zionist immigrants set up agricultural settlements on purchased land. "From the very beginning," wrote Ariel Hecht, an Israeli analyst of land tenure in Palestine, "it was clear to the leaders of the Zionist movement that the acquisition of land was a sine qua non towards the realisation of their dream."[4] Land was not acquired in a random fashion. The effort, wrote Israeli General Yigal Allon, was "to establish a chain of villages on one continuous area of Jewish land."[5] The Arabs, soon realizing that the immigrant's aim was to establish a Jewish state, began to oppose Zionism.[6] As early as 1891 Zionist leader, Ahad Ha'am, wrote that the Arabs "understand very well what we are doing and what we are aiming at."[7]

In 1901 the World Zionist Organization formed a company, the Keren Kayemeth (Jewish National Fund), to buy land for Jewish settlers.[8] According to its charter, the Fund would buy land in "Palestine, Syria, and other parts of Turkey in Asia and the Peninsula of Sinai."[9] The aim of the Fund was "to redeem the land of Palestine as the inalienable possession of the Jewish people."[10] Fund director, Abraham Granovsky, called "land redemption" the "most vital operation in establishing Jewish Palestine."[11]

The Fund's land could not be sold to anyone and could be leased only to a Jew, an "unincorporated body of Jews," or a Jewish company that promoted Jewish settlement. A lessee was forbidden to sublease.[12] Herzl considered land acquisition under a tenure system that kept it in Jewish hands as the key to establishing Zionism in Palestine. "Let the owners of immovable property believe that they are cheating us," he wrote, "selling us things for more than they are worth. But we are not going to sell them anything back."[13] The Fund thus kept land as a kind of trustee for a future state.[14]

The Fund purchased large tracts owned by absentee landowners. Most of this land was tilled by farmers whose families had held it for generations with possessory rights recognized by customary law. Regrettably for many of these families, in the late nineteenth century Turkey had instituted a land registration system that led to wealthy absentees gaining legal title to land, often by questionable means. After this occurred, the family farmers continued in possession—as tenants—and considered themselves to retain their customary right to the land, although that was no longer legally the case.[15]

At the turn of the century the better farmland in Palestine was being cultivated. In 1882 a British traveler, Laurence Oliphant, reported that the Plain of Esdraelon in northern Palestine, an area in which the Fund purchased land, was "a huge green lake of waving wheat."[16] This meant that the Fund could not acquire land without displacing Arab farmers. A delegate to a 1905 Zionist congress, Yitzhak Epstein, warned: "Can it be that the dispossessed will keep silent and calmly accept what is being done to them? Will they not ultimately arise to regain, with physical force, that which they were deprived of through the power of gold? Will they not seek justice from the strangers that placed themselves over their land?"[17]

An element of the Zionist concept of "land redemption" was that the land should be worked by Jews. This meant that Arabs should not be hired as farm laborers. While this policy was not uniformly implemented, it gained adherence. In 1913 Ha'am objected to it. "I can't put up with the idea that our brethren are morally capable of behaving in such a way to men of another people . . . if it is so now, what will be our relation to the others if in truth we shall achieve power?"[18]

But Herzl viewed the taking of land and expulsion of Arabs as complementary aspects of Zionism. It would be necessary, he thought, to get the Arabs out of Palestine. "We shall try to spirit the penniless population across the border by procuring employment for it in the transit countries, while denying it any employment in our own country. . . . Both the process of expropriation and the removal of the poor must be carried out discreetly and circumspectly."[19] Some Zionist leaders advocated moving Palestine Arabs to neighboring countries by force if necessary.[20] Moshe Menuhin, a student at the Herzlia Gymnasium in Palestine during the early twentieth century, recalled years later that "it was drummed into our young hearts that the fatherland must become ours, 'goyim rein' (free of Gentiles)."[21]

In 1909 the World Zionist Organization formed the Palestine Land Development Company, Ltd., which became the main purchasing agency for the Fund.[22] As land purchases increased, so did Arab opposition to them and, consequently, to Zionism itself.[23] At various locations in northern Palestine Arab farmers refused to move from land the Fund purchased from absentee owners, and Turkish authorities, at the Fund's request, evicted them.[24] Arabs formed societies in Jerusalem and Nablus to raise funds to purchase land that might otherwise be sold to Zionists, and Arab newspapers warned of the danger that Zionism posed to Palestine.[25] In Haifa Arabs formed a society in 1910 to lobby Turkey to prohibit land sales to Zionists,[26] and Arabs boycotted goods produced by the settlers.[27] In 1914 Arabs in Tiberias protested when settlers tried to buy the Huleh marshes, which contained mineral deposits.[28] At times dispossessed Arab farmers raided settlements built on their former lands and Zionist settlers formed a militia that it called Hashomer to defend them.[29]

The indigenous Jews of Palestine also reacted negatively to Zionism. They did not see the need for a Jewish state in Palestine and did not want to exacerbate relations with the Arabs. In 1903 a Zionist group in Palestine tried to convene a "Jewish National Assembly," but they got little response from the indigenous Jewish communities, which were in Jerusalem, Safad, Tiberias, and Hebron.[30]

Zionism emerged just as European nations were dividing Africa.[31] Taking advantage of the European interest in colonization, Herzl sought the backing of European governments in establishing a Jewish state. To European leaders he argued that Zionism would serve their interests in the Middle East.[32] "For Europe," Herzl said, "we could constitute part of the wall of defense against Asia; we would serve as an outpost of civilization against barbarism."[33] Yet Palestine was only one of several possible sites discussed for settlement. In 1903, at Herzl's request, Britain offered Uganda as a Jewish state.[34] The 1903 Zionist congress voted to send a commission there but let the matter drop.[35] In 1904 Herzl approached King Victor Emmanuel III of Italy and asked for Tripoli (north Africa) as a Jewish state. The king refused.[36] To the sultan of the Ottoman Empire, Abdülhamid II, Herzl argued that Jews would help prevent an Arab uprising against the empire.[37]

Herzl approached Britain because, he said, it was "the first to recognize the need for colonial expansion." According to him, "the idea of Zionism, which is a colonial idea, should be easily and quickly understood in England."[38] In 1902 Herzl approached Cecil Rhodes, who had recently colonized the territory of the Shona people as Rhodesia. "You are being invited to help make history," he said in a letter to Rhodes. "It doesn't involve Africa, but a piece of Asia Minor; not Englishmen, but Jews. How, then, do I happen to turn to you since this is an out-of-the-way matter for you? How indeed? Because it is something colonial."[39]

Britain had already shown interest in Palestine. In 1839 Lord Palmerston as foreign secretary had opened a consulate in Jerusalem, instructing it to protect the Jews. Then in 1840 Palmerston proposed to the Ottoman Empire that it encourage settlement of European Jews in Palestine and that Jews be permitted to make complaints against Ottoman officials through the British embassy in Constantinople.[40] While nothing came of this plan, the British consul at Jerusalem carried out Palmerston's directive to assist Jews.[41] When anti-Jewish violence erupted in Damascus in 1840, Britain extended protection to Jews in Palestine.[42]

In encouraging the Jews to look to Britain for aid, Palmerston was following a technique already being used by rival powers. Cultivating a population group was a technique of European intervention in the Middle East in the nineteenth century. France already had client populations in the Levant, and Russia courted the Orthodox population.[43] A protected minority, it was hoped, would be loyal to the protecting power,[44] so Palmerston encouraged Jewish dependence on Britain.[45] This policy, however, was not risk-free. Conflict on protection of minorities precipitated the Crimean War of 1854–56.[46]

The Zionist movement hoped to build on this earlier British interest and on its contemporary needs in the Middle East. After Herzl's death in 1904 Chaim Weizmann assumed the lead.[47] A research chemist, Weizmann did military research for Britain during World War I and gained a position in the British admiralty through Lord Balfour, who was then foreign secretary.[48] Like Herzl, Weizmann argued that sponsorship of Zionism could help Britain. "Should Palestine fall within the British sphere of influence," he wrote to the *Manchester Guardian* in 1914, "and should Britain encourage a Jewish settlement there, as a British dependency, we could have in twenty to thirty years a million Jews out there, perhaps more; they would develop the country, bring back civilization to it and form a very effective guard for the Suez Canal."[49]

As Britain was taking territory from the Ottoman Empire in World War I, Weizmann increased his efforts. In 1917 he convinced Balfour to propose to the cabinet a policy statement in support of Zionism.[50] At Balfour's request Weizmann and Lord Rothschild, who headed the Zionist Federation in Britain, drafted the statement. Balfour convinced the cabinet to approve the statement, which Balfour then issued as a letter to Rothschild. The letter said that Britain "viewed with favor the establishment in Palestine of a national home for the Jewish people, it being clearly understood that nothing should be done which might prejudice the civil and religious rights of existing non-Jewish communities in Palestine, or the rights and political status enjoyed by Jews in any other country."[51] The letter became known as the Balfour Declaration. The next month Britain captured Jerusalem.

The cabinet issued the declaration because it thought that Zionism would help Britain.[52] It hoped that Jewish settlement of Palestine under British auspices would strengthen Britain there.[53] Louis Brandeis, the president of the Zionist Federation of America, said that from his contact with British officials during World War I he became convinced that it was "as much to the interest of Great Britain as to our interest" that "Palestine should be developed by Jews."[54] Sir Ronald Storrs, Britain's military governor of Jerusalem and later of Palestine, said that Zionism "blessed him that gave as well as him that took by forming for England 'a little loyal Jewish Ulster' in a sea of potentially hostile Arabism."[55]

Moreover, the War had demonstrated the importance of oil, and Britain wanted to build a pipeline from Arabian oil fields west to Haifa.[56] Britain's Palestine expert, Sir Mark Sykes, saw in Zionism a vehicle for extending British influence in the Middle East.[57] In 1916 Sykes negotiated with France the secret Sykes-Picot Agreement, which arranged the postwar partition of the Ottoman Empire. The agreement gave Britain the right to build a port at Haifa[58] and called for joint Anglo-French control of Palestine.[59] The cabinet feared competition from France and thought that a Jewish presence in Palestine under British protection would help it solidify control.[60] It also thought that Jewish settlement in Palestine would give Britain a solid base to counterbalance France's control of Lebanon and Syria.[61]

Prime Minister David Lloyd George viewed a Jewish "garrison-colony" in Palestine as a buffer for Egypt and the Suez Canal,[62] a view Weizmann encouraged by offering a Jewish Palestine as "an essential link in the chain of the British Empire." He said that Britain needed, "somewhere in the countries abutting on to the Suez Canal, a base on which, in case of trouble, she can rely to keep clear the road of Imperial communication."[63] A foothold in Palestine would provide protection for Britain's vital Cape-to-Cairo and Cairo-to-India routes.[64]

Britain also had interests relating to the prosecution of World War I, which had not yet ended. It needed to combat pacifism in Russia—Britain's ally—because the Bolshevik party was threatening a separate peace with Germany. The cabinet hoped that, since the Bolshevik Party counted many Jews as members and was anti-Zionist, British support for Zionism would draw Russian Jews away from Bolshevism.[65]

Finally, Britain had a problem gaining the sympathy of neutral-state Jews for its war effort because of Russian anti-Jewish policies.[66] Weizmann said that Britain, in issuing the Balfour Declaration, sought "to win the sympathy of world Jewry, especially of the American Jews."[67] Lloyd George said later that the Zionist leaders had promised, in return for the declaration, to "do their best to rally Jewish sentiment and support throughout the world to the Allied cause." He was satisfied that they had kept their word.[68]

After the decline of colonialism Britain's sponsorship of Zionism would engender dispute over its character. Zionism had been used, said some, as a cover for British imperialism.[69] The political scientist Hannah Arendt, a refugee from Nazi Germany who worked in Jewish relief organizations, found Zionism a movement that originally was idealistic. But she said that "by taking advantage of imperialistic interests," Zionism had "sold out at the very first moment to the powers-that-be." In a reference to Palestine's Arabs, she said that Zionism had "felt no solidarity with other oppressed peoples."[70]

In response, it was argued that British sponsorship did not color Zionism. "Since when," asked the Zionist legal scholar, Nathan Feinberg, "does a humanitarian project cease to be humanitarian and become reprehensible simply because those who support it are likely to derive some political benefit?"[71]

The Balfour Declaration referred to a Jewish "national home" in Palestine. The Zionist aim was to establish a state, as set forth in Herzl's *Der Judenstaat*. "National home" had been used instead of "state" by the first World Zionist Congress, because, with Jews only a small minority in Palestine, political reality dictated a formulation in less forthright terms. The congress conceived "national home" as a step toward statehood.[72]

Britain understood that the World Zionist Organization sought statehood, however, and did not object. Weizmann said that British officials assured him that "national home" meant "a Jewish State."[73] Representing the World Zionist Organization at the Versailles Conference in 1919, Weizmann declared that "when the Jews formed the large majority, they would be ripe to establish such a Government as would answer to the state of the development of the country and to their ideals."[74] Indeed, in the British cabinet Lord Curzon opposed issuance of the Balfour Declaration because he understood the aim to be statehood. He stated, "Here is a country with 58,000 Arabs and 30,000 or is it 60,000 Jews (by no means all Zionists). . . . Acting upon the noble principles of self-determination and ending with a splendid appeal to the League of Nations," we "draw up a document" that is "an avowed constitution for a Jewish state."[75]

The Balfour Declaration was also inexplicit on another point —the territory to which it applied. The declaration referred to a "national home" to be created "in" Palestine. This formulation suggested that it might encompass less than the entire territory of Palestine. But Brandeis told Balfour that, despite this formulation, the organization wanted a state encompassing all Palestine.[76] At Versailles it said that it wanted a state in all of Palestine, plus a strip of southern Lebanon and a strip east of the Jordan River.[77]

Balfour said that Zionism's critics invoked self-determination to argue that Palestine should belong to the majority of its existing population. He conceded that "there is a technical ingenuity in that plea" but argued that "the case of Jewry in all countries is absolutely exceptional. . . . The deep, underlying principle of self-determination really points to a Zionist policy, however little in its strict technical interpretation it may seem to favour it."[78]

"In Palestine," Balfour said, "we do not propose even to go through the form of consulting the wishes of the present inhabitants of the country." Balfour's rationale for disregarding Arab rights was that "Zionism, be it right or wrong, good or bad, is rooted in age-long traditions, in present needs, in future hopes, of far profounder import than the desires of prejudices of the 700,000 Arabs who now inhabit that ancient land."[79] British officials understood that Zionist colonization would take land and resources from Palestine's Arabs. According to Hugh O'Beirne, "All we can do" is to "devise a settlement which will involve as little hardship as possible to the Arab populations."[80]

At the urging of Brandeis, U.S. President Woodrow Wilson had responded to a September 1917 inquiry from Britain by saying that he favored Zionism.[81] Yet Wilson had made self-determination of peoples a major U.S. aim in World War I. Self-determination for peoples of the former Austro-Hungarian and Ottoman empires was seen at the 1919 Versailles Conference as necessary to a lasting peace.[82] A journalist at Versailles, Herbert Gibbons, noted the opposition of Palestine's Arabs to Zionism and asked: "How can we reconcile such a policy in Palestine with the principles for the *world-wide* maintenance of which we have announced that we are fighting?"[83]

Wilson's secretary of state, Robert Lansing, viewed Wilson's backing of self-determination as "fraught with danger." "Will not the Mohammedans of Syria and Palestine rely on it?" he worried. "How can it be harmonized with Zionism, to which the president is practically committed?"[84] In January 1919 a Palestinian Arab Congress was convened in Jerusalem to plan strategy to prevent the takeover of Palestine by the Zionist movement. Delegations represented the major towns of Palestine. Some delegates sought independence for Palestine with British guarantees against Zionist immigration, while others thought that uniting Palestine with Syria would provide better protection against Zionism.[85]

In 1919 Wilson dispatched a fact-finding commission to Palestine. Known as the King-Crane Commission, its report to Wilson confirmed Arab fears. It said that "the Zionists looked forward to a practically complete dispossession of the present non-Jewish inhabitants of Palestine, by various forms of purchase." It recalled Wilson's position in World War I had been that one of the Allies' aims was that territorial settlements should be based on "the free acceptance" by "the people immediately concerned, and not upon the basis of the material interest or advantage of any other nation or people which may desire a different settlement for the sake of its own exterior influence or mastery." The commissioners said that "if that principle is to rule, and so the wishes of Palestine's population are to be decisive as to what is to be done with Palestine," then "the non-Jewish population of Palestine—nearly nine-tenths of the whole—are emphatically against the entire Zionist program."[86]

To respond to this criticism, Weizmann minimized the danger to the Palestine Arabs. He told the Versailles Conference that the "Zionists wished to settle Jews in the empty spaces of Palestine."[87] But elsewhere Weizmann said that Palestine should become "as Jewish as England is English, or America is American."[88]

British and U.S. officials in Palestine foresaw difficulty. The King-Crane Commission telegrammed President Wilson: "We doubt if any British Government or American official here believes that it is possible to carry out Zionist program except through support of large army."[89] Anstruther MacKay, who served as Britain's military governor in Palestine during World War I, said that without military intervention from outside "the scheme of a Jewish state, or settlement, is bound to end in failure and disaster."[90]

A Jewish "national home," it was feared by Arabs and by many Jews, would lead to an ethnically based state. "How could a Jewish Palestine allow complete religious freedom, freedom of intermarriage, and free non-Jewish immigration, without soon losing its very reason for existence?" asked Morris Cohen, an American civil libertarian and an anti-Zionist. "A national Jewish Palestine," he feared, "must necessarily mean a state founded on a peculiar race, a tribal religion, and a mystic belief in a peculiar soil. . . . Zionists are quite willing to ignore the rights of the vast majority of the non-Jewish population of Palestine."[91]

At the time of World War I Zionism still enjoyed little support among Jews. At the Versailles Conference Weizmann claimed to speak for the 96 percent of European Jews who lived in Eastern Europe.[92] "A million Jews," he said, "staff in hand were waiting the signal to move" to Palestine.[93] But in 1927 Weizmann acknowledged that "the

Balfour Declaration of 1917 was built on air . . . I trembled lest the British Government would call me and ask: 'Tell us, what is this Zionist Organisation? Where are they, your Zionists?' . . . The Jews, they know, were against us; we stood alone on a little island, a tiny group of Jews with a foreign past."[94] In the United States few Jews were Zionists.[95] The World Zionist Organization delegation to the Versailles Conference claimed to represent the Jewish population of Palestine,[96] but indigenous Jews there still outnumbered Zionist settlers and opposed Zionism.[97]

2

Zionist-Arab Conflict Under the British

Mandate: The Struggle for Land

Palestine belongs to the Arabs in the same sense that England belongs to the British and France to the French. —Mahatma Gandhi *

In an attempt to prevent wars like the one just ended the Versailles Conference created an international organization of nations, called the League of Nations. One source of international tension was the status of the colonies that Germany and Turkey had held. The peoples of many of those colonies, especially Turkey's colonies, were demanding independence. Yet the Versailles Conference did not opt for independence. Instead, in Article 22 of the covenant it adopted for the League of Nations in 1919, it characterized the peoples of the former German and Ottoman colonies as "not yet able to stand by themselves under the strenuous conditions of the modern world." It said that the states administering them should promote "the well-being and development of such peoples," bearing "a sacred trust of civilization." Administering states, which it referred to as mandatory powers, were to be accountable to the League of Nations.

An assembly of delegates elected that year from Syria, Palestine, and Lebanon, called the General Syrian Congress, denounced Article 22. The delegates said that Article 22 "relegates us to the standing of insufficiently developed races requiring the tutelage of a mandatory power." Fearing that Britain would try to implement the Balfour Declaration, they also rejected "the claims of the Zionists for the establishment of a Jewish commonwealth."

Though Article 22 denied independence to the people of Palestine and other dependent territories, it did recognize them as having an international status. In 1931 the Institute of International Law, a leading academic group, said that a mandate community was a subject of international law, meaning that it had the capacity to bear rights and responsibilities.[2] In 1947 the UN Special Committee on Palestine stated that the mandate system gave "international recognition" to self-determination.[3] By prohibiting the states that took territories from Germany and Turkey from holding them as colonies, the International Court of Justice would say in 1971 that the League rejected the legality of annexation.[4] The League of Nations' Permanent Mandates Commission, which oversaw mandate administration, said that mandatory powers had no right of sovereignty but that the people under the mandate held ultimate sovereignty.[5]

Administering states bore specific responsibilities[6] and the condition of tutelage was temporary.[7] The "ultimate objective," the International Court of Justice would later say, was "the self-determination and independence of the peoples concerned."[8] In determining the fate of the territory after the expiration of the mandate, the wishes of the population were to be the key factor.[9] The League divided the mandate territories into three classes, depending on its assessment of how close the territory was to readiness for independence. Class "A" mandates were the closest to independence, class "C" mandates the farthest from independence. The League made Turkey's former colonies, including Palestine, Class "A" mandates, which it defined as those whose "existence as independent nations can be provisionally recognized."[10]

An opinion rendered in 1920 in a dispute that the League of Nations was handling indicated that self-determination was considered a legal right. The dispute related to the Aaland Islands, which lie between Finland and Sweden. The inhabitants of the Aaland Islands were Swedish. In 1809 Sweden ceded the islands, along with Finland, to Russia. When Finland became independent of Russia in 1917 the islanders asked Finland to return the islands to Sweden. A committee of jurists appointed by the League to give an opinion on the matter said that self-determination did not apply to a people located in a state that, like Finland, is "definitively constituted." The jurists thus concluded that the islanders had no right to separate from Finland. But the jurists said that in a situation of unresolved sovereignty self-determination would apply. They stated that if "territorial sovereignty" is lacking, then "the principle of self-determination may be called into play." Referring to "the principle of recognizing the rights of peoples to determine their political fate," they said that a people in a situation of unresolved sovereignty had a right to choose between "the formation of an independent State" and merger with an existing state.[11]

In 1922, at Britain's request, the League of Nations gave it a mandate to administer Palestine. The document formalizing the relationship was called the Mandate for Palestine, which was a treaty between the League and Britain. The mandate included the words of the Balfour Declaration, just as it was adopted by the British cabinet in 1917.[12] Objections were raised in Britain that to make the Balfour Declaration governing policy in Palestine would violate the self-determination right of the people of Palestine.[13] In the House of Lords a group of members moved that Britain reject the mandate because of the inclusion of the Balfour Declaration. They put their motion to a vote and it carried by 60 votes to 29.[14]

But the British government ignored the Lords and accepted the mandate. The League thus gave its endorsement to the concept of a Jewish national home in Palestine.[15] The scope of that endorsement, however, remained unclear. The Balfour Declaration referred to the "historical connection" of the Jews to Palestine, and Weizmann construed this phrase to mean "that we have the right to establish our national home in Palestine."[16] But it is not clear that "right" was intended. The World Zionist Organization had asked the Versailles Conference to use the phrase "historical right" instead of "historical connection." The conference refused, precisely to avoid recognizing a right.[17]

The League asked the World Zionist Organization to set up an agency to oversee Jewish immigration and settlement. The mandate instrument said that "an appropriate Jewish Agency shall be recognized as a public body for the purpose of advising and cooperating with the Administration of Palestine in such economic, social and other matters as may affect the establishment of the Jewish national home."[18] As its first high commissioner in Palestine, Britain appointed Herbert Samuel, a proponent of Zionism. Weizmann expressed "the hope that Sir Herbert will continue to give his services to the Zionist cause for a long time to come."[19] Weizmann kept convincing Britain of Zionism's utility. He said that Britain had "an interest in Palestine" and a "double and tenfold interest in a Jewish Palestine."[20] He was concerned that some British political figures, like the members of the House of Lords, did not agree. "Maybe the British Empire does need us, but so far not all the factors of British policy have sufficient knowledge of that fact. We try to make them comprehend it."[21]

Norman Bentwich, Britain's attorney general in Palestine, said that Britain as the mandatory power must advance the interests of the Palestine population. The "capitalistic exploitation which marked the development of Africa and the Far East under the protection of European States in the nineteenth century," he declared, was prohibited by the Mandate for Palestine.[22] He said that the mandate system meant the "right of nationalities, great and small, in the East as in the West, to live their national life, and the duty of the greater States to train them to that end."[23] But it was unclear how that would occur in Palestine if a Jewish national home were to be created there.

Backed by the Balfour Declaration, the Jewish National Fund stepped up its land purchasing.[24] In 1920 the World Zionist Organization founded the Palestine Foundation Fund (Keren Hayesod) to finance settlement of land purchased by the Jewish National Fund.[24] From the Hashomer militia, Zionist settlers formed what they called Haganah (self-defense force) to protect their land.[25] Brandeis said proudly that the Arabs "soon realized" that the force "was not to be trifled with."[26] A major function of the Haganah was to decide where the Fund should buy land and build settlements. "A special branch of the General Staff determined the location of each village," said General Allon, to ensure that they would be arrayed in a militarily defensible pattern.[27]

In 1920 the Histadrut, the General Confederation of Hebrew Workers in the Land of Israel, was founded as a nucleus for state-building, with David Ben-Gurion as secretary-general.[28] The Histadrut sought to create an economic infrastructure for a Jewish state and to promote Jewish settlement.[29] Its founding was later called "a central event in the process of the rebirth of the Hebrew people in the fatherland." While the Histadrut organized workers, it was—as explained by Pinhas Lavon, who later would be its secretary-general's secretary—"not a workers' trade union." The Histadrut also tried to organize Arab workers, to convince them not to oppose Zionism.[30] In 1921 Arabs rioted in Jaffa, their largest city, to protest Zionist land purchases. Recognizing the strength of this Arab reaction, Britain in 1922 clarified that the Balfour Declaration did not mean a Jewish state, but rather a "national home," and that the "national home" would not encompass all of Palestine.

Some Zionists were concerned that in its quest to create a Jewish state the Zionist movement was running roughshod over the Arabs. "We think," wrote Ahad Ha'am in a letter to the editor of the newspaper *Ha'aretz* in 1922, "that the Arabs are all savages who live like animals and do not understand what is happening around. This is, however, a great error. . . . What do our brethren do in Palestine? . . . Serfs they were in the lands of the Diaspora and suddenly they find themselves in freedom, and this change has awakened in them an inclination to despotism. They treat the Arabs with hostility and cruelty, and even boast of these deeds; and nobody among us opposes this despicable and dangerous inclination."[31]

The Palestine Arabs saw themselves as subjects of the British Empire and feared becoming subjects of "a protegé—the Zionist movement—of this empire."[32] Quincy Wright, a leading international lawyer, reported after a 1925 visit that the Palestine Arabs regarded the Balfour Declaration as "a gross violation of the principle of self-determination proclaimed by the Allies."[33] Wright found that the Zionist settlers rationalized their takeover on what they argued was "the Jew's superior capacity to utilize the land and resources of Palestine. . . . As Englishmen occupied the lands of the American Indian through their superior ability to utilize them, so someone is going to occupy Palestine. If the Jews did not, the Italians would."[34] Wright found the Balfour Declaration and the mandate to be "political decisions" that were "difficult to reconcile with the claim of the Arab population to self-determination."[35]

During the 1920s the British government permitted the Jewish Agency to bring settlers into Palestine. The settlers needed land so the Jewish National Fund—as earlier—through its Palestine Land Development Company purchased land primarily from absentee owners.[36] Arab tenant farmers, however, often refused to vacate this land. Purchasers sued in the British courts, which stated that the farmers had no right to remain.[37] Nevertheless, the British government recognized the displacement as a problem, and in 1929 it enacted the Protection of Cultivators Ordinance, which required purchasers to compensate evicted tenant farmers.[38]

The settlement and land purchases, undertaken now with British backing, heightened the concern of the Palestine Arabs that their country might be taken from them. In 1929 conflict over access to the Holy Places in Jerusalem led to attacks by Palestine Arabs on Jewish settlements, resulting in the deaths of 133 Jews.[39] A British commission appointed to study the incidents (the Shaw Commission) found the cause of the discontent to be "the twofold fear of the Arabs that by Jewish immigration and land purchase they may be deprived of their livelihood and in time pass under the political domination of the Jews."[40]

The Jewish Agency denied that land purchases were displacing Arab tenant farmers.[41] It said, moreover, that the purchases were lawful and were made from willing sellers. "A Jew must be able to buy land from an Arab," according to Weizmann, "and must not be made responsible for what may or may not happen to the willing seller."[42] But the Fund was purchasing prime agricultural land.[43] To the Palestine Arabs the purchases represented a colonialist seizure of their land, even though the land was handed over by willing sellers.[44] They pointed out that in many other colonial situations land was acquired by purchase.[45]

The Shaw Commission found that the farmers' situation was "acute." It declared, "there is no alternative land to which persons evicted can remove."[46] It found "an acceleration of a process which results in the creation of a large discontented and landless class" and "no further land available which can be occupied by new immigrants without displacing the present population." The commission called for policy changes to avert "further calls upon the police to carry out evictions of large bodies of cultivators with no alternative land to which they can be moved or upon which they can settle."[47] It recommended limits on Zionist land purchases[48] and on immigration to Palestine.[49]

Britain's high commissioner for Palestine, John Chancellor, recommended total suspension of Jewish immigration and land purchase to protect Arab agriculture. He said, "all cultivable land was occupied; that no cultivable land now in possession of the indigenous population could be sold to Jews without creating a class of landless Arab cultivators." He recommended legislation "to insure that the indigenous agricultural population shall not be dispossessed of its land and to prevent the creation of a class of landless peasantry." The Colonial Office rejected the recommendation.[50]

A follow-up British government investigation later in 1930 (the Hope Simpson Commission) also found Arab landlessness as a result of Zionist land purchases. "Of 688 Arab families which cultivated in the villages of the Vale of Esdraelon which were purchased and occupied by Jews," said the commission, "only 379 are now cultivating the land."[51] "It is an error to imagine that the Government is in possession of large areas of vacant lands which could be made available for Jewish settlement. In fact free areas are negligible in extent."[52]

But Britain did not act on this finding. In a letter to Weizmann, dated February 13, 1931, Prime Minister Ramsey MacDonald said that Britain would not limit Jewish immigration or settlement and would not restrict land sales to Jews.[53] A new British inquiry in 1932, using a stricter definition of displacement, found Arab landlessness less significant than had the Shaw and Hope Simpson commissions.[54] But Arthur Ruppin, who headed land purchasing for the Fund, acknowledged that his land purchasing dispossessed Arab farmers. In 1930 he said, "What remains is densely populated land";[55] and in 1936: "On every site where we purchase land and where we settle people the present cultivators will inevitably be dispossessed." There is "no alternative, but that lives should be lost. It is our destiny to be in a state of continual warfare with the Arabs."[56]

As Zionist settlement progressed, Ben-Gurion acknowledged the rights of the Palestine Arabs that were in jeopardy. In a 1931 lecture in Berlin he said, "we are entirely for the right to self-determination of all peoples, of all individuals, of all groups, and it follows that the Arab in Palestine has the right to self-determination." He said that the Arabs' desire for self-determination "will create serious difficulties for us," but that "this is not a reason to deny their rights."[57]

In the early 1930s, as anti-Semitism grew in Germany, Britain allowed immigration at levels that doubled the Jewish population of Palestine between 1931 and 1935.[58] That influx increased the Jewish share of Palestine's population to 30 percent. With the population increase, Britain allowed substantial new land purchases.[59]

Some displaced Arab farmers took jobs as agricultural laborers in Zionist settlements, but the Histadrut, trying to create a Jewish society in Palestine, picketed Jewish employers who hired Arabs. In some cases it sent mobile units to work sites to evict Arab workers by force.[60] A picket organizer explained, "we stood guard at the orchards to prevent Arab workers from ever getting jobs there." The

Histadrut also encouraged Jews not to purchase Arab products. Boycott organizers poured kerosene on Arab tomatoes, attacked Jewish housewives in the markets and smashed the Arab eggs they bought.[61] As a result of this pressure, many Zionist settlers stopped hiring Arab farm workers.[62]

These tactics were later described by a British government inquiry as "a movement to intimidate those Jewish farmers who employ Arab labour." The picketing and pressure led the government to adopt the Prevention of Intimidation Ordinance of 1927.[63] The Arab Executive—an Arab political group—was one of the more prominent elements that protested the Jewish labor policy.[64]

But the Jewish Agency Constitution of 1929 required that only Jews be hired on Jewish National Fund land. Its policy stated, "the Agency shall promote agricultural colonization based on Jewish labour, and in all works and undertakings carried out or furthered by the Agency, it shall be a matter of principle that Jewish labour shall be employed."[65] The Fund drafted a model lease that stipulated: "The lessee undertakes to execute all works connected with the cultivation of the holding only with Jewish labour. . . . Where the lessee has contravened the provisions of this Article three times the Fund may apply the right of restitution of the holding, without paying any compensation whatever."[66]

Attorney General Bentwich called the Jewish labor policy "economic apartheid"and said that it strengthened Arab resistance to Zionist immigration.[67] In 1931 British historian Arnold Toynbee said that the land purchases and Jewish labor policy were creating "an exclusive preserve for the Jews, what in South Africa is called segregation."[68] The Hope Simpson Commission said that Fund land "ceases to be land from which the Arab can gain advantage either now or at any time in the future. Not only can he never hope to lease or to cultivate it, but, by the stringent provisions of the lease of the Jewish National Fund, he is deprived forever from employment on that land."[69] A British-U.S. inquiry found that the Jewish labor policy widened the economic difference between Jew and Arab by keeping Arabs from many jobs.[70]

The Hope Simpson Commission said that the Jewish labor policy violated Britain's obligation under Article 6 of the Mandate for Palestine to protect "the rights and position of other sections of the population." The commission said the "persistent and deliberate boycott of Arab labour in the Zionist colonies is not only contrary to the provisions of that article of the Mandate," but "a constant and increasing source of danger to the country."[71]

There was a certain idealism, to be sure, behind the Jewish labor policy. It was viewed by some not as segregation but as a measure to avoid a society of European Jews exploiting Arab workers.[72] Advocates of the policy argued that it negated any colonial aspect in Zionism, since exploitation of local labor is a hallmark of colonialism. Others countered that colonists had not hired local labor in some colonial situations, such as in North America, the East Indies, Australia, and New Zealand.[73]

As its land purchases increased, the Jewish National Fund acquired tracts in close proximity to each other to create a geographic nucleus for a state.[74] In the 1930s it bought land in the Haifa area, along the Tel Aviv–Jerusalem road, in the Tel Aviv area, and in the Galilee.[75] The Jewish Agency established what it called "stockade and watchtower" settlements on purchased land.[76] These were fortified enclaves in areas where Jews had not lived previously, erected to facilitate the establishment of a state.[77]

Land acquired by the Jewish National Fund could serve as a base for a state because it could not be alienated. In this respect the Fund continued the policy it established before World War I. The 1929 Jewish Agency constitution stipulated that land acquired by the Fund "shall be held as the inalienable property of the Jewish people."[78] The Fund retained ownership and leased to Jews only.[79] By a 1933 amendment to its Memorandum of Association, subleasing was authorized,[80] but its model lease prohibited a lessee from subleasing "to a person or a company to whom the Fund according to its Memorandum of Association is prohibited from leasing its land."[81] The Memorandum of Association permitted leasing only to Jews, unincorporated bodies of Jews, and Jewish-owned companies.[82]

The Palestine Land Development Company tried to lease land east of the Jordan River from Emir Abdullah, the ruler under British mandate of Transjordan. In 1933 a deal was struck. Abdullah backed out of the deal, however, when the Arab press revealed it. Still, the company secretly paid Abdullah some of the agreed-upon rent moneys in what amounted to a political payment. Abdullah had shown himself willing to make an accommodation with Zionist ambitions, and the Jewish Agency cultivated the relationship.[83]

3

Things Fall Apart:

The Collapse of the British Mandate

All the King's horses, and all the King's men. . . .

The Jewish Agency became a state within a state in Mandate Palestine.[1] Besides being a landowner on a large scale, it financed agricultural settlement and held industrial and commercial enterprises. It was, said the Anglo-American Committee of Inquiry, which Britain and the United States sent to Palestine in 1946, "one of the most successful colonizing instruments in history."[2] Through its access to European wealth and technology and its influence in British political life, the Agency exercised more influence over British policy than did the Arabs.[3] Arab fear that the Agency might seek statehood culminated in 1936 in an Arab revolt against Britain. With a movement based largely in the rural population, the Arabs hoped to pressure Britain to stop Zionist migration and land purchases. Committees emerged in Arab towns to organize commercial strikes and campaigns for nonpayment of taxes.[4] Arab groups raided Zionist settlements, causing civilian deaths.[5] The Haganah, now attached to the Jewish Agency, raided Arab villages, also causing civilian deaths and demolishing houses.[6] In 1937 a new Zionist military group formed called the Irgun Zvei Leumi (National Military Organization), with the aim of using more overt force against the Arabs. For example, Irgun planted bombs in Arab markets.[7]

Britain gave itself extraordinary powers in 1937 to punish Arab rebels by enacting the Defense (Emergency) Regulations, which permitted incarceration without charge and expulsion from the country.[8] As it had done after the 1929 Arab protests, the British government appointed an inquiry commission, the Peel Commission, which issued its report in 1937, and—like the Hope Simpson Commission of 1931—it found land displacement to be the prime Arab concern.

The Peel Commission stated that the criteria for landlessness used in the 1932 land survey were "unduly restrictive," resulting in an understatement of the number of landless Arabs displaced by Zionist land purchases.[9] The commission also declared that Arabs continued to be displaced from land they cultivated[10] and that they could not find alternative land.[11] "The Arab peasant" had "neither the capital nor the education necessary for intensive cultivation. The Jew has. But the lack of these two essential requisites does not justify the expropriation of the Arab to make room for the richer and more enterprising colonist."[12] Arabs demanded a prohibition of land purchases by Zionist organizations, but the purchases continued.[13] A British official described a "filthy tin-can settlement where the evicted Arab peasants huddle under the orange trees."[14]

The Peel Commission also made an important political recommendation. It suggested the partition of Palestine into Arab and Jewish states, the Arab state to be placed under Emir Abdullah of Transjordan.[15] The Peel Commission envisaged the removal—by mutual agreement—of the Arabs who would fall within the envisaged Jewish state and of the Jews who would fall within the envisaged Arab state. According to the commission, there would be 225,000 Arabs in the Jewish state, but only 1,250 Jews in the Arab state.[16] The disparity in numbers indicated that the commission contemplated giving the Jewish state much Arab-populated territory, but not giving the Arab state any Jewish-populated territory.

The Arab Higher Committee, which had been formed in 1936 by several Arab political parties as a voice for Arab interests, called the partition proposal a violation of the Arabs' "basic natural rights" and of their self-determination.[17] The Jewish Agency applauded it but did not abandon its aim of taking all of Palestine. Ben-Gurion viewed a Jewish state in a part of Palestine as a stepping-stone, "a powerful instrument for the total fulfillment of Zionism, an instrument for the redemption of all the Land of Israel."[18] If the Arabs objected to the Agency's expansion beyond the area of partition, Ben-Gurion declared, "our army will be among the world's outstanding."[19] He told the Zionist Executive that "after the formation of a large army in the wake of the establishment of the state, we will abolish partition and expand to the whole of Palestine."[20]

By the "Land of Israel," Ben-Gurion meant Mandate Palestine plus Transjordan and portions of Syria and Lebanon.[21] He told the

World Zionist Congress in Zurich in July 1937: "The mandate in the motherland does not cover the totality of Greater Israel. Have we therefore renounced the right to settle the part of the land of Israel situated outside the zone of the mandate?"[22]

Some Zionist leaders advocated military means to statehood. Irgun leader Vladimir Jabotinsky asked, "Has it ever been known that a people would willingly give up its soil? No more would the Palestine Arabs yield their sovereignty without force."[23] Golda Meir, who headed the Histadrut's political department, said in 1937 that only through war could Zionism establish a state in Palestine.[24]

The Jewish Agency welcomed the Peel Commission's proposal of a population transfer. It began to plan for removal of the Arabs, establishing a Population Transfer Committee.[25] Weizmann urged Britain to buy out Palestine Arabs and relocate them in Transjordan to make more room for Zionist settlement.[26] Ben-Gurion was less optimistic about securing consent to a removal of so many Arabs. He proposed "transferring the Arab populations with their consent or without, and then to enlarge Jewish colonization."[27] "We must expel Arabs and take their places,"[28] but he saw no need to pay compensation.[29] Joseph Weitz, a Jewish National Fund official who directed Zionist settlement, wrote in 1940: "Among ourselves it must be clear that there is no place in the country for both peoples together. . . . With the Arabs we shall not achieve our aim of being an independent people in this little country." Weitz wanted "at least the western part [west of the Jordan River] of Eretz Israel without Arabs." He saw "no other way but to transfer the Arabs from here to the neighbouring countries; transfer all of them, not one village or tribe should remain."[30]

In a 1938 speech to the Workers Party of Eretz Israel (Mapai), of which he was a founder, Ben-Gurion acknowledged the Arab perception of Zionism that had led to the Arab revolt. "We are the aggressors, and they defend themselves." By this time Ben-Gurion was the chairman of the Jewish Agency, and he acknowledged that for the Arabs Palestine "is theirs, because they inhabit it, whereas we want to come here and settle down, and in their view we want to take away from them their country."[31]

Mahatma Gandhi also understood the Arab reaction to Zionism but drew conclusions different from Ben-Gurion's. In 1939 Gandhi, who was trying to secure Britain's withdrawal from India, said, "It is wrong and inhuman to impose the Jews on the Arabs. What is going on in Palestine today cannot be justified by any moral code of conduct. The mandates have no sanction but that of the last war." In a reference to the Peel Commission's partition proposal he said, "It would be a crime against humanity to reduce the proud Arabs so that Palestine can be restored to the Jews, partly or wholly as their national home."[32]

Zionist military prospects were enhanced by the Arab revolt because Britain allowed Jews to arm themselves legally for the first time, and 20,000 Jews came to possess arms. The Haganah began to manufacture arms and to bring them clandestinely from Europe, storing them in secret locations.[33] At the same time Britain disarmed the Arab population to prevent another outbreak of violence. Sentiment for Zionism within European Jewry grew in the 1930s as a result of Nazi policy toward Jews, but most Jews still opposed it.[34] The Jewish Agency and World Zionist Organization tried to ensure that Jews emigrating from Europe would go to Palestine.

When Nazi anti-Jewish policy became apparent, Ben-Gurion anticipated the necessity for Jewish emigration from Germany. He saw an opportunity to get Jews to Palestine and a danger that they might be accepted elsewhere. "Britain is trying to separate the issue of the refugees from that of Palestine," he said, and "it is assisted by anti-Zionist Jews," by which he meant Jews who urged Western countries to accept Jewish refugees. "The dimensions of the refugee problem demand an immediate, territorial solution; if Palestine will not absorb them, another territory will. Zionism is endangered."[35]

In 1938 a thirty-one-nation conference was held in Evian, France, on resettlement of the victims of Nazism. The World Zionist Organization refused to participate, fearing that resettlement of Jews in other states would reduce the number available for Palestine.[36] The German Zionist organization, in its negotiations with Germany to secure emigration of Jews, maneuvered to get the Gestapo to force Jews emigrating from Germany to go to Palestine.[37] Ben-Gurion was also concerned, as he said in a letter to the Zionist Executive in 1938, that "if Jews will have to choose between the refugees, saving Jews from concentration camps, and assisting a national museum in Palestine, mercy will have the upper hand and the whole energy of the people will be channelled into saving Jews from various countries." In that situation Ben-Gurion feared "Zionism will be struck off the agenda not only in world public opinion, in Britain and the USA, but elsewhere in Jewish public opinion. If we allow a separation between the refugee problem and the Palestine problem, we are risking the existence of Zionism."[38]

In November 1938 the British government rejected the Peel Commission's recommendation to partition Palestine. The government explained that partition was "impracticable," by which it meant it could not be forced on the Palestine Arabs.[39] In May 1939 it issued a white paper as a new statement of policy. A single independent state should come into being in Palestine within ten years to be "governed in such a way as to ensure that the essential interests of each community are safeguarded." Immigration of Jews was to be limited to a total of 75,000 for the next five years, and thereafter there was to be no more immigration without the acquiescence of the Arab community. The government again recognized landlessness among Arabs as a critical problem and for the first time called for radical measures to curb it, saying that land sales in areas of extreme land shortage should be prohibited altogether, while in other sectors they should be regulated.[40]

The Jewish Agency took the new policy as an abandonment of Zionism and issued an angry rejection. The Agency said that "Jews would fight rather than submit to Arab rule."[41] The day it was issued the Irgun bombed the Palestine Broadcasting Service office in Jerusalem and attacked the Immigration Office.[42] Mass demonstrations were organized within the city.[43] The Jewish Agency began to organize a military wing to fight the British army,[44] and the Irgun undertook a series of bombings aimed at Arabs—in a movie house, in coffee houses, in public squares.[45] It set a time bomb at the vegetable market in Haifa, killing eighteen Arabs.[46]

Within three months World War II broke out, and the Jewish Agency and the Irgun suspended anti-British agitation, deciding instead to cooperate with Britain against Germany.[47] That shift displeased some Irgun members, who split from the Irgun to continue armed action against Britain. They called their organization Fighters for the Freedom of Israel, which became known by its Hebrew acronym, LEHI, or the Stern Gang, after its founder, Avraham Stern.[48]

Disillusioned with Britain because of the white paper, the Jewish Agency began to look to the United States for support.[49] The Agency needed a new major power to back it and the United States was in any event replacing Britain in the Middle East.[50] Ben-Gurion said of that period: "I no longer doubted that the center of our political work in the international arena had shifted from Britain to the United States, which had firmly grasped world leadership and in which the largest and most influential Jewish concentration in the Diaspora was to be found."[51]

During World War II the Jewish National Fund continued to purchase land.[52] The Haganah, though cooperating with Britain, stole arms from British depots in the Middle East and stockpiled them in Palestine for use after the war.[53] Arab groups also stockpiled weapons.[54]

In May 1942 the American Emergency Committee for Zionist Affairs, meeting at the Biltmore Hotel in New York, declared that its aim was "that Palestine be established as a Jewish commonwealth."[55] This was the first open declaration of an aim to establish a state and to do so in all of Palestine.[56] In October 1944 the American Zionists at their Atlantic City convention called for a "free and democratic Jewish commonwealth" in "the whole of Palestine, undivided, and undiminished."[57] This formulation was adopted in August 1945 at a London meeting of the World Zionist Conference, the policymaking body of Zionism.[58] Meanwhile, LEHI kept up armed attacks to force Britain out of Palestine. In 1944 it tried unsuccessfully to assassinate High Commissioner Harold MacMichael in Jerusalem, but in Cairo it succeeded in assassinating Lord Moyne, the British resident minister in the Middle East.[59]

World War II left a legacy that would influence Palestine's future. As a result of the Nazi genocide, many Jews feared to remain in Central and Eastern Europe. In Poland violence against Jews continued even after the war ended. Arnold Toynbee thought that Britain and the United States should have admitted them since they had been persecuted by another Western country.[60] But no state was willing to accept them.[61]

The Jewish Agency was anxious to get the refugees to Palestine but it was not clear whether a substantial number of them wanted to go there. A U.S. government report found that of the refugees expressing a desire to go to Palestine in 1945, many decided to do so "because they realize[d] that their opportunity to be admitted into the United

States or into other countries in the Western Hemisphere [was] limited, if not impossible."[62]

The Jewish Agency did not encourage Western governments to accept these refugees. To the contrary, it lobbied to deny their admission.[63] Morris Ernst, an advisor to President Franklin Roosevelt, worked unsuccessfully to gain permission for the refugees to enter the United States. He found opposition from U.S. Zionist leaders who wanted to leave the displaced Jews no option other than Palestine. The leaders attacked Ernst "as if I were a traitor," he said. *New York Times* publisher Arthur Sulzberger shared Ernst's view. "Why in God's name should the fate of all these unhappy people be subordinated to the single cry of Statehood?" he asked. Sulzberger said that these "unfortunate Jews" were "helpless hostages for whom statehood has been made the only ransom."[64] Roosevelt reportedly took the decision to refuse admittance to Jewish refugees because of opposition from U.S. Zionist organizations.[65]

In October 1944 Egypt, Iraq, Saudi Arabia, Yemen, Transjordan, Syria, and Lebanon formed the League of Arab States at a meeting in Alexandria, Egypt.[66] In a resolution on Palestine the new organization deplored "the horror and suffering which the Jews of Europe have endured" but said that their situation should not be resolved by inflicting "another injustice at the expense of the Palestinian Arabs."[67] The Arab states found it unfair to "make the Arabs pay for Germany's crimes."[68]

Ben-Gurion visited the United States in 1945 and established a businessman's group that sent arms for the Haganah.[69] As the War ended, the Jewish Agency began a campaign to drive Britain out of Palestine.[70] The Haganah had instituted conscription in the early 1940s and, through thefts from British arms depots, it had increased its hidden stockpile of arms and ammunition.[71] The Irgun joined LEHI, with the secret encouragement of the Haganah.[72] The Haganah began military operations of its own, the three groups coordinating their attacks on bridges, railways, and British army personnel.[73] The most spectacular operation was the Irgun's dynamiting—with Haganah consent—of the British headquarters, located in the King David Hotel in Jerusalem, in July 1946.[74]

While fighting Britain, the Jewish Agency negotiated secretly for a territorial settlement with Abdullah, who in 1946 became king when Britain gave Transjordan its independence.[75] The Agency also kept up the secret payments to Abdullah it had begun in 1933.[76] Abdullah, encouraged by the Peel Commission's suggestion of attaching part of Palestine to Transjordan, hoped to annex a portion of Palestine.[77] The Agency also established new settlements, particularly in the Negev, in preparation for the declaration of statehood. Jewish National Fund Director Granovsky said in October 1946 settlements founded within the past year had resulted in "penetrating boldly and energetically into new districts and decisively changing the map of Palestine."[78] Also in 1945 the Haganah undertook clandestine military maneuvers, which involved simulated assaults on Arab villages.[79]

A major point of tension between Britain and the Jewish Agency was the Agency's efforts to bring Jews into Palestine clandestinely, in violation of the limits set for immigration by Britain. An Agency underground apparatus organized ship transport to Palestine from Mediterranean ports, and the United States pressured Britain to admit more Jews.[80] But Britain took strict measures to stop the immigration and deported Jews who entered Palestine illegally.

To quell the Jewish Agency revolt, Britain used the Defense (Emergency) Regulations. In 1946 Dov Joseph, a future minister of justice of Israel, denounced them before the Jewish Lawyers Association. "There is no guarantee to prevent a citizen from being imprisoned for life without trial," he said. The government may "banish any citizen at any moment." A decision to banish, he complained, was taken administratively: "a man does not actually have to commit an offense; it is enough for a decision to be made in some office for his fate to be sealed." The regulations authorized "collective responsibility," he complained. "All of the six hundred thousand settlers could be hanged for a crime committed by one person."[81]

Yaacov Shapira, another future minister of justice in Israel, said the regulations led to a situation "unparalleled in any civilized country. Even in Nazi Germany there were no such laws." To call the military tribunals that conducted trials under the regulations "courts," he declared, was "mere euphemism."[82] Moshe Dunkelblum, a future judge of the Supreme Court of Israel, said the regulations "violate the basic principles of law, justice, and jurisprudence. They abolish the rights of the individual and grant unlimited power to the administration.[83] The Jewish Lawyers Association demanded repeal of the regulations.[84]

In 1946 the United States and Britain sent the Anglo-American Committee of Inquiry to Palestine to make recommendations for future policy. The committee said that Palestine should be neither Jewish nor Arab but should have a single government. The constitution should protect Jewish rights, so the Jewish minority would not be under the control of the Arab majority, and a UN trusteeship was proposed to facilitate the transition to independence.[85]

The Jewish Agency cited its revolt as proof that Zionism was not a tool of Britain.[86] But other colonizing populations had revolted against the metropole. "The fact that the Jewish community in Palestine afterward fought the British," wrote American journalist I. F. Stone, "is no more evidence of its not being a colonial implantation than similar wars of British colonists against the mother country, from the American Revolution to Rhodesia."[87] Richard Crossman, a British member of the Anglo-American Committee of Inquiry, wrote that despite the revolt the Arabs viewed the "Zionist invasion" as "an act of national and economic oppression of a colonial people."[88]

The Zionist movement continued to press for Palestine as a Jewish state. In February 1947 Ben-Gurion told Britain's foreign minister Ernest Bevin that the Jewish Agency wanted "a Jewish state embracing the whole of western Palestine," meaning the area west of the Jordan River.[89] Desperate for a solution, Britain toyed with reviving partition, urging the Jewish Agency to table a partition proposal. But the Agency refused.[90] In April 1947 Britain announced that it would leave Palestine; it had tired of the Agency's revolt, particularly the recent attacks by the Irgun against British soldiers and officers. It was unable to find a formula to balance the competing Zionist and Arab interests, and so it asked the newly established United Nations to propose a solution.[91]

4

A Portrait by Picasso:

The UN Recommendation of Partition

All the nations assemble as one,
The peoples gather.
—*Holy Bible*, Isaiah 43:9

When Britain asked the United Nations to make recommendations on the status of Palestine, five Arab states asked the UN General Assembly to take up the Palestine issue as a matter of "the termination of the Mandate over Palestine and the declaration of its independence."[1] They were concerned that Britain's open-ended request for a recommendation on the future governance of Palestine invited the General Assembly to link the issue of Jewish refugees in Europe with that of Palestine's status. They feared that the question of legal entitlement would be forgotten. But the General Assembly rejected the Arab approach and took up Britain's request, appointing an eleven-nation Special Committee on Palestine.[2] The General Assembly gave the Special Committee a broad mandate, which the committee construed as permitting it to consider Jewish refugees in Europe in formulating a recommendation on Palestine.[3]

In its discussions the General Assembly relied on the Jewish Agency to speak for the Jews of Palestine.[4] By 1947 many more Jews supported Zionism than before World War II, both in Europe and in Palestine, but the U.S. delegate, Warren Austin, cautioned the General Assembly that the Jewish Agency did not speak for all Jews, or even for all Jews in Palestine.[5] The Arab Higher Committee—convinced that the Special Committee would not give due consideration to Arab rights—did not cooperate with it, even though Arab-state representatives testified before it.

The United States, pressed by the Jewish Agency to support the partition of Palestine, had yet to state a public position. Under Secretary of State Dean Acheson said that partition held "domestic advantages for us," by which he meant securing the Jewish vote in the 1948 presidential election. But, even so, Acheson said that partition carried "too great a weight of international difficulty to put across."[6] Secretary of State George Marshall also saw a conflict between domestic and international considerations. He said that formulation of a U.S. position was "extremely complicated" because of "factors of internal politics."[7]

In September 1947 the Special Committee reported back to the General Assembly.[8] The committee acknowledged that the self-determination right of the Palestine Arabs had been violated by the inclusion of the Balfour Declaration in the League of Nations Mandate for Palestine Arabs. The committee further stated that the principle of self-determination, internationally recognized after World War I, was "adhered to with regard to other Arab territories" but was "not applied to Palestine, obviously because of the intention to make possible the creation of the Jewish National Home there." The "Jewish National Home" and the "*sui generis* Mandate for Palestine," it said, "run counter" to the principle of self-determination.[9]

The Special Committee did not question the validity of the League's approach, even though a self-determination right had just been written into Article 1 of the UN Charter. Three members of the Special Committee proposed a federal state with Jewish and Arab components, while a majority of seven members suggested the partition of Palestine into a Jewish state and an Arab state with an economic union between them. None favored a single state in Palestine, the preferred solution of the Arab Higher Committee.

The decision of the majority to propose partition reflected a linkage of the refugee and Palestine questions. Weizmann correctly stated that the United Nations "was motivated pre-eminently by the purpose of solving once and for all the Jewish question in Europe, to get rid of the concentration camps and of the aftermath of Hitler's holocaust."[10] But others viewed this as a convenient solution for a problem that should have been handled otherwise. Morris Ernst, Roosevelt's advisor, decried "the hypocrisy of closing our own doors while making sanctimonious demands on the Arabs."[11] Pakistan's UN delegate commented, sarcastically: "Australia, an overpopulated small country with congested areas, says no, no, no; Canada, equally congested and overpopulated, says no; the United States, a great humanitarian country, a small area, with small resources, says no . . . they state: let them go to Palestine, where there are vast areas, a large economy and no trouble; they can easily be taken in there."[12]

There was "neither merit nor justice," said Toynbee, in "compensating victims at the expense of innocent third parties."[13] The Palestine Arabs were "innocent of the crimes committed against the Jews by the Germans under the Nazi regime." Toynbee thought that if a state were to be created as compensation, it "should have been carved out of Central Europe." A "guilty Western people's territory was held to be sacrosanct, because, though guilty, they were Westerners. . . . An innocent non-Western people's territory could, it was held, legitimately be given away to the Jews by the victorious Western powers. This amounts to a declaration of the inequality of the Western and the non-Western sections of the human race. It is a claim that Westerners are privileged, however guilty they may be."[14] A U.S. diplomat found "no necessary connection between the humanitarian problem of succoring the displaced persons of Europe and the political problem of creating a new nationalist state in Palestine."[15]

The Jewish Agency welcomed the partition recommendation, while the Arab Higher Committee rejected it.[16] The Jewish Agency geared up its parastate institutions for an early assumption of power and began troop mobilization.[17] The Haganah was placed under the control of David Ben-Gurion, who was still chairman of the Jewish Agency.[18] The Palestine Arabs had no program of conscription or military training,[19] but the Arab League took a decision to resist, by force if necessary, any effort to implement partition in Palestine.[20] In October 1947 the League resolved to send troops only if the Jewish Agency invited foreign troops on its side,[21] and it decided to provide military aid to local militia of the Palestine Arabs.[22] Though militarily weak, Palestine's Arabs planned to resist the expected attempt by the Jewish Agency to take over Palestine.[23] Loy Henderson, the U.S. State Department official responsible for Middle Eastern affairs, advised Secretary of State George Marshall to approach the matter cautiously. He said that the partition plan ignored "self-determination and majority rule." The United States, Henderson said, was "under no obligations to the Jews to set up a Jewish State. The Balfour Declaration and the Mandate . . . provided not for a Jewish State, but for a Jewish national home."[24]

King Abdullah, who commanded the only Arab army of any size, continued his secret negotiations with the Jewish Agency over a division of Palestine.[25] On November 17, 1947, Abdullah met Golda Meir, who headed the Jewish Agency's political department, in a small town on the Jordan River. Abdullah said that Transjordan would not intervene militarily against a Jewish state, if one was established by the Agency.[26] He also asked the Agency to increase its financial subsidy to him.[27] In addition to a direct payment, the Agency was paying the expenses in New York of Omar Dajani, the man who represented Transjordan at the United Nations.[28]

After receiving the Special Committee's report, the General Assembly constituted an Ad Hoc Committee on the Palestine Question to frame the Palestine issue for plenary debate, composed of all UN member states.[29] The ad hoc committee set up a subcommittee 1 to draw up a detailed plan for partition and a subcommittee 2 to draw up a plan for a single Palestine state.[30] Subcommittee 2 asked the ad hoc committee to urge the General Assembly to seek an advisory opinion from the International Court of Justice before adopting any resolution on Palestine.[31] It wanted the Court to determine whether the Balfour Declaration violated self-determination of the Palestine population, whether the indigenous population of Palestine had a right to determine the status of Palestine, and whether the General Assembly had the power to suggest or to enforce a territorial settlement for Palestine.[32] A Jewish Agency lawyer, Shabtai Rosenne, thought the questions "one-sided."[33] The ad hoc committee narrowly defeated the request of the subcommittee 2 for an advisory opinion.[34] That led members of subcommittee 2 to castigate the majority for giving insufficient weight to the "juridical aspects of the Palestine question."[35]

Subcommittee 1 approved the Special Committee's partition plan, with some changes, and the ad hoc committee voted to recommend partition to the General Assembly. The resolution asked the Arab Higher Committee and the Jewish Agency to establish states with an economic union between them, including common rail transport, postal system, and currency. A two-year phase-in period was envisaged to establish this infrastructure. Jerusalem was to be included in neither state but to be administered under an international regime. The suggested boundary between the two states was long and intricate—not intended as a defensible international border.[36] The proposed boundaries of the Jewish State—according to Robert McClintock, a U.S. State Department official—were "predicated on the assumption that there would also be an Arab State in Palestine linked to the Jewish State by economic union." He likened the partition map to "a portrait by Picasso."[37]

The proposed Jewish state would have had 56 percent of Palestine. Jews owned 6 percent of the land and made up 30 percent of the population, most of them mandate-period immigrants.[38] Ernest Bevin, Britain's foreign secretary, noted the difficulty of drawing boundaries because of the sparseness of Jewish population. "It is impossible to find in all Palestine, apart from Tel Aviv and its environs . . . any sizable area with a Jewish majority."[39] In the envisaged Jewish state Jews would have been in a minority—499,020 Jews to 509,780 Arabs.[40] In the proposed Arab state there would have been only 9,520 Jews to 749,101 Arabs.[41] The plan thus gave much Arab-populated territory to the Jewish state, but little Jewish-populated territory to the Arab state.

On November 25, 1947, the ad hoc committee approved the partition recommendation of subcommittee 1, by a vote of 25 to 13, with 17 abstentions. While sufficient to carry the plan in the subcommittee, this margin was short of the two-thirds majority that would be required for passage in the General Assembly. By this time the United States had emerged as the most aggressive proponent of partition. Most European countries, including the Soviet Union, supported it, but most Third World countries viewed it as an infringement of Arab rights.[42] The United States got the General Assembly to delay a vote "to gain time to bring certain Latin American republics into line with its own views."[43] U.S. officials, "by direct order of the White House," used "every form of pressure, direct and indirect," to "make sure that the necessary majority" would be gained, according to former Under Secretary of State Sumner Welles.[44] Members of the U.S. Congress threatened curtailment of economic aid to several Third World countries.[45]

As a last-minute compromise, and as a major concession, several Arab states proposed a plan for a federated government in Palestine. Similar to the Special Committee's minority proposal, this plan called for a federation with Jewish and Arab components.[46] Colombia asked the General Assembly to refer the matter back to the ad hoc committee for further efforts at producing a solution acceptable to both the Arabs and the Jews of Palestine.[47] There was little reason in the fall of 1947 to believe that the delicate political arrangement contemplated by the partition plan could find the necessary level of cooperation between the Jewish and Arab communities.

But the General Assembly proceeded to a vote on the partition plan. On November 29 it adopted a draft resolution embodying the partition plan as Resolution 181. The resolution narrowly gained the required majority of two-thirds—33 in favor, 13 opposed, and 10 abstaining. Included in the countries that switched their votes from November 25 to November 29 to provide the two-thirds majority were Liberia, the Philippines, and Haiti. All heavily dependent on the United States financially, they had been lobbied to change their votes. Liberia's ambassador to the United Nations complained that the U.S. delegation threatened aid cuts to several countries.[48] Some delegates charged U.S. officials with "diplomatic intimidation."[49] Without "terrific pressure" from the United States on "governments which cannot afford to risk American reprisals," said an anonymous editorial writer, the resolution "would never have passed."[50] The fact such pressure had been exerted became public knowledge, to the extent a State Department policy group was concerned that "the prestige of the UN" would suffer because of "the notoriety and resentment attendant upon the activities of U.S. pressure groups, including members of Congress, who sought to impose U.S. views as to partition on foreign delegations."[51] Zionists packed the public gallery during the November 29 meeting to urge adoption of the partition plan.[52] Several delegates said the resolution "would have been carried in no other city than New York."[53]

Resolution 181 was a political solution, a Zionist lawyer, Benjamin Akzin, wrote at the time, "not a verdict of a court of law."[54] An Arab lawyer, Nabil Elaraby, chided the General Assembly for having acted without examining the question of legal claims to Palestine.[55] In subsequent self-determination disputes—over Namibia (South-West Africa) and Western Sahara—the General Assembly would seek advisory opinions from the International Court of Justice.[56] "The Arabs," declared an Arab jurist of Resolution 181, "have had to pay for and expiate the outrage committed against mankind in Treblinka,

Auschwitz, and elsewhere."[57] A Yugoslav jurist objected that Resolution 181 reflected the view that "so-called 'civilized' people were stilled entitled to determine the fate of the 'uncivilized,' and that the territories and interests of dependent nations were objects to be manipulated—in short the blindly obstinate arrogance which we call the 'colonial spirit'!"[58]

A U.S. military officer, Commander E. H. Hutchison, who later chaired the Israel-Jordan Armistice Commission, said that in adopting Resolution 181 the major powers "overran the rights of the indigenous population of Palestine—the Arabs. Every step in the establishment of a Zionist state" was "a challenge to justice."[59]

The Jewish Agency accepted Resolution 181. The Jewish Agency proceeded with its plans to establish a Jewish state, although it did not promise to limit itself to the area proposed in Resolution 181.[60] On November 30 the Arab Higher Committee rejected Resolution 181.[61] It hoped that the General Assembly might reconsider the issue and recommend an alternate solution. The Arab League also still hoped for a political solution and made no preparations for intervention. Meeting in Cairo in December, the League kept to its October plan of aiding Palestinian irregulars rather than intervening directly.[62] The mufti of Jerusalem, Haj Amin al-Husseini, who headed the Arab Higher Committee, opposed Arab League military intervention. He feared correctly that King Abdullah of Transjordan wanted part of Palestine.[63] The Arab states feared each other's motives and territorial ambitions;[64] within the Arab League, Abdullah objected to the formation of an independent Palestinian state,[65] and Syria organized a force of irregulars under the command of Fawzi al-Kaukji for immediate intervention in Palestine, as a counterweight to Abdullah's plan of annexation.[66]

The Palestine Arabs were not well organized administratively or politically and had little military capability.[67] Disarmed by Britain after their 1936 revolt,[68] they had no full-time military force, no military unit structure, and no unified command.[69] The arms they had been able to accumulate in the 1940s were no match for those of the Haganah, which was "one of the largest and best-trained underground armies in modern history."[70] Richard Crossman said the Arabs knew that if Britain withdrew without a political solution, the Haganah would overrun the country.[71]

The day after Resolution 181 was adopted the Jewish Agency called on all Jews age seventeen to twenty-five to register for military service in the Haganah.[72] It began purchasing armaments in the United States,[73] and the Haganah operations chief prepared a map showing "the strategic characters of every Arab village."[74] The Arab Higher Committee made no military decisions but called on Palestine Arabs to hold a three-day commercial strike to protest the partition plan.[75]

5

Chaos on the Ground:

Palestine in a Power Vacuum

And the Lord said to Moses in the plains of Moab by the Jordan at Jericho, "Say to the people of Israel, When you pass over the Jordan into the land of Canaan, then you shall drive out all the inhabitants of the land from before you, . . . and you shall take possession of the land and settle in it, for I have given the land to you to possess it. . . . But if you do not drive out the inhabitants of the land from before you, then those of them whom you let remain shall be as pricks in your eyes and thorns in your sides, and they shall trouble you in the land where you dwell."—*Holy Bible*, Numbers 33:50–56

Outraged at the General Assembly's partition recommendation, Palestine Arabs held street demonstrations in Palestine during the three-day commercial strike.[1] Groups of Arabs attacked Jews and vice versa, resulting in deaths on both sides.[2] The Haganah restrained Jewish crowds[3] and the Arab Higher Committee counseled against violence by Arabs.[4] Demonstrations were also held in other Arab countries to protest Resolution 181.

The Arab Higher Committee planned no major military action before British withdrawal, now scheduled for May 1948.[5] But local Arab irregulars loyal to the Arab Higher Committee staged armed attacks on transport convoys that carried supplies to Zionist settlements and Jewish-populated towns. These attacks resulted in more deaths.[6] In mid-December the Irgun and LEHI, which were still attacking the British army, launched major attacks against Arabs.[7] Irgun and LEHI operatives threw bombs into Arab shops and street crowds.[8] "The Jews again appeared today to be on the offensive," the *New York Times* reported in a December 12 dispatch, "roughly two-thirds of the incidents being initiated by them, and in their operations they showed evidence of planning, something absent in general from the Arab attacks."[9] In its December 13 dispatch the *New York Times* reported: "The day's total casualties were twenty-one Arabs and three Jews killed. . . . More than eighty Arabs were wounded and three Jews were seriously wounded."[10] Though the Jewish Agency disclaimed responsibility for Irgun and LEHI killings, British High Commissioner Alan Cunningham and the U.S. Central Intelligence Agency both reported that the Haganah, Irgun, and LEHI had coordinated strategy.[11]

The Irgun leader, Menachem Begin, took pride in this offensive. "For three days, from 11th to 13th December," he recounted, the Irgun "hammered at concentrations of rioters and their offensive bases," by which he meant Arab towns and villages. Begin continued, "we attacked at Haifa and Jaffa; at Tireh and Yazar. We attacked again and again in Jerusalem. . . . Enemy casualties in killed and wounded were heavy."[12] In its attack on Tireh village the Irgun killed thirteen people.[13] LEHI also targeted Arab civilians. In the words of a British officer, Major R. D. Wilson, LEHI made "bestial attacks on Arab villages, in which they showed not the slightest discrimination for women and children, whom they killed as opportunity offered."[14] "The hope for a decrease in tension, arising from Arab reaction to the United States decision on partition of Palestine, seemed destroyed by the Irgun Zvai Leumi terrorist bombings of Arabs yesterday," the *New York Times* reported in its December 14 dispatch.[15]

Ben-Gurion laid a plan to destroy Arab transport. He hoped to force the evacuation—"because of hunger"—of Haifa and Jaffa, two major Arab cities. We can "starve them out," he wrote on December 14.[16] As Britain turned over the policing of some Jewish-populated areas to a Jewish police force,[17] the Jewish Agency proceeded with its plans to establish a state, which it was thought might be named Judea.[18]

On December 18, 1947, the Palmach—the shock force of the Haganah—attacked the Arab village of Khissas, killing five adults and five children.[19] The Jewish Agency publicly commended the action.[20] Of that attack, Christopher Sykes, a contemporary observer, wrote "something of the evil spirit of the terrorists," meaning the Irgun and LEHI, "was entering Haganah." The Khissas attack was "in no sense the sudden deed of hotheads," but "part of a considered policy which had been preceded by debate, and was finally ordered by the highest authorities of the Jewish Agency and Haganah." He felt "this Haganah crime precipitated the next phase of the war."[21]

The next day the Haganah dynamited the house of the village

elder of Qazaza village in central Palestine, killing several inhabitants.[22] At that point the Jewish Agency and the Haganah formally
announced a policy of reprisals against Arab civilians.[23] The Central
Intelligence Agency called these Haganah attacks "terrorist raids
against the Arabs similar in tactics to those of the Irgun Zvai Leumi
and the Stern Gang [LEHI]."[24]

The Haganah justified its attacks on Arab civilians as reprisals
for acts committed by inhabitants since Jewish civilians were being
killed in attacks on convoys. A pattern quickly developed. "While
the Jews are suffering mainly through sniping at their road convoys,"
reported *The Times* of London, "the Arabs have lost many lives
through Jewish assaults on their villages."[25]

At a December 26 meeting of Haganah leaders, Ben-Gurion said a
"major offensive against the Arabs" would "greatly reduce the percentage of Arabs in the population of the new state." His biographer
commented that "this might be called racialism," but that "the whole
Zionist movement actually was based on the principle of a purely
Jewish community in Palestine." He quoted Ben-Gurion as saying the
fewer Arabs in the new Jewish state, "the better he would like it."[26]

As Arab militia continued attacks on convoys, the Jewish Agency
used armored buses to get supplies through safely.[27] The irregulars
also attacked supply trains, and British troops began to ride the trains
to thwart attacks.[28] The British army took food supplies to the Old
City of Jerusalem into the Jewish Quarter, which the irregulars were
trying to blockade.[29] In Haifa the Irgun threw bombs into a crowd of
Arab workers at the gates of the Haifa oil refinery, killing several of
them. Arab workers who were not injured by the bombs immediately
assaulted Jewish workers at the refinery, killing a number of them.[30]
The Haganah attacked the nearby village of Balad ash Sheikh and
killed inhabitants in reprisal.[31]

In January 1948 Syria-based irregulars called the Arab Liberation
Army, under Fawzi al-Kaukji, entered Palestine and attacked Zionist
settlements. They were counterattacked by Zionist forces and by the
British army and the Royal Air Force.[32] They received only mixed
support from Arab villages, which feared Haganah reprisals,[33] since
the Haganah continued attacks on villages and also attacked Arab
farmers in their fields.[34]

On January 5 LEHI set a bomb in Jaffa in a building that housed the Arab Higher Committee, killing an estimated thirty people, including Arab refugees who had been temporarily housed in the building.[35] The same day the Haganah set a bomb in the Semiramis Hotel in an Arab district of west Jerusalem that killed twenty-six people. The Haganah said it had erroneous information that the hotel housed Arab irregulars.[36] The British government issued a statement denouncing the attack as a "dastardly and wholesale murder of innocent people." The Jewish Agency replied that the British government had not similarly criticized killings done by Arabs. British officials rejoined that Arab elements had not carried out organized attacks on buildings containing women and children.[37]

The Irgun began to direct its attacks at major Arab population centers. According to Irgun leader Begin, at a meeting of the Irgun command in late January four targets were selected: Jerusalem, Jaffa, the Lydda-Ramleh area, and the Triangle.[38] Lydda and Ramleh are adjoining towns in central Palestine; the Triangle is an area in northern Palestine, between the Arab towns of Nablus, Jenin, and Tulkarm. To promote this action, Irgun Radio called for greater cooperation between the Haganah and itself.[39]

In Cairo the Arab League announced that when Britain withdrew it would intervene militarily to occupy all of Palestine.[40] But Abdullah told the Jewish Agency privately that his intention remained firm not to interfere with the establishment of a Jewish state.[41] And Britain—whose officers still commanded Abdullah's Transjordan legion—encouraged Abdullah in his plans to annex part of Palestine, but to avoid attacking Jewish-populated areas.[42] Far from being concerned about Abdullah's intention to send troops into Palestine, the Agency encouraged him to do so. It hoped that Abdullah could convince the Palestine Arabs to accept a Jewish state and that he might physically prevent the Arab Higher Committee from establishing an Arab state.[43]

As the British administration prepared to leave Palestine, the Jewish Agency assumed authority.[44] By February it had a "complete blueprint of government" and began actual administration.[45] Arabs were beginning to flee from some rural areas and some urban districts, and on February 5, 1948, Ben-Gurion ordered that Jews be settled in conquered and abandoned Arab areas. The Haganah rocketed

Arab neighborhoods in Jerusalem, causing many Arab residents to flee.[46] On February 6 the Arab Higher Committee told the UN Palestine Commission, which had been appointed in Resolution 181 to supervise partition, that any attempt "to establish a Jewish state in Arab territory" would be "an act of aggression which will be resisted in self-defense by force."[47]

Speaking to the Mapai party's central committee on February 7, Ben-Gurion expressed satisfaction at the exodus of Arabs. "Since Jerusalem's destruction in the days of the Romans," he said, "it hasn't been so Jewish as it is now." In "many Arab districts" in the western part of Jerusalem "one sees not one Arab. I do not assume that this will change." And "what had happened in Jerusalem," he continued, "could well happen in great parts of the country. . . . Certainly there will be great changes in the composition of the population in the country."[48] "For the Arabs of the Land of Israel," according to Ben-Gurion, "there remains only one function: to flee."[49] On February 12, 1948, after a Jewish woman was shot in the Talbieh district of Jerusalem, a Haganah loudspeaker van drove through the neighborhood ordering the Arab residents to evacuate. Many of them did.[50]

On March 5, 1948, the UN Security Council adopted a resolution asking its five permanent members—Britain, France, China, the USSR, and the United States—to make recommendations on how partition might be implemented.[51] But the strongest supporter of partition, the United States, was having second thoughts. The State Department's policy planning staff, in a report to the secretary of state, noted the Palestine Arabs' rejection of partition. The staff expressed fear that, in light of that rejection, U.S. support for partition ran counter to the Palestine Arabs' right of self-determination. The staff suggested the United States abandon the partition recommendation.[52]

On March 19 the United States suggested to the Security Council that partition be abandoned. It advised the council to ask the General Assembly to set up a temporary trusteeship over Palestine until the two parties reached a settlement.[53] On April 1, at the urging of the United States, the Security Council asked the General Assembly to "consider further the question of the future government of Palestine"; in other words, to seek a solution other than partition.[54] The council did not seriously consider the possibility of using UN troops to force partition on the Palestine Arabs.[55]

Thus, the United Nations abandoned the partition idea scarcely four months after laboring long and hard to approve it. The abandonment of partition is not surprising, however, in light of the Arab rejection of it. The General Assembly had approached the Palestine issue with the aim of making proposals that the parties might accept.[56] In Resolution 181 it had recommended the adoption and implementation of the partition plan and asked the inhabitants of Palestine to take "such steps as may be necessary on their part to put this plan into effect."[57]

When it posed the Palestine question to the General Assembly in 1947, Britain had asked the assembly to exercise its power of recommendation. In its request it referred to the assembly's powers under Charter Article 10, which gives the assembly the power to make recommendations.[58] In Resolution 181 itself, the assembly had made reference to charter provisions giving it a power of recommendation by stating that it "considers that the present situation in Palestine is one which is likely to impair the general welfare and friendly relations among nations."[59] The phrases "general welfare" and "friendly relations" are drawn from Charter Article 14, which gives the General Assembly the power of recommendation.

Member states viewed Resolution 181 as a recommendation.[60] In the Security Council discussion that led to the abandonment of Resolution 181, the United States said that General Assembly recommendations have only "moral force."[61] Britain told the Security Council it would not implement partition so long as Arab or Jewish authorities objected.[62] Syria,[63] Egypt,[64] Saudi Arabia,[65] Yemen,[66] Pakistan,[67] and Iraq[68] told the council they did not consider the partition recommendation binding on them.

Resolution 181 contemplated voluntary compliance in its mechanism for selecting provisional leaders of the two projected states. A UN commission, "after consultation with the democratic parties and other public organizations of the Arab and Jewish States," was to "select and establish in each State as rapidly as possible a Provisional Council of Government."[69] Since this cooperation did not materialize, Resolution 181 remained a recommendation only.[70]

Resolution 181 also requested the Security Council "determine as a threat to the peace" any attempt "to alter by force the settlement envisaged by this resolution."[71] This provision was later cited as indicating that the General Assembly intended "a solution to be imposed by force," and therefore "not a simple recommendation."[72] But this appeal was not more than a recommendation.[73] The assembly used the term "request," an indication it was aware of the limit of its power.[74] The United States, commenting on the assembly's request to the council, said that the charter "does not empower the Security Council to enforce a political settlement made "pursuant to a recommendation of the General Assembly."[75]

Moreover, the General Assembly, when it asked the Security Council to deal with a possible attempt to alter by force the settlement envisaged in Resolution 181, contemplated a situation in which the two parties were creating the two states voluntarily but where an outside party might intervene militarily. U.S. representative Warren Austin said this provision referred to an attempt to frustrate partition "on the part of states or people outside Palestine."[76] Resolution 181 did not purport to convey title to territory,[77] and since partition had not been accepted by the parties no territorial rights were created.[78] Resolution 181 had failed;[79] it was a "dead letter."[80]

6

Whose Land to Give? The UN Power over Palestine

Ma è ancora casa di altri.
(But it is still the home of other people.)
Response of King Victor Emmanuel III of Italy, January 23, 1904,
to Theodor Herzl's request for a Jewish state in Tripoli

Moshe Shertok (later Moshe Sharett), head of the Jewish Agency political department, said in the United Nations that the General Assembly was legally competent to determine the future status of Palestine and that its Resolution 181 carried binding force.[1] But the General Assembly of the United Nations is not a legislature for the world. The UN Charter, in Articles 10, 11, and 14, gives it only the power of recommendation. The assembly makes binding decisions only on internal UN matters, like setting the budget or electing members of the International Court of Justice.[2] Thus, even if the assembly had intended to impose partition, it is not clear it had the legal authority to do so.

Leading early students of the UN Charter said that in adopting Resolution 181 the General Assembly had only the power of recommendation. Hans Kelsen, citing Resolution 181, wrote that General Assembly recommendations "do not constitute a legal obligation to behave in conformity with them."[3] Leland Goodrich and Edvard Hambro, also citing Resolution 181, stated that "recommendations have no obligatory character."[4] Clyde Eagleton said that "a resolution of the General Assembly, such as that for the partition of Palestine, is no more than a recommendation" and "can have no legally binding effect upon any state whatsoever."[5] The U.S. deputy representative to the Security Council said during the Palestine debate that the General Assembly had the power only to recommend a settlement.[6]

A lawyer from the UN secretariat, F. Blaine Sloane, argued to the contrary, saying that Resolution 181 carried binding force. He stated that the General Assembly has the power to decide the status of territory whose sovereignty is unclear. In areas "where sovereignty is not vested in a member State," the General Assembly, "acting as the agent of the international community," may take "a binding decision."[7] On this view, Resolution 181 gives Israel valid title to Palestine. But few lawyers agreed with him. By the UN charter, the General Assembly is given no power over territory any broader than its general power of recommendation.[8] The assembly, according to Ian Brownlie, a later student of the charter, has no "capacity to convey title," since it "cannot assume the role of territorial sovereign." Even as regards disposition of territory, Brownlie wrote, the assembly "only has a power of recommendation."[9] The assembly, wrote Elihu Lauterpacht, another leading student of the charter, could not "give the Jews and the Arabs in Palestine any rights which either did not otherwise possess."[10]

It has been argued by some scholars, however, that even if the General Assembly has no power over territory generally, it has decisionmaking power over territory that was under a League of Nations mandate. Emile Geraud, a former legal officer of both the League of Nations and United Nations, said that the United Nations succeeded to the League's power over mandate territory.[11] The assembly, stated Allan Gerson, possesses an "adjudicative role" to terminate a mandate that is "beyond its normal recommendatory role."[12]

This argument relies largely on the International Court of Justice advisory opinions on Namibia (South-West Africa) of 1950 and 1971.[13] The court said in 1950 that the competence to determine and modify the international status of a League of Nations mandate territory rested with the mandatory, "acting with the consent of the United Nations."[14] Nathan Feinberg, a legal scholar of the Hebrew University in Jerusalem, argued that Resolution 181 was an agreement between Britain and the United Nations to change the status of Palestine.[15]

In 1971 the International Court of Justice discussed the legal significance of General Assembly Resolution 2145, which affirmed the right of the people of Namibia to independence and decided that South Africa's mandate "is therefore terminated, that South Africa has no other right to administer the Territory and that henceforth South-West Africa comes under the direct responsibility of the

United Nations."[16] The court upheld the legality of that resolution, stating: "To deny to a political organ of the United Nations which is a successor of the League in this respect the right to act, on the argument that it lacks competence to render what is described as a judicial decision, would not only be inconsistent but would amount to a complete denial of the remedies available against fundamental breaches of an international undertaking."[17] Gerson cited this language to argue that the General Assembly has the power to determine the status of a League of Nations mandate territory and that Resolution 181 was such a resolution and was binding.[18]

What the court found, however, was that the General Assembly had supervisory power over the South-West Africa mandate. The court made it clear that this power "derived from" Article 10 of the charter, "which authorizes the General Assembly to discuss any questions or any matters within the scope of the Charter and to make recommendations on these questions or matters to the Members of the United Nations."[19] Thus, the power it found in the assembly to supervise former mandate territories is only a power to make recommendations.

The issue in the two Namibia advisory opinions, moreover, was different from that raised by the situation in Palestine. South Africa had declared an intent to incorporate the mandate territory. The court said that South Africa could not do so without consent of the General Assembly. The court recognized the people of the territory as a "jural entity," possessing rights under the mandate. It could have found, as did dissenting Judge Fitzmaurice, that South Africa was precluded from incorporating the territory solely by virtue of terms of the mandate instrument, which forbade incorporation.[20] The instrument was a treaty between the League and South Africa,[21] and it survived the League's demise in the court's view.[22] That obligation flowed not to the United Nations or any of its organs, but rather to the other members of the League and to the people of South-West Africa, who were a third party beneficiary of the mandate instrument.[23]

The court said that Resolution 2145 fell within what it found to be a power of the General Assembly to supervise former League mandates.[24] If the court had not found supervision to be within the assembly's competence, South Africa would have had only an obligation to make reports on South-West Africa "for information purposes."[25] But the court found supervision to be an essential aspect of the mandate system: "The obligation incumbent upon a mandatory State to accept international supervision and to submit reports is an important part of the Mandates System."[26]

The court had not been asked by the General Assembly, however, whether the assembly had supervisory functions over the South-West Africa mandate. The assembly had asked only whether South Africa was required to conclude a trusteeship agreement with the assembly, and whether South Africa could modify the status of South-West Africa unilaterally.[27] To answer these questions, the court had no need to state whether the General Assembly had supervisory functions.

The court's statement that the assembly exercised "supervisory functions" made little sense in the context of the League's demise and the founding of the United Nations. Judge McNair, dissenting, said that "the succession of the United Nations to the administrative functions of the League of Nations in regard to the Mandates could have been expressly preserved and vested in the United Nations" by an appropriate provision in the UN Charter. But, he noted, "this was not done."[28] McNair also stated: "The United Nations did not succeed to the rights of the League of Nations as to the former mandated territories. . . . There is no legal continuity in the relations of these two systems."[29]

The United States had agreed with McNair's view in a Security Council discussion of Resolution 181 in 1948. "The United Nations does not automatically fall heir to the responsibilities either of the League of Nations or of the Mandatory Power in respect of the Palestine mandate. The record seems to us entirely clear that the United Nations did not take over the League of Nations Mandate system."[30]

Subcommittee 2 also said the United Nations "has not inherited the constitutional and political powers and functions of the League of Nations" and is not "the successor of the League of Nations insofar as the administration of mandates is concerned." In addition, UN powers over mandate territories are limited "by the specific provisions of the Charter," and "neither the General Assembly nor any other organ of the United Nations" is competent to "recommend or enforce" a "solution with regard to a mandated territory."[31]

One reason that the United Nations could not succeed to the League's power of supervision is that the supervision to which mandatory powers agreed under the League of Nations mandate system was significantly less onerous than what the court said could be imposed on South Africa. The League's supervision over mandates was exercised by its council, which functioned on unanimity.[32] All the mandatory powers were council members. France, Britain, Japan, and Belgium were members themselves, and Britain represented the interests of the mandatory powers that belonged to the Commonwealth— South Africa, Australia, and New Zealand. Thus, each mandatory power possessed a veto on a decision regarding its performance.[33]

The General Assembly in this situation operates by two-thirds majority voting.[34] Thus, a decision adverse to the mandatory power could be taken over its negative vote. A state which assumed a League mandate did not consent to such a procedure. There would be an "excess of supervision if the decision of the General Assembly reached by a two-thirds majority," stated Judge Lauterpacht of the International Court of Justice, "had the same legal and binding force as unanimous resolutions of the Council of the League of Nations."[35]

Even if the General Assembly had supervisory power over a former League of Nations mandate territory, that would not give it the power to determine the territory's future status.[36] With trusteeship, the UN analogue to the League of Nations mandate system, the assembly has no power to make decisions binding on an administering state. "The Trusteeship Agreements," stated Judge Lauterpacht, "do not provide for a legal obligation of the Administering Authority to comply with the decisions of the organs of the United Nations in the matter of trusteeship. Thus there is no legal obligation, on the part of the Administering Authority, to give effect to a recommendation of the General Assembly to adopt or depart from a particular course of legislation or any particular administrative measure. States administering Trust Territories . . . have often asserted their right not to accept recommendations of the General Assembly." That right "has never been seriously challenged."[37]

In its advisory opinion on Namibia, the International Court of Justice did not decide whether the General Assembly has the power to decide on the future status of a mandate territory against the wishes of the inhabitants, which is the issue if it is asserted that Resolution 181 is a binding decision. In the Namibia situation the decision of the assembly—to prohibit South Africa from incorporating the territory—was in accord with the wishes of the population. But Resolution 181 foresaw a territorial solution unacceptable to the majority of Palestine's inhabitants. The Namibia advisory opinions do not suggest the assembly has the power to adopt a territorial solution against the wishes of the inhabitants.

If Resolution 181 were considered a binding determination of future status, it would violate the Palestine Arabs' right of self-determination. Some have argued that it did not violate the right of self-determination of the Palestine Arabs since it recognized the claims of both the Arab and Jewish communities in Palestine.[38] But since partition was against the will of the majority of inhabitants, the right to self-determination was violated.[39] The Palestine National Covenant, which was adopted in 1968 as a statement of principle by the Palestine Arabs, construed Resolution 181 as a binding decision. On that basis it considered it "null and void" since "it was contrary to the wish of the people of Palestine and its natural right to its homeland, and contradicts the principles embodied in the Charter of the United Nations, the first of which is the right of self-determination."[40]

Moreover, the population of Palestine has specific rights under the UN Charter. The charter states that the rights of a people under a League of Nations mandate may not be altered to its detriment.[41] The charter contemplated that League mandates would be converted into trusteeships. Article 80 stated that nothing in the charter's chapter on trusteeship could alter the rights "of any states or any peoples or existing international instruments to which Members of the United Nations may respectively be parties." Thus, the rights of the Palestinian people under the mandate instrument are preserved. Arab states, in arguing that partition would violate the rights of the Palestine Arabs, relied on Article 80.[42]

Subcommittee 2 said that a partition of Palestine against the consent of the population would violate that population's rights. The United Nations "cannot make a disposition or alienation of territory, nor can it deprive the majority of the people of Palestine of their territory and transfer it to the exclusive use of a minority in their country."[43]

There is one other difference between the Namibia case and the

Palestine case. The League had made Palestine a class "A" mandate, but it made South-West Africa a class "C" mandate. The covenant described a community under a class "C" mandate as "best administered under the laws of the Mandatory as integral portions of its territory," whereas a class "A" mandate was to be governed separately.[44] Thus, even if the International Court of Justice had decided that the assembly had the power to resolve the status of mandate territory against the wishes of its inhabitants, that would not give the assembly a similar power over Palestine.[45]

It has been argued that even if the Palestine Arabs once had a right to self-determination, they forfeited it by not establishing a state as recommended in Resolution 181.[46] But Resolution 181, as indicated, proposed a solution that would violate the Arabs' right to self-determination. They cannot be considered to have forfeited their right to self-determination by rejecting a proposal which would have violated that right.

One other argument has been made to reach the conclusion that Resolution 181 was binding. The argument is that even if the General Assembly did not have the power to issue a binding decision on the future status of Palestine, the Security Council "re-affirmed" Resolution 181 and thereby made it binding.[47] The council, unlike the assembly, has the power under the UN Charter to make decisions that are binding on member states.[48] Security Council Resolution 42 is cited, in which the council asked its five permanent members to make recommendations regarding "instructions which the Council might usefully give to the Palestine Commission with a view to implementing the resolution of the General Assembly."[49] Security Council Resolution 46 is also cited, in which the council called on each of the two parties to refrain from actions that might frustrate the claims of the other.[50] From Resolution 54 language is cited in which the council decided a truce should remain in force "until a peaceful adjustment of the future situation of Palestine is reached."[51]

None of this language implies an affirmation of Resolution 181 by the Security Council. In April 1948, when the Security Council became aware that Resolution 181 was unrealistic, it abandoned it.[52] Even if the council had "re-affirmed" Resolution 181, that would not render it binding. While the council has decisionmaking power on some subjects, it does not have a power to dispose of territory.

Part Two

The 1948 War and the

Establishment of Israel

7

Sten Guns and Barrel Bombs:

The Realization of the Zionist Dream

Run for your lives . . . in the name of Allah!
—Haganah Loudspeaker Message

"We needed weapons urgently," said Golda Meir, "but before we could buy anything, we needed money . . . millions of dollars. And there was only one group of people in the whole world that we had any chance of getting these dollars from: the Jews of America." Meir toured the United States and by her account raised $50 million, which was used by the Haganah to buy arms clandestinely in Europe.[1] Overall in 1948 Zionist fund-raisers collected $150 million from U.S. Jewry.[2]

The Arab irregulars directed their efforts at protecting Arab-populated sectors.[3] But the Jewish Agency did not restrict itself to Jewish-populated sectors, or even to the area projected for a Jewish state in Resolution 181, which included many Arab-populated sectors. In early March the Haganah command agreed on a set of war objectives it called "Plan D." The plan called for "control of the area given to us by the UN in addition to areas occupied by us which were outside these borders."[4] The latter phrase referred to Zionist settlements in parts of Palestine projected in Resolution 181 for an Arab state. The formulation in Plan D was vague but if read broadly could include most of Palestine. The Irgun and LEHI, meanwhile, still proclaimed their goal as not only Palestine but Transjordan as well.[5]

Plan D called for the destruction of Arab villages, the expulsion of Arabs, and Jewish settlement to replace them.[6] The Haganah stepped up attacks on Arab villages, killing inhabitants and blowing up houses. The attacks became so intense that Elias Sasson, director of the Arab division of the Jewish Agency political department, expressed concern at a departmental Agency meeting on March 25 that the Agency might not be able to prove "that we weren't the aggressors."[7] Ezra Danin, a senior Haganah intelligence service officer, said at the same meeting that the military operations had caused a "mass exodus from all places."[8] This exodus was a result of attacks by the Haganah, Irgun, and LEHI, and of fear of more attacks.[9] By late March most of the Arab rural population on the coastal plain had fled.[10] On April 6, 1948, Ben-Gurion was self-congratulatory: "We have hit the Arab guerrillas hard, villages have been emptied in panic, even from Haifa one-third of its Arabs have fled."[11]

Against the Haganah, Irgun, and LEHI, the Arab irregulars were ineffective. In addition to their weakness in numbers, equipment, and training, the two Arab forces were at odds with each other. The Arab Liberation Army sided with King Abdullah and therefore did not cooperate with the irregulars loyal to the Arab Higher Committee.[12]

One of the first operations undertaken to implement Plan D was Operation Nachson, which aimed at ensuring Jewish Agency access to the important Jerusalem – Tel Aviv highway.[13] On April 9 the Irgun and LEHI captured the village of Deir Yassin, just west of Jerusalem on the Jerusalem – Tel Aviv highway. Shortly after taking Deir Yassin, Irgun and LEHI soldiers killed 250 of its civilian inhabitants.[14] The Irgun claimed it had killed the inhabitants while taking houses by force, but witnesses said they killed them after fighting ended.[15] Toynbee called the killings "comparable to crimes committed against the Jews by the Nazis," since a large number of civilians were killed outside a combat situation.[16]

The Irgun announced that the action was the first step in the conquest of Palestine and Transjordan.[17] It paraded surviving Deir Yassin inhabitants in trucks in Jerusalem the same day as a demonstration to Jerusalem's Arabs.[18] Later that day it killed these survivors.[19] The Haganah too utilized the Deir Yassin killings. It proclaimed in Arabic from loudspeaker vans in Jerusalem, "unless you leave your homes, the fate of Deir Yassin will be your fate."[20] The apparent aim was to frighten other Arabs into leaving Palestine.[21] Memory of Irgun attacks on Arab civilians in 1936 heightened the Arabs' apprehension. After the Deir Yassin killings, many Arabs, particularly in unprotected rural areas, left for neighboring countries.[22] A week after the Deir Yassin killings, the United States denounced Irgun and LEHI attacks on Arab civilians since the adoption of Resolution 181 as "widespread terrorism and wilful murder which had shocked the entire world."[23]

The Haganah, Irgun, and LEHI secretly coordinated strategy in the early months of 1948.[24] But two days after the Deir Yassin attack the Irgun and Haganah concluded a formal pact of cooperation.[25] The Haganah agreed to try to keep the press from denouncing Irgun terrorism and to ask Britain to stop demanding the disbanding of Zionist terrorist organizations.[26] The Irgun and Haganah thereafter held regular strategy conferences.[27]

Jewish Agency forces effectively used psychological warfare to supplement direct force.[28] Haganah radio spread rumors that cholera and typhus would break out in April and May in Arab areas.[29] It announced—falsely—that smallpox had been reported in Jaffa as a result of the arrival of Syrian and Iraqi irregulars.[30] The Jewish Agency organized "whispering campaigns" to have Jews advise Arab neighbors to leave.[31]

When they attacked Arab towns, Haganah units used barrels filled with explosives, a device that had been developed by the Irgun.[32] As explained by Leo Heiman, a Haganah officer, they sent these barrel bombs "crashing into the walls and doorways of Arab houses" to encourage the residents to flee. The bombs "exploded with a furious sound, like an erupting volcano, sending up sheets of flame and pillars of nauseating smoke." Then the Haganah personnel brought up jeeps with loudspeakers which broadcast tape-recorded horror sounds. "These included shrieks, wails, and anguished moans of Arab women, the wail of sirens and clang of fire-alarm bells, interrupted by a sepulchral voice calling out in Arabic: 'Save your souls, all ye faithful! Flee for your lives! The Jews are using poison gas and atomic weapons. Run for your lives in the name of Allah!'"[33]

On April 17, 1948, the Security Council called for a truce in the Palestine fighting.[34] But the Zionist forces pressed their attack. That same day the Palmach, an elite unit of the Haganah, attacked Tiberias, the first Zionist assault on a major town in the Galilee. Using barrel bombs and loudspeaker warnings, the Palmach set the entire Arab population of Tiberias to flight.[35] "A hasty exodus of Arabs from Tiberias continued all day long, and scores of Arab trucks, carrying panic-stricken foreign Arabs and local families, moved out in long convoys," reported the *Palestine Post*.[36] The Haganah began to demolish villages it captured. After taking Beit Surik and Biddu, villages north of Jerusalem, it "levelled every house except the two Mosques. More than 100 buildings were destroyed."[37]

On April 21 the Haganah and Irgun attacked Haifa, the terminus of the Iraqi oil pipeline. According to the *Palestine Post*, a Zionist daily, the Haganah "said that the Arabs had been warned by leaflets in Arabic for two days" to "evacuate women, children and old men immediately." The Haganah said that it repeated the warning from loudspeaker trucks.[38] The messages threatened dire consequences if the warnings were ignored.[39] The Haganah lobbed mortars into densely populated neighborhoods in Haifa, rolled barrel bombs into alleys, and played horror recordings.[40] The combination of bombings and threats succeeded in setting the population to flight. The "barrages making loud explosive sounds" and the "loudspeakers in Arabic," according to an assessment by the Haganah intelligence branch, "proved their great efficacy when used properly (as in Haifa particularly)."[41]

The flight of Arab residents from Haifa reached the level of panic even before the main attack.[42] In "whatever transport they could find, many of them on foot—men, women, and children—moved in a mass exodus toward the port area," the *Palestine Post* reported. "Then thousands stormed the gate and streamed to the seaside to be taken to Acre by Army landing crafts."[43] Some shouted "Deir Yassin" as they left, reported Menachem Begin, proud at the impact of his Irgun's mass killing two weeks earlier.[44]

As families fled, the Haganah directed gunfire at them to keep them moving.[45] British officials reported "indiscriminate and revolting machine gun fire" by the Haganah "on women and children" as they ran for the docks. They said there was "considerable congestion" of "hysterical and terrified Arab women and children and old people on whom the Jews opened up mercilessly with fire."[46] Haganah commander Ben Zion Inbar recalled: "we manned the biggest mortar which our forces had at that time—a three-inch mortar—and when all the Arabs gathered in this area we started firing on them. When the shells started falling on them, they rushed down to the boats and set off by sea for Acre."[47] (Acre is another coastal town, to the north of Haifa.)

An account was later disseminated that Haifa's Arabs fled not from fear but because local Arab leaders decided on an evacuation to avoid living under Zionist rule.[48] Arab leaders in Haifa did meet with Haganah officers but only after the population was already in flight.[49]

At that meeting the Haganah offered a truce that the Arab leaders rejected; the leaders instead asked the British commander to ensure the safety of those fleeing.[50]

A few days later the Irgun attacked Jaffa.[51] For three days, beginning April 26, it shelled residential districts, causing civilian casualties and terrifying the population.[52] The Haganah joined the attack on April 29. The result was a "mass exodus" by sea and overland.[53] The panic flight was caused both by "the repute which propaganda had bestowed" on the Irgun, and by the scale of the bombardment, according to Irgun leader Begin.[54] Shmuel Toledano, a Haganah intelligence officer who would later be a member of Israel's parliament (Knesset), recited the same two reasons for the Arab flight from Jaffa. "First, because the Etzel [Irgun] had been shelling Jaffa for three weeks before the Haganah entered, making the Arabs very much afraid; some already began to leave as a result of that shelling by Etzel." Second, "there were rumours, based on the Etzel's reputation," that "the minute the Jews entered the town, the inhabitants would all be slaughtered."[55] The Irgun fired at fleeing residents.[56]

The Palmach was the military force primarily responsible for the Galilee, and its commander, Moshe Dayan, said that the new state must be "homogeneous," with as few Arabs as possible.[57] From many villages in the Galilee the Palmach removed entire populations by force. In Er Rama village, which it captured April 24, it ordered inhabitants to assemble in the square and forced nearly all the residents to go north into Lebanon.[58] On May 1 it captured the village of Ein ez Zeitun after rolling explosive-filled barrels down a hill into the village and throwing in hand grenades. The Palmach then forced all the inhabitants to the edge of town, ordered them to leave, and fired over their heads as they went.[59]

In late April the Haganah also attacked Arab sectors of Jerusalem and took the Sheikh Jarrah and Katamon districts, resulting in the flight of Arab residents.[60] In early May the Palmach took two more major towns in the Galilee. The Palmach shelled Safad, and when the fall of the town became imminent the Arab residents fled.[61] Yigal Allon, the Palmach commander, said of the assault on Safad: "The Arab population fled. We did everything to encourage them to flee."[62] The Palmach then attacked Beisan. Its shelling led some of its Arab population to flee, and after taking the town it expelled most of the rest.[63] Allon said the Haganah "saw the need to clean the inner Galilee, to cause the tens of thousands of sulky Arabs who remained in Galilee to flee." He convinced village elders to urge villagers "to escape while there is still time."[64] In the Galilee village of El Bassa, which it captured May 14, the Palmach forced the population into the village church, where it shot and killed a number of youths. It then forced the other inhabitants out of the village.[65]

As the expulsion drive gained momentum, the UN General Assembly continued to work toward a trusteeship, as advised by the Security Council. Nonetheless, the Jewish Agency continued to insist on partition, viewing Resolution 181 as giving it a legal right to statehood. On April 9 Weizmann referred to Resolution 181 as a "grant of independence" for a Jewish state.[66] At the United Nations, Jewish Agency representative Moshe Shertok said that in Resolution 181 the General Assembly had "conferred statehood" on both Jews and Arabs.[67] As a result of the recent hostilities a Jewish state "already existed," making discussion of a trusteeship moot. He chided the United States, which had proposed trusteeship, juxtaposing that policy with the U.S. support for UN membership of recently independent Arab states. It was "incongruous for the United States to endorse the claims of those relatively primitive societies to sovereignty and membership in the United Nations and yet advocate further tutelage for both peoples of Palestine."[68] The Arab Higher Committee said that if no trusteeship were established, it would declare statehood.[69] But the committee had little chance of holding territory, since the Jewish Agency was rapidly advancing and King Abdullah was planning to incorporate part of Palestine.

British journalist Harry Levin, working for the Haganah, wrote on April 28 of the accelerating Arab flight from Palestine: "it has become panic . . . all over the country, even from places not directly in the fighting line."[70] The *Palestine Post* reported the Arabs of Palestine were "in panic flight."[71] In a speech to the Jewish National Council on "the success of Jewish arms," Ben-Gurion said "the Arabs had left 100 villages, and 150,000 of them were on the move."[72] By mid-May 300,000 Arab refugees had fled from the territory occupied by the Zionist forces.[73] The Haganah intelligence branch said the "main cause of the movement of population" was "hostile operations," which, it added, accounted for 55 percent of the flight. It attributed another 15 percent to fear engendered by prior terror attacks.[74]

Despite its January decision to send troops into Palestine upon Britain's withdrawal, the Arab League had made no preparations for intervention. In early April it was encouraged by the General Assembly's abandonment of the Resolution 181 partition plan and hoped for a political solution. But by late April the Zionist forces had captured Haifa and Jaffa, and the flight of Palestine's Arabs was becoming evident in neighboring Arab states. Pressure built on Arab governments to protect the Palestine Arabs, and on April 29 the League decided to intervene.[75]

As the Palestine Arabs fled, the Arab Higher Committee and Arab governments, in radio broadcasts, urged them to remain in place.[76] The Arab Higher Committee broadcast particular appeals to Arab civil servants to remain at their posts, and these broadcasts were reported in the *Palestine Post*.[77] In an April 24 broadcast the committee characterized as "cowards" any who "deserted their homes."[78] In Jerusalem on April 27 the local national committee appealed to residents to stay.[79] In a Palestine Broadcast Service message Anwar Nuseibeh, secretary of the Arab Higher Committee, urged Arab Jerusalemites to "remain calm and avoid chaos."[80] The Haifa national committee issued at least twelve communiqués urging the population of Haifa to remain,[81] and the Haganah radio reported these appeals.[82] A Haganah internal report said that "the Arab institutions attempted to struggle against the phenomenon of flight and evacuation."[83]

The Arab Higher Committee urged Arab states not to grant entry permits to Palestine Arabs.[84] A radio message on May 4 by King Abdullah asked Palestine Arabs who had left to return and praised those who had stayed.[85] Egypt announced on May 5 that Palestine Arab men aged eighteen to fifty would not be admitted into Egypt.[86] As reported by the Haganah radio, Lebanon ordered all Palestine refugees aged eighteen to fifty to leave Lebanon within forty-eight hours.[87]

A U.S. State Department official, Robert McClintock, accurately predicted on May 4, 1948, what would occur upon British withdrawal, scheduled for May 14: "In light of the Jewish military superiority which now obtains in Palestine, the Jewish Agency will prefer to round out its State after May 15 and rely on its armed strength to defend that state from Arab counterattack." If the Agency were to use force to establish a state, McClintock said, "the Jews will be the actual aggressors against the Arabs. However, the Jews will claim that they are merely defending the boundaries of a state which were traced by the UN."[88]

By May 14, the date set for Britain's renunciation of authority, the General Assembly had not finalized its trusteeship recommendation. Instead, it proposed a truce and appointed a mediator "to promote a peaceful adjustment of the future situation of Palestine." At the same time it relieved of its duties the commission it had established in Resolution 181 to supervise partition.[89]

On May 14, 1948, Britain renounced authority in Palestine, and its troops were in the final phase of withdrawal. The Arab Higher Committee did not proclaim statehood, but the Jewish Agency did, issuing a Declaration of the Establishment of the State of Israel. "By virtue of our natural and historic right and on the strength of the resolution of the United Nations General Assembly," the declaration read, we "hereby declare the establishment of a Jewish state in Eretz-Israel, to be known as the State of Israel."[90] Thus, the Agency ignored the General Assembly's abandonment of partition and insisted that Resolution 181 gave them legal entitlement.

Similarly, when the Jewish Agency informed the United Nations of its declaration, it cited Resolution 181 as "recognition by United Nations" of a "right of Jewish people to establish their independent state."[91] Abba Eban, addressing the United Nations on behalf of the Agency, called Israel "the first state to be given birth by the United Nations."[92] Two Zionist lawyers said at the time that Israel was established "in pursuance of the United Nations Resolution," which was not "a mere act of international ratification of the existence of a new State which had already established itself." They said the "international decision had preceded the emergence of the State and thus may be said to have been its legal foundation."[93]

The declaration did not specify any borders for Israel. But in a message to President Truman urging him to recognize Israel, the Agency said it was proclaiming statehood "within frontiers approved by the General Assembly of the United Nations in its Resolution of November 29, 1947."[94] Use of the designation "Eretz Israel" suggested, however, that broader claims might be intended. Truman immediately extended de facto recognition of Israel. That recognition led—according to Dean Rusk, director of the State Department's Office of Special Political Affairs—to "pandemonium" on the floor of the UN General Assembly, since delegates (including U.S. delegates) felt that the United Nations should establish a temporary trusteeship.[95]

8

Kaftans and Yarmulkes:

The Claim of Ancient Title to Palestine

I have been a stranger in a strange land.
—*Holy Bible*, Exodus 2:22

In addition to Resolution 181, the Jewish Agency relied for its claim to Palestine on self-determination and ancient title."[1] Its declaration's reference to "our natural and historic right" was to a claim of right based on the Hebrew kingdom that existed during the first millenium B.C. in a portion of Palestine. The declaration recited that "Eretz-Israel was the birthplace of the Jewish people."[2]

The Jewish Agency said that modern Jewry is the successor to the ancient Hebrews, who had been forced out of Palestine by the Romans. "We are in Palestine as of right," said Ben-Gurion. "We are at home there. Ever since the Jewish people has existed, Palestine has been, remains and will remain their national home—and to one's home one can always return as of right without having to ask anybody else's leave."[3] The "exile of eighteen hundred years that began with the Roman conquest" and "the destruction of the Jewish state," argued Moshe Avidán, Israeli ambassador to Chile, "does not invalidate the historic and natural right of the Jewish people over its ancestral land."[4] Zionist lawyers said the Agency's claim was "sanctioned by the principle of self-determination."[5]

The Jewish Agency based its claim on self-determination.[6] The League of Nations Covenant, as already indicated, treated self-determination as a right of dependent peoples to the extent of prohibiting new colonization. By 1948 the UN Charter had come into force, and it used language on self-determination that was stronger than that of the League's Covenant. The UN Charter took the League's requirement on states administering former Turkish and German colonies and applied it to all states administering colonies. The charter, like the covenant, viewed administration of a nonself-governing territory as a "sacred trust" and required an administering state to make reports to the United Nations.[7] The charter stated that "equal rights and self-determination of peoples" was a "principle" of the United Nations.[8] But there was a question whether that charter declaration on self-determination made it a right.

The term "principle" was used in the Chinese, Spanish, English, and Russian versions of the charter. Some commentators argued that as a "principle," self-determination was not a right, but only an "aspiration."[9] "Principle," however, can mean a legal obligation.[10] The prohibition in Article 2 of the UN Charter against use of force is called a "principle." "The Organization and its Members," states Article 2, "shall act in accordance with the following Principles. . . . (4) All Members shall refrain in their international relations from the threat or use of force."

A complication in construing "principle" here is that the drafters of the UN Charter were not consistent in the five official languages in which they drafted the charter. The French text of the charter referred to self-determination as a "right" rather than a "principle." All five texts are official. When treaty texts vary, they must be reconciled.[11] If "principle" is ambiguous, "right" is not, and, therefore, "principle" must be read to mean a "right."

Subsequent UN practice confirmed that the charter's reference to self-determination was to a right. In 1950 the General Assembly asked for the UN Commission on Human Rights to "ensure the right of peoples and nations to self-determination."[12] In 1952 it referred to "the right of peoples and nations to self-determination as a fundamental human right."[13] Thus, self-determination did exist as a norm of law when the Jewish Agency made its claim to territory in Palestine in 1948.

It remains to apply that principle to the Agency's claim. Occupation and dominion are the key considerations in international law in a claim to territory, though in the twentieth century, when aggression was outlawed, naked possession was no longer sufficient.[14] But the initial consideration in a claim to territory is longevity of control over it. In Palestine the earliest period for which there is solid evidence as to the identity of the occupants is the second millenium B.C. At that time the most significant population group in Palestine was the

Canaanites.[15] They may have been associated with peoples who migrated to Palestine from the Arabian peninsula around 3500 B.C.[16] Because of the Canaanites, Palestine in the second millenium B.C. was, called the Land of Canaan. Other population groups in Palestine in that era included the Babylonians, Sumerians, Accadians, Phoenicians, Hebrews, and Philistines (from whom the name Palestine derives).[17]

Hebrews constituted a substantial community in Palestine by the twelfth century B.C. and formed a state around 1000 B.C.—in the area that the Arabs today call the West Bank of the Jordan River.[18] The coastal plain continued to be occupied by the Philistines.[19] In 930 B.C. the Hebrew state split into a northern state called Israel, in Samaria, and a southern state called Judah, in Judea.[20] Hebrews constituted a majority in Judea, though it is uncertain whether they did in Samaria.[21] The Hebrews were driven out as rulers of Samaria by Assyria around 720 B.C. and as rulers of Judea by Babylonia around 590 B.C.[22] Some Hebrews, particularly from the upper classes, were deported to Babylonia, while the peasantry remained.[23] Many of these deportees returned to Judea around 500 B.C.[24]

The Hebrews regained dominance in Judea around 150 B.C.[25] They came to be called Jews because of their association with Judea.[26] At that period they extended their control over much of modern-day Palestine.[27] The Romans took over in 63 B.C., though Jews remained the majority population of Judea until many of them were expelled by the Romans in A.D. 133.[28] The population of Palestine thereafter was a mixture of Philistines, Canaanites, Greeks, and Romans.[29]

In the seventh century A.D. Arabs from the Arabian peninsula conquered Palestine. The population absorbed their Arabic language, and most adopted their Islamic religion, although some remained Christians.[30] Of the Jews who still lived in Palestine, some retained Judaism as their religion. But the Arab conquest had little impact on the ethnic composition of Palestine. The number of Arabs who came to Palestine was small, and they were absorbed into the local population. Therefore, as of 1880—the time just before the onset of Zionist immigration—the majority population of Palestine, though Arabized, descended from the Canaanites and other groups that inhabited Palestine in the second millenium B.C.[31] That population numbered about 450,000, while there were about 20,000 Jews.[32]

A difficulty with the Jewish Agency's claim was that claims to territory based on ancient title have not generally been recognized. During the House of Lords debate of the Balfour Declaration in 1922, Lord Sydenham said the Zionists "have no more valid claim to Palestine than the descendants of the ancient Romans have to this country."[33] The U.S. King-Crane Commission stated that the claim, "often submitted by Zionist representatives, that they have a 'right' to Palestine, based on an occupation of two thousand years ago, can hardly be seriously considered."[34]

To support the Zionist historical claim, Julius Stone argued that "no identifiable people now survives which can demonstrate any special relation to Palestine prior to the centuries of Jewish statehood there."[35] As indicated above, the Palestine Arabs derive from peoples who occupied Palestine before the time of the Hebrew kingdom. Thus, if ancient title were recognized, it would not necessarily support a Zionist claim.

The International Court of Justice rejected a concept of original, or ancient, title. In a dispute between Britain and France over two islands in the English Channel controlled by Britain in modern times, France claimed "an original feudal title." The court stated that France's ancient title "could today produce no legal effect."[36] If ancient title were recognized, the result would be perpetual war, as communities claimed the land that belonged to their ancestors.[37] Ancient title would require the dismemberment of many existing states.[38]

Even if ancient title were recognized, the Jewish Agency would still need to establish its connection to the population that inhabited Palestine in ancient times. A World Zionist Organization delegate to the Versailles Conference in 1919 referred to Palestine as the land of the Jewish people's "ancestors."[39] But this assertion was questioned. Joseph Reinach, an anti-Zionist Jewish member of the French parliament, argued in 1919 that Jews of "Palestinian origin" form only a "tiny minority" of contemporary Jewry. He said that the Jews "have been as zealous as proselytizers as Christians and Moslems"; that in ancient times they converted many Arabs, Greeks, Egyptians, and Romans, and made converts later in Asia, north Africa, Italy, Spain, and Gaul. Most "Russian, Polish and Galician Jews," he said, "descend from the Khazars, a Tatar people from the south of Russia who converted to Judaism in mass at the time of Charlemagne."[40]

A people claiming territory bears a burden to prove the facts underlying its claim.[41] Ben-Gurion said that "race" does not unite Jewry since the ancient people "dissipated after so much dispersion."[42] But the Jewish Agency usually argued the opposite—that the Jews did not mix with other peoples. "Intermarriage has brought few additions," stated Louis Brandeis. "Therefore the percentage of foreign blood in the Jews of today is very low. Probably no important European race is as pure."[43]

Many Jews who remained in Judea and the Galilee converted to Christianity and lost their identity as Jews.[44] Many Jews who left Palestine intermarried, resulting in "an influx of non-Jewish genes into the Jewish groups from the earliest times to the present in most places and ages," in the words of Raphael Patai and Jennifer Patai Wing, two leading students of the subject.[45] In early times proselytism brought non-Jews into Judaism in Babylon, Syria, Arabia, Phoenicia, and Egypt.[46] In the last several centuries B.C. and the early centuries A.D. the substantial Jewish communities around the Mediterranean included many converts. In Europe Gallo-Romans converted to Judaism.[47] Proselytism continued in Europe into the Middle Ages,[48] with much of the large Jewish community in Spain consisting of converts.[49] The substantial Jewish population of southern Arabia, particularly in Yemen, was composed largely of Arabs who converted to Judaism,[50] for in Islamic countries Jews frequently converted their Arab slaves.[51] The Jews of China have always been predominantly Chinese, and the Falashas of Ethiopia predominantly African.[52]

In the area north of the Caspian and Black seas the sizable kingdom of the Khazars adopted Judaism as a state religion in the eighth century.[53] Large sections of the population converted,[54] and the Khazars adapted the Hebrew alphabet to write their Turkish-related language.[55] Khazars migrated into Slavic-speaking areas,[56] particularly after the Mongols destroyed Khazaria in the eleventh century.[57] A Khazar subgroup called the Kabars, who also followed Judaism,[58] accompanied the Magyars westward and founded Hungary.[59] Khazars migrated to Poland and Lithuania, establishing Jewry there.[60] The presence of some fair-complexioned persons in Eastern European Jewry is cited to show Khazar descendance, since there were fair-complexioned persons among the Khazars.[61] There is similarity as well between Khazars and Eastern European Jews in male attire, particularly the long kaftan robe, the yarmulke skullcap, and the large round fur-trimmed hat.[62]

A competing theory is that Eastern European Jewry is made up largely of Jews who migrated from Western Europe to escape persecutions that accompanied the Crusades (eleventh century) and the Black Death (fourteenth century),[63] or that such eastward migrations supplemented the Khazar-Jewish population.[64] There is no contemporary evidence, however, of eastward migration of Jews during the Crusades or the Black Death.[65] But evidence of such migration is sketchy,[66] and most scholars find the East European Jews to be predominantly Khazar-descended.[67]

One aspect of the Jewish Agency's historical claim was that, although few Jews remained in Palestine, Jews retained a strong psychological attachment to it.[68] The Agency's declaration recited that "the people kept faith with" Israel "throughout their dispersion" and "never ceased to pray and hope for their return to it and for the restoration in it of their political freedom."[69] The declaration alludes here to a religious doctrine that Palestine was promised to the Jews.[70] Until the development of Zionism in the late nineteenth century, however, the biblical promise was not taken as a promise of a territorial state.[71] The idea of establishing a Jewish state in Palestine emerged only in the nineteenth century.[72]

Israeli officials later would repeat this position. Ben-Gurion said that "the Romans, the Persians, the Byzantines, the Arabs, the Mongols, the Crusaders, the Turks have reigned in the country," but that "in the eyes of generations of Jews, it was Eretz-Israel." The "uniqueness of the country in the soul of the Jewish people and in Jewish history" is "a fact as solid as iron that thousands of years of alienation and revolution have not been able to root it out."[73] Levi Eshkol, as prime minister of Israel in the 1960s, would say that "Israel in dispersion maintained its spiritual and material links with this country." This "historical and spiritual right" has been "confirmed by international law and forged on the anvil of reality." He found "no parallel in the annals of the nations to this unique bond between our people and its land."[74] Judge Moshe Silberg of the Supreme Court of Israel would state that "our spiritual presence in this land was far more intensive than the physical presence" of those who inhabited it. "We prayed in exile for the dew and the rain," he said, "not in the rainy seasons of Poland and the Ukraine but in the rainy season of the land of Israel."[75]

Ben-Gurion argued that though Jews were absent from Palestine they made "incessant efforts" to return.[76] But British historian Hugh Trevor-Roper disputed Ben-Gurion's interpretation. The Jews were not "constantly prepared for a return to the Holy Land," he wrote, nor was Zionism "the end to which all creation, in those two thousand years, had been groaning and travailing." The Jews "might suffer terrible persecutions and pogroms in Russia or Poland," but "somehow when they left, with the Holy Land on their lips, their feet carried them" to "Germany or England or America."[77]

Prior to the nineteenth century few Jews migrated to Palestine,[78] though there was no prohibition on migration after the Arab conquest in the seventh century. The Ottoman Empire did not prohibit Jewish immigration, but European Jews who migrated to the Ottoman Empire typically went to Constantinople, Damascus, or Cairo, where economic opportunities were greater than in Palestine.[79] The fact of psychological attachment to a territory does not yield territorial rights; and the criteria of occupation and dominion used in international law require a more concrete connection.

9

Arab vs. Zionist: War of

Independence or War of Aggression?

And those who, when
An Oppressive wrong is inflicted
On them, (are not cowed
But) help and defend themselves.
—*Holy Quran*, xlii, 39

To bolster its territorial claim, the Zionist movement downplayed the size and longevity of the Arabs' residence in Palestine. This was expressed in a phrase that became popular that the movement sought "a land without people for a people without land."[1] But the Arab population had been stable for hundreds of years. There was no substantial in-migration in the nineteenth century.

The Jewish Agency argued that the Palestine Arabs did not constitute an ethnic group separate from other Arabs and, therefore, had no self-determination right and in particular no right to Palestine.[2] The Agency pointed out that in the early twentieth century Palestine Arabs did not seek independence for Palestine but for a single Arab state or for a Syrian state of which they would form a part. Thus, it depicted the idea of a separate Palestine as artificial, invented to defeat Zionist claims.[3] Golda Meir, as prime minister of Israel, declared that "there is no such thing as Palestinians." She said, "it was not as though there was a Palestinian people in Palestine considering itself as a Palestinian people and we came and threw them out and took their country away from them. They . . . did not exist."[4] By this, Meir meant that Palestine Arabs did not consider themselves different from the Arabs of neighboring areas.

To be sure, the Palestine Arabs did, in the early twentieth century, seek a single Arab state and later an affiliation with Syria. While Turkey ruled, many Arabs sought the establishment of a single Arab state. Syria was a dominant force in Arab nationalism, and affiliation with Syria appealed to many Palestine Arabs.[5] Syria also seemed to have the strength to defend the Palestine Arabs against Zionism.[6] That orientation, however, "did not mean that they regarded themselves as Syrians."[7] Though Palestine had not been administered by Turkey as a single unit, Palestine had its identity from ancient times and was considered as a territorial unit into modern times by its inhabitants—and by Europeans—who referred to it either as Palestine or as the Holy Land.[8] When France and Britain divided the Arab territories into the mandates of Syria, Lebanon, Iraq, Palestine, and Transjordan after World War I, pan-Arabism gave way in Palestine to the espousal of independence for Palestine alone.[9] Arabs came to identify themselves as Syrian Arab, Iraqi Arab, or Palestinian Arab.[10]

The issue of Palestinian distinctiveness is not relevant, however, to claims to Palestine. The basis for a claim to territory is longtime occupation. For this purpose it does not matter whether the Palestine Arabs are distinct from neighboring peoples. The fact that they may have constituted part of a larger nation cannot be used to defeat their right to their territory.

Another argument made by some scholars in opposition to a right of self-determination for the Palestine Arabs was that to recognize their right would involve denying self-determination to the Jews. Arab self-determination "should not be applied to the territorial area of Israel," argued Michael Reisman, "for it would involve a comparable deprivation of the Israelis who themselves have their own historical trauma and have established a state for reasons which are well known."[11] The solution, say scholars like Julius Stone, is for Jordan to be the Palestinian Arab State.[12] These views overlook the Palestine Arabs' strong claim based on occupation and dominion and the correspondingly weak claim of the Zionists on these grounds.

If the Jewish Agency did not have a right based on history—and if the United Nations conferred no rights upon it—and if the indigenous population of Palestine (predominantly Arab) had a right to self-determination, then the Jewish Agency's right to use force to take control of Palestine is in doubt. As the Arab Higher Committee viewed the matter, "the people of Palestine" were "an independent nation." It said that the "majority of the population of Palestine, the 1,300,000 Arabs," considered that "the Jewish minority—whether

the 300,000 Palestinian citizens or the 400,000 foreigners—is a rebel-
lious minority which has revolted against the sovereignty of the majority of the population of the country." Thus, the committee thought
"that any attempt to create any foreign government in Palestine" was
"an act of rebellion."[13] This view was expressed in more colorful
terms some years later by Mohammed Bedjaoui, an Arab jurist who
would become a judge of the International Court of Justice. "Who is
the aggressor? The intruder who, without right or title, has taken
possession of another's house and cries foul play whenever an attempt
is made to evict him?" Bedjaoui asked. "Or the rightful owner, who
has been clamoring for his rights for nearly half a century and asks
for nothing but the restitution of his property?"[14]

The Arab Higher Committee was not a state. But, like the Jewish Agency, it was recognized by the League of Nations as representing the interests of its community in Palestine. "Communities under
mandate" were "subjects of international law" with "a patrimony
distinct from that of the Mandatory State," the Institute of International Law said in 1931. They possessed "a national status," and they
could acquire rights or be held to their obligations.[15] As the entity
representing the majority population of Palestine, the Arab Higher
Committee had a strong claim to be the bearer of sovereignty. And
Palestine, as it emerged from the mandate upon Britain's renunciation, possessed many attributes of statehood. It had a border internationally recognized;[16] its inhabitants carried Palestinian citizenship;[17]
it had a body of law deriving from Ottoman law enforced in its
courts;[18] and it had been a party in its own name to treaties.[19]

The Jewish Agency could also be considered in itself to be an
outside force. Thus, Cherif Bassiouni suggested by way of analogy
that if "a hypothetical group of people" were to steal an atomic bomb
and to try to drop it on a particular state, this would be an armed
attack warranting self-defense within the meaning of Article 51 of
the UN Charter.[20] This conclusion arguably follows from the fact that
Article 51 permits self-defense "if an armed attack occurs" but does
not specify that the attack must be carried out by a state.[21]

The view that an attack by a private group is an "armed attack"
under the UN Charter has been challenged, however.[22] Aggression is
generally considered to occur only when the attacking entity is a
state.[23] If an attack by a private group on a state were deemed an
attack by a state, then a state using force to defend itself would be

required to inform the UN Security Council, since Article 51 of the UN Charter requires a state using force in self-defense to report to the council. But there is little precedent for reporting to the council by a state repelling an attack by a private group.

Even if an attack by a private group is not an attack as defined by the UN Charter, it nonetheless may lawfully be opposed by force. A state has the right to defend itself from armed action by private groups, whether they originate in the state or enter from outside.[24] Thus, if the Arab Higher Committee were a territorial sovereign, it would have a right to use force against the Jewish Agency, which would have been asserting by armed force a right to sovereignty in the committee's territory.

The Jewish Agency's military action of 1947–48 has also been analyzed as the action of a state, on the ground that the Agency had public-law status with the League of Nations. Under this analysis, the Zionist forces were agents of that public-law body who took up arms against the majority population of Palestine. Their action, therefore, constituted an armed attack by a state warranting self-defense by the majority population.[25]

The Security Council's approach to the 1948 war lends support to this view, at least to the extent that the council seemed to consider the Jewish Agency a state for this purpose. On May 14, 1948, the Jewish Agency, anticipating Arab-state intervention, brought to the Security Council a complaint of aggression against the Arab League. The Security Council treated it as a state-to-state complaint. This approach, according to international law specialists Myres McDougal and Florentino Feliciano, suggested that a conflict involving a newly organized territorial body politic on the one side and established states on the other is treated like a conflict between established states.[26] While the council was acting in response to the hostilities between Israel and the Arab League, its approach suggests that the Jewish Agency should be deemed a public-law body even with regard to its hostilities with the Palestine Arabs.

It was also plausibly suggested that the Jewish Agency's imposition of statehood amounted to a forced colonization of Palestine. The Agency had been allowed to develop a Jewish settler population by Great Britain, and it then revolted against Britain. The UN Charter did not require administering states to divest themselves of their colonies.[27] But, like the League of Nations Covenant, it barred new colonization. By outlawing aggression and requiring the promotion of self-determination, the charter prohibited the taking of a people's territory by force. In the post-charter era no state claimed a right to acquire new colonies. If the Jewish Agency had no right to statehood, the colonialist aspect of its venture was unmistakable.

"Left to themselves," wrote a contemporary observer of the 1948 situation, "the Arabs of Palestine would be impotent against the Jewish State."[28] When the Arab-state forces entered Palestine May 15, 1948, the Jewish Agency, now representing the provisional government of Israel, told the United Nations that the intervention constituted aggression.[29] But the UN Security Council made no determination on that score.[30] The United States submitted a draft resolution that would have characterized the intervention as a breach of the peace, but it was voted down.[31] The council merely asked "all Governments and authorities, without prejudice to the rights, claims or positions of the parties concerned, to abstain from any hostile military action in Palestine."[32] Without assigning fault, it found "that the situation in Palestine constitutes a threat to the peace" and called for a cease-fire.[33]

The Arab states characterized their intervention as a defense of the majority population of Palestine.[34] Egypt cited atrocities against the Palestine Arabs[35] and a need to stop "Zionist terrorist gangs who persisted in attacking the peaceful Arab inhabitants."[36] Transjordan had been "compelled to enter Palestine to protect unarmed Arabs against massacres."[37] The Arab Higher Committee had invited the League forces to "assist" the committee "in maintaining law and order."[38] The intervening states also stressed they were entering Palestine at the committee's request. Egypt "was asked by the abundantly expressed will of the people of Palestine to offer aid to the new State."[39] Syria stated that the Arab majority in Palestine, in requesting Arab-state intervention, was exercising its right of self-determination.[40] Saudi Arabia sent forces into Palestine "to help their brothers, the Palestinian Arabs, only after they have been requested to do so by the majority of the inhabitants of the country."[41]

Despite Israel's charge of aggression, it was not clear that the Arab League forces were invading the territory that Israel claimed, which was the territory designated for a Jewish state in Resolution 181. The chiefs of staff of the Arab armies had informed their governments that the Arab League did not have the necessary troop strength or aircraft to defeat the Zionist forces. Realizing that, League officials hoped a show of force might convince the major powers to act on behalf of the Palestine Arabs.[42] Egypt conducted some air raids over Tel Aviv,[43] but the Arab League forces did not launch a serious ground attack into the areas the General Assembly had suggested for a Jewish state.[44] Transjordan, in particular, aimed at taking the West Bank, leaving the rest of Palestine to the Jewish Agency.[45] Upon entering Palestine, Transjordan indicated it would try only to stop farther advances by Zionist forces into Arab-populated sectors.[46] King Abdullah ordered his forces not to enter the area designated for a Jewish state in Resolution 181.[47] Transjordan's forces were headed by British officers, and they were under instructions to resign if the king ordered attacks into the area designated for a Jewish state.[48] The only major battle between the Arab Legion and the Zionist forces occurred around Jerusalem, which, according to Resolution 181, was to be internationalized. When that occurred, Britain withdrew from the legion both its officers and its funding.[49]

If the aim of the Arab-state forces was to prevent further atrocities, its intervention might be justifiable as humanitarian intervention. There is a doctrine, on which Israel would rely in 1976 in sending troops into Uganda to rescue kidnapped Israelis, that permits troop intervention to save persons from imminent harm.[50] While that doctrine was and still is controversial in international law, the factual basis of a need to protect human life was strong. The Haganah, Irgun, and LEHI had already killed substantial numbers of Palestine Arab civilians, even with British troops in Palestine. The prospect was very real that with Britain out of Palestine they would kill civilians more freely.

While the Arab states limited themselves for the most part to the territory designated in Resolution 181 for an Arab state, they made no formal commitment to observe that limitation, and the Arab Higher Committee claimed jurisdiction over all of Palestine.[51] If the aim of the Arab League was to uphold the right of the Palestine Arabs to sovereignty in all of Palestine, then the legality of the intervention would depend on the rights to Palestine of its Arabs and Jews.

If the hostilities amounted to a domestic rebellion by the Jewish

Agency against the Arab Higher Committee as the lawful bearer of sovereignty in Palestine, the law in force at the time did not provide clear guidelines. There had been outside intervention in the civil wars in Russia (1918–19) and Spain (1936–38), despite international efforts to limit it.[52] The law of the period did not clearly prohibit intervention, particularly on the side of the lawful government.[53]

If the rebel group was aided by outside states, then the right of other states to aid the lawful government was stronger still.[54] The Jewish Agency's challenge to the Arab Higher Committee was, arguably, being aided morally by the states that proposed a Jewish state in part of Palestine through Resolution 181, and materially by states —like Czechoslovakia—that permitted arms to be sold to the Jewish Agency.

The Jewish Agency was even more clearly being aided by outside private elements—through financial contributions—and one leading scholar found this gave the Arab states a right to intervene. "The Jewish community in Palestine," wrote Michael Akehurst, "was being used by foreign interests to commit indirect aggression against Palestine. The Arab states were protecting Palestine against such subversion; it is generally agreed that one state may protect another against subversion, under the rule of collective self-defense." The subversion was outside aid to the Jewish Agency, according to Akehurst. "The Zionist victory was due in no small measure to the money, weapons and men which the Zionists received from overseas."

The aid, Akehurst continued, "came mainly from private individuals and private organisations rather than from governments." While "most instances of collective self-defense against subversion relate to subversion by foreign governments," a state, "should have as much right to defend another state against subversion from foreign private interests as it has to defend another state against subversion from foreign governments, particularly as private interests are often as powerful as governments." Akehurst cited the 1960 secession of Katanga Province in the Congo, in which "a number of states regarded the assistance allegedly given by western capitalists to the secessionary movement in Katanga as a form of subversion, and claimed a right to defend the Congo against such subversion."[55]

The Arab Higher Committee would have a right to request intervention only if it enjoyed the necessary status in Palestine to do so. It has been objected that Palestine was not an independent state and the Arab Higher Committee was not a legitimate government authorized to seek foreign aid.[56] But Palestine possessed, as indicated, an international status as representative of a people enjoying a right to statehood. The Arab Higher Committee represented the Arab population of Palestine and, therefore, had a right to request assistance.[57]

Israel objected to the Arab Higher Committee's request to Transjordan on the ground that Transjordan did not recognize the Arab Higher Committee. In mid-May 1948 King Abdullah, arguing that a truncated Palestine state was not viable, stated that the Arab Higher Committee no longer represented the Palestine Arabs.[58] Abdullah's nonrecognition of the Arab Higher Committee did not impair its request for intervention, however. The other Arab League states recognized the Arab Higher Committee, and the committee had the right to issue the invitation, regardless of the king's view. The Arab Legion entered with consent of the Arab Higher Committee, which rendered their entry lawful even if King Abdullah was not responding to the committee's invitation.[59]

The request was also challenged on the ground that the Arab League had decided in September 1947 to intervene if necessary to prevent partition, prior to any invitation from the Arab Higher Committee. This decision, it was argued, showed the aggressive character of the invasion.[60] But, as indicated, the League's intentions were uncertain through late 1947 and early 1948. It did not make a definite decision to intervene until April 1948. In any event, the league never contemplated intervening without the consent of the Arab Higher Committee. On December 8, 1947, the League indicated that if it intervened, it would do so "with the full consent of Palestine Arabs."[61]

The Arab League states also justified their intervention as lawful action of a regional organization.[62] The UN Charter authorizes action against breaches of the peace by regional bodies, and the Arab League probably qualified as such a body. Article 6 of the pact of the League states that in case of "aggression or threat of aggression by a State against a member State," the League's council should "determine the necessary measures to repel this aggression."[63] This justification faced two problems, however, and the matter was never resolved by the Security Council. The first was that Article 6 required aggression by a state. It would thus be necessary to decide that Israel was a state. Since the Security Council was dealing with the dispute on the assumption Israel was a state, this might not be too great an obstacle. A second problem was that Article 6 required the aggression be against a member state, and Palestine was not a member state. Had the Arab Higher Committee had an opportunity to form a state, it would have joined the league, but the fact remained it was not a member.

10

Exodus: The Departure

of the Palestine Arabs

We did everything to encourage them to flee.
— Yigal Allon, Commander, Palmach

The concerns of the Arab League were not frivolous. "British with-drawal freed our hands," explained the Haganah's intelligence branch in an analysis of the events.[1] In Jerusalem on May 15, 1948, Haganah loudspeaker vans urged the Arab population to flee. "Take pity on your wives and children and get out of this bloodbath," they proclaimed. "Surrender to us with your arms. No harm will come to you. Or get out by the Jericho road, that is still open to you. If you stay, you invite disaster."[2] The Jericho road leads to Jordan. "The evacuation of Arab civilians had become a war aim," said Haganah officer Uri Avnery, who would later become a member of Israel's parliament (Knesset).[3]

On May 15–16 the Haganah shelled Acre, where thousands of Arabs from Haifa and elsewhere had taken refuge. Most residents of Acre had fled during the Haganah's encirclement of the city that began in late April, and as the city fell more of them fled.[4] The Arab Legion moved into Jerusalem, where it tried to take back territory captured by the Haganah, but its only success was in capturing the Jewish Quarter inside the walls of the Old City.[5] In June the Haganah reorganized itself as the Israel Defense Force (IDF), absorbing the Irgun and LEHI,[6] and consequently the IDF outnumbered the combined forces of Arab armies.[7] Arms and ammunition the Jewish Agency purchased in Czechoslovakia began to arrive.[8] Meir attributed the Haganah's success in this period to these purchases of "shells, machine guns, bullets—and even planes."[9]

The Arabs of Palestine were "ejected and forced to flee into Arab territory," wrote Edgar O'Ballance, an historian of the war. "Wherever the Israeli troops advanced into Arab country, the Arab population was bulldozed out in front of them."[10] It "typically sufficed," recalled Avnery, "to fire a few shots in the direction of Arab villages to see the inhabitants, who had not fought for generations, take flight."[11] In the town of Beisan some of the Arab population remained after the Palmach's attack in May. In June the IDF drove these remaining Beisan residents to the Jordan River and forced them to cross.[12] In July the IDF captured the major adjoining towns of Ramleh and Lydda in central Palestine. By decision of Ben-Gurion, it sent loudspeaker vans to order the inhabitants to evacuate. The IDF forced 60,000 residents, nearly the entire population of the two towns, to march east to the town of Ramallah, which was under Jordanian control.[13] The Haganah fired mortars to encourage the Ramleh and Lydda inhabitants along the road.[14] It spared one small group of Lydda residents from the expulsion, the town's railroad employees, since it needed them to run the railroad.[15] But Israel's policy, wrote O'Ballance, "was now openly one of clearing out all the Arab civil population before them."[16]

On July 16 the Haganah's Seventh Brigade captured Nazareth with little fighting,[17] but strong Arab leadership there prevented panic flight when the town fell.[18] Ben Dunkelman, commander of the Seventh Brigade, met with Nazareth officials and concluded a written surrender document in which he agreed not to expel the population.[19] Ben-Gurion arrived in Nazareth and reportedly asked why the Arabs were still there.[20] Dunkelman said he received an order about that time from the IDF command to expel the Nazareth population. He refused and, as a result, was ordered to withdraw the Seventh Brigade from Nazareth, to be replaced by other forces that would carry out the expulsion.[21] But after replacing the Seventh Brigade, IDF command reconsidered the matter. Expulsion from such an important Christian site would attract attention in the West.[22] To avert negative reaction, the command decided not to expel the population.[23] It did, however, try to expel small groups of Nazarenes over the next few weeks.[24] The nonexpulsion of the Nazareth population has been cited to prove that the IDF did not precipitate the Arab exodus from Palestine.[25] But Nazareth was a special case. The IDF did push out nearly all the Arabs in the territory it was capturing.[26]

Around Jerusalem the IDF and Arab Legion fought during July, but neither side was able to improve its position.[27] In mid-July the

IDF attacked the village of Jaba, near Haifa, and expelled all 8,000 inhabitants, firing at fleeing civilians.[28] It repeated this scenario in many Galilean villages.[29] In the Galilean town of Saffuriya IDF airplanes dropped barrels filled with explosives, metal fragments, nails, and glass. The population fled in panic.[30] To prevent the inhabitants' return, the IDF blew up houses in this and many other Galilean villages.[31] Count Folke Bernadotte, the UN mediator, complained of the demolitions, which he said were done "without apparent military necessity."[32]

Israel's expulsion policy generated modest opposition from left-wing Zionists.[33] Aharon Cizling, a left-wing member of the provisional government, complained about the expulsions and the demolition of Arab houses, leading the cabinet to issue an order on July 6 that read: "Except in the course of actual fighting, it is forbidden to destroy, burn or demolish Arab towns and villages, or to expel Arab inhabitants from their villages, neighborhoods and towns, or uproot inhabitants from their homes without express permission of an order from the Minister of Defense, in each and every case."[34] Expulsion and demolition continued, however.[35]

In August the government formalized its policy of demolishing villages to make it impossible for expelled inhabitants to reclaim them.[36] To prevent return by the inhabitants, the IDF set land mines around abandoned villages.[37] It quickly brought in Jews to settle many of the abandoned areas.[38] Count Bernadotte asked the government to repatriate refugees, but it refused.[39] As one reason for its refusal the government denied expelling the Arabs in the first place. Foreign Minister Moshe Shertok told Bernadotte "the war brought in its wake a mass exodus, mostly spontaneous."[40] But Bernadotte persisted on the issue. Disagreeing with Shertok's analysis of the reason for the departure, he reported to the United Nations that the "exodus of Palestinian Arabs resulted from panic created by fighting in their communities, by rumours concerning real or alleged acts of terrorism, or expulsion."[41]

As the IDF forced Arabs out of towns and villages, reported the *Economist*, it "systematically stripped" them of their personal belongings.[42] Soldiers removed furniture and housewares from abandoned Arab homes and took off doors, windows, lintels, bricks, roof tiles, and floor tiles[43] in what one observer called an "orgy of looting."[44] Bernadotte reported "large-scale looting, pillaging, and plundering" of Arab-owned property by the IDF, and he said that compensation should be paid for what was taken.[45] On September 17 three members of LEHI assassinated Bernadotte in Jerusalem, apparently because of his concern for the rights of the Arabs. LEHI leader Itzhak Shamir, according to several of the assassins, authorized the assassination.[46]

In October 1948 the IDF attacked more Galilean villages, typically taking them without resistance. In the village of Elabun it gathered the inhabitants and shot and killed thirteen young men.[47] It then expelled the rest of the residents, except for a small number of elderly and the village's Greek Orthodox residents. "The priests," an Israeli police report explained, "complained bitterly about the expulsion of the villagers and demanded their return."[48] In the village of Safsaf the IDF ordered the population to line up, then blindfolded seventy adult males and shot them to death. The other villagers fled.[49] In the village of Hula, just north of the Lebanon-Palestine border, Zionist forces confined seventy males in a building and killed them with submachine guns.[50] The IDF forced out the population of the villages of Ikrit and Biram,[51] and in the village of Gish IDF soldiers took valuables from the villagers. When the villagers demanded receipts, the soldiers took several of them outside the village to be shot and killed them.[52] UN observers in the Galilee reported these killings and expulsions, despite efforts by the IDF to keep them from investigating.[53] The Red Cross reported that, in villages whose population was not expelled, able-bodied men were put into hastily organized prison work camps.[54]

In October 1948 the IDF also conquered the Negev desert. It forced out most of the Arabs by destroying villages and killing inhabitants.[55] On October 22 it captured Beersheeba, the major town in the Negev, from the Egyptian army and expelled the town's population.[56] In the major coastal town of Majdal much of the population fled as the IDF approached.[57] On October 28 an IDF unit composed of former LEHI members captured the village of Dawaymeh, near Hebron. No fighting had occurred in Dawaymeh but soldiers said later they believed the villagers were responsible for killing one hundred Jews the previous year at a nearby settlement.[58] The unit killed several hundred civilians in Dawaymeh,[59] including seventy-five elderly men in a mosque. According to witnesses, Israeli soldiers beat women and children to death with sticks and blew up houses with people inside.[60]

Some Arabs forced out of their localities fled beyond the borders of Palestine, while others fled to the Gaza Strip or east central Palestine, which would later be known as the West Bank of the Jordan River. Some fled to other locations in the area controlled by the IDF. A report from Haifa by an Israeli intelligence officer gave figures for the so-called "internal refugees" in six northern villages.[61] The internal refugees had no homes in the localities where they took refuge and no source of income.[62]

UN mediator Count Folke Bernadotte reported shortly before his assassination that "almost the whole of the Arab population fled or was expelled from the area under Jewish occupation."[63] Of the major Arab towns of Palestine that it captured, the IDF depopulated nearly all of them, with the exception of Nazareth. Figures on populations before and after the expulsion are: Jaffa 70,000 to 3,600; Haifa 70,000 to 2,900; Jerusalem 70,000 to 3,500; Lydda-Ramleh 34,920 to 2,000; Acre 15,000 to 3,500; Tiberias 5,300 to virtually none; Safad 9,530 to virtually none;[64] Beisan 5,180 to virtually none;[65] and Beersheeba 6,500 to virtually none.[66] The Arab urban population on December 31, 1948, according to an Israeli government count, was only 36,814.[67]

The IDF also virtually depopulated the rural areas.[68] An IDF report of October 1948 on the Galilee recited: "In all the villages where we fought the population has already fled, but many more will still flee." A government report said that 600,000 had fled.[69] It is estimated that in the area Israel took in 1948 there had been 900,000 Arabs in 1947. Of these, only 120,000 remained, according to the first Israeli census. Of these 120,000, half were Bedouins in the Negev, living in sparsely populated areas where there was no heavy fighting. That means that in the densely populated areas only 60,000 Arabs remained out of 840,000.[70] And of these, 20,000–30,000 were internal refugees.[71] So of 840,000 Arabs in the densely populated areas, very few remained where they had formerly lived. To the Arabs, wrote a student of colonialism, Zionism had become "a prolonged and tragically successful invasion" conducted by "an alien people under Western imperialist auspices, ending in the expulsion of most of the people whose country it was."[72]

11

To Justify a State:

Israel as a Fact

I have found you an argument; I am not obliged to find you an understanding.
—Samuel Johnson, June 1784, in James Boswell, *Life of Samuel Johnson*

In the fall of 1948 Israel's provisional government prepared to invade the West Bank.[1] Militarily, Israel had the capacity to take the West Bank from Abdullah's Arab Legion,[2] but a West Bank invasion held political risks. If Israel took the West Bank and did not expel its population, the Jews would be a minority in their new state.[3] So the invasion plan proceeded on the assumption the IDF would force out the West Bank population. A West Bank invasion-expulsion would, however, greatly intensify the Arab refugee problem, over which Israel was already under pressure at the United Nations.[4] Israel had maintained good standing at the United Nations, despite the expulsions, but a West Bank invasion might jeopardize its application for UN membership.[5] Britain, it feared, might intervene on Transjordan's side.[6] Weighing these concerns, the provisional government canceled the invasion.

On November 29 the provisional government applied for UN membership.[7] Under the UN Charter a state is admitted to membership by an affirmative vote in both the Security Council and the General Assembly. The Security Council took up Israel's application on December 17. In the council discussion Britain voiced concern that Israel had not responded to the UN request for an explanation of the assassination of its mediator, Count Bernadotte. Britain also said that before it could support Israeli membership it needed clarification of Israel's position on the internationalization of Jerusalem and on repatriation of the Arab refugees. Israel's application was put to a vote and was rejected.[8]

On December 11 the UN General Assembly established a conciliation commission to urge the parties "to achieve a final settlement." At the same time it asked Israel to repatriate the refugees. It said that "the refugees wishing to return to their homes and live at peace with their neighbors should be permitted to do so at the earliest practical date, and that compensation should be paid for the property of those choosing not to return and for loss of or damage to property which, under principles of international law or in equity, should be made good by the Governments or authorities responsible."[9] But the provisional government refused repatriation, declaring that it was not responsible for the Arabs' flight. Ben-Gurion denied that Israel expelled any Arabs and said the departure of the Arabs had been organized by the Arab states or by Britain.[10] Ben-Gurion repeated that claim in later years, stating that the Zionist military had told Arabs to remain in place and the Arabs had "fled under orders of Arab leaders."[11]

In a few localities the Arab Higher Committee and Arab Legion did advise evacuation in the face of imminent attack.[12] But Ben-Gurion produced no evidence of any general departure orders to the Palestine Arabs from any Arab authority, and subsequent investigators found none.[13] Ben-Gurion did not mention the repeated appeals from Arab authorities for the Palestine Arabs to remain in place.[14] Legal scholar Nathan Feinberg, who supported Ben-Gurion's explanation, cited a statement attributed to Monsignor George Hakim, the Greek Orthodox Archbishop of Galilee: "The refugees had been confident that their absence from Palestine would not last long, that they would return within a few days—within a week or two. Their leaders had promised them that the Arab armies would crush the 'Zionist gangs' very quickly and there was no need for panic or fear for a long exile."[15] Feinberg said this statement acknowledged that the Palestine Arabs left because Arab authorities suggested it. Monsignor Hakim acknowledged the statement but said he did not mean that Arabs left in response to appeals. "At no time did I state that the flight of the refugees was due to the orders, explicit or implicit, of their leaders, military or political."[16]

In December 1948 the provisional government set a plan to conquer the Gaza Strip and Sinai Peninsula. It had the military capacity to accomplish this goal.[17] In late December the IDF made major gains against Egypt in the Sinai,[18] but Britain got word of the invasion and threatened to intervene.[19] The United States also threatened to withdraw its support for Israel's membership in the United Nations and warned against any further IDF offensives.[20] Under that pressure Ben-Gurion withdrew the IDF from Egyptian territory and canceled plans to take Gaza and the Sinai.[21]

At the same time Ben-Gurion withdrew the IDF from southern Lebanon, where it had penetrated. The Litani River, an important water source, flowed through southern Lebanon. General Yigal Allon criticized Ben-Gurion's decision to withdraw, complaining that the IDF had been "on the crest of victory" from "the Litani in the north to the Sinai desert in the southwest. A few more days of fighting would have enabled us to liberate the entire country."[22]

In the spring of 1949 Israel concluded individual armistice agreements—though not peace treaties—with Egypt, Lebanon, Transjordan, and Syria.[23] Under the armistice lines drawn in these agreements, Israel retained the territory it had taken militarily with minor adjustments.[24] The most protracted negotiations were between Israel and Syria, ending in a settlement that included the creation of a demilitarized zone between them.[25] By the agreements Israel held 77 percent of Palestine—all sectors except the Gaza Strip and the West Bank of the Jordan River. The agreements specified that the armistice lines were not international borders and that their acceptance did not imply recognition of a right to any piece of territory.[26] The only exception was the Israel-Lebanon armistice, which implied recognition of what had been the border between Mandate Palestine and Mandate Lebanon by saying that "the Armistice Demarcation Line shall follow the international boundary between Lebanon and Palestine."[27]

In March Israel resubmitted to the Security Council its application for membership, and this time the council approved it.[28] The General Assembly then took up the application, but many members had the same concerns Britain had expressed in the Security Council. Some were concerned as well that Israel had claimed no borders; this raised the question of whether it might intend to take further territory. If it did, Israel might not meet the membership requirement in Article 4 of the charter that it be "a peace-loving state." The assembly's ad hoc political committee asked Israel to appear to address these matters.[29]

In a statement to the committee on May 5 Abba Eban, Israel's representative, said that Jerusalem's status should be defined by international consent but that internationalization should apply only to the holy sites and that Israel might claim sovereignty over the "Jewish part" of the city. On the refugee question, Israel said the situation "was a direct consequence of the war launched by the Arab States" and, therefore, the matter should be solved by resettlement of the refugees in Arab states. It agreed to compensate Palestine Arabs whose property had been taken and promised to respect the property of the Palestine Arabs who remained in the territory it held. Israel regretted not having identified the assassins of Count Bernadotte but it would continue efforts to do so. On the question of borders, this should be determined by negotiation between it and the Arab states.[30]

Though some members expressed concerns over Israel's explanations, the General Assembly on May 11 approved Israel's application for membership, thereby admitting it to the United Nations. Its resolution approving the application noted its own Resolution 194 that called on Israel to repatriate the refugees and referred to the explanations given by Israel.[31]

In an attempt to work out a final settlement of the Palestine conflict, the conciliation commission got Israel, the Arab states, and the Arab Higher Committee to negotiate in Lausanne during May, but little came of the effort.

During 1948 few states had recognized Israel.[32] But in 1949 more did so. This recognition and the admission to UN membership led to a new argument for Israel's legitimacy. Even if there had been no lawful basis to establish Israel, its recognition became an argument for its legitimacy.[33]

It is not generally accepted, however, that recognition can legitimize a state that asserts sovereignty over territory to which it is not entitled. A "vice in title," wrote Ian Brownlie, cannot be "cured by recognition."[34] Daniel O'Connell stated that "a mere adding up of assents is of no greater juristic value than a particular assent, and since unanimous action is improbable, validation can never be international but can only be vis-à-vis the assenting states."[35] Thus, recognition confers no objective status.

Some scholars, like Quincy Wright, pointed to Israel's admission to the United Nations as a fact that constituted recognition by other states.[36] But admission to UN membership does not imply recognition by all member states or even by those voting for admission.[37] The UN Charter does not require a member state to recognize another member state.[38] Many states that do not recognize Israel are UN members.

Another theory that has been asserted to legitimize Israel is that Britain created a "legal vacuum" when it left Palestine.[39] Palestine became a "terra delicta"[40] or "terra nullius,"[41] in which Israel created itself through "auto-emancipation."[42] When in such a situation a community "asserts its independence," said O'Connell, it "acquires capacity if it has the qualifications for Statehood."[43] This sovereignty-vacuum theory relies on the concept in international law that sovereignty may be established by exerting control over unoccupied territory.

The sovereignty-vacuum theory as applied to Israel has been criticized as smacking of colonialism since it assumes the indigenous population had no rights.[44] Israel itself has never used this argument since it claimed a prior-existing right. Palestine was not open to occupation by whoever might take it in 1948.[45] An inhabited territory, said Brownlie, "cannot be regarded as *terra nullius* susceptible to appropriation by individual states in case of abandonment by the existing sovereign."[46] When mandate territory is abandoned, sovereignty is still located somewhere.[47] The International Court of Justice made this point in the case involving Spain's departure from its colony of Western Sahara. When Spain relinquished sovereignty, Western Sahara was not *terra nullius* since there was a people in occupation.[48]

A theory suggested by André Cocâtre-Zilgien is that Israel is the lawful successor to the Jewish Agency. After Britain's withdrawal, he wrote, the "only authority remaining in place" was, "in fact and even in law, the Israeli authority."[49] But while the Jewish Agency had the status of a public body, it represented only a minority of Palestine's population. Thus, it could not have been deemed the bearer of sovereignty in Palestine.

That theory is similar to another that has been posited to justify Israel's existence, namely, that Israel is legitimate because it exists in fact.[50] Reliance is placed on the legal maxim *uti possidetis*, which says that one owns what one possesses.[51] But the international community has not followed such a rule. Rhodesia maintained a factual existence as an independent state 1965–80 but was deemed illegitimate since its government denied self-determination to a segment of the population.[52] Title to territory can be established by long-standing possession, a doctrine known as acquisitive prescription. But the possession must be peaceful and unchallenged. It does not apply "where possession has been maintained by force in the face of persistent and violent opposition."[53] A U.S. claim of acquisitive prescription to the Chamizal tract, long in dispute between it and Mexico, was denied by an arbitration panel because the possession had not been "undisturbed, uninterrupted, and unchallenged." Mexico had "constantly challenged and questioned" U.S. control.[54] In the Palestine case the possession has been persistently challenged both by neighboring states and by the Palestine Arabs.

Israel's factual existence did not make clear the extent of its territory. While the Jewish Agency declared statehood within the borders proposed for a Jewish state in Resolution 181,[55] the provisional government of Israel asserted that the resolution's rejection by the Arab Higher Committee and the military intervention by the Arab states freed it of that limitation. When Transjordan cited the resolution in a discussion over borders in May 1949, Foreign Minister Shertok told Transjordan that Resolution 181 had no legal force since the resolution had assumed the two parties would voluntarily establish their states.[56] With respect to the territory it took outside that designated for a Jewish state in Resolution 181, Israel claimed it acted in self-defense against the Arab states and filled a "sovereignty vacuum" there.[57] That position is dubious, however, since Israel's claim to self-defense was weak.[58] And even acting in self-defense, a state does not have the right to territory it occupies while repelling the attack, since self-defense is justifiable only as self-protection.[59]

In October 1949 Israel told the United Nations that it "asserts its title to the territory over which its authority is actually recognized," by which it presumably meant the territory within the 1949 armistice lines. "Although some of the invading Arab armies still stand on the soil of Palestine," it stated, "Israel is not advancing any further territorial claims. But of the territory now constituting the State of Israel, there can be no cession."[60] This claim to the territory on Israel's side of the armistice lines is doubtful, however, since the armistice agreements stated that the lines were not international borders.[61] Many specified that Israel's borders were undetermined.[62] For operational purposes, however, they regarded the territory on the Israeli side of the armistice lines as Israel's.[63]

States recognizing Israel did not recognize Israeli sovereignty over west Jerusalem.[64] They typically cited UN resolutions proposing an international status for Jerusalem.[65] In December 1949 the General Assembly recommended placing Jerusalem under a "permanent international regime," supervised by the Trusteeship Council.[66] But the Knesset soon declared west Jerusalem Israel's capital.[67] Few states located embassies there, however, and Tel Aviv remained the effective capital.[68]

Part Three

The Status of Arabs

in Israel

12

The Real Conquest:

The Repopulation of Palestine

And he gathered them together into a place called in the
Hebrew tongue Armageddon.—*Holy Bible*, Revelation 16:16

The armistice line was not well patrolled, and some Arab refugees
returned clandestinely.[1] The government of Israel called them
"infiltrators," and the Knesset passed a law against "infiltration."[2]
The authorities reexpelled those it found, and in some cases these
were substantial groups.[3] Internal refugees as well tried to return to
their villages, and the IDF tried to stop them.[4] It expelled many internal refugees by trucking them to the armistice line and forcing them
to cross.[5] In some cases it cited security considerations, particularly
in expelling persons living near the armistice line, while in other
cases it cited the need to make room for Jewish immigrants.[6]

Much of this expulsion was from the Galilee, the largest con-
centration of Arabs inside the armistice lines.[7] In February 1949 the
IDF expelled 700 internal refugees from the Galilee town of Kfar Yasif.[8]
It also expelled half the inhabitants of Kfar Anan village,[9] the adult
males of Gish village,[10] and the inhabitants of Hisam, Qatia, and
Jauneh villages.[11] In August it expelled several thousand Arabs from
Baqa el Gharbiya, a village in the Little Triangle area Transjordan had
ceded to Israel in their armistice agreement.[12] In November it expelled
500 Arabs from Galilee and 150 Bedouin Arabs from the Beersheeba
area.[13]

In August 1950 the IDF expelled the 14,000 remaining inhabitants of Majdal, who were the last substantial Arab population on
Israel's southern coast. It trucked them to the Gaza border over a
three-week period and forced them to cross. The government then
renamed the town by its ancient name of Ashkelon[14] and moved
Jewish immigrants into it.[15] The ministry of defense had decided

that removing the Arabs from Majdal and repopulating it with Jews would be "desirable from the security viewpoint."[16] In February 1951 the IDF forced the inhabitants of thirteen Arab villages in Wadi Ara (Little Triangle area) into the West Bank.[17] On November 17, 1951, it expelled the inhabitants of the village of Buwaishat, dynamiting their homes.[18] In 1951 the IDF also expelled large numbers of individual Arabs from the Galilee, typically forcing male heads of families or eldest sons to cross into the West Bank.[19] The IDF continued collective expulsions of villagers in the Galilee over the next two years.[20] In September 1953 the IDF expelled the residents and dynamited the houses of the villages of Um-el-Faraj[21] and Biram.[22] It also forced thousands of Bedouin Arabs in the Negev Desert beyond the armistice lines.[23]

The expulsion of Palestine's Arabs opened the possibility of creating a Jewish state. But still it was necessary to bring Jews there. In 1948 the government of Israel formulated plans to recruit several hundred thousand Jews from Europe and the Middle East.[24] The immigrants, editorialized the *Economist*, would "take the place of the outgoing Arabs."[25] Ben-Gurion said that immigration was intended to "save Jews from destruction."[26] But the government was concerned more about creating a Jewish-populated state and about its military potential.[27] The "real reason" for immigration drives, the U.S. ambassador, James G. McDonald, quoted Israeli officials as saying, was that Israel was "underpopulated and surrounded by actual and potential enemies." Israel "must be filled up as rapidly as possible."[28] It controlled "large conquered but unoccupied spaces from which the Arabs of Palestine had been evicted," and it feared "the Arabs would never forget and never forgive the wrongs done to them until justice was done."[29] Only an implantation of a Jewish population could protect the territory.[30] It would also make it less likely Israel could be pressured into permitting a return of the Arab refugees.[31]

Despite his statement about saving Jews, Ben-Gurion voiced a security rationale for immigration. "We have conquered territories, but without settlements they have no decisive value. Settlement . . . is the real conquest."[32] Israel needed "mass immigration in swift tempo." He said that "nothing is as forceful for security as intensifying immigration."[33] Without immigrants, he declared, Israel could not "last for long."[34] The Soviet Union and its Eastern European allies freely permitted Jewish emigration for Israel from 1948 to 1950 to provide recruits for the IDF.[35]

Immigration also provided a justification for Jewish statehood. The "ingathering of the exiles" was the rationale for a Jewish state in Zionist ideology.[36] A state of "seven hundred thousand Jews," said Ben-Gurion, referring to the Jewish population in Palestine at the time, "cannot be the climax of a vigil kept unbroken through the generations and down the patient centuries." Even if "unperturbed by external dangers, so empty a State would be little justified, for it would not change the destiny of Jewry, or fulfill our historic covenant."[37]

The government hoped to bring in European Jews liberated from Nazi concentration camps.[38] The Zionist underground in Eastern Europe encouraged Jews to migrate to Palestine.[39] But when Britain's withdrawal in 1948 ended the limits on Jewish immigration to Palestine, no large influx resulted. Even though the Eastern European governments did not impede emigration, few Eastern European Jews went to Israel.[40] A study published in 1948 concluded that 80 percent of the displaced Jews wanted to emigrate to the United States.[41]

Ben-Gurion said that Israel had room for all of Eastern Europe's 3 million Jews.[42] The government made great efforts to encourage Jews in Eastern Europe to migrate to Israel. Its immigration agent in Romania reported in 1950: "Working through the local leadership and every reliable Jew we have met, we are urging the Jews to make applications for emigration and for passports."[43] Agents tried to get emigrating Jews to Israel. In Poland Israeli officials would "send the people directly to the port, so they would not be able to stop en route," reported Samuel Eliashiv, Israel's ambassador to Czechoslovakia.[44] Israel's consul in Warsaw, Israel Carmel, found that persuasion was difficult. "The awakening of the Jews of Poland will not happen by itself," he reported in 1949. "They must be motivated and organized."[45]

The government also recruited Jews from Arab states.[46] It sent agents to convince Jews to immigrate to Israel. There too it did not meet a ready reception. The Jewish Agency had operatives in Arab states during the early 1940s to encourage Jews to move to Palestine, but few had done so. Jews had, to be sure, occupied a subordinate status in the Arab world, though the situation varied from country to country. Jews did not experience in the Arab world the enmity they found in Europe.[47] "For many centuries," according to Henry A. Byroade, assistant secretary of state for Near Eastern, South Asian, and African affairs of the U.S. Department of State, "Jews and Arabs lived side by side in the Middle East in relative harmony."[48] In some Arab countries, like Iraq, Jews occupied positions of wealth and political power that put them well above the average person. In Yemen, on the other hand, many Jews were quite poor.[49]

Mob attacks on Jewish quarters took place in several Arab countries in 1947 after the General Assembly vote on Resolution 181.[50] These were motivated by the perceived injustice of the Resolution. In Damascus mobs attacked not only Jewish quarters but institutions they perceived as responsible for Resolution 181, including the U.S. and French legations and the Syrian Communist Party headquarters.[51] In early 1948, as military confrontation became likely, Arab states grew suspicious of Jews who supported Zionism and restricted them in various ways.[52] The expulsion of Palestine Arabs in 1948 created resentment in the Arab world, particularly as the refugees went to Arab countries and recounted what had occurred to them. With the Jewish Agency purporting to be carrying out its policy in the name of world Jewry, some of this resentment was directed against the indigenous Jewish populations in the Arab states.[53] The Arab League issued a statement February 9, 1948, in which the member states agreed to suppress anti-Jewish activity in their countries.[54] But mob attacks against Jews took place, and governments undertook discriminatory administrative and legislative measures of various kinds. Still, the Jews of the Arab world did not flock to Israel. Zionism had made little headway there before 1948, and even after 1948 the reaction was mixed. Even those who approved of Zionism did not necessarily want to migrate to Israel. For most Arab-state Jews, migration to an unknown situation in a newly established country was riskier than staying where they were. Further, they heard stories of discrimination in Israel by European Jews against Arab-state Jews.

The recruiters, who were associated with the Israeli intelligence agency Mossad, were active in Arab states and encouraged Jews to immigrate to Israel. Both Arab and Western states expressed concern that Israel's recruiters artificially generated a desire for immigration to Israel. In Yemen, in 1949–50, Israeli agents organized the departure for Israel of almost all indigenous Jews. They told the Yemeni Jews, most of whom were deeply religious, that the third kingdom of Israel had arrived. En route to Israel, the Yemeni Jews reportedly sang (referring to Ben-Gurion) "David, David, king of Israel!"[55]

In Iraq most of the country's Jews migrated to Israel in 1950–51. Israel organized in Iraq an underground group called the Movement to promote migration of Iraqi Jews to Israel. To frighten Iraqi Jews into departing, the Movement set off a series of bombs in Baghdad, including one at a synagogue, killing a number of Jews in the process.[56] The Movement distributed leaflets urging Jews to flee to Israel.[57] Israel denied setting the bombs, for which two members of the underground were convicted by an Iraqi court. But after one such bombing, leaflets referring to it and urging Jews to leave for Israel were distributed within hours, suggesting they had been printed prior to the bombing.[58] Wilbur Crane Eveland, a U.S. Central Intelligence Agency officer who was in Baghdad at the time, concluded that the Movement had set the bombs, as did resident British officials.[59] While Israel denied responsibility for the bombings,[60] its role was later indirectly acknowledged after Israeli agents set bombs in Cairo, making it appear that the act had been done by Arabs. The defense minister said this tactic had first been tried in Iraq.[61]

The assistant secretary of state for Near Eastern, South Asian, and African affairs in the U.S. Department of State, George McGhee, criticized Israel for its Iraq operation. "It was one thing to take Jews from all over the world who were in distress," he said, "but it was another matter entirely to attempt to create circumstances which would stimulate immigration of Jews from areas where they were living in peace."[62] When Israel undertook a campaign to get Iranian Jews to immigrate to Israel, the director of the office of Near Eastern affairs in the U.S. Department of State, G. Lewis Jones, told Teddy Kollek, of Israel's embassy in Washington, that the United States "would not favor a deliberately generated exodus there," as he put it, "along the lines of the ingathering from Iraq." Kollek justified Israel's Iraq operation as beneficial for Iraq, stating it was "better for a country to be homogeneous."[63] In Yemen and Iraq, Israeli agents arranged transportation for the Jews to ensure their destination would be Israel. This was a major problem for Israel since, of Jews leaving Arab states at this period, many went to countries other than Israel.[64]

By 1951, 684,000 Jews entered Israel as immigrants, more than

doubling the previous Jewish population of Palestine. Half came from
Europe, including 100,000 from displaced person camps in Germany,
Austria, Italy, and Cyprus. The other half came from Arab countries,
mainly Yemen, Iraq, Morocco, and Algeria.[65] The government of Israel
portrayed the influx of Jews from Arab states as a product of persecu-
tion. "Parallel to the exodus of half a million Arabs from Israeli territory, 700,000 Jews fled Arab countries due to repression and persecu-
tion of all kinds, emigrating to Israel." It depicted it as "a kind of
exchange of population."[66]

In 1952 the Knesset wrote the policy of promoting mass immigration into legislation: "The mission of gathering in the exiles, which
is the central task of the State of Israel and the Zionist Movement in
our days, requires constant efforts by the Jewish people in the Diaspora; the State of Israel, therefore, expects the cooperation of all Jews
as individuals and groups, in building up the State and assisting the
immigration to it of the masses of the people."[67]

In Morocco, Israeli agents went from house to house in poor
Jewish quarters warning of anti-Semitism that would follow the anticipated independence of Morocco from France. There were, in fact,
acts of violence against Jews during that period in Morocco. As in
Iraq, a clandestine Zionist organization was established as an "underground railroad" for potential emigrants. Of Jews emigrating from
Morocco at that time, the well-to-do predominantly chose Europe,
while the less affluent predominantly chose Israel.[68] The Moroccan
interior minister said that Moroccan Jews "were driven to Israel by
the fear psychosis" spread by these agents.[69] About 30,000 emigrated
to Israel. The repression in Morocco did not materialize, and in Israel
these immigrants encountered discrimination from European Jews.[70]
About 5,500 returned to Morocco.[71]

The government gave itself broad legal authority to govern the Arabs,
whom Ben-Gurion called a "potential fifth column."[72] The Knesset
adopted legislation putting into effect the Defense (Emergency) Regulations that Britain had enacted for Palestine in 1937.[73] The regulations gave the government the power to expel a person,[74] to detain a
person indefinitely without trial,[75] to restrict a person's movement,[76]
and to restrict travel into or out of any area declared closed.[77] They
permitted the censoring and suppression of newspapers,[78] the banning of organizations,[79] and a broad ban on speech by making it an

offense to try to influence public opinion in a manner likely to prejudice public safety, or to possess written material of such content.[80]
They also permitted curfews on towns and the demolition of houses
inhabited by persons accused of offenses.[81]

The regulations were considered to be in force under a statute
the Knesset adopted to retain in force all enactments Britain had
used in Palestine. The statute read: "The law which existed in Palestine on 14th May, 1948 shall remain in force."[82] But just before its
departure, the British government had repealed certain laws, including the Defense (Emergency) Regulations. On May 12, 1948, it issued
an Order in Council that repealed "Orders in Council specified in the
Schedule to this Order . . . to the extent specified in the second column of the Schedule." The schedule included the Palestine (Defence)
Order in Council 1937 (the original enactment of the 1945 regulations), and the second column specifies "the whole Order." The May
12 Order in Council by its terms came into force at midnight May
13–14.[83] The British government later confirmed that the 1948 Order
in Council repealed the regulations.[84] Thus, the regulations were not
in force on May 14, 1948, and, therefore, were not covered by the
statute preserving the British law in force.

The government of Israel understood that Britain had repealed
the regulations. This is evident from its effort in 1949 to remedy the
defect. In that year the Knesset adopted the Law and Administration
Ordinance (Amendment) Law in which it construed Article 11 of the
ordinance to exclude "unpublished laws"—which it defined as laws
adopted between November 29, 1947, and May 15, 1948—which were
not published in the *Palestine Gazette*, despite being a law of a cate-
gory whose publication was "obligatory or customary."[85] The Order
in Council repealing the regulations had not been published by May
15, 1948, and was, therefore, rendered of no effect by this amendment. Under British law, however, the Order in Council was effective
to render the regulations void on May 14, 1948.[86]

The regulations were by their terms in force only during a
government-declared emergency, so the Knesset authorized the government to declare an emergency in Israel[87]—which it did—and
which it has continued in force ever since. Haim Cohn, as attorney
general in 1950, proposed repeal of the regulations. He reported that
other government officials "decided it was better to have this sort of
regulation in a British law than in an Israeli one."[88] The government

used the Defense (Emergency) Regulations almost exclusively against Arabs.[89] In a 1959 report Israel's state controller criticized this selective application.[90] He said there was "something improper about this law, which was drafted with the intention of its being applicable to all the inhabitants of the country, whereas in fact it is only enforced against some of them."[91]

13

The Present Are Absent:

The Fate of the Arabs' Land

Enter not houses other than
Your own, until ye have
Asked permission and saluted
those in them.
—*Holy Quran*, xxiv, 27

The provisional government used the Arabs' land, dwellings, and possessions for its Jewish population, and primarily for recent immigrants. Ben-Gurion ordered that abandoned Arab housing be allocated to Jews.[1] By April 1949, he reported to the Knesset, the government had settled 150,000 Jews in Arab housing.[2] In Jerusalem the government gave the better Arab houses to government officials.[3] In Jaffa many Jewish immigrants occupied Arab housing before the government could organize the process.[4]

The government also took housing from Arabs who remained inside the armistice lines. In Haifa in July 1948 the IDF forced out Arab residents of the Carmel ridge area to make room for Jews.[5] It forced Arabs from their homes in Acre, into what became an Arab ghetto.[6] Many "internal refugees" tried to return to their homes. Their land, like that of the Arab "external refugees," was considered "absentee" property and was controlled by the custodian of absentee property, who rented it to Jews—the rent money going to the government.[7] Many internal refugees had no housing, living in tin shacks or burial caves.[8] As late as 1958, 20,000 internal refugees lived in makeshift housing near Arab towns.[9] Nazareth, which received many internal refugees in 1948, still had three refugee neighborhoods in substandard housing in the 1980s.[10]

The expelled inhabitants of Ikrit and Biram, two Galilean villages, sued in court for the right to return to their villages, whose lands had been distributed to kibbutzim (Jewish agricultural collectives.[11] In 1951 the Ikrit villagers obtained a return order from the Supreme Court to the minister of defense.[12] The minister refused, and the IDF demolished Ikrit.[13] The Biram villagers also sued, but in 1953, while their case was pending, the IDF sent airplanes that bombed all of Biram's buildings, leveling the entire village. The kibbutzim kept the land.[14] Ben-Gurion explained that "these are not the only villagers living a long way from their home villages. We do not want to create a precedent for the repatriation of refugees."[15] The government had closed Ikrit and Biram under the 1949 Emergency Regulations Law.[16] In 1963 and again in 1972 it extended the closure order under the Defense (Emergency) Regulations.[17] In 1981 the Ikrit villagers again petitioned the Supreme Court; the court cited Ikrit's proximity to Lebanon and said that security considerations still warranted their exclusion.[18] The villagers continued unsuccessfully to petition the government,[19] and expelled residents of other villages did so as well, also with no success.[20]

The Defense (Emergency) Regulations provided a full set of regulations for martial law rule, and the government imposed martial law.[21] It did so by declaring Arab-populated sectors to be "closed areas" under Article 125 of the regulations.[22] It established three martial-law zones—the northern area (which encompassed the Galilee), the central area (which encompassed the so-called Little Triangle area), and the Beersheba area (Negev Desert).[23] About 85 percent of the Arabs inside the armistice lines inhabited these three zones.[24] The only substantial numbers of Arabs not included were those in predominantly Jewish urban areas.[25]

The military government instituted a nighttime curfew[26] and a permit requirement for travel.[27] The military government divided the Galilee into fifty-eight sectors for travel purposes. This meant, in effect, that any travel outside an Arab's home village required a permit.[28] To obtain a pass, an Arab applied to a military office, often waiting hours in a queue.[29] On the roads the IDF set up checkpoints and inspected Arabs for their passes. It fined or imprisoned Arabs found without a pass, or with an expired pass, or on a route different from that prescribed in the pass.[30] The military government required a permit not only for short-term travel but for a change of residence. An Arab who resided in a locality without permission might be evicted, with confiscation of property. One observer, analogizing to South Africa, called the system one of "bantustans."[31]

Arabs had to carry identity papers, and soldiers on occasion forced large numbers of Arabs out of their houses for identity checks. Soldiers would typically gather a group of residents in an open field where they might keep them—men, women, and children—for a number of hours without food, drink, or toilet facilities.[32] The authorities frequently denied travel permits Arab farmers needed to take their produce to traditional market towns. This forced them to sell in their home village to Jewish merchants who could travel without a pass. The Arab farmer would receive only a fraction of the value of the produce.[33]

Arabs could not approach government ministries with grievances, as only military authorities had jurisdiction over them.[34] To challenge an order of the military government, Arabs had to go to a military court, as the civilian courts did not have jurisdiction to hear their petitions.[35] Avnery called the martial law over Israel's Arabs "a colonial regime enforced by colonial law."[36]

The Jewish National Fund continued to purchase land from Arabs after 1948,[37] but these purchases lost their significance because the government began to confiscate large tracts.[38] The Knesset in 1949 enacted the Emergency Land Requisition (Regulation) Law, which authorized expropriation "for the defense of the State, public security, the maintenance of essential supplies or essential public services, the absorption of immigrants or the rehabilitation of ex-soldiers or war invalids."[39] Another 1949 law permitted the minister of agriculture to take control of "waste" (uncultivated) land.[40] The land of Arab refugees could be seized as "waste" land.

The Absentees' Property Law, adopted in 1950, permitted confiscation of the land of a person deemed an "absentee." It defined "absentee" to include any Palestinian who in 1948 left the land to go either to another state or to an area of Palestine held by Arab League forces.[41] The original draft of the Absentees' Property Law would have defined as absentees only those who remained outside the 1949 armistice lines, but as enacted it not only meant that absent external refugees but internal refugees and returning external refugees were deemed "absentees."[42] Forbidden to return to their homes even though they were living in Israel, they were referred to as "present absentees."[43]

The requirement of having left the land was construed to mean leaving for even a short period. As a result, land was confiscated from Arabs living on their land but who may have been absent for a few days during the fighting. The military government used Arab informants, of whom it cultivated a substantial number, to notify it what Arabs, though living on their land, might be deemed absentees, so their land could be confiscated.[44]

The Absentees' Property Law was implemented only against Arabs.[45] Because of the breadth of the definition of absentee, some Jews would have qualified, but the government did not invoke the law against them.[46] The government gave most of the land it confiscated as absentee to Jewish farmers. According to Mordechai Schattner, custodian of absentee property, between 1948 and 1953 the government established 370 new Jewish settlements, 350 of them on land it confiscated as "absentee."[47]

The custodian's office received complaints from absentees who "see their property in the hands of others and can't bear it." Some absentees offered exorbitant rents to lease back their own land. But the policy was to refuse them, for fear of difficulty in getting them to vacate. Thousands of Jewish settlers had occupied these lands.[48]

The Absentees' Property Law permitted confiscation but did not give the government title to the land seized. In 1953 the Knesset adopted the Land Acquisition (Validation of Acts and Compensation) Law,[49] which gave the government title to the land it had confiscated as "absentee."[50] Arabs protested the law, as it sought to bring finality to the land seizures.[51] It was condemned by the philosopher Martin Buber as bringing about a "robbery of the land" of Palestine's Arabs.[52] It provided for compensation, but most Arabs refused it, preferring to preserve their claim to the land.[53] The rate of compensation offered was sufficiently low that Prime Minister Moshe Sharett (formerly Moshe Shertok) called it "robbery."[54]

Article 125 of the Defense (Emergency) Regulations was also used to confiscate land. It permitted the closing of any area for security purposes and expulsion of its inhabitants.[55] The government closed substantial tracts under Article 125 and expelled their inhabitants. Once the Arabs were gone, the minister of agriculture confiscated the land as "uncultivated."[56] Shimon Peres, who later would be prime minister of Israel, said this use of Article 125 was not in fact security-related but was "a direct continuation of the struggle for Jewish settlement and Jewish immigration."[57]

The system of martial law, by restricting the Arabs' movement, helped the government take and control confiscated land. Ben-Gurion said "the military regime came into existence to protect the right of Jewish settlement in all parts of the state."[58] One consequence of the system of travel passes was that it kept Arabs from reoccupying their confiscated lands.[59]

The government typically confiscated valley lands, leaving Arabs with rocky hillsides.[60] It took major tracts in the Little Triangle area, which came under its control by cession from Transjordan in 1949.[61] The government confiscated water pumps in abandoned Arab orange groves and gave them to Jewish farmers.[62] Members of kibbutzim and moshavim in the Galilee took over flocks of cattle and sheep left by departing Arabs.[63] The government confiscated over 85 percent of the land of the Bedouin Palestinians of the Negev Desert[64] and concentrated the remaining Bedouins into small, largely uncultivable areas.[65] If an animal wandered off, a Bedouin might need a permit to look for it—a permit obtainable only by traveling to a military official a considerable distance away.[66]

Under a 1965 statute the government confiscated as absentee the extensive Moslem charitable lands (waqf), much of which was used for cultivation on a long-term basis.[67] This statute provided for the waqf land to be administered for charitable purposes by local boards of trustees appointed by the government.[68] It was not clear on what theory these lands were considered absentee since even though many of the farmers had departed, the authority owning them had not.[69]

All land was confiscated from those Palestine Arabs who were refugees beyond the 1949 armistice lines. Of the land belonging to Arabs who remained, 65 percent was confiscated by the mid-1950s.[70] The value of the land taken from the Palestine Arabs was estimated at 100 million Palestinian pounds.[71] It included stone quarries, 10,000 acres of vineyards, 25,000 acres of citrus groves, 10,000 business establishments, 95 percent of what became Israel's olive groves,[72] and 50,000 apartments.[73] Of 859,000 Arabs who had lived within the territory on Israel's side of the 1949 armistice lines, 684,000—by Toynbee's estimate—lost homes and property.[74]

The government of Israel emptied about 400 Arab towns and villages.[75] It demolished many of them and planted forests to eradicate traces of habitation.[76] Defense Minister Moshe Dayan, referring to Zionist land acquisition both before and after 1948, said there was not a single settlement in Israel "which was not built on the site of a previous Arab settlement."[77]

The government continued in later years to confiscate Arab agricultural land on a piecemeal basis.[78] In the Negev the government confiscated the land of 8,000 farmers in 1980 to construct a military air base to replace evacuated airfields in the Sinai Peninsula.[79] Confiscations in the Galilee led to organized citizen protests.[80] The government also continued to purchase land, particularly in the Galilee.[81] According to a Jewish Agency report on the Galilee, the fact that the population there was 70 percent Arab posed "a major threat to the character of the area as part of the Jewish state, to Jewish control thereof, and even to Israeli sovereignty over it." The report called for more Jewish settlements as "mini-lookouts."[82]

14

Hewers of Wood:

Arab Commerce, Agriculture, and Labor

What are kingdoms but great robberies?
—St. Augustine*

In addition to their land, the Arabs of Palestine lost their economic infrastructure. The exodus of the Arab urban population in 1948 destroyed their commercial-industrial base.[1] The government took over fully equipped plants. In Ramleh it distributed 600 shops to Jewish immigrants. In Lydda it seized 1,800 truckloads of property, including a button factory, a carbonated drinks plant, a sausage factory, an ice plant, a textile plant, a macaroni factory, 7,000 retail shops, 500 workshops, and 1,000 warehouses. It confiscated cabinetmaking shops, locksmith works, turneries, ironworks, and tinworks, which it then leased or sold to Jews. Some of the Arab property was appropriated privately by what became a class of newly prosperous merchants and speculators.[2] The UN Palestine Conciliation Commission tried unsuccessfully to work out a monetary compensation system for Arabs whose property had been taken.[3]

The government sequestered as "enemy property" the bank accounts of expelled Arabs, saying it would release them only if the Arab states made peace with Israel.[4] Under a program worked out by the UN Palestine Conciliation Commission, it returned a small percentage of these funds in the late 1950s and early 1960s.[5]

The Arabs were left with a few small towns and villages. Only in the Galilee were towns and rural areas sufficiently contiguous to allow economic interchange.[6] In Nazareth, the largest Arab-populated city following the 1948 war, tile and match factories were no longer viable.[7] The modest industrial potential that remained was eroded by land confiscation. To found the Jewish town of Carmiel in the Galilee, the government confiscated quarries of high-quality marble that had provided a livelihood for hundreds of persons.[8] The armistice line with Transjordan cut Arab manufacturers and merchants from their traditional connections in the territory that had become the West Bank. The Arabs became dependent on the Jewish economy for industrial and consumer products.[9]

The government promoted economic development for the Jewish sector but not for the Arab sector.[10] It used martial law powers to prevent the development of Arab industry. It denied Arabs permits to start businesses in areas closed to Arab habitation. The Israel Land Authority denied a permit to an Arab to open a marble quarry in Carmiel, on grounds that the area was closed to non-Jews.[11]

The government did not make available to Arab entrepreneurs the financial subsidies and loans it gave to Jews.[12] The ministry of the interior allocated to Arab towns only a fraction of the funding it allotted to Jewish towns.[13] Jewish towns received funds from Zionist agencies abroad, but the government did not permit outside funds to Arab towns.[14] Industry could not develop in Arab towns because the government did not fund sewage treatment, roads, or education.[15] The primary and secondary schools for Jews and Arabs, which were separate, showed "a marked disparity in quality," the U.S. Department of State said in a human rights report, because the government allocated greater resources per student into the Jewish system.[16]

Much industrial development was undertaken by the Histadrut, whose industrial arm, Koor Industries, Ltd., advertised itself as "Israel's largest industrial complex."[17] Koor, which accounted for one-fourth of Israel's industrial output, located no plants in Arab towns.[18] In 1985 it made plans for the first time to begin investment in Arab areas but did not carry them through.[19]

In the Encouragement of Capital Investments Law of 1959, the Knesset granted incentives for investment in areas designated by the ministers of finance and of industry and commerce as "development areas."[20] The two ministers designated forty Jewish-populated areas as development areas.[21] However, they did not give that designation to any Arab localities, even the most economically depressed.[22] The government used the development area designation in particular to provide a livelihood for Jewish immigrants and to place Jews along Israel's borders as a security measure.[23]

Through market and price controls, the government prevented the modest Arab agriculture that survived the land confiscations from competing with Jewish agriculture.[24] Government purchasing agencies paid more to Jewish farmers than to Arab farmers for similar products.[25] By statute the government marketing boards that set prices included representatives of the World Zionist Organization and Jewish Agency, which are dedicated to promoting the welfare of Jews.[26] Thus, the Knesset called for World Zionist Organization and Jewish Agency participation on the Peanut Production and Marketing Board,[27] the Vegetable Production and Marketing Board,[28] the Egg and Poultry Board,[29] and the Fruit Production and Marketing Board.[30]

A tobacco-purchasing agency (Alei Tabak) was established, owned jointly by the Jewish Agency, the Jewish National Fund, and the government. It was given a monopoly in tobacco purchasing and marketing[31] and bought tobacco from Jewish growers at a price higher than that at which Arab farmers could sell—a lower price set by the government.[32] The Agency[33] and Histadrut[34] provided financial assistance to kibbutzim or moshavim, but not to Arab farmers. Arab farmers were, and still are, excluded from membership in kibbutzim and moshavim.[35]

By the 1959 Water Law the Knesset declared all water in Israel "public property" and authorized the minister of agriculture to designate "rationing areas."[36] The minister's Water (Use of Water in Rationing Areas) Regulation of 1976 rationed water in the entire country.[37] The regulation gave Arabs only 2 percent of the water allotted for agriculture,[38] though they farmed 20 percent of the cultivated land, half of it in the arid Negev Desert.[39] The rationing system deprived Arab farmers of water they needed to compete with Jewish agriculture.[40]

The national water authority, Mekorot, manages Israel's water, a scarce and critical resource. Mekorot was founded in 1937 by the Jewish National Fund, the Jewish Agency, and a subsidiary company of the Histadrut, to supply water to Jewish settlements,[41] and under the Water Law it is owned jointly by the government and its three founders.[42] In the Water Law the Knesset also created a Water Board under the ministry of agriculture to oversee water use in agriculture and placed on the board a representative of the World Zionist Organization.[43] Mekorot did not supply to Arab agriculture even the small amount to which it was entitled under the minister's regulations.[44] Control of water by the Zionist institutions has been called one of the "legal structures of apartheid."[45]

Arab labor experienced a radical transformation after 1948. Land confiscation deprived Arabs of the agriculture that had been their mainstay.[46] As a result, Arab farmers were forced into wage employment in the Jewish economy,[47] and so the government created labor exchanges to put Arabs into jobs.[48] A pattern developed of Arabs commuting from their home areas to jobs in Jewish areas.[49] Arab villages became bedroom communities.[50] The Arab village of Taibe, for example, had 4,900 inhabitants and 8,250 acres of land in 1949. By 1976 it had 15,000 inhabitants but only 4,750 acres of land, the decline resulting from confiscation. In 1949 one-half of the population was employed in agriculture—in 1976, only 10 percent. The displaced farmers worked in the Jewish sector in construction, agriculture, or food service.[51] Through land confiscations the Little Triangle, which had been a major agricultural area, became fully dependent on the Israeli economy.[52] The few remaining members of a pre-1948 Arab trade union, the Arab Workers Congress, tried to reorganize, but the government arrested its leadership, thus effectively suppressing it.[53]

Military authorities used the pass system to control the flow of labor into the Jewish economy.[54] In periods of unemployment in the Jewish economy the authorities withheld permits to protect Jewish jobs.[55] They initially issued permits valid for one day only, but as the need for Arab labor increased in the late 1950s they issued longer-term permits.[56] By the mid-1960s the government no longer feared Arab labor but rather needed it. As a result, it ended martial law in 1966.[57] It did so by issuing a general permit for citizens to enter and leave the "closed areas."[58] It did not, however, revoke the orders declaring the Arab areas "closed" and thereby maintained the legal structure for martial law. The Defense (Emergency) Regulations were retained.

While Israel's legislation treated Arabs as workers the same as Jews in many respects, the labor laws discriminated against them in several ways. Under the 1963 Severance Pay Law, the Knesset made workers employed for at least one year in the public or private sector eligible for severance pay if they were "dismissed" from their employment.[59] It deemed a worker who resigned voluntarily to take up residence in an "agricultural settlement" or "development area" to have been "dismissed" and, therefore, to be entitled to severance pay.[60] The Severance Pay Law authorized the minister of labor to define "agricultural settlement" and "development area" for these purposes.[61]

By a 1964 regulation the minister of labor defined "development area" to include sixty Jewish-inhabited areas. He defined "agricultural settlement" to mean either a kibbutz or moshav (both Jewish-inhabited), or other settlement (*yishuv*), most of whose inhabitants are employed in agriculture.[62] Since most workers in Arab towns are employed in the Jewish sector this definition excludes Arab towns. The effect of the regulation was that only a Jew could resign to take up residence in one of the specified locations.

The Histadrut adopted a decision to admit Arabs in 1953 but did not implement the decision until 1959.[63] This exclusion limited an Arab's ability to gain employment.[64] In 1959 the Histadrut admitted Arabs as members—though it did not allow them to participate in Histadrut national elections until 1966[65]—but even so Arabs have not achieved a prominent role in the Histadrut.

The government permitted private employers to require IDF service as a prerequisite for employment, and some prospective employers required prior IDF service.[66] IDF itself excluded Arabs from many jobs on security grounds,[67] as did the Histadrut, a major employer. The Histadrut in one instance refused to hire Arab workers in a refrigerator plant because the plant was close to a factory producing military communications equipment.[68] Of 600 managers operating Histadrut firms, none to date is an Arab.[69]

Like government ministries, the Histadrut set up an "Arab affairs" department for its Arab members after it began admitting Arabs, but it then abolished this department in 1987.[70] In integrating Arabs into its general structure in 1987 the Histadrut established a division for organization and labor councils to administer trade union councils. It forbade Arab members to run for office on these councils, however, permitting them only to vote for Jewish candidates.[71]

15

The National Institutions: The

Legislation that Makes Israel Jewish

Good laws lead to the making of better ones; bad ones bring about worse.
—Jean-Jacques Rousseau, *Social Contract*

The state the Jewish Agency created in Palestine mirrors the Zionist philosophy. Signers of the Declaration of the Establishment of the State of Israel identified themselves as "representatives of the Jewish Community of Eretz-Israel and of the Zionist Movement." The declaration called Israel a "Jewish State" and thus defined it as such.[1] Its mission was to be a state for world Jewry.[2]

The Knesset repeated this view of Israel in legislation. In a 1952 law it declared that "Israel regards itself" as "the creation of the entire Jewish people."[3] In a 1985 law it excluded from eligibility for Knesset membership any candidate who rejects "the existence of the State of Israel as the state of the Jewish people."[4] Also in 1985 the Knesset amended its rules for submission of legislation in order to prohibit the tabling of a bill that "negates the existence of the State of Israel as the state of the Jewish people."[5] The government has referred to Israel as having a "Zionist character,"[6] while the World Zionist Organization has called Israel the "supreme expression of the will of the Jewish nation for redemption."[7]

The Jewish character of Israel was reflected as well in state symbols. The 1949 Flag and Emblem Law used a Jewish symbol, the Star of David, in the state flag of Israel,[8] thereby reflecting the "identification between the new state and the Jewish people."[9] The Flag and Emblem Law used a Jewish candelabra, the menorah, as the state emblem.[10] The menorah, which appears in the Talmud, evoked the memory of the destruction of the second temple by the Roman emperor Titus in A.D. 70. Its use as Israel's emblem suggested "a return of the Jews to political existence as an independent nation."[11]

The national anthem adopted by the government was the Hatikvah, formerly the anthem of the Zionist movement.[12] Its words mention return to "Zion and Jerusalem."[13] The Knesset titled Israel's immigration law the Law of Return, suggesting that Israel is a state to which Jews are returning.[14] For Arabs, even those who are citizens of Israel, this legislation identifying Israel as Jewish indicates that they are not part of the constituency whom the state represents.[15] The concept of a Jewish state reflected in Israel's legislation made Arabs "aliens in their own land." They are not "wholly part of a nation conceived as a Jewish state."[16]

The Knesset early on rejected proposals for an explicit legislative provision that Jewish law would be applied in Israel.[17] In the state courts of Israel, judges use Jewish religious law in construing Israeli law.[18] By statute the Knesset required a judge "faced with a legal question" who "finds no answer to it in statute law or case-law or by analogy" to "decide it in the light of the principles of freedom, justice, equity and peace of Israel's heritage."[19] Since Israel is defined legislatively as a Jewish state, "Israel's heritage" means Jewish heritage, though there is disagreement whether this phrase refers to Jewish law only or to concepts emanating from Jewish history.[20] According to Supreme Court Justice Menachem Elon, "when Jewish law is cited in a civil court it has no religious import, but is simply a reflection of our national history and culture."[21]

   While judges in Israel have made rulings that contradict Jewish law,[22] they have frequently referred to it, for example, in determining rules for the division of the property of a partnership[23] and in determining the validity of a deathbed will not properly witnessed.[24] The Supreme Court has cited the Talmud as a source of the principle of political tolerance.[25]

   The Knesset uses Jewish law in formulating its statutes. Attorney General Haim Cohn said that in legislative drafting "special regard" is given to ancient Jewish law. "Whenever our experts find in Jewish law a provision which we can adapt to the needs of our modern and progressive country, we give it priority over the provisions of other law systems."[26] Referring to the declaration's definition of Israel as a Jewish state, Cohn said that legislators thereby "are told to look to the ancient prophets for their orientation."[27] The ministry of justice established a Jewish law department to advise Knesset committees on the approach of Jewish law to pending bills.[28] The drafters' commentary on the Succession Law of 1952 indicated that the drafters based their proposals "as far as possible upon Jewish Law, and in a number of matters—and among them the more basic, such as maintenance out of the estate—we regard our proposals as a kind of continuation of Jewish Law."[29] Describing a pending agency bill in 1964, Minister of Justice Dov Joseph said that drafters would find "inspiration" in the "rich legal sources of the Jewish people," and "so far as they find in these sources material appropriate for a modern statute book," they would "give it preference in language and content over other approaches less just or practical."[30] In Knesset debate over proposed laws members have frequently remarked over the correspondence of provisions to Jewish law.[31] The Chamber of Advocates Law called on the chamber, which controls the practice of law in Israel, to do research in Jewish law.[32] It did not mention any other body of law that the advocates should study.

In its legislation on rabbinical courts the Knesset gave them jurisdiction in marriage and divorce over all resident Jews, not only those Jews who adhere to Judaism. "Matters of marriage and divorce of Jews in Israel, being nationals or residents of the State," the law said, "shall be under the exclusive jurisdiction of rabbinical courts."[33] This provision subjected all Jews to religious authority, whether or not they ascribed to Judaism. During the mandate period, rabbinical courts had jurisdiction over religious Jews only.[34]

A primary mechanism to assure the Jewish character of Israel was the role given to the institutions that had built up the Jewish community in Palestine in the early twentieth century. The Knesset gave a key role in Israel's governmental scheme to the Zionist organizations, or "national institutions" as they are generally called.[35] After Israel was established, the World Zionist Organization/Jewish Agency continued to function as the political arm of the Zionist movement to mobilize Jewish support worldwide for Israel. "The Zionist Organization," said Ben-Gurion, "is able to achieve what is beyond the power and competence of the State, and that is the advantage of the Zionist Organization over the State."[36]

In its 1952 World Zionist Organization/Jewish Agency (Status) Law the Knesset declared the executive body of the World Zionist Organization, the Zionist Executive, to be a "juristic body" that "takes care as before of immigration and directs absorption and settlement projects in the State."[37] The specifics of its relationship with the government are treated in a covenant between it and the government, called for by Article 7 of the Status Law.[38]

The Status Law made the Agency a partner of the government in the performance of many essential government services. For the state of Israel, the World Zionist Organization and Jewish Agency provide a valuable legal mechanism. They disseminate the kind of information normally disseminated by a government press office, but with the appearance of objective information. They enter into relations with other organizations in host countries and thereby create goodwill for Israel. They maintain contact with Jewish communities on behalf of Israel but on a nominally unofficial basis.[39]

The national institutions allowed Israel to establish a worldwide fund-raising apparatus under the guise of charity. In a number of countries this yielded important financial benefits. In the United States, where substantial sums were collected for Israel, persons making contributions were entitled to deduct these sums from their income for taxation purposes. This was allowed on the rationale that the purposes are charitable, whereas if contributions were made directly to the government of Israel no deduction would be allowed.[40]

The World Zionist Organization/Jewish Agency viewed itself as working for Israel. In a 1952 resolution it stated it operated "in the interests of the State of Israel within the Diaspora."[41] It described itself as "the representative of the Jewish people in all matters relating to organized participation of the Jews of the Diaspora in the development and upbuilding of the country."[42] Its functions included "organization of immigration, the transfer of immigrants and their property to Eretz Israel, . . . absorption of immigrants," "agricultural settlement," "acquisition and amelioration of land by the Jewish National Fund," and "development projects."[43]

In 1971 the World Zionist Organization/Jewish Agency split into two organizations. The Jewish Agency took responsibility for activities in Israel—rural settlement, immigrant absorption, youth training, and, later, urban rehabilitation. The World Zionist Organization (wzo) became responsible for Zionist political activity and the promotion of immigration to Israel from the West.[44] Policy for the two organizations is set by the World Zionist Congress.

Since the 1971 reorganization the Jewish Agency has been controlled equally by Jews in and outside Israel.[45] The 1971 reorganization required amendment of the 1952 Status Law. The amendment states that the two bodies coordinate their activities with the government through a government-WZO committee and a government–Jewish Agency committee: "Two committees shall be set up for the coordination of activities between the Government and the World Zionist Organisation and the Jewish Agency for Israel."[46]

Until 1968 the two organizations alone were responsible for immigrant absorption, to the exclusion of the government. In that year the government established a ministry of immigrant absorption but the Jewish Agency—through its immigration and absorption department—works with the ministry,[47] handling the bulk of the task, administratively and financially.[48]

The Agency is given other functions in legislation adopted by the Knesset. The Agency nominates one member of the National Board for Planning and Building, which oversees construction work.[49] It nominates one member of the Committee for the Protection of Agricultural Land, which prevents encroachment on agricultural land.[50] As already indicated, it has, by statute, a role on governmental agricultural marketing boards and in operating Mekorot, the state water authority.[51] Participation on these bodies involves the Agency in decisionmaking for government agencies.

In 1977 the government announced an urban neighborhood improvement program called Project Renewal. It was to be undertaken jointly with the Agency, which was to raise the funds. Neighborhoods selected for renewal by the government and the Agency numbered about eighty and were all Jewish-inhabited.[52] One Arab neighborhood sought participation but was denied on the ground that its Arab majority precluded Agency funding. The majority of the funding for the project was contributed by the government rather than by the Agency, which meant that the Agency's restriction on funding directed the government's contribution to Jewish neighborhoods only.[53] In the late 1980s, however, some Project Renewal funds were used in Arab neighborhoods.[54]

16

Holding the Soil:

Arab Access to Land

Get off this estate.
What for?
Because it's mine.
Where did you get it?
From my father.
Where did he get it?
From his father.
And where did he get it?
He fought for it.
Well, I'll fight you for it.
—Carl Sandburg, *The People, Yes*

Like the World Zionist Organization/Jewish Agency, the Jewish National Fund continued to function after the establishment of Israel. It continued to purchase land under statutory authority.[1] The Fund remained a subordinate body of the World Zionist Organization and Jewish Agency.[2] To define the Fund's role in Israel, the Knesset adopted the Jewish National Fund Law. The law recognized the creation of a new Jewish National Fund, which had by that time been incorporated in Israel, "to continue the activities of the existing company, which was founded and incorporated in the Diaspora."[3] The new company held Fund land inside the 1949 armistice lines. The British-incorporated company continued to exist and to hold Fund land elsewhere.[4] The activities of the Israel-incorporated Fund were further defined in a 1961 "covenant" between the Fund and the government of Israel.[5] The Keren Hayesod (Foundation Fund) was also incorporated under Israeli law and was renamed "Keren Hayesod—United Israel Appeal."[6]

The Fund describes its role as using "charitable funds" in ways "beneficial to persons of Jewish religion, race or origin."[7] Its leadership is appointed by the World Zionist Organization and its personnel are recruited from the Zionist movement.[8] While the Fund's principal function involved land, it assumed a major role in road-building, where it emphasized considerations of military strategy. In 1967 the Fund would claim credit for facilitating Israel's military victory over Jordan by building roads for use by tanks.[9]

The government owns 76 percent of the land within the 1949 armistice lines, while the Jewish National Fund owns 16 percent.[10] The U.S. Department of State cited this tenure system in a report on human rights in Israel, since it affects the right of Arabs to own and use land in Israel. "Title to 93 percent of the land in Israel is held by the State or quasi-public organizations in trust for the Jewish people," the department stated. "According to law, anyone may purchase the remaining seven percent of privately-owned land through ordinary commercial transactions."[11] Of the 7 percent, some is encumbered by deed clauses prohibiting sale to persons other than Jews,[12] but Arabs own most of that 7 percent, or about 5 percent of the land inside the armistice lines.[13] The government holds title to much of the Negev Desert, and the Fund holds 50 percent of the non-Negev land within the 1949 armistice lines, including most of Israel's prime agricultural land.[14]

Once the state or Fund acquires land, either is prohibited from alienating it.[15] By law, "the ownership of Israel lands, being the lands in Israel of the State, the Development Authority or the Keren Kayemet Le-Israel [Fund], shall not be transferred either by sale or in any other manner."[16] The Fund's charter also prohibits it from alienating land it owns.[17] Thus, land acquired by the state or Fund remains in perpetuity in the ownership of one or the other. In this way the law ensures the original Zionist goal of "redemption of the land."

Most of the land held by the Fund and government is land confiscated from the Palestine Arabs. As a result of this legal prohibition against land alienation, that land cannot be reacquired by them, even by purchase. As explained by Abraham Granovsky, for many years the chairman of the board of the Fund, "a great rule was laid down, which has a decisive and basic significance—that the property of absentees cannot be transferred in ownership to anyone but national public institutions alone, namely, either the State itself, or the original Land Institution of the Zionist Movement."[18]

The Fund uses its land to advance Zionist goals. It leases land for housing for Jews[19] and for kibbutzim, which accept only Jews as members.[20] The Fund's 1954 charter requires it to purchase land "for the purpose of settling Jews on such lands" and to "make donations" and to "promote the interests of the Jews."[21]

The Fund's charter omits the provision of its 1907 charter prohibiting the leasing of land to non-Jews.[22] The 1954 charter permits the Fund to lease "on such terms and in such manner as it may deem fit,"[23] but it specifies the Fund's objective as purchase of land "for the purpose of settling Jews."[24] The earlier proviso permitting leasing to Jews only was omitted because "the undesirable impression might be created of so-called racist restrictions," according to a Fund memorandum. "Even without these explicit prohibitions," the memorandum read, "the Fund Board of Directors will know how to administer the work of the institution in accordance with the explicit object as specified in the aforementioned clause which remains unchanged."[25] The Fund, however, as before 1954, leases to Jews only.[26] The Fund's standard lease contract requires a lessee "to carry out the work related to the cultivation of the Leasehold only and exclusively by Jews."[27] Arabs, therefore, are excluded from using or living on Fund land.[28]

Land owned by the Fund and by the state is administered by the Israel Lands Administration.[29] The administration's director is appointed by the government, after consultation with the Fund.[30] Policy for the administration is set by the Israel Lands Council, established in the same statute, and the government appoints the council.[31] Under the 1961 "covenant" between the government and the Fund, it appointed six Fund representatives and seven government representatives.[32] Only in rare cases has state land been leased to Arabs.[33]

The covenant gave the Fund the exclusive right and obligation for land reclamation and afforestation.[34] Accomplished by the Fund's Land Development Administration, this task includes land drainage, tree planting, and the opening of new border areas for settlement.[35] The Fund's regulations limiting the use of land to Jews are applicable to this state-owned land as well as to Fund-owned land.[36]

A 1973 Fund report indicated that the Knesset enacted the 1960 land legislation after securing the Fund's agreement to it. It stated that the legislation made the Fund's policies on land use into state policy: "Following an agreement between the Government of Israel and the Keren Kayemeth Leisrael, the Knesset in 1960 enacted the Basic Law: Israel Lands which gives legal effect to the ancient tradition of ownership of the land in perpetuity by the Jewish people . . . the principle on which the Keren Kayemeth Leisrael was founded. The same law extended that principle to the bulk of Israel's State domains."[37] The Fund's power over state land means that its Zionist principles are government policy.[38]

Subleasing of Fund Land is also controlled. The Fund's charter provides that, once the Fund leases land, "no lessee shall be entitled to effect any sublease" without Fund approval.[39] Nevertheless, some lessees of Fund and state agricultural land sublet it to Arab farmers without approval.[40] To prevent that, the Knesset in 1967 enacted the Agricultural Settlement Law, which prohibited subleasing or sharecropping arrangements without the authorization of the minister of agriculture.[41] Avnery and an Arab Knesset member, Tawfiq Toubi, objected that the purpose was to prevent subleasing to Arabs.[42] Fund Director Shimon Ben-Shemesh confirmed Avnery and Toubi's suspicion by arguing in favor of the law precisely because, he said, it was necessary to keep Jewish lessees from subleasing Fund land to Arabs.[43]

As a sanction for unauthorized subleasing, the Agricultural Settlement Law called for the payment of a fine or for the forfeiture of lease rights.[44] Land has been confiscated when sublet to Arab farmers.[45] To ensure enforcement of the law, the director of the Galilee office of the Jewish Agency's Settlement Department sent a notice in 1975 to the settlements it had established. The notice warned that it is a violation of the law and of Settlement Department regulations to lease state or Fund land to Arabs as sharecroppers, or to rent orchards to Arabs for picking and marketing of fruit. The department mentioned in the notice that in 1974 it had pressed legal charges against Jews who violated these regulations.[46]

Since the Fund promotes land use by Jews over Arabs, it contributes to the segmentation of Israeli society.[47] This separationism in land use has been compared to land tenure in South Africa. There the sectors for blacks and whites are delineated and neither may purchase land in the area of the other. South Africa's Native Land Act of 1913 set aside 7 percent of the territory for the African population and prohibited them from acquiring land in the other 93 percent.[48] In 1936 the Native Trust and Land Act increased the land available to Africans to 13 percent.[49] The South African law protects the 13 percent as African land, whereas Israel's legislation excludes the Arabs from Fund and state land but does not exclude Jews from the Arabs' land. In that respect, Israel's land tenure system is less favorable to the Arabs than is South Africa's to the Africans.

The governmental character of the national institutions is reflected in the fact that the Israel penal code deems an employee of the World Zionist Organization, the Jewish Agency, the Jewish National Fund, or the Keren Hayesod—United Israel Appeal as a "public servant"[50] in provisions on bribery, abuse of office, and impersonation or insult of a public servant.[51] Similarly, under the covenant between the Zionist Executive and the government, the national institutions enjoy immunity from taxation on the same basis as government agencies and have the power to issue administrative orders to carry out investigations.[52]

The fact that the Knesset has given the national institutions extensive governmental functions means that the Zionist doctrine is professed officially by the state.[53] The role of the national institutions results in national discrimination because, as stated by Hebrew University Professor David Kretzmer, "while entrusted with tasks which are *par excellence* tasks of a governmental nature, their mandate restricts them to dealing with the Jewish sector of the Israeli population."[54] A Fund official acknowledged that "the Government would have to look after all citizens if they owned the land; since the JNF [Jewish National Fund] owns the land, let's be frank, we can serve just the Jewish people."[55] Another Fund official suggested all state lands be transferred to the Fund so Arabs would not ask to use them.[56] The national institutions can discriminate in favor of Jews without the state itself being seen as discriminating.[57]

17

The Law of Ingathering:

Nationality and Citizenship

Integration is to be avoided.
—Abba Eban

Another area of Israeli legislation where differences between Jews and Arabs are found is nationality and citizenship. In the 1950 Law of Return the Knesset gave "every Jew" a "right to come to this country."[1] In the 1952 Nationality Law it conferred Israeli citizenship automatically on a Jew who settles in Israel and who does not reject it.[2] The Nationality Law does not refer to any nationality defined by the geographic borders of Israel.[3] This unrestricted right of immigration for Jews is deemed a basic aspect of the concept of a Jewish state.[4] Ben-Gurion said Israel "is not a Jewish State only because Jews constitute a majority, but a State for Jews wherever they are, and for every Jew who wants to be here." He characterized the Nationality Law as embodying "a central purpose of our state, the purpose of the ingathering of exiles."[5]

This philosophy drew criticism on the ground it was unfair to the Palestine Arabs. Henry Byroade, U.S. assistant secretary of state for Near Eastern, South Asian, and African affairs, criticized Israel in 1954 for regarding itself as a "headquarters" of "worldwide groupings of peoples of a particular religious faith who must have special rights within and obligations to the Israeli state."[6]

Which Jews Israel represents is not clear.[7] The signers of the Declaration of the Establishment of the State of Israel rejected a proposal to amend the term "Jewish state" to "sovereign independent Jewish state" because they did not want to imply that the state was independent of Jews outside Israel.[8] Thus, Israel purports to represent world Jewry. In 1971 the Knesset broadened citizenship rights for Jews by amending the Nationality Law to grant citizenship to any

Jew abroad who expressed a desire to settle in Israel.[9] Its intent was to grant citizenship to Soviet Jews who desired to settle in Israel.[10] Tawfiq Toubi criticized the amendment on the ground it separated citizenship from the territory of the state of Israel.[11]

Palestine Arabs displaced in 1948 have no right under Israeli law to return. The Nationality Law grants citizenship to a person who maintained continuous residence in Israel from May 14, 1948, to July 14, 1952, or who legally returned during that period if, in addition, the person registered as an inhabitant by March 1, 1952, under the 1949 Registration of Inhabitants Ordinance.[12] This provision was intended to apply to Palestine Arabs[13] but it excludes from citizenship Arabs who departed in 1948 unless they returned legally before July 14, 1952. The government, however, permitted only a few to legally return.

The rationale for this exclusion was that Palestine Arabs who departed in 1948 were disloyal. The legal advisor to the foreign ministry, using the government's version of the 1948 departure of Palestine's Arabs, said it was a sign of "disloyalty towards the State of Israel" to have "participated in the Arab exodus from Palestine organized by the Arab leaders in 1948."[14]

For Jews, proof of continuous residence from May 14, 1948, to July 14, 1952, was not required by the Nationality Law, since any Jew is automatically entitled to citizenship. In this way the law made a clear distinction between Jew and Arab widely viewed as discriminatory.[15] Of those Arabs who did not leave in 1948, many were unable to prove continuous residence from May 14, 1948, to July 14, 1952, and thus were refused citizenship.[16] A child born of such stateless parents was also stateless. In 1968 the Nationality Law was amended to grant citizenship to such a stateless child if the child applied between the ages of 18 and 21 and had not been convicted of a "security offense" or been sentenced to a term of five or more years' imprisonment after conviction on any offense.[17] In 1980 it was amended again to remove the restrictions of the original Nationality Law for those Arab residents of Israel and to grant them citizenship as of that time.[18]

Even with the 1968 and 1980 amendments, the law retains distinctions between Jew and Arab. The legal route for acquiring citizenship is still governed by different legislation, since a Jew acquires citizenship by virtue of being a Jew, regardless of place of residence.[19]

Further, the 1980 amendment grants citizenship only to those Arabs who were citizens of Palestine in 1948[20] and who have necessary documents to prove so.[21]

The United States characterized the Law of Return and Nationality Law as conferring "an advantage on Jews in matters of immigration and citizenship."[22] Others have said the two laws establish a "legal apartheid"[23] and have compared them to racial categorization in South Africa.[24] It has been argued in response that the two laws, while favoring Jews, do not discriminate against any particular nationality[25] and that it is not necessarily discriminatory to favor particular groups in granting citizenship.[26] Certain other states, it is pointed out, prefer members of ethnic groups in citizenship.[27] Human rights norms permit ethnic preference in citizenship, "provided that such provisions do not discriminate against any particular nationality."[28] These justifications are challenged on the basis that, while the two laws do not contain explicit discrimination against a particular nationality, the reality of their implementation in Israel is to discriminate against the indigenous population, the Palestine Arabs.

Jews are said to form a "nation"[29] because of a self-perception of commonality[30] and a perception by others.[31] Supreme Court Justice Moshe Silberg said that in view of "the exclusive status of the Jews in the world" and of "the fact that we are always so different from others," Jewry must be considered "as a people or nation."[32] It is objected by others that the link among Jews is religion, not "nationhood."[33] The government and Supreme Court of Israel both view Jewishness as something other than birth as a Jew, because they consider that a Jew who opts for a religion other than Judaism is not a Jew. For instance, a Jew who had converted to Catholicism applied for citizenship under the Law of Return. The ministry of the interior refused on the ground of his Catholicism,[34] and the Supreme Court upheld the refusal, Judge Silberg stating that "a Jew who has become a Christian is not deemed a Jew."[35] Judge Zvi Berenson quoted a statement made at the United Nations on behalf of the Jewish Agency by Moshe Sharett, later a prime minister of Israel. Sharett said that to be a Jew "it is essential that the person has not converted to another religion. He need not be an active, pious Jew. He is still considered a Jew. But if he converts to another religion he can no longer demand to be recognized as a Jew. The religious test is decisive."[36]

That conclusion was written into statute law in 1970. The Knesset amended the Law of Return to define a Jew as "a person who was born of a Jewish mother or has become converted to Judaism and who is not a member of another religion."[37] This definition was followed in 1977 to deny status as a Jew to a Jewish woman who converted to Christianity.[38] By using religious affiliation as a criterion, the Knesset suggests that Jewry is not a nation.

The United States has also taken the position that Jewry does not constitute a nation. It was explained—regarding a possible relation to Israel of Jews who are U.S. citizens—that the U.S. government "does not recognize a legal-political relationship based upon the religious identification of American citizens. . . . Accordingly, the Department of State does not regard the 'Jewish people' concept as a concept of international law."[39]

A second obstacle to Jewish nationhood is the fact that Jews do not inhabit a single territory but are nationals of many states.[40] Because of the nationality of Jews in various states, early Zionist diplomats used the term "Jewish people," rather than "Jewish nation," though they intended the "Jewish people" be considered a "nation" in the international law sense of a group having collective rights.[41]

Even though there is no "Jewish nation," it is possible there could be an "Israeli nation," made up of those Jews, or perhaps those Jews and Arabs, living in Israel. The government and courts of Israel have said, however, that there is no "Israeli nation." In 1972 a Jewish Israeli asked to change the "nationality" notation in his identity card from "Jewish" to "Israeli." Israel's identity cards call for nationality, and the designation used for Jewish Israelis is "Jew."[42] The interior ministry denied the request, and the applicant sued. The Supreme Court also denied the request, stating there is "no Israeli nation separate from the Jewish people. The Jewish people is composed not only of those residing in Israel but also of Diaspora Jewry."[43] Chief Judge Simon Agranat stated that the creation of an Israeli nation would negate the aspiration on which Israel was established. The court's decision reinforced the concept that Israel exists not for those within its territory but for persons wherever they are located who make up the "Jewish nation." That definition of Israel's constituency excludes Arabs, even if they are citizens of Israel.

The Jewish people Israel aspires to represent is primarily the European Jews who founded Zionism at the turn of the century. Israel does not seek to assimilate into the Arab world but to maintain its separate identity.[44] Arab-state Jews are to be Europeanized to the farthest extent possible. Israel's onetime UN representative, Abba Eban, said that for Israel "integration" is "to be avoided." He evoked a "danger lest the predominance of immigrants of Oriental origin"—by which he meant Jews from Arab states—might "force Israel to equalize its cultural level with that of the neighboring world. So far from regarding our immigrants from Oriental countries as a bridge toward our integration with the Arabic speaking world, our object should be to infuse them with an Occidental spirit, rather than to allow them to draw us into an unnatural Orientalism."[45]

18

Divide and Conquer:

Arabs in Israel's Political System

I preferred "separate development."
—Yehoshua Palmon, Adviser on Arab affairs, government of Israel

Arab citizens of Israel have the right to vote and to be elected to the Knesset,[1] and many Arabs support an Arab-Jewish Communist party sharply critical of the government on important issues.[2] Arabs are regularly elected to the Knesset and participate actively in its debates. Arab Knesset members have only a limited ability, however, to influence policy on basic issues, like the repatriation of the Arab refugees. They cannot exert significant influence over the executive branch of government, whose functionaries are committed to Zionism. The government, the Jewish Agency, the Histadrut, and the army all promote a Zionist view. As a result, the ability of the Arabs to influence policy is limited.[3] Few Arabs serve in high bureaucratic posts. No Arab has been a cabinet minister. Of 1,839 leading government officials in 1980, only 16 were Arab.[4] Arabs are less able than Jews to develop with bureaucrats the relationship necessary to secure favorable action.[5] For Arabs the government is "alien";[6] each ministry has an "Arab affairs" department,[7] and Arabs approaching a ministry must contact it rather than the official who handles the issue in question.

As a result of the 1948 expulsion, the number of Arabs eligible to vote (17 percent of the electorate) cannot threaten Zionist policies in Israel.[8] And by keeping the Arabs economically dependent, the government prevented them from exercising political power even in proportion to their reduced numbers. Arabs have never held more than eight of the 120 seats in the Knesset.[9] The military government in Arab areas pressured Arabs to vote for Zionist parties[10] and in particular for the ruling Mapai party.[11] "Through the military government," said Teddy Kollek, who had been elected mayor of Jerusalem, "Arab votes were secured."[12] The system of permits and closed zones resulted in a dependence of Arab citizens on the military government. That dependence extended to the Arabs' political activity. Mapai created lists of Arabs to run as Mapai candidates in general elections.[13] A 1959 Mapai internal memorandum titled "Recommendations for Dealing with the Arab Minority in Israel" explained the purpose of creating these lists was to ensure Arab politicians "would not consolidate into an independent Arab bloc."[14]

Military authorities threatened land confiscation or loss of work permits to Arabs who supported the Communist party.[15] A complaint to the UN Human Rights Commission in 1961 by a group called the Third Force Movement recited that the military governors "see to it that a worker who has expressed sympathy with the anti-Zionist party should get no permit to go to look for work, and he and his family should remain unemployed and hungry."[16]

Military authorities controlled elections to local office as well. In Arab towns they thwarted the election to municipal councils of Arab candidates viewed as hostile, and even of candidates of Zionist parties other than Mapai.[17] In some instances, when candidates it deemed hostile were elected, the military authorities dissolved the municipal council[18] and expelled the candidates from the country,[19] or cut allocations to the municipal budget.

The government's purpose in introducing elections in Arab municipalities was to prevent the development of unity under the traditional Arab leadership. The 1959 Mapai party memorandum claimed success in achieving this effort, which it referred to as its "communal policy." The "government's policy has sought to divide the Arab population into diverse communities and regions. . . . The municipal status of the Arab villages, and the competitive spirit of local elections, deepened the divisions inside the villages themselves. The communal policy and the clan divisions in the villages prevented Arab unity."[20]

Yehoshua Palmon, the government's advisor in the 1950s on Arab affairs, described in a 1983 interview how he had implemented the government's policy toward the Arabs. "I behaved toward them as a wolf in sheep's clothing—harsh, but outwardly decent," he said. "I opposed the integration of Arabs into Israeli society. I preferred separate development." Palmon understood "separate development" excluded Arabs from the political process. "True, this prevented the

Arabs from integrating into the Israeli democracy. Yet they had never had democracy before. Since they never had it, they never missed it. The separation made it possible to maintain a democratic regime within the Jewish population alone."[21]

Despite the pressure from the military government, some Arabs tried to form their own political parties, and when they did, the government blocked them.[22] It was "a principle of the military authorities not to tolerate nationalistic organising within the area under its control."[23] When nationalists organized meetings aimed at forming Arab political organizations, the military government stopped them.[24] It denied them travel permits,[25] put them under house arrest, or expelled them from the country.[26]

An Arab political organization was formed in the 1950s under the name Al-Ard (The Land). Concerned over its activity, the government confiscated its publications in 1960 and arrested its leaders.[27] In 1964, however, Al-Ard presented a list of candidates to stand election to the Knesset, under the name Arab Socialist List. The district commissioner of Haifa denied the group the right to form, on the ground "its aim was to undermine the existence and security of the State of Israel."[28]

The district commissioner acted under Articles 84 and 85 of the Defense (Emergency) Regulations, which permit the banning of "unlawful associations," groups found to be detrimental to state security.[29] The Supreme Court upheld the denial, Judge Alfred Witkon stating that Al-Ard's platform "expressly and totally negates the existence of the state of Israel in general and its existence within its present boundaries in particular."[30] Al-Ard did not call for the elimination of Israel, though it did advocate a Palestinian state.[31] It called for "recognition" of the UN General Assembly Resolution 181 which recommended partition of Palestine and would thereby "maintain the rights of both Israeli-Jewish and Palestinian Arab people and would strengthen the stability and peace of the area."[32] Following the Supreme Court decision, the minister of defense declared Al-Ard an "illegal association."[33]

In 1965 a group of ten Arabs sought to stand for the Knesset as the Arab Socialist List. Of the ten, five had been Al-Ard members.[34] The Central Elections Committee rejected the list as "an unlawful association, because its promoters deny the integrity of the State of Israel and its very existence."[35] The committee did not have evidence of illegal acts done or threatened by the candidates.[36] The Supreme Court of Israel affirmed the Central Election Committee's rejection of the Arab Socialist List.[37] Judge Simon Agranat said the committee must protect "the continuity and perpetuity" of Israel as a "sovereign Jewish state."[38] Judge Yoel Sussman said the list's aim was the "destruction of the state."[39] Judge Haim Cohn dissented on the ground the election law did not authorize exclusion of candidates for their views.[40]

During the 1981 election campaign the government invoked the Defense (Emergency) Regulations to prohibit nationalist political congresses planned for the Arab towns of Nazareth and Shfar'am. These congresses had been called to form an Arab political party.[41] In 1984 the Central Elections Committee disqualified a list of Knesset candidates presented by an Arab-Jewish coalition, the Progressive List for Peace, which advocated a West Bank–Gaza state and negotiations between Israel and the Palestine Liberation Organization (PLO).[42] The candidates stood for election, however, after a favorable ruling from the Supreme Court.[43] The court found that the Progressive List for Peace, unlike the Arab Socialist List of 1965, did not seek to destroy Israel[44] and did not deny its right to exist.[45]

The Knesset in 1985 wrote the prohibition against Arab nationalist candidates into statute law by prohibiting participation in Knesset elections by candidates who reject "the existence of the State of Israel as the state of the Jewish people."[46] Avnery said the purpose was to "prevent Arabs from taking part in Israeli democracy."[47] Toubi said the law showed Israel to be an "apartheid state."[48]

The Arab population of Israel had loyalties to extended families, loyalties that divided them from each other. In addition, they were not all of the same religion. While most were Muslim, some belonged to the Druze sect of Islam, and others were Christian. The government of Israel was cognizant of these differences and their potential from its standpoint. "The government's policy," said the 1959 Mapai party memorandum, "has sought to divide the Arab population into diverse communities and regions." The "communal policy and the clan divisions in the villages prevented Arab unity."[49] The government sought "forced segmentation of the population (Druze, Christian villages, townsfolk)" through the co-optation of "positive elements."[50]

One aim of government activity was to foster discord between

Christian and Moslem Arabs.[51] It particularly cultivated the Druze Arabs, to split them from other Arabs.[52] The Druze are Arabs who formed a sect within Islam in the eleventh century.[53] They live in their own villages, making up 8 percent of the Arab population within the armistice lines.

The government gave the Druze Arabs preferences over other Arabs.[54] In 1948 it did not expel Druze Arabs to the same extent as other Arabs;[55] in fact, it managed to convince some Druze Arabs even to fight on the Zionist side.[56] Others of them cooperated with Zionist forces by convincing non-Druze Arabs to surrender.[57] The government put Druze Arab areas under martial law, as with other Arab areas, but it terminated martial law for them in 1962, four years earlier than for other Arab areas.[58] Even before it ended martial law, the government exempted Druze Arabs from the requirement of securing permits for travel.[59]

Though the conscription law of Israel contained no ethnic criteria, the minister of defense did not draft Arabs into the IDF, due to fears about their loyalty.[60] The IDF did not accept Arabs as volunteers, except for Bedouin Arabs.[61] In 1956, however, the minister began to draft Druze Arabs,[62] and when that occurred twelve hundred Druze Arab sheikhs protested. But the IDF successfully drafted Druze Arab soldiers and used them to oppose other Arabs—to drive Bedouin Arabs out of the Negev Desert to Jordan and to shoot Arab refugees attempting to reenter Israel clandestinely from Egypt.[63] The IDF service of Druze Arabs engendered confrontations with other Arabs during the 1956 war between Israel and Egypt, as the non-Druze Arabs viewed the role of the Druze Arabs as traitorous. As a result, fistfights between Druze and non-Druze Arabs were reported.[64] Some Druze Arabs refused to be drafted and have been prosecuted.[65] One fringe benefit of IDF service was that it made Druze Arabs eligible for many financial benefits the government gives on the basis of veteran status.[66] Druze Arab eligibility for these benefits created a further gulf between Druze and non-Druze Arabs.

Druze Arabs have benefited in other ways. The government gave larger budget allocations to Druze Arab villages than to other Arab towns,[67] though less than to Jewish towns.[68] The Histadrut admitted Druze Arabs into membership in 1957, two years before other Arabs,[69] thereby making it easier for them to get jobs.

The government also gave Druze Arabs a legal status separate from other Arabs. In 1957 the ministry of religious affairs recognized the Druze as a religious community separate from other Moslems,[70] though they had not had separate status under Ottoman or mandate law[71] and had functioned as part of the Moslem religious community.[72] The major religious communities in Israel are governed by religious courts in domestic relations and matters of personal status.[73] In 1962 the Knesset established Druze religious courts separate from the Islamic courts.[74] It let the Druze Arabs have more qadis (religious judges) per capita than other Arabs.[75] One consequence of separate religious status was that a Druze Arab and a non-Druze Arab may not contract marriage in Israel, since all marriage is ecclesiastical, and religious authorities marry only persons of their own religion.[76]

The 1959 Mapai party memorandum claimed success in co-opting the Druze Arabs. "The policy of communal division bore fruit," it stated. The policy "succeeded in creating barriers, albeit sometimes artificial ones, between certain parts of the Arab community, as in the case of the mistrust between the Druze and the other Arab communities. This policy enabled the state to prevent the formation of a unified Arab bloc and left considerable leeway for the leaders of the respective communities to concern themselves with their communal affairs, instead of general Arab ones."[77]

The government in 1970 changed the administrative structure for Druze Arabs. It directed government ministries to deal with Druze Arabs by ordinary channels rather than in the "Arab affairs" departments through which other Arabs are required to approach the government.[78] On the identity cards the government requires of all citizens nationality is noted, and for Druze Arabs the ministry of the interior uses "Druze" rather than "Arab," regardless of the preference of the individual Druze.[79] In 1977 the government removed Druze Arab schools from the jurisdiction of the education ministry's department that handles Arab schools.[80] In Druze Arab schools the government uses a special curriculum that teaches children about the differences between Druze and other Arabs in a way that promotes division.[81]

Despite granting them certain privileges, the government discriminated against Druze Arabs in many of the ways it discriminates against other Arabs. In the early 1950s it confiscated their lands to the same degree as it did those of other Arabs.[82] It does not permit them to purchase housing in locations closed to Arabs.[83] Like other Arabs, Druze are excluded from employment in security-related jobs.[84] In 1987 the government declared an intent eventually to treat Druze Arabs equally with Jews in all respects;[85] but the reaction of the Druze Arabs to the favoritism policy was mixed. Many welcomed the benefits,[86] while recognizing the effort to separate them from other Arabs.[87] Although many Druze Arabs opposed the policy, it kept Druze and non-Druze Arabs from uniting as a political force.[88]

19

Protecting Privilege:

Arabs and Governmental Services

We has met the enemy, and it is us.
—Walt Kelly, *Pogo*

The government and the national institutions provide a variety of services to the population of Israel, and often the two collaborate to provide services. One important field of such collaboration is the creation of new residential settlements and the construction of housing.[1] The government plans and finances new settlements in coordination with the Jewish Agency, and, in conformity with its charter, the Agency organizes settlements for Jews only.[2] By 1968 the government and national institutions had built twenty-eight new towns for Jews in the Negev and Galilee areas,[3] primarily for immigrants.[4] The aim was to put "a large Jewish population" in areas where Jews were few.[5] "The history of immigrant housing," wrote Israel Shaham, assistant director-general of budget and finance in the ministry of housing, "is actually the history of public housing in Israel."[6] The government's housing policy has been aimed largely at establishing Jewish population concentrations. Conversely, it has put few resources into housing for Arabs.[7]

The Jewish National Fund, Jewish Agency, and Histadrut all build housing.[8] The ministry of housing built two major new towns in the Galilee—Upper Nazareth (adjoining the original Nazareth) and Carmiel. By its regulations the ministry refused to sell housing in these towns to Arabs,[9] unless they had served in the Israel Defense Force, police, or prison service.[10] As a result, few Arabs qualified.[11] The ministry of defense does not draft Arabs, except for Druze Arabs, and does not accept them as volunteers.[12]

Asked in the Knesset why the ministry refused to sell housing in Carmiel to Arabs, Minister of Housing Joseph Almogi replied that

Carmiel was not built for the people in the surrounding area.[13] Jewish purchasers may, however, lease or sell this housing to Arabs, since an Arab lessee or purchaser does not acquire rights in the land.[14] As a result, many Arabs have leased or purchased housing in upper Nazareth and Carmiel.[15] At other locations where it built housing, the ministry did not restrict ownership to Jews, but it has not built housing in Arab areas.[16]

In 1967 the government expanded the Jewish Quarter of the Old City of Jerusalem, evicting 650 Arab residents.[17] A government corporation, the Company for the Restoration and Development of the Jewish Quarter in the Old City of Jerusalem, Ltd., built new housing there. In a public offering the company stated it would sell to new immigrants who were residents of Israel, or to resident citizens of Israel who had served in the IDF or had received an exemption from IDF service, or had served in a Jewish organization prior to May 14, 1948.

Muhammed Bourkan, a former Arab resident of the Jewish Quarter, applied to purchase an apartment. Bourkan, like most East Jerusalem Arabs, was a citizen of Jordan. When the company refused to sell to Bourkan, he sued in the Israel Supreme Court, where the company acknowledged its policy of selling to Jews only. The court found no unlawful discrimination, reasoning that the expulsion and exclusion of Arab residents were justified by the expulsions in 1948 of Jewish residents of the Quarter by the Arab Legion.[18]

The government has tried through administrative measures to keep Arabs from moving into Jewish areas. Meir Shamir, director of the Israel Land Registration Office, told a meeting of the Government Committee to Evaluate Land Policy that "we have been operating according to governmental consensus on this issue all along. I am not authorised to tell you whether there is any such government decision written down anywhere. But these are guidelines we have received—not to encourage mixed peripheral areas."[19]

The government uses Jewish housing for strategic purposes. In the 1950s it created settlements in border areas, and after 1967 it built large apartment complexes in East Jerusalem in "a ring of Jewish settlement" around Arab areas,[20] to create "a Jewish-populated buffer zone between Arab Jerusalem and the West Bank."[21] It oriented sales to Jews, though it did not refuse Arabs. The Galilee has been a focus of attention for the national institutions and government since it is the area of the greatest Arab population density inside the armistice lines.[22] In the 1980s the government and national institutions established new "lookout" settlements for Jews in the Galilee to increase the Jewish population there.[23]

The ministry of housing makes loans to the general public for the purchase of housing.[24] Two categories of people get preferential rates. Persons immigrating to Israel under the Law of Return are eligible to rent at a reduced rate and then to purchase the housing on preferential terms.[25] Zionist institutions abroad, like the Zionist Organization of Canada, make loans available at advantageous rates to persons immigrating under the Law of Return.[26]

By regulations of the ministry of housing if the loan applicant is a veteran, the loan is given for a larger percentage of the purchase price, part of the loan is interest-free, and the applicant is freed of a requirement that interest be adjusted for inflation.[27] The regulations define "veteran" as a person who holds a military identification number, or that person's parent, sibling, child, or spouse. Since no length of service is required, all persons who enter the military qualify. "Veteran" also includes any person who receives an individual exemption from military service. The ministry of defense issues individual exemptions only to persons subject to the draft, which means, with minor exceptions, only to Jews. The regulations also include as a veteran a person who was issued a military service postponement, which the ministry of defense typically gives to Orthodox Jews.[28] The definition of veteran thus includes nearly all Jews, regardless of whether they served in the IDF.

The ministry of housing gives preferential financing to certain applicants for the housing it builds in "development areas." These preferences are available by regulation to "a person who has served, or whose parent, sibling, or child has served in the IDF, police, or prison service."[29] Such persons are eligible for grants or loans to purchase the housing, or for rent subsidies in rental housing.[30] The broad definition—requiring no minimum military service and including the designated relatives—indicates that this benefit is not a reward for military service.

The government has continued the practice it started in the 1950s of giving Arab municipalities less budget funding than Jewish municipalities for roads, sewage, and other public services.[31] This underfunding has exacerbated the housing situation of Arabs. Nazareth, an Arab-populated town, is an example. Gur-Arie, the prime minister's advisor on Arab affairs, said Arabs from Nazareth were moving into Upper Nazareth because of the poor housing in Nazareth. As the reason for what he called a "serious housing problem in Arab Nazareth," he said that "we are conducting a war against the Nazareth Municipality which is a part of the Communist Party [Rakah] and the standard of services there is very low. So those who can afford it obviously prefer to pay more than a Jew does and move to a place with better services."[32] Nazareth is an example of an Arab town receiving low budget allocations.

Discrepancies have appeared in the government's policy toward people who build houses in violation of regulations that require a building permit. Much housing is built in Israel without a permit, and the government frequently bulldozes houses built by Arabs without a permit.[33] It has not, however, typically bulldozed houses built by Jews without a permit,[34] even though, according to a study done at the Technion architecture and town planning faculty in Haifa, 75 percent of the houses built without a permit are built by Jews.[35]

Many individual Jews discriminate against Arabs in the sale or rental of housing. In one reported instance a Jew who signed a preliminary agreement to sell an apartment withdrew upon discovering the purchaser was Arab.[36] The government has adopted no legislation to prohibit private discrimination in housing and the courts have not found it illegal.[37] The chief rabbi of the Sephardic community, Mordechai Eliahu, whose position is established by statute,[38] ruled in 1985 that Jewish law forbids a Jew to sell or lease housing to an Arab in any area of Israel where Jews live or are preparing to live.[39] The chief rabbi of Acre, a town that includes Arabs and Jews, ruled that Jewish law forbids Jews to live in proximity to Arabs.[40]

Beyond housing, the government of Israel provides a number of welfare benefits to the public.[41] It places conditions on some of them, such as a recipient's having some relation to a person who has served in the Israel Defense Force. In a human rights report on Israel, the U.S. Department of State wrote that Arabs "do not qualify for many of the important economic and social benefits that derive from military service."[42] To encourage births, the ministry of labor and social welfare makes child support payments to parents, under the National

Insurance Law.[43] The 1949 Discharged Soldiers (Reinstatement in Employment) Law[44] was amended in 1970 to authorize the ministry, through the National Insurance Authority, to make an additional child support payment to "soldiers." The amendment defined "soldier" as "a person who is serving or has served in the Defence Army of Israel, the Police or the Prison Service," or who served in one of the Zionist military formations (Haganah, Irgun, or LEHI) prior to the establishment of Israel.[45] Avnery objected in the Knesset that the aim was not to reward for IDF service but to "encourage births among one part of the population of Israel and to effect the opposite among the other part."[46]

In 1970 the minister issued regulations under the amendment. He adopted the Regulations on Grants for Soldiers and Their Families, which provided grants for the third child and any additional children at a level approximately equal to the amount payable under the National Insurance Law.[47] Thus, a qualifying person receives double the ordinary amount.[48] The minister's 1970 Regulation broadened the 1970 amendment's definition of soldier to include the "spouse, children, or parents of a soldier."[49] Eligibility thus defined does not depend on actual military service.

The ministerial committee on the interior and services, acting without statutory authorization, provides this supplementary child support payment to parents who have not served in the IDF but are students in Jewish seminaries.[50] The result of the 1970 amendment, the 1977 Regulation, and the committee decision for seminarians was that nearly all Jews qualified for the additional payment, while almost no Arabs did.[51]

Universities in Israel are private. They are forbidden by government regulation to discriminate in the admission of students on the basis of "race, sex, religion, national origin, or social status."[52] But on security grounds, the universities do not admit Arab applicants to certain faculties.[53] Scholarships are given by the Office of Absorption of the Jewish Agency; Arabs are not eligible to compete for them, as they are available to persons immigrating under the Law of Return.[54] Certain privately funded scholarships are open only to students with IDF service.[55]

For higher education the government provides tuition loans and grants to "veterans," and to persons who reside in a "development town" or "renewal neighborhood." Guidelines for distribution of these loans and grants were adopted by a commission appointed in 1982 by the minister of education and culture and chaired by Moshe Katzav, deputy minister of housing.[56] The commission defined "veteran" to include the parent or sibling of a person who served in the IDF. A student from a family of four or more children and who was eligible as a veteran for a supplemental allowance for a child was made eligible for a grant covering half tuition.[57]

With minor exceptions, "development towns" and "renewal neighborhoods" are inhabited by Jews only. The guidelines made a resident of either one eligible for a loan for one-third of university tuition. The loan was to be forgiven if the student resides in the development town or renewal neighborhood after graduation for a period equal to the period of study.[58] The criterion of development town or renewal neighborhood residence and the expansive definition of "veteran" made most Jews, but few Arabs, eligible for preferences in university tuition.

In 1987 the government decided to establish a dual tuition system — a lower rate for those who have served in the IDF, a substantially higher rate for others.[59] While in theory each university sets its own fees, the universities in fact set fees as decided upon by the government because of the substantial government subsidies they receive. The decision was criticized in the press as "apartheid policy."[60]

In elementary education the Knesset legislated in 1953 that the purpose of elementary education was to teach "the values of Jewish culture" and "loyalty to the State and the Jewish people." This purpose covered even "non-Jewish educational institutions," whose curriculum is prescribed by the minister of education.[61] The state funds an Orthodox Jewish private school system but does not fund schools for other religions.[62]

The Jewish Religious Services Budgets Law of 1949 and the Jewish Religious Services Law of 1971 called for local religious councils to submit budgets to the minister of religious affairs. The budgets are financed one-third by the central government and two-thirds by the local government.[63] There are no such statutes for other religions.[64] The Jewish religion thus was given preferential treatment.[65] The government allocates funds for Muslim and Christian religious services, but at a level far less than their proportion in the population, and without a legislative mandate.[66] By statute, the Knesset gave legal status to the chief rabbinate and empowered and obligated it to undertake "activities aimed at bringing the public closer to the values of tora (religious learning) and mitzvot (religious duties)."[67] No other religion has a body with similar legal status, empowerment, or obligations.[68]

The ministry of absorption provides funds to immigrants and "returning residents."[69] Nearly all immigrants are Jews, as a result of the application of the Law of Return and the Nationality Law. Immigrants receive economic assistance for housing and job placement.[70] "Returning residents" are Israeli citizens who have resided abroad for at least two years. They are eligible for job placement assistance and for a loan for travel to Israel and for shipment of their personal effects. From 1969 to 1987, under a regulation of the ministry of absorption, only Jews were deemed "returning residents" to qualify for these benefits. In 1987 the attorney general ruled that this exclusion was discriminatory against Arabs.[71]

By the Specified Goods Tax and Luxury Tax Law, the Knesset authorized the minister of finance to designate classes of persons for favorable treatment when they bring goods into Israel after residence abroad.[72] Under this authorization, the minister issued the Purchase Tax Order (Exemption), which called for a lower import duty to be collected from a returning national than from a returning resident.[73] The order defined "returning national" to include only a person who, "if the person were not an Israeli national the Law of Return would apply to him."[74] Thus, only a Jewish citizen of Israel is a returning national.[75] An Arab citizen of Israel is a returning resident and pays higher customs duty.[76] By making eligibility under the Law of Return the criterion, the minister used an explicitly ethnic basis of distinction.

20

Some Are More Equal:

Ethnic Distinctions in the Law of Israel

Zionism is a form of racism.
—UN General Assembly

Even after it ended martial law rule in Arab-populated sectors in 1966, the government of Israel applied the Defense (Emergency) Regulations primarily against Arabs. It used the regulations to prosecute Arabs before military rather than civilian courts[1] and to subject individual Arabs to town arrest.[2] To prevent demonstrations against land confiscations in the Galilee in 1976, it issued notices that villages where demonstrations were planned were still "closed areas" under Regulation 125.[3] In 1979 the Knesset repealed two provisions of the regulations—those on deportation and administrative detention—but retained the power of administrative detention with certain safeguards for the detainee.[4] In 1982 the government invoked the regulations to ban planned publication of an Arab scientific periodical. The Supreme Court approved the ban, saying that under the regulations the government need not state its reason.[5] In 1986 the government used the regulations to prohibit an Arab cleric from traveling abroad for public speaking.[6]

Beyond the Defense (Emergency) Regulations, the Knesset adopted other legislation to suppress Arab nationalism. In 1980 the Knesset amended the Prevention of Terrorism Ordinance to prohibit "any act manifesting identification or sympathy with a terrorist organisation in a public place or in such manner that persons in a public place can see or hear such manifestation of identification or sympathy, either by flying a flag or displaying a symbol or slogan or by causing an anthem or slogan to be heard, or any other similar overt act clearly manifesting such identification or sympathy as aforesaid." That law empowered the government to declare an organization to be terrorist.[7] It declared as terrorist the Palestine Liberation Organization (PLO) and thirteen other Palestinian organizations, including the component organizations of the PLO.[8] Under this law a court convicted two Arab students of producing a pamphlet supporting the PLO,[9] and Arabs have been arrested for flying a PLO flag.[10] The ministry of justice filed charges under this law against Faisal Husseini, head of the Arab Studies Society in Jerusalem.[11] It alleged that in a newspaper interview Husseini had said that the PLO was the only legitimate representative of the Palestinian people.[12]

In 1980 the Knesset gave the minister of the interior the power to revoke the citizenship of "a person who has done an act constituting a breach of allegiance to the State of Israel."[13] Since the government defined the PLO as a terrorist organization, a show of support for it would apparently constitute a breach of allegiance. In a 1980 law on nonprofit societies, the Knesset precluded registration of a society "if any of its objects negates the existence or democratic character of the State of Israel."[14] The law was criticized by several members of the Knesset as being aimed against political organizing by Arabs.[15]

In 1986 the Knesset adopted a statute that forbade "contact" with any person holding an executive position in "an organization that the Israeli government has declared a terrorist organization."[16] This law prohibited contact for any purpose, unless based on family ties or on participation in an academic conference.[17] The government prosecuted both Jews and Arabs for meeting with PLO officials.[18] A note in explanation of the 1986 amendment in the Knesset indicated that one purpose was to prevent political contact between Arabs and Jews that might lead to pressure for recognition of Arab rights: "Recent contact of Israelis with activists and official representatives of terrorist organizations have [sic] grown both numerous and frequent. This phenomenon is causing Israel serious harm, both politically and in the area of security, and cannot be tolerated. Therefore, we propose to outlaw such contacts, if held knowingly and without lawful authority."[19]

Israel has no constitution that might take precedence over legislation that is discriminatory in nature. The Declaration of the Establishment of the State of Israel called for equality of rights, but Israel's courts did not deem the declaration to be a source of law.[20] The courts have no power of judicial review of legislation and, therefore, no power to overturn discriminatory laws.[21] Thus, the laws defining Israel as a Jewish state and giving Jews a preferred status cannot be challenged in the courts of Israel.

The possibility of enacting a constitution or a bill of rights has been debated in Israel. A draft bill of rights proposed by the ministry of justice in 1987 would have forbidden discrimination on a wide variety of bases with the stipulation it not affect legislation enacted prior to entry into force of the new constitution. Thus, the Defense (Emergency) Regulations and prior laws of the Knesset would not be affected. Further, the proposal stated that "a legal provision which derives from Israel being a Jewish state shall not be regarded as discriminatory."[22]

Although the Supreme Court of Israel has no power to review legislation, it does review actions of officials,[23] and Arabs frequently use this procedure.[24] Judges of the Supreme Court are appointed for life and are independent of the executive.[25] On occasion the court has annulled government decisions in security-related situations, like a 1989 case in which, for the first time, it countermanded a decision by the censor against the publication of an item proposed for release. The court ruled the censor could not prohibit a newspaper article containing criticism of the head of the state security agency, the Mossad.[26]

But the court rarely questioned officials who took measures against Arabs for reasons of government policy or state security.[27] With administrative detention, the Knesset instituted judicial review in 1979. But it said the review should be conducted in closed session and it need not follow the rules of evidence.[28] The IDF, in particular, has not always obeyed the Supreme Court. In July 1951 the court ruled that Arabs, formerly residents in the Galilee village of Ikrit from which the IDF had excluded them in October 1948, were entitled to return. The IDF, defying the ruling, prevented the residents from returning.[29]

The racial distinctions found in Israel's legislation have led some commentators to call Arabs second-class citizens in Israel.[30] These distinctions are criticized in Israel.[31] Racial discrimination as a matter of state policy violates the customary law of human rights binding on all states.[32] The UN Charter prohibits discrimination by a state on the basis of race.[33] The International Convention on the Elimination of All Forms of Racial Discrimination, to which Israel is a party, prohibits any "distinction, exclusion, restriction or preference" based on "race, colour, descent, or national or ethnic origin" which has the "purpose or effect of nullifying or impairing the recognition, enjoyment or exercise, on an equal footing, of human rights and fundamental freedoms in the political, economic, social, cultural or any other field of public life."[34]

Some commentators, who argue that a Jewish state is justified, argue further that if that is so then a preferred legal status for Jews over Arabs is justified as well.[35] Resolution 181, on which they rely, called for a constitution in the two prospective states to guarantee "to all persons equal and nondiscriminatory rights in civil, political, economic and religious matters."[36] Resolution 181 did not contemplate a state in which Jews would enjoy a privileged status.[37]

The UN General Assembly, in part because of the legislative discrimination against Arabs under Israeli law, adopted a resolution in which it called Zionism "a form of racism."[38] This characterization has been strongly criticized.[39] But the opinion that Zionism as practiced in Israel reflects racial animus against the Palestine Arabs is widely held in the world community. In particular, those states previously subject to foreign authority view the Palestine Arabs as being in the situation in which they found themselves prior to independence. The nonaligned countries called Zionism an "imperialist ideology."[40] The Organization of African Unity said that "the racist regime in occupied Palestine and the racist regimes in Zimbabwe and South Africa have a common imperialist origin."[41] The African Charter on Human and Peoples' Rights, in naming in its preamble concepts that involve a denial of rights, listed "colonialism, neocolonialism, apartheid, zionism."[42]

Israel reacted sharply at the United Nations in 1961 when Iraq accused it of being an apartheid state.[43] But a number of Israel's legislative enactments give ethnically based preferences in important areas of national life.[44] By prohibiting the return of expelled Arabs while giving Jews ready entry, by segregating land ownership and use, by providing social services to Jews on a preferential basis, by allowing the national institutions to carry out governmental functions, and by providing special power under the Defense (Emergency) Regulations to suppress opposition to discriminatory treatment, Israel has created a complex of rules that constitutes something more than casual discrimination.

Apartheid was defined by McDougal, Lasswell, and Chen as "a complex set of practices of domination and subjection, intensely hierarchized and sustained by the whole apparatus of the state, which affects the distribution of all values."[45] The International Convention on the Suppression and Punishment of the Crime of Apartheid prohibited "racial segregation and discrimination" undertaken to dominate a racial group.[46] As an exaggerated form of racial discrimination, apartheid is, like racial discrimination, prohibited by customary international law.[47]

The racial distinctions in Israel's legislation have been called a natural and intended result of the colonization of Palestine,[48] inherent in the ideology of Zionism.[49] Maxime Rodinson, a leading Arabist, wrote that to create a Jewish state in an Arab Palestine on the basis of the Zionist concept "could not help but lead to a colonial-type situation" and to "a racist state of mind."[50]

The Organization of African Unity said that Israel and South Africa share "a common imperialist origin."[51] Each won independence after armed struggle against British rule, then "coped with the problem of keeping their native populations in subordinate status, and perforce resorted to comparable, though not identical, measures."[52] Both are, in the view of a leading African political scientist, "discriminatory ideologies whose implementation inevitably and logically necessitated strategies of repression and ethnic exclusivity."[53]

Other human rights analysts rejected the analogy. Tom Franck argued that South Africa has "almost nothing in common" with Israel,[54] and John Norton Moore denied "that a class of citizens within Israel is denied self-determination as with apartheid in South Africa."[55] But Haifa University psychology professor Benjamin Beit-Hallahmi found the analogy appropriate. He said that "the real problem facing the Israeli settlers" was "the natives." White South Africans were "in the same situation."[56] Former South African prime minister John Vorster viewed Israel's government as confronting a situation similar to South Africa's. Israel was faced with an "apartheid problem" as concerned its Arab inhabitants, he said. "We view Israel's position and problems with understanding and sympathy."[57]

There is a common religious ideology for the Zionist claim in Palestine and the Afrikaner claim in South Africa.[58] In Afrikaner nationalism blacks, as the offspring of Ham, were pagans destined to serve the "new Israelites" as "hewers of wood and drawers of water." Both Afrikaaners and Zionists considered the land to be theirs by divine right.[59]

Some analysts have described Israel's discrimination as less formal than South Africa's. "Whereas South Africa has laws clearly identifiable as racist, Zionist racism is informal, *de facto* and deceptive."[60] While South Africa has been more rigid in some aspects of segregation, particularly in housing, Israel has been more rigid in others. Unlike South Africa, Israel expelled most of the indigenous population. Its segregation in land ownership and use is more thoroughgoing, and the performance of governmental functions by Israel's national institutions has no counterpart in South Africa. Arnold Toynbee, referring to Israel, said that "a racialist state is as bad and as dangerous in the Middle East as it is in southern Africa." He found it "wrong" that "people feel differently about the rights and wrongs of the existence of the state of Israel versus white South Africa."[61]

Part Four

The 1967 War, the West Bank and the Gaza Strip

21

No Peace: War Always

on the Horizon

For war breeds war again.
—John Davidson, *War Song*

The 1949 armistice agreements left the Gaza Strip and the West Bank in an uncertain status, Gaza administered by Egypt and the West Bank by Transjordan, and both with a substantial number of refugees. In Gaza the refugees outnumbered the indigenous population. In 1949 Transjordan became the Hashemite Kingdom of Jordan, "Hashemite" after the ruling family, and "Trans" being dropped to indicate that, with the inclusion of the West Bank, the country spanned both sides of the Jordan River. In 1950 Jordan's parliament incorporated the West Bank, fulfilling King Abdullah's long-held objective.[1] But the parliament said it took the step "without prejudicing the final settlement of Palestine's just case within the sphere of national aspirations, inter-Arab cooperation and international justice."[2] It thus acknowledged the self-determination right of the Palestine Arabs. The Arab states and many Palestine Arabs opposed the merger, which was recognized by only Pakistan and Great Britain.[3]

Egypt did not incorporate the Gaza Strip but administered it as "an inseparable part of the land of Palestine."[4] The Egyptian administration continued the law of Palestine in force and issued court judgments "in the name of the people of Palestine."[5] A Gaza constitution adopted in 1962 was declared to be in force "until a permanent constitution for the State of Palestine is promulgated."[6] Egypt's minister of war appointed a governor-general and an eleven-member executive council to administer Gaza.[7] Limited legislative competence was given to a legislative council that consisted of twenty-two elected members, eleven members appointed by the governor-general, the eleven members of the executive council, and the governor-general.[8]

To stop Arab refugees from returning from Lebanon, Syria, Jordan, and Egypt, the IDF began attacks on villages across the armistice line. Jordan claimed that during 1950 Israel made over one hundred such raids.[9] During 1950 and 1951 the UN Truce Supervision Organization, which had been established to monitor the armistice agreements, and the UN Security Council dealt with repeated charges that Israel had made incursions across the armistice lines.[10] Egypt interfered with the shipment through the Suez Canal of goods destined for Israel, and the Security Council asked it to let the goods pass.[11] Israel also charged armistice violations, but of the many mutual complaints the United Nations resolved most of them against Israel.[12]

Meanwhile, groups of refugees began military raids into Israel, without overall coordination and without direction from the Arab governments.[13] Jordan, where most of the attacks originated, made strenuous efforts to prevent them.[14] Israel met raids with reprisal attacks,[15] often on targets where civilians were in close proximity. Israel viewed its reprisal attacks as justifiable self-defense[16] and also aimed at "teaching a lesson."[17] It wanted to deter not only the guerrillas, but also the Arab governments, which it charged with aggression for allowing the guerrillas to operate.[18]

Ben-Gurion said in 1953 that Israel was "in danger of peace" and that a state of war was necessary to achieve "the fusion of communities," by which he meant the migration of Arab-state Jews to Israel and the settlement of the Palestine Arabs in Arab states.[19] Ben-Gurion's reference to the danger of peace indicated his belief that hostilities needed to be maintained so the Arab states would be suspicious of their Jewish populations, which he hoped would result in their migrating to Israel.

Arab states regularly complained of the reprisals to the UN Security Council, which routinely rejected Israel's claims of self-defense.[20] The council said that "reprisals have proved to be productive of greater violence rather than a deterrent to violence."[21] Israel's reprisal attacks, because of their severity, were credited with escalating the guerrilla raids.[22] The Security Council condemned Israel for many such attacks.[23] In 1953 the IDF conducted a reprisal raid on the West Bank town of Qibya, killing sixty-six civilians.[24] The IDF unit, commanded by Ariel Sharon, blew up houses with the inhabitants inside.[25] UN military observers arriving two hours after the raid said that "bullet-riddled bodies near the doorways and multiple bullet hits on the doors of the demolished houses indicated that the inhabitants had been forced to remain inside until their homes were blown up over them." They reported that "witnesses were uniform in describing their experience as a night of horror, during which Israeli soldiers moved about in their village blowing up buildings, firing into doorways and windows with automatic weapons and throwing hand grenades."[26] Ben-Gurion issued a statement claiming that the Qibya operation had been conducted by private Israeli citizens, not by the IDF.[27] Foreign Minister Moshe Sharrett told Israel's cabinet the raid was a "monstrous bloodbath" which "exposed us in front of the whole world as a gang of blood-suckers, capable of mass massacres."[28] The Security Council said the raid on Qibya violated the UN Charter. It also called on Jordan, which had promised to try to stop future guerrilla raids,[29] to prevent "crossing of the demarcation line by unauthorized persons, often resulting in acts of violence."[30]

Most Security Council resolutions on Israel's reprisal raids contained no such cautionary language. Denouncing a 1955 attack on the Egyptian army in the Gaza Strip, in which the IDF killed thirty-eight Egyptian soldiers, the council found a "prearranged and planned attack ordered by Israel authorities . . . committed by Israel regular army forces against the Egyptian regular army force," which it condemned as a violation of the Egypt-Israel 1949 armistice and of the UN Charter.[31] The council condemned a 1955 IDF attack on Syrian military posts in which fifty-six Syrians were killed.[32] The council rejected Israel's argument of retaliation for smaller Syrian attacks, saying that "military action in breach of the General Armistice Agreements" was unlawful, "whether or not undertaken by way of retaliation."[33] U.S. assistant secretary of state Henry Byroade criticized Israel's attacks: Israel had developed "the attitude of the conqueror" and the belief that force and "retaliatory killings" were the "only policy" its "neighbors would understand."[34]

Moshe Dayan, Israel's chief of staff, saw a domestic political purpose in the reprisal policy. He said that reprisals "make it possible for us to maintain a high level of tension among our population and in the army. Without these actions we would have ceased to be a combative people and without the discipline of a combative people we are lost. We have to cry out that the Negev is in danger, so that young men will go there."[35]

At the same time, Dayan recognized the justice of the refugees' view that force was permissible to regain their homeland. Delivering a eulogy for a friend killed in a refugee raid across the Gaza border in 1956, he said: "Let us not today fling accusations at the murderers. Who are we that we should argue against their hatred? For eight years now, they sit in their refugee camps in Gaza, and before their very eyes we turn into our homestead the land and the villages in which they and their forefathers have lived."[36]

During the early 1950s, according to Prime Minister Moshe Sharett, the IDF establishment made contingency plans to invade and occupy the West Bank.[37] In 1951 Ben-Gurion formulated a plan to seize the Gaza Strip and approached Britain to ask its acquiescence. The British government objected, and Ben-Gurion dropped the plan.[38] In 1954, according to Sharett, the IDF sought a way to initiate a war with Egypt in order to take the Gaza Strip.[39] In 1955 Ben-Gurion asked the cabinet to approve an invasion of the Gaza Strip. After five days of discussion the cabinet rejected the proposal, concerned over the likely U.S. reaction.[40]

But in 1956 Israel, together with France and Britain, invaded Egypt and occupied the Gaza Strip and the Sinai Peninsula.[41] During the invasion General Itzhak Rabin, as commander of Israel's northern region, expelled from the Galilee to Syria four thousand villagers whom the IDF had earlier removed from their homes in connection with water diversion projects.[42] The Security Council did not condemn the tripartite invasion of Egypt because France and Great Britain, as permanent council members, enjoyed power of veto. It did, however, call an emergency special session of the General Assembly, finding "that a grave situation has been created by action undertaken against Egypt."[43] In a memorandum to the UN secretary-general Israel proposed to take over the administration of the Gaza Strip,[44] but the secretary rejected the idea.[45] Israel withdrew from the Gaza Strip and Sinai Peninsula under strong international pressure, particularly from the United States.[46] The United Nations put an emergency force (UNEF) on the Egyptian side of the 1949 armistice line to assure there were no further hostilities.

In Egypt few Jews had emigrated in the wake of the establishment of Israel, though anti-Jewish sentiment had been manifested there at the time, including violence against Jews. As well, Israel's Mossad secret service had been urging Egyptian Jews to migrate to Israel. "It's true that we encouraged the Jews to leave," one Mossad agent explained. "We believed that if they did not leave at once it would be too late. We really believed it. . . . Also the State needed them."[47] After the 1956 invasion, however, the bulk of Egyptian Jewry did leave Egypt. The government of Egypt ordered many Jews to leave,[48] fearing subversive acts. Egypt's fear stemmed from bombings carried out in Egypt in 1954 by an Israeli underground. The government of Israel had ordered the bombings to convince Britain to keep its troops there and to convince the United States and Britain that Egypt's nationalist president, Gamel Abdel Nasser, was a risky ally.[49] The underground agents bombed U.S. and British property in Alexandria and Cairo, following which they were captured and convicted. In an Israeli court proceeding on an unrelated matter in 1960 it came to light that Israeli officials had forged the name of then Defense Minister Pinhas Lavon on the order for the bombings.[50]

The guerrilla raids and reprisal attacks continued into the 1960s. In 1962 the UN Security Council condemned an IDF attack into Syria across the Sea of Galilee as a "flagrant violation" of Syrian territory.[51] It condemned a 1966 IDF attack into the West Bank village of Samu, where an IDF force of 4,000 in armored cars and tanks, with air support, killed fifty people, and demolished 140 buildings.[52] Deploring "the loss of life and heavy damage to property" resulting from the attack, the council characterized it as "a large-scale and carefully planned military action." It said "that actions of military reprisal cannot be tolerated," and threatened that, "if they are repeated, the Security Council will have to consider further and more effective steps as envisaged in the Charter to ensure against the repetition of such acts."[53]

Guerrilla action in the 1950s had been undertaken by small groups of refugees. During that period the Palestine Arabs looked primarily to Arab states to secure their return to Palestine. In 1964 the Arab states formed the Palestine Liberation Organization (PLO).[54] It asserted a right to use "all possible means to retain their human dignity and restore their usurped rights."[55] In the early 1960s a group of Palestine Arab refugees formed another organization, called the

Palestine National Liberation Movement.[56] Better known by its acronym, Fatah, this group thought reliance on the Arab states was unrealistic and therefore the Palestine Arabs would have to conduct their own military operations against Israel. In 1965 Fatah began raids into Israel against weapons depots and IDF patrols.[57] Egyptian President Nasser declared the military action premature, and Arab states impeded Fatah operations.[58]

In April 1967 the IDF undertook cultivation of land in the demilitarized zone along the Israel-Syria armistice agreement. Israel claimed sovereignty in the portion of the demilitarized zone that fell on its side of the 1949 armistice line, which ran through the middle of the zone. Syria protested that claim of sovereignty as a violation of the armistice agreement.[59] The Security Council had previously agreed with Syria on this point and had criticized Israel for activities it had undertaken in the zone.[60] To stop the cultivation, Syria attacked into the demilitarized zone April 7, and Israel subsequently retaliated.[61]

These border incidents continued,[62] and General Itzhak Rabin, as Israel's chief of staff, declared Israel's security dependent on the overthrow of the Syrian government.[63] On May 11 Prime Minister Levi Eshkol said in a speech that "in view of the fourteen incidents of the past month," Israel "may have to adopt measures no less drastic than those of April 7."[64] On May 13 Eshkol said in a radio interview that "the focal point of the terrorists is in Syria, but we have laid down the principle that we shall choose the time, the place and the means to counter the aggressor."[65] Syria complained to the Security Council about these threats.[66] The threats may have been made for domestic political purposes,[67] but Israeli officials repeated them in private to journalists and to Soviet diplomats, thereby making the threats appear to Arab leaders as serious.[68] Israel apparently meant the threats.[69]

Syria sought help from Egypt, with which it had a mutual defense agreement, exaggerating the level of Israeli troop activity near the Israel-Syria armistice line.[70] These exaggerations were repeated to Egypt by the USSR in an apparent effort to influence Egypt to make a show of force to protect Syria.[71] The UN Truce Supervision Organization investigated and reported that there was no Israeli troop buildup near Syria.[72] But President Nasser became convinced by the Soviet warning that an Israeli attack on Syria was imminent.[73]

Tanks were absent from Israel's May 15 Independence Day parade in Jerusalem,[74] which suggested they were being massed for an attack.[75] The Soviet government stated that "Israeli forces, drawn up to the Syrian border, have been put in a state of battle readiness."[76] The Soviet misapprehension may have been based in part on leaks by the Israeli government to the USSR that Israel was in fact planning to attack Syria.[77]

On May 16 Egypt asked the United Nations to move the UNEF, and the UN commander said the request was for withdrawal of "all UN troops which install OPS [observation posts] along our borders." Secretary-General U Thant requested clarification[78] and said that Egypt requested total withdrawal,[79] specifically from Sharm el-Sheikh, which commands the entrance to the Gulf of Aqaba, through which Israel had access to its southern port of Eilat.[80] "I pointed out," said Thant, "that if the intention were a temporary withdrawal of UNEF from the armistice demarcation line, the request was 'unacceptable,'" and "that UNEF 'cannot now be asked to stand aside in order to become a silent and helpless witness to an armed confrontation between the parties.' If complete withdrawal were intended, and if that intention were properly communicated to me, I would have 'no choice but to order the withdrawal of UNEF from Gaza and Sinai as expeditiously as possible.'"[81] But Nasser later said he had asked for withdrawal "only from a part of the border running from Rafah to Eilat," but not "from Gaza and Sharm el-Sheikh, which controls the entrance to the Gulf."[82]

According to General Rabin, Nasser had requested the UNEF withdrawal "only from the portion of the border from Rafah to Kuntilla, and he suggested that the UN soldiers be regrouped at Gaza and at Sham el-Sheikh." But "unfortunately," according to Rabin, "Thant made him choose—to keep the international force at all their positions or, on the other hand, to request their total and definitive withdrawal."[83] On May 18 Egypt requested total withdrawal.[84] Nasser said in a 1970 interview that Thant "decided to withdraw all the 'blue hats,'" thus "forcing me to send Egyptian forces to Sharm el-Sheikh."[85] Thant appears to have led Nasser to make a request for total withdrawal.[86]

Israel said that Egypt requested the withdrawal to initiate war with Israel. But Indar Jit Rikhye, the UN commander, reported that Egypt gave as its reason that it contemplated "action against Israel, the moment it might carry out any aggressive action against any Arab country."[87] Thant proposed the United Nations arrange a settlement. Egypt accepted the idea, but Israel rejected it.[88] Thant asked Israel to accept the UNEF on its side of the 1949 armistice line. Israel declined.[89] "If only Israel had agreed to permit UNEF to be stationed on its side of the border, even for a short duration," wrote Thant, "the course of history could have been different. Diplomatic efforts to avert the pending catastrophe might have prevailed; war might have been averted."[90] While Israel's rejection of Thant's offer has been attributed to the inefficacy of the UNEF being stationed on Israel's side of the armistice line,[91] the more probable inference is that Israel was not concerned about an Egyptian attack[92] and that the UNEF withdrawal "did not constitute a serious threat to Israel's security."[93]

22

Mortal Danger?

The 1967 Israel-Arab War

Appearances often are deceiving.— Aesop, *The Wolf in Sheep's Clothing*

As tension grew, Israel announced a full military mobilization on May 19, including a call-up of its reserves.[1] On May 22 Egypt announced that it would close the Straits of Tiran to Israeli-flag vessels and to any vessels carrying strategic goods to Israel.[2] The Straits of Tiran led into the Gulf of Aqaba, which provided access to Israel's southern port of Eilat. Egypt said its purpose was to prevent Israel from transporting strategic goods it might use in an attack on Syria. It cited Israel's threats against Syria and the presumed Israeli troop buildup facing Syria.[3] Egypt took the decision because of the removal of the UNEF from Sharm el-Sheikh, evidently concerned that with the UNEF gone, Israel might transport strategic goods to Eilat.[4]

Citing the Egyptian action, Israel said it faced "economic strangulation." But Egypt did not restrict non-Israeli-flag vessels carrying nonstrategic materials, or Israeli-registered vessels chartered to a non-Israeli carrier.[5] During the two years preceding June 1967 no Israeli-flag vessel had used the port of Eilat.[6] Most of Israel's commerce used Mediterranean ports.[7] The most significant cargo for which Israel used Eilat was oil, which was carried on non-Israeli flag vessels.[8] This would have constituted the major detriment to Israel from the closure.

Egypt at this time also moved troops toward the Israel-Egypt armistice line. Its aim, it declared, was to deter Israel from attacking Syria.[9] On May 22 General Rabin reported to Israel's cabinet that the Egyptian forces were in a defensive posture, that they were not being deployed to attack.[10] The IDF concluded that Nasser meant to intervene in case of an Israeli attack against Syria.[11] U.S. intelligence likewise did not expect Egypt to attack in the absence of an Israeli invasion of Syria. On May 26 the United States communicated that assessment to Israel.[12] On May 20 Jordan concluded a defensive treaty with Egypt, and on June 3 Egypt withdrew some of the troops from the Israel-Egypt armistice line.[13] Egypt's belief that Israel might attack Syria had apparently motivated its troop concentration, its request for UNEF withdrawal, and its closure of the Straits of Tiran to Israeli shipping.[14]

On June 4 the cabinet of Israel authorized an invasion of Egypt.[15] On the morning of June 5 Israel's air force bombed Egyptian aircraft on the ground at their bases, destroying 300 of Egypt's 340 combat aircraft.[16] At the same time Israel sent ground troops through the Gaza Strip into the Sinai Peninsula.[17] Israel's attack, which took Egypt by surprise, followed a long and well-rehearsed plan.[18] "Sixteen years' planning had gone into these initial 80 minutes," said Brigadier Mordechai Hod, commander of Israel's air force. "We lived with the plan, we slept on the plan, we ate the plan. Constantly we perfected it."[19]

Jordan retaliated later in the morning of June 5 with shelling in the Jerusalem area[20] and made air strikes farther into Israel.[21] In so doing, Jordan acted in response to Israel's attack on Egypt in exercise of the right of collective self-defense permitted under Article 51 of the UN Charter.[22] On June 5 the United States sent Israel ammunition and jet fighters.[23] Although the United States did not acknowledge a direct role in the fighting, it sent reconnaissance aircraft that traced nighttime movement of Egypt's ground troops to facilitate daytime Israeli air attacks on them.[24] The Egyptian troops were forced to move at night because, with their air force destroyed, they had no protection against air strikes.[25] The air strikes were important in Israel's rapid victory.[26]

Israel's air force attacked Jordan's and Syria's aircraft in the manner it had done to Egypt's and by the evening of June 5 it had destroyed the air warfare capacity of all three.[27] Messages intercepted by a U.S. intelligence ship—according to Wilbur Crane Eveland of the Central Intelligence Agency—indicated that Israel did not plan to limit its attack to Egypt.[28] Israel intercepted and "doctored" Egypt's communications to Jordan and Syria, Eveland said, to make them believe Egypt had repelled Israel's invasion.[29] Israel apparently wanted the Arab states to believe they had a chance to win, so they would continue fighting.[30]

By the time a cease-fire was effected June 8 Israel had taken the West Bank, the Gaza Strip, and the Sinai Peninsula.[31] On June 9 Israel attacked Syria, which had shelled targets in Israel June 5–8 but had not otherwise engaged in the war.[32] After occupying Syria's Golan Heights, Israel stopped its attack June 10, under pressure from the United States.

In the Security Council on June 5 Egypt charged Israel with aggression,[33] as did the USSR.[34] But Israel claimed that Egypt had struck first. It told the council that "in the early hours of this morning Egyptian armoured columns moved in an offensive thrust against Israel's borders. At the same time Egyptian planes took off from airfields in Sinai and struck out towards Israel. Egyptian artillery in the Gaza Strip shelled the Israel villages of Kissufim, Nahal-Oz and Ein Hashelosha. Netania and Kefar Yavetz have also been bombed. Israeli forces engaged the Egyptians in the air and on land, and fighting is still going on."[35]

The next day Foreign Minister Abba Eban repeated this version of events to the council. "On the morning of 5 June, when Egyptian forces engaged us by air and land, bombarding the villages of Kissufim, Nahal-Oz and Ein Hashelosha," he said, "we knew that our limit of safety had been reached, and perhaps passed. In accordance with its inherent right of self-defence as formulated in Article 51 of the United Nations Charter, Israel responded defensively in full strength." Eban said that "approaching Egyptian aircraft appeared on our radar screens."[36] Eshkol, in a speech to the Knesset, said that the "existence of the Israeli state" had "hung in the balance."[37]

In fact, Egypt had not attacked by land or air and none of its aircraft had approached Israel. Neither the Security Council nor the General Assembly could take a stand on the hostilities. The United States, according to President Lyndon Johnson, was aware that Israel had initiated the hostilities,[38] but it supported Israel's claim that Egypt had attacked it. With its permanent members split on the issue, the Security Council condemned neither side for aggression. The General Assembly on July 4 defeated a Soviet-proposed resolution that would have named Israel the aggressor.[39]

On July 7 Eshkol acknowledged that Israel had struck first, abandoning Israel's position that Egypt had initiated the hostilities. But Eshkol said Israel's attack had been a "legitimate defense," in anticipation of an Egyptian attack on Israel.[40] Israel argued that the "massive concentration of Arab forces on Israel's borders" endangered "its very existence."[41]

To support its view that Egypt had been about to attack it, Israel cited Egypt's request for the departure of the UNEF, its closure of the Straits of Tiran, its positioning of troops near Israel, its May 30 alliance with Jordan, and verbal threats by President Nasser.[42] Israel's change of argument created skepticism about both its versions of the facts. "At first Israel claimed that the Arab armies had attacked her first," wrote Michael Akehurst. "If this Israeli claim is false, why did Israel tell a lie?"[43] But Israel's assertion it was about to be attacked was widely accepted.[44]

Various Israeli officials said later, however, that Israel had not in fact anticipated an imminent attack by Egypt when it struck June 5.[45] General Rabin, consistent with his reports to the cabinet in May 1967, said, "I do not believe that Nasser wanted war. The two divisions he sent into Sinai on May 14 would not have been enough to unleash an offensive against Israel. He knew it and we knew it."[46] Rabin said Nasser massed troops to deter an attack by Israel on Syria to appear as "the savior of Syria and thus win great sympathy in the Arab world." Rabin said the forces Nasser sent into Sinai May 20–22 were not planning an offensive against Israel.[47]

General Matitiahu Peled, a member of Israel's general staff during the 1967 war, said that "the thesis according to which the danger of genocide weighed on us in June 1967, and that Israel struggled for its physical existence is only a bluff born and developed after the war."[48] Peled confirmed that Rabin had told the cabinet Egypt had not planned to attack. "Our General Staff," he said, "never told the government that the Egyptian military threat represented any danger to Israel."[49]

Ezer Weizman, chief of the general staff branch, said that had Egypt attacked, Israel would have defeated it—"maybe thirteen hours would have been needed instead of only three—that Jordan had offered little opposition, and that Syria posed no "real threat," which is why Israel waited "three days before attacking it."[50] Weizman said that "a country does not go to war only when the immediate threat of destruction is hovering." Explaining Israel's decision to strike, he said, "We entered the Six-Day War in order to secure a situation in which we can manage our lives as we see fit without external pressures." He called the 1967 war "a direct continuation" of the 1948 war.[51]

Menachem Begin, when prime minister, said that "the Egyptian Army concentrations in the Sinai approaches do not prove that Nasser was really about to attack us. We must be honest with ourselves. We decided to attack him." Begin gave an analysis similar to Weizman's of Israel's motive. He said Israel's aim was to "take the initiative and attack the enemy, drive him back, and thus assure the security of Israel and the future of the nation."[52]

Even if Israel had expected Egypt to attack, it is not clear a preemptive strike is lawful.[53] The UN Charter, Article 51, characterizes armed force as defensive only if it is used in response to an "armed attack." Most states consider this language to mean that a preemptive strike is unlawful.[54] India, for one, asserted in General Assembly discussion of the June 1967 hostilities that preemptive self-defense is not permitted under international law.[55] Most authorities agree with that view,[56] though some say force may be used in anticipation of an attack that has not yet occurred but is reasonably expected to occur imminently.[57] Israel did not face such a situation.

Israel also claimed that Egypt's partial closure of the Straits of Tiran gave it a right to use force against Egypt.[58] It called the closure an "armed attack" against Israel. In the UN General Assembly Eban said that blockades are "acts of war. To blockade, after all, is to attempt strangulation."[59] A blockade, to be sure, is an aggressive act.[60] But from Egypt's viewpoint the purpose was to keep Israel from getting strategic material it might use to invade Syria.[61]

It is doubtful Egypt's action of May 22 was a blockade as that term is generally understood. The navigable channel through the Straits of Tiran is only one mile from Egypt's shore, well within its territorial waters. No state had ever been deemed to have set up a blockade for stopping foreign shipping in its own territorial waters.

Israel also said that all states enjoyed a right under customary international law to passage through the Straits of Tiran and Israel was entitled to use force to secure passage. Egypt denied the existence of any such customary law right.[62] It argued that Egypt and Israel had been in a state of war since 1948 and that, as a result, Egypt was not required to afford Israel rights to which Israel might have been entitled in peacetime.[63] Israel contended that the 1949 Israel-Egypt armistice had terminated the state of war.[64] But an armistice, according to the accepted view, does not terminate a state of war.[65] The Israel-Egypt armistice, in particular, had not been viewed as having terminated the state of war between the two.[66] And the right to exclude a belligerent's shipping, justifiable as a war measure, continues even after an armistice.[67]

Israel argued that no state of war existed with Egypt on the additional theory that a state of war between two UN member states is impossible, since the charter prohibits aggressive war.[68] Most states reject that view, however, as it would mean that when two states fight, no law would govern the hostilities.[69]

Egypt also argued in defense of its action that the Straits of Tiran was not in fact a strait and, therefore, it did not have to permit vessels of other states to pass through. It said that only a passage between two areas of the high seas is a strait.[70] The Straits of Tiran lead from the high seas into a bay, the Gulf of Aqaba.[71] The 1958 Geneva Convention on the Territorial Sea and Contiguous Zone had defined "strait" to include a passage between the high seas and a bay,[72] but Egypt had refused to sign the convention, precisely because of that provision.

The question of a right of passage through the Straits of Tiran had been discussed at the conference leading to the Geneva Convention. A majority of delegates said there was a right of passage through them in customary international law, but others disagreed.[73] U.S. secretary of state John Foster Dulles conceded at the time the "plausibility from the standpoint of international law" of Egypt's position.[74] Arthur Dean, the head of the U.S. delegation at the Geneva conference, said the convention's position that a passage from the high seas to a bay is a strait was a "new rule," which was clearly aimed at the Straits of Tiran.[75] Thus, the general view was that the convention did not reflect customary law on this point.[76] Saudi Arabia, which holds the eastern shore of the Gulf of Aqaba, argued that the gulf was a closed or "historic" sea and, therefore, not open to passage.[77] That argument was not made by Egypt and was rejected by Israel.[78]

Some authorities thought Egypt had violated Israel's rights by its partial closure of the Straits of Tiran,[79] while others disagreed.[80] Even if Israel had a right to passage through the Straits, however, it was probably not entitled to attack Egypt to assert that right. The

Egyptian refusal to permit passage would give rise to a dispute whose resolution would need to be sought by peaceful means.[81] The closure is not an "armed attack." Further, under the doctrine of proportionality in use of force, even if Israel had the right to use force, it would have had to use only enough to secure its right of passage. It is not clear Israel would be entitled to undertake a full-scale invasion of Egypt.

Déjà Vu: Israel's Control

of the West Bank and Gaza

To win a war is as disastrous as to lose one! We shall not survive war, but shall, as well as our adversaries, be destroyed by war.
—Agatha Christie, *An Autobiography, X*

During the 1967 war 350,000 Palestine Arabs were displaced from the West Bank and Gaza Strip,[1] a figure that represented 25 percent of the population of the two areas. As the IDF attacked their localities, some residents fled in fear, recalling the 1948 killings,[2] and the flight was heavy from the West Bank town of Qibya, site of the 1953 killings.[3] The Jordanian army's rapid retreat contributed to the fear, and in some localities the IDF forced civilians out.[4]

The IDF aerial bombardment led many civilians to flee. The U.S. embassy in Jordan reported during the fighting: "IDF Air Force yesterday and again today hit many civilian targets on West Bank where there are absolutely no military emplacements."[5] Aerial bombardment by the IDF caused 35,000 inhabitants of three refugee camps near Jericho to flee.[6] Of West Bank Arabs who took refuge in Jordan, 57 percent cited the bombardment as the reason for their departure.[7] In a few situations the IDF dropped napalm on civilians,[8] and on refugees east of the Jordan River—people who had fled from the Jericho area.[9]

In Qalqilya the IDF drove residents out by force after destroying 850 of the town's 2,000 houses.[10] The IDF blew up the entire villages of Emmaus, Yalu, and Beit Nuba—near Jerusalem[11]—and drove the villagers toward Jordan.[12] Others who saw these refugees joined them out of fear.[13] In some localities the IDF forced Arab residents onto trucks and drove them to the Jordan frontier,[14] in others it used loudspeakers to order people to leave.[15] A UN representative relayed "persistent reports of acts of intimidation by Israeli armed forces and of Israeli attempts to suggest to the population by loud-speakers mounted on cars, that they might be better off on the East Bank."[16] In some towns soldiers fired their guns, knocked on doors, and searched the same houses for arms, night after night. IDF officers suggested that those with military training and their families should leave "for their own safety."[17] In some areas the IDF pointedly made buses and trucks available, day after day, to transport to the Jordan River any Arabs who feared to remain.[18] At the United Nations, Israel denied expelling Arabs. In a note to the secretary-general on June 22 it stated: "Any allegation that Israel has been expelling residents from their homes and thus creating a new refugee problem is untrue."[19]

As soon as Israel had secured control over the West Bank and Gaza Strip, Prime Minister Eshkol, referring to them as "the new areas," said Israel would retain them for security reasons.[20] "Be under no illusion that the State of Israel is prepared to return to the situation that reigned up to a week ago. . . . The position that existed until now shall never again return."[21] Eshkol ordered the foreign ministry and bureau of statistics to omit the 1949 armistice lines from maps.[22] In the General Assembly Eban said, "the suggestion that everything goes back to where it was before 5 June" was "totally unacceptable."[23] Information Minister Israel Galili said that Israel could not return to the 1949 armistice lines, that the "armies, tanks and planes of the United Arab Republic, Jordan, Syria and Iraq" had "nullified the armistice agreements."[24] Defense Minister Moshe Dayan said that Israel should not "in any way give back the Gaza strip to Egypt or the western part of Jordan to King Hussein."[25]

While these statements might be consistent with an intent to return the territories as part of a future settlement, their likely meaning was that Israel intended to retain them for the foreseeable future.[26] General Weizman said the war had served "Zionist objectives," that "our national instincts led us to take advantage of it beyond the immediate military and political problems it came to solve."[27] According to Eban, Israel had anticipated Jordan's defense of Egypt because of the two countries' May 30 treaty of defense.[28] Jordan's minister of information, Abdel-Hamid Sharaf, had declared on June 4 that Jordan would fight Israel if Israel invaded Egypt.[29] For Israel, attacking Egypt thus opened the prospect of taking both the Gaza Strip and the West Bank and thereby securing the portion of Palestine eluded in 1948.

Mordecai Bentov, a cabinet minister who attended the June 4 cabinet meeting and supported the decision to invade Egypt,[30] said Israel's "entire story" about "the danger of extermination" was "invented of whole cloth and exaggerated after the fact to justify the annexation of new Arab territories."[31]

Many Israeli leaders considered the West Bank and Gaza a part of Israel it should have taken in 1948.[32] For Itzhak Shamir, a former LEHI leader and future prime minister, the war was "a historical and revolutionary turning point" in Jewish history that "put the stamp of permanency on the state's borders." He continued, "a fragmented country with fragile borders and a divided capital became a stable nation with a reasonable defence capacity, with its eternal capital united."[33] Supreme Court Judge Moshe Silberg said, "Something happened in June 1967 in Israel. Under the rushing noise of the wings of history, in the cruel storm of war, a sudden encounter took place between the people and the land."[34]

As after the 1948 war, the government began to settle Israelis in the newly acquired territory. In September the World Zionist Organization founded the first settlement.[35] "No political victory, no proclamation," it declared, "can convert these territories into Jewish territories if they are not settled by Jews."[36]

The UN Security Council called for a cease-fire in the 1967 hostilities, but as a result of the position taken by the United States it did not issue a clear call to Israel to withdraw.[37] In November 1967, in its Resolution 242, the council asked Israel to withdraw but in the context of an envisaged general settlement with Arab states.[38] The United States blocked an alternative resolution proposed by Latin American states to make an unconditional call on Israel for withdrawal.[39] In the drafting of Resolution 242 it blocked the placement of the word "the" before "territories" from which Israel was to withdraw, thereby leaving it unclear whether withdrawal was to be from all the territories it had occupied, or only from some portion.[40]

By conditioning Israel's obligation to withdraw on recognition of Israel by the Arab states, the Security Council in effect made the attainment of self-determination by the Palestine Arabs contingent on acts by others. This was a dubious approach since the exercise of a right cannot be conditioned on acts that may or may not be taken by a group of states. The International Court of Justice said as much when it ruled on the question of whether member states of the United Nations could vote against the admission of new states as members on the ground that they wanted other states to be admitted as part of a package. The court said admission was a right for a state satisfying the criteria set in the UN Charter and, therefore, a member state could not make an affirmative vote conditional on other considerations.[41]

Viewed from another perspective, Resolution 242 sought to force Arab states to recognize Israel's control over the territory inside the 1949 armistice lines in exchange for Israel's withdrawal from the Gaza Strip and West Bank.[42] Syria criticized Resolution 242 for neglecting "the uprooted, dispossessed people in exile."[43] The Organization of African Unity said Resolution 242 failed to guarantee the rights to which the Palestinian people are entitled.[44]

Since Resolution 242 called on Israel to withdraw from the West Bank and Gaza Strip, but from no further territory, it was interpreted by some as an implied recognition of Israel's sovereignty within the 1949 armistice lines. "It would appear," wrote Konstantin Obradovič, "that the international community has tacitly resigned itself to the fruits of the 1948 conquest remaining finally in Israeli hands, although in strictly legal terms, that should obviously not be the case."[45]

It is questionable, however, that Resolution 242 had this effect. Resolution 242 sought to deal with the recent hostilities and did not address the question of Israel's borders. The Security Council adopted Resolution 242 under Chapter 6 of the UN Charter, which gives it the power to recommend solutions for disputes.[46] The council did not act under Chapter 7, which gives it the power to make decisions binding on member states to resolve breaches of the peace.[47] Thus, whatever its meaning, Resolution 242 was not binding on UN member states.

In any event, in 1980 the Security Council issued an unconditional call on Israel to withdraw from the Gaza Strip and West Bank. "Reaffirming that acquisition of territory by force is inadmissible," it referred to "the overriding necessity to end the prolonged occupation of Arab territories occupied by Israel since 1967, including Jerusalem."[48] The General Assembly also called for unconditional withdrawal. It said that "the acquisition of territory by force is inadmissible" and that "Israel must withdraw unconditionally from all the

Palestinian and other Arab territories occupied by Israel since 1967, including Jerusalem."[49] The UN Commission on Human Rights characterized the occupation from a human rights perspective as "a fundamental violation of the human rights of the civilian population of the occupied Arab territories."[50]

After the 1967 war Israel treated east Jerusalem differently from the rest of the West Bank. The Knesset quickly adopted a law stating that "the law, jurisdiction and administration of the state" of Israel "shall extend to any area of Eretz Israel designated by the Government by order."[51] Using this law, the government declared Israeli law applicable to an area that included east Jerusalem, plus adjacent West Bank territory of approximately equal size.[52] The government merged this newly enlarged east Jerusalem area with west Jerusalem.[53] Justifying the incorporation, Eshkol said, "Israel without Jerusalem is Israel without a head."[54] The action was condemned by the UN Security Council and General Assembly as annexation and, therefore, a violation of the rights of the Palestine Arabs.[55] The annexation of east Jerusalem was not recognized by other states and was condemned as unlawful.[56] In 1980 the Knesset declared "Jerusalem, complete and united" to be "the capital of Israel." The Knesset denominated this law a "basic law," giving it quasi-constitutional rank.[57] The Security Council and General Assembly declared the 1980 law a nullity.[58]

A number of theories were suggested to justify Israel's temporary or permanent retention of the West Bank and Gaza Strip, but all were based on the view that Israel acted in self-defense. One theory was that a state taking territory in self-defense may lawfully annex it.[59]

As already indicated, however, a state that uses force in self-defense may not retain territory it takes while repelling an attack.[60] If Israel had acted in self-defense, that would not justify its retention of the Gaza Strip and West Bank.[61] Under the UN Charter there can lawfully be no territorial gains from war, even by a state acting in self-defense.[62] The response of other states to Israel's occupation showed a virtually unanimous opinion that even if Israel's action was defensive, its retention of the West Bank and Gaza Strip was not.[63]

Another thesis was that Israel's taking of the West Bank and Gaza Strip was necessary and proportional in relation to its security needs and that this necessity did not immediately subside.[64] But even if Israel had responded to an imminent attack in 1967, it quickly eliminated any threat to itself. At that point its defensive right would have ceased and it would have been obligated to withdraw.[65]

It was also asserted that Israel might lawfully retain the Gaza Strip and West Bank, pending a peace agreement between itself and the Arab states.[66] Others argued it might lawfully retain them permanently on the theory that Jordan had not held lawful title and, therefore, there was no sovereign power to whom the territories could revert. Israel, it was said—particularly because it took the territories defensively—had a better claim to title than anyone else.[67] That argument ignored, however, the generally recognized proposition that uncertainty over sovereignty provides no ground to retain territory taken in hostilities. Even if Jordan held the West Bank on only a de facto basis, Israel could not, even acting in self-defense, acquire title.[68] The argument also overlooked the fact that the Palestine Arabs as a collectivity had a sound claim to the Gaza Strip and West Bank on the basis of their right of self-determination.

24

More Land: Confiscation

and Settlements

The right of conquest has no foundation other than the right of the strongest.
—Jean-Jacques Rousseau, *Social Contract*

After taking the Gaza Strip and West Bank in 1967, the government of Israel replicated there many of the policies it had used since 1948 to acquire land.[1] It applied the same land confiscation laws.[2] The Jewish National Fund began acquiring land in the Gaza Strip and West Bank in conjunction with the government.[3] In addition, and unlike its system inside the 1949 armistice lines, the government authorized individual Israelis to buy land in the West Bank and Gaza Strip.[4] Through confiscation and purchase, Israeli interests acquired half the land area of the Gaza Strip and West Bank. Added to the land taken within the 1949 armistice lines, this gave Israel the ownership of 85 percent of the land area of Palestine.[5] Thus "the Zionist movement," said Meron Benvenisti, an Israeli former vice-mayor of Jerusalem, had "achieved its maximum territorial goal: control over the entire area of Mandatory Palestine."[6]

Israel referred to the Gaza Strip as Gaza District and to the West Bank by the ancient names of Judea for the sector around Jerusalem, and Samaria for the northern sector.[7] Development planning was undertaken jointly by the government and the World Zionist Organization. In 1983 the organization and the ministry of agriculture jointly prepared the Master Plan and Development Plan for Settlement in Samaria and Judea.[8] The organization and the Jewish Agency financed and organized civilian settlements.[9] The Jewish National Fund built roads to service the settlements and to facilitate troop movement.[10] The Master Plan envisaged the eventual incorporation of the West Bank into Israel, aiming "to disperse maximally large Jewish population in areas of high settlement priority, using small national inputs and in a relatively short period by using the settlement potential of the West Bank to achieve the incorporation [of the West Bank] into the [Israeli] national system."[11]

In a court action challenging the construction of a settlement in the West Bank, the Supreme Court of Israel said that the cabinet, in approving the settlement, was "decisively influenced by reasons stemming from the Zionist world-view of the settlement of the whole land of Israel." Judge Moshe Landau cited an affidavit of the attorney general that quoted Prime Minister Menachem Begin as affirming "the Jewish people's right to settle in Judea and Samaria." Judge Landau said this "view concerning the right of the Jewish people" was "based on the fundamentals of Zionist doctrine."[12] Government officials said that settlement construction was aimed at creating a presence to prevent the Palestine Arabs from forming a state.[13] In promoting settlement the government also sought to use the settlements as physical obstacles to separate Arab towns from one another and to decrease the possibility of united political action against the occupation.[14] In the 1980s the government was allocating $300 million annually for settlement construction and maintenance.[15]

In a court case over its right to take private land to build a settlement, the government said in an affidavit that the establishment of the projected settlement was

"part of the security conception of the Government which bases the security system inter alia on Jewish settlements. In accordance with this concept all Israeli settlements in the territories occupied by the IDF constitute part of the IDF's regional defence system. . . . In times of calm these settlements mainly serve the purpose of presence and control of vital areas, maintaining observation, and the like. The importance of these settlements is enhanced in particular in time of war when the regular army forces are shifted, in the main, from their bases for purposes of operational activity and the said settlements constitute the principal component of presence and security control in the areas in which they are located."[16]

Supreme Court Judge Alfred Witkon justified the establishment of settlements on confiscated Arab land on the ground that "Jewish settlements in occupied territories serve security needs" and aid the IDF. "Terrorist elements," he said, "operate with greater ease in an area solely inhabited by a population that is indifferent or sympathizes with the enemy, than in an area in which one also finds people likely to observe the latter and report any suspicious movement to the authorities."[17]

The Supreme Court of Israel upheld one confiscation of a tract of privately owned land after the ministry of defense said the purpose was to form a defensive line of three settlements to protect the Tel Aviv airport. The settlement, the ministry claimed, would permit observation of the airport and deployment of military forces. The area was near an important junction that might serve as an alternate route from Tel Aviv to Jerusalem and a settlement there could protect road traffic during unrest in the West Bank.[18]

In one instance the Supreme Court ruled illegal the construction of a projected settlement, to be called Elon Moreh, on private land confiscated for that purpose. The military government of the West Bank, supporting the settlement, argued that it would promote security. The settlers, however, told the court their purpose was to assert a territorial claim to the West Bank. The objective of the settlers undermined the claim of the military government, and as a result the court ruled the settlement illegal.[19]

Just as in the 1930s the Jewish Agency settled land in preparation for statehood, so after 1967 the government of Israel settled the Gaza Strip and West Bank as a step toward permanent control. In the West Bank it elaborated a strategy for locating settlements. The Labor Party, which held power in 1967, developed a plan to build settlements in strategic locations, and the first area to be settled was the Jordan Valley, which forms the eastern border of the West Bank.[20] Settlement there placed Israelis between Jordan and the West Bank's Arab population.

The Likud Party, which came to power in 1977, took a broader view of settlements. The Likud was more explicit in declaring the West Bank to be a part of Israel. It asserted the right to establish settlements at any location in the West Bank, on the ground that it formed part of Eretz-Israel, over which it asserted Israeli sovereignty. On the issue of possible annexation by Israel of the West Bank, the Likud prime minister, Menachem Begin, said, "you can annex foreign land. You cannot annex your own country. Judea and Samaria," he said, "are part of the land of Israel, where the nation was born."[21] Itzhak Shamir, who succeeded Begin as prime minister in 1983, pledged in his inaugural speech to continue what he called the "holy work" of settlement in the West Bank.[22]

Israel's land acquisition and settlement activity in the West Bank and Gaza Strip created "an elaborate network of vested interests."[23] The International Commission of Jurists, citing the "permanent character" of many of the settlements and "pronouncements of Israeli leaders to the effect that they are permanent," viewed the settlements as "a step towards eventual assertion of sovereignty over the territories or part of them." It said this policy violated the self-determination right of the Palestine Arabs.[24] Despite the desire to assert permanent control, many in Israel were concerned that if Israel annexed the West Bank and Gaza Strip, the Jewish majority in Israel's population would be reduced so substantially as to threaten the Jewish character of Israel.[25]

Though the Supreme Court of Israel found most of the settlements to be legal, other states considered them unlawful. The international community held Israel, in its administration of the West Bank and Gaza Strip, to the standards set by human rights law and by the law of belligerent occupation. The law of belligerent occupation, sometimes called humanitarian law, applied since Israel had come into control of the West Bank and Gaza Strip through hostilities. The law of belligerent occupation provides a variety of protections for an occupied population, while ceding to the occupying power the right to protect its temporary tenure. The principal embodiment of the law of belligerent occupation is the 1949 Geneva Convention Relative to the Protection of Civilian Persons in Time of War, to which Israel and the neighboring Arab states are parties.[26]

The Geneva Convention requires an occupying power to change the existing order as little as possible during its tenure. One aspect of this obligation is that it must leave the territory to the population it finds there. It may not bring in its own people to populate the territory. This prohibition is found in the convention's Article 49, which states: "The Occupying Power shall not deport or transfer parts of its own civilian population into the territory it occupies." On the basis of Article 49 many states criticized Israel for establishing and maintaining the settlements. Israel responded that the settlers themselves had established the settlements and, therefore, it had not "transferred" its own people. To that it was replied that Israel funded the settlements and that it had used the IDF to establish many of them. One particular use was that the government placed many recent immigrants in the settlements. In 1987 the UN Human Rights Commission criticized it for the "settlement of alien populations brought from other parts of the world in the place of the original Palestinian owners of land."[27]

Israel also argued that the Geneva Convention was not applicable to its administration of the West Bank and Gaza Strip. It pointed out that Article 2 of the convention refers to the territory of a High Contracting Party and said that this means the convention applies only to territory lawfully held by a contracting party. Jordan did not have good title to the West Bank and Egypt did not have good title to the Gaza Strip.[28] However, it would apply de facto those provisions of the convention it deemed "humanitarian." The Supreme Court of Israel followed that position, applying certain provisions of the convention but not others.[29] It did not find Article 49 to be a "humanitarian" provision.

Israel's view that the Geneva Convention did not apply to its occupation of the Gaza Strip and West Bank was rejected by other states. They argued that, according to Article 1 of the convention, it applies "in all circumstances," and, according to Article 2, it applies to "all cases of declared war or of any other armed conflict." All states that indicated a view on the matter, other than Israel, found the convention to be applicable to Israel's occupation of the Gaza Strip and West Bank.[30]

An earlier treaty on belligerent occupation is the Hague Regulations of 1907.[31] Article 46 of the Hague Regulations states that private property should not be confiscated. Much of the land confiscated in the West Bank and Gaza Strip was taken from private persons. While Israel is not a party to the regulations, they are generally taken to reflect the customary law of nations and, therefore, to be binding on all states. Israel concurs that the Hague Regulations are binding as customary law.[32] After the Supreme Court in the Elon Moreh case said that private West Bank or Gaza Strip land could not be confiscated in the absence of a security justification, the government began confiscation of nominally state-owned land. Much of the land of the West Bank was under a tenure system that was in a technical sense state ownership, though individual families had occupied the land for generations and, so long as they paid taxes on it, were considered its owners.[33]

In 1978 Israel concluded a treaty with Egypt, the Camp David agreement, that required Israel to return the Sinai Peninsula to Egypt.[34] The agreement also made provision for the West Bank and Gaza Strip, calling for limited autonomy for the Arab population, a continued Israeli military presence, and a prohibition against any Palestinian military force.[35] It contemplated, as construed by Israel, permanent control by Israel of the West Bank and Gaza Strip.[36] The West Bank and Gaza population rejected the Camp David agreement, on the grounds they had had no role in its elaboration and it did not contemplate self-determination. The UN General Assembly agreed that the agreement violated the Palestine Arabs' right to self-determination.[37] The agreement was criticized for tending to preserve Israel's control in such a way it would not be forced to bring the two populations into its own political system.[38] It strengthened Israel's tenure in the territories, it was said, by splitting Egypt politically from the other Arab states, thereby freeing Israel to take stronger measures against the Palestine Arabs in the West Bank and Gaza Strip.[39]

Israel's military government in the West Bank and Gaza Strip was comparable in many respects to the military government it had established after 1948 in its own Arab-populated sectors. Rule was by military decree and direct control was exercised by military personnel. Court cases went to military tribunals. Israel did not allow the West Bank or Gaza Strip population any territory-wide governance, though it did to a limited extent at the local level. In the Gaza Strip it permitted no elections for local positions,[40] but in the West Bank it permitted local elections in 1972 and 1976, though it cancelled subsequent elections because it feared more strongly nationalist candidates would be elected. "If we let them run for elections," said the military governor, General Benjamin Ben-Eliezer, in 1981, "the result would be very clear—once and for all to bury the Camp David peace process."[41] The government dismissed a number of nationalist-oriented mayors elected in 1976 and expelled several others.[42]

Israel also did not allow any governing institutions for the 100,000 Arabs of east Jerusalem. After it incorporated east Jerusalem into Israel the Knesset made east Jerusalem residents eligible to vote in Jerusalem municipal elections.[43] But few did so because of their objection to the incorporation.[44]

As it had done after 1948 with the Arabs under its control, the government tried to direct local Arab politics in the Gaza Strip and West Bank. In the Gaza Strip it promoted Moslem fundamentalist groups that opposed the Palestine Liberation Organization. The military governor for Gaza, General Itzhak Segev, said the government gave him a budget to finance fundamentalist mosques.[45] The government tried to keep aid from private outside development agencies from benefiting supporters of the PLO.[46]

In the West Bank, Israel's military administration created a local Arab political structure, separate from that of the Arab elected officials, which it called "village leagues."[47] Its purpose, reported the U.S. Department of State, was to "transfer patronage and authority from elected and established Palestinian nationalist leaders whom Israel objects to as being supporters of the Palestine Liberation Organization." It gave the leagues arms and financial assistance.[48]

The government tried, said the State Department, "to interpose the Leagues as an intermediary between the inhabitants and the occupation authorities by refusal to accept requests for such services as the registration of births or marriages, building permits, bridge crossing permits, and family reunion applications without the participation of the local league." Village league members "often exacted fees for their services. Many West Bankers," the department reported, "complained that the Leagues' expanding activities undermine the elected Arab political structure."[49]

For its citizens who settled in the West Bank and Gaza Strip— numbering 65,000 and 2,700 respectively[50]—the government provided a separate system of government. It established "area councils" over groups of settlements.[51] To govern the settlers, the military governors issued military orders that repeated verbatim the texts of various Israeli laws. In this way the settlers were freed from the local law of the West Bank or Gaza Strip with respect to education, personal status, health, and labor. They gained a kind of extraterritoriality.[52] For most legal purposes Israeli settlers living in the West Bank or Gaza Strip were deemed in Israeli law to be residents of Israel,[53] rather than of the West Bank or Gaza Strip. This separation resulted in separate legal regimes for settlers and for Arabs. It also curtailed the power of the Arab municipal authorities. Arabs continued to function under the prior existing law and institutions—which meant Jordanian law and courts in the West Bank and Palestinian law and courts in the Gaza Strip—except to the extent they were superseded by military orders and military courts.

For lawsuits between settlers the government created courts in the settlements, and it made the judgments of these courts enforceable in courts inside the 1949 armistice lines.[54] The government also authorized settlers to sue one another in courts inside the armistice lines.[55] Arab courts continued to function in the Gaza Strip and West Bank, but the settlers did not file there since the government provided non-Arab alternatives.[56] If an Arab wanted to sue a settler, the Arab courts would, in theory, have jurisdiction. But they had no enforcement mechanism to compel an appearance in court by a settler defendant.[57]

Arab police abstained from entering the settlements to investigate crime or make arrests.[58] In criminal matters the settlers were made subject to Israeli law and courts rather than to the local law and courts. Criminal cases against settlers are to date prosecuted either in Israeli courts within the 1949 armistice lines,[59] in settlement courts,[60] or, rarely, in Israeli military courts.[61] Arab courts still do not try settlers.[62] In a 1984 directive to West Bank prosecutors and judges the government ordered Arab courts not to try settlers:

> Reference is made to document No. 3/63 dated 11 January 1979, in which the legal advisor has interpreted the law on the West Bank whereby it is not possible to execute judgments from West Bank courts made against holders of Israeli identity cards who are living inside Israel (to include Jerusalem and its suburbs). . . . Therefore, . . . West Bank courts should not register any criminal case (to include traffic cases) against holders of Israeli identity cards unless written authorization is obtained from me.[63]

Settlers had been issued Israeli identity cards; thus, by this directive they were not to be tried in Arab courts. The exclusion of criminal jurisdiction over settlers left Arabs unprotected from physical attacks by settlers, which occurred with some frequency.[64] Israeli authorities rarely prosecuted the perpetrators of these attacks.[65]

The separation in applicable law and court jurisdiction between the settlers and the Arab populations of the West Bank and Gaza Strip has been characterized as "a form of legal apartheid,"[66] since the Apartheid Convention prohibits dividing a population on racial lines for administrative purposes.[67]

25

More Hewers of Wood:

Commerce, Agriculture, and Labor

Another such victory over the Romans, and we are undone.
—Pyrrhus, King of Epirus, Plutarch, *Lives*

The 1949 armistice lines cut the West Bank off from Mediterranean ports and separated the port of Gaza from its traditional hinterland in the area south of Jaffa.[1] The expulsion of the Palestine Arabs in 1948 left 150,000 refugees in the Gaza Strip and 400,000 in the West Bank. For Gaza that represented a doubling of its population, and it became one of the most densely populated areas in the world. Furthermore, history would prove that neither Gaza nor the West Bank could incorporate this influx into their economies successfully.

As in the Galilee in the early 1950s, the government's land confiscations in the West Bank and Gaza Strip radically altered their economies. "The taking of land for settlements and for military use in the occupied territories," said the U.S. Department of State, "strongly affected the lives of Arab residents." Many of them, it said, "had to leave farming to become day laborers."[2] They took jobs in Israeli settlements or inside the 1949 armistice lines.[3] By the 1980s one-third of the work force commuted to jobs inside the 1949 armistice lines.[4]

The government let employers pay these workers lower wages than they paid Israelis, and they paid 20–30 percent less to Arabs than they paid Israelis for similar work.[5] The Histadrut took 1 percent of the salary of these guest workers but did not admit them as members and did not provide them services.[6] Israel's National Insurance Law limited many employment-related benefits to residents of Israel.[7] This limitation excluded Gaza and West Bank guest workers.[8] By Israeli regulation they were required to cross back over the armistice line by 1:00 A.M.[9] Therefore, they could not become residents of Israel.[10]

The National Insurance Law provides only three benefits to workers who are not Israeli residents—on-the-job injury compensation,[11] wages and severance pay given in the event of the bankruptcy of the employer,[12] and maternity payments to a worker or to the wife of a male worker. Maternity benefits, however, are conditioned on the birth taking place in Israel,[13] with the result that few West Bankers or Gazans receive them, since most women give birth in their home area.[14]

Other important benefits are conditioned on Israel residency —unemployment compensation,[15] off-the-job injury compensation,[16] care for a long-term illness,[17] compensation for lower limb dysfunction,[18] pension payable to survivors,[19] income support (where income falls below a stipulated minimum),[20] and days off for mourning and weddings.[21] Thus, the West Bank and Gaza guest workers are by law ineligible for these benefits.

As for old-age pensions, a West Banker or Gazan working inside the 1949 armistice lines receives only a "retirement pension"—which is quite small—but not the much larger "comprehensive pension" since that pension is conditioned on residence in Israel.[22] To qualify even for the retirement pension a West Banker or Gazan must work at least ten years.[23] This requirement excludes many West Bankers and Gazans since employers are not required to keep records of their employment.[24]

Even though the National Insurance Law limits important benefits to Israeli residents, nonresident workers are assessed wage deductions as if they were eligible to receive them.[25] Thus, West Bank and Gaza workers are assessed wage deductions to the same extent as resident workers.[26] This difference in treatment was characterized by a Hebrew University sociologist, Michael Shwartz, as an "apartheid practice."[27]

The government of Israel acknowledged that West Bank and Gaza workers are entitled to some return for that portion of their wage deductions for which they do not receive benefits. Therefore, it began to transfer a percentage of the deductions made from their salaries into a special fund.[28] It stated that it will turn these moneys over in the event of a political settlement for the West Bank and Gaza Strip.[29] It refused a request from Ephraim Sneh, head of Israel's civil administration in the West Bank, that it spend these moneys in the West Bank.[30]

Some West Bankers and Gazans working inside the 1949 armistice lines do not receive even those benefits ordinarily available to nonresidents. This is so because they contract for employment directly with Israeli employers, rather than through government labor exchanges.[31] Employers do not report the employment and thus do not make wage deductions for benefits. Employment is arranged in this fashion in part because employers avoid insurance deductions and in part because the workers avoid the Israeli income tax and the Histadrut representation fee.

Although Gaza and West Bank Arabs who work inside the 1949 armistice lines are not considered residents of Israel, the Knesset deemed Israeli settlers living in the Gaza Strip or the West Bank to be residents of Israel. Thus, whether these Israelis work inside the armistice lines or in the Gaza Strip or West Bank, they qualify for the benefits denied to the West Bank and Gaza Arabs.[32]

As it had done after 1948 in Arab-populated areas, the government of Israel adopted policies in the West Bank and Gaza Strip that had the effect of obstructing Arab industrial initiatives. It closed the thirty banks operating there, which limited access to capital for Arab entrepreneurs.[33] The lack of Arab banking facilities for credit and financial transactions hurt industrial development.[34] The government also limited the import by West Bank and Gaza industry of capital from the Arab countries.[35] Instead, Israeli banks began to operate in the Gaza Strip and West Bank, to the further detriment of Arab development.

In 1981 the government permitted the reopening of the Bank of Palestine in Gaza but prohibited it from dealing in non-Israeli currencies.[36] In 1986 it permitted another bank to open in Gaza[37] and allowed the Jordanian Amman-Cairo Bank to open one branch in Nablus in the West Bank. It imposed on these banks, however, close controls not used on the Israeli banks operating in the two areas.[38]

In economic planning Israeli officials took the lead.[39] The government did not let West Bank or Gaza Arabs establish any institutions to set economic policy[40] or to set tariffs that might protect local industry.[41] The government expanded West Bank roads, but largely for its own security needs[42]—such as a 1984 highway construction plan that called for highways linking Israeli settlements, but bypassing Arab towns.[43]

The government invested little in the Arab economy.[44] On the contrary, it thwarted development projects that might make the econ-omies of the territories more independent.[45] Uncertainty about the future political status and about the possibility of military decrees that might impede their work made Arab entrepreneurs view invest-ment as hazardous.[46] The climate was not conducive to risk-taking.[47]

By an extensive system of control the government of Israel kept Arab industry from injuring Israeli production. Itzhak Rabin, who as defense minister was in charge of the West Bank and Gaza Strip, said his government tried to keep West Bank and Gaza industry from com-peting with Israeli industry.[48] In actual fact, the government directed Arab industry to make it complement Israeli industry. It encouraged production of goods that enjoyed a weak demand in the occupied territories and of goods that had a comparative advantage with the Israeli economy since Israel was the principal client. In industry it imposed production specialization through subcontracting by Israeli firms to Arab firms.[49] Subcontracting allowed Israeli firms, particu-larly in textile and confection, to use the cheaper Arab labor;[50] but it did not provide a stable base for the West Bank or Gaza Strip since subcontracting diminished during downswings in production.[51]

The government began to use the West Bank and Gaza as a pro-tected market for Israeli manufactured goods. Through high tariffs and rigid policies of import licensing, it ensured the marketing in the West Bank and Gaza Strip of high-priced and low-quality Israeli products.[52] As a result, the West Bank and Gaza soon came to receive nearly all their imports from Israel.[53] At the same time a much lower percentage of their own production was exported to Israel because of quotas and other restrictions the Israeli government set.[54]

Functioning within the Israeli economy, West Bank and Gaza industry could not compete since Israeli industry enjoyed substan-tial government subsidies and credit.[55] It also had to compete with the production of Israeli settlements in the West Bank and Gaza, which, like Israeli industry, was subsidized by the government.[56] To make matters worse for Arab industry, the government gave Israeli industry financial incentives to invest in the West Bank and Gaza,[57] which led to the construction of six Israeli industrial parks in the West Bank; the World Zionist Organization's 1982 Plan of One Hun-dred Thousand Settlers projected seven more industrial parks;[58] and, finally, the government directed outside development aid away from sectors that might compete with Israeli producers.[59] In particular, it made it difficult for voluntary economic-development agencies to bring in heavy equipment that might have helped Arab industry.[60]

A principal mechanism the military government devised for directing Arab industry into desired channels was to require a license for the establishment of any new business. As a matter of practice, it did not license new Arab businesses likely to compete with Israeli industry.[61] By various regulations the government restricted the construction of new factories.[62] For many years it denied a permit sought by Arab entrepreneurs to open a cement plant in Hebron and a citrus plant in Gaza.[63] These refusals to license new businesses moved the UN Economic and Social Council to call upon Israel "to facilitate the establishment of a cement plant in the occupied West Bank and a citrus plant in the occupied Gaza Strip."[64] The denial was apparently motivated by a desire to protect Israeli producers.[65]

A major industry in Gaza is fishing. The government undermined that industry by establishing zones in the Mediterranean Sea in which it did not permit Arab trawlers to fish,[66] while Israeli fishing vessels were allowed to fish in the same waters. It justified the regulations on the ground that guerrilla groups might use fishing boats to approach the Gaza coast. To keep the Gaza fishing industry from competing with Israel's, it restricted the sale inside the 1949 armistice lines of fish caught by Gaza fishing vessels.[67] Most Gaza fishermen went out of business as a result of these restrictions.[68]

Similarly in agriculture, the government of Israel oriented West Bank and Gaza production to meet the needs of Israel's economy.[69] To prevent competition with Israeli farmers, it prohibited the production of melons in the West Bank and limited the production of tomatoes and cucumbers in the West Bank and the planting of citrus trees in Gaza.[70] Israel's controls on the export to Israel of West Bank and Gaza agricultural products, according to the U.S. Department of State, "restrict the market opportunities" of West Bank and Gaza farmers.[71] The minister of agriculture prohibited or restricted the sale inside the 1949 armistice lines of major West Bank and Gaza products, like grapes and dates, to forestall competition with Israeli producers.[72] Israel's agricultural officer for the Gaza Strip explained that the government erected "a legislative structure and mechanism of separation" to prevent the free marketing inside the 1949 armistice lines of produce from the territories.[73] To enforce the prohibitions, agricultural inspectors on occasion confiscated fruits and vegetables being brought by West Bank farmers into Jerusalem, a major market.[74] The government imposed customs duties to prevent entry of perishable food items.[75] It undermined the citrus industry of the Gaza Strip by imposing a high tariff on Gaza citrus exports,[76] by setting administrative restrictions on exports,[77] and by mandating taxes that favored Israeli producers.[78] It limited Gaza citrus exports to other countries.[79]

At the same time, said Israel's agricultural officer for the Gaza Strip, "the leftover produce from Israel" was "flooding the territories, without regard for the interests of local agriculture."[80] The government did not regulate the marketing of Israeli produce on the West Bank.[81] West Bank farmers protested the low market prices for vegetables, blaming Israeli produce that entered the West Bank duty-free.[82]

The aquifer underlying the hilly West Bank contains most of the water available underground on the coastal plain, which is inside the 1949 armistice lines. Control of the West Bank, therefore, gave Israel the ability to assure its own water supply. The government gave control of the West Bank and Gaza Strip water to the National Water Authority, Mekorot, so this water could be managed according to Israel's needs. The government permitted West Bank Arabs to drill new wells only for domestic consumption,[83] denying their requests to drill for irrigation.[84] It placed meters on Palestinian wells to check daily consumption.[85]

The government did allow, however, the drilling of deep wells to serve Israeli users inside the 1949 armistice lines or in West Bank settlements. Many of these wells were drilled near shallower Arab wells, thereby drying them up.[86] This deprived Arab farmers of water and put many of them out of business.[87] Arab farmers were forced to let formerly productive land go unused because water, previously available for irrigation, was siphoned off by Israeli wells.[88] Israeli settlers came to use water far out of proportion to their numbers in the West Bank, taking about 20 percent of the water consumed while constituting 3 percent of the population.[89] The UN General Assembly, referring to this situation, called on Israel to end its "illegal exploitation of the natural wealth, resources and population of the occupied territories."[90]

In the Gaza Strip as well the government prohibited the digging of new wells by Arabs but let Israeli settlers do so.[91] It allowed these wells to be dug deeper than Arab wells, both to supply the settlements and to send the water inside the 1949 armistice lines.[92] According to a UN study, the settlements "use the limited water resources of the West Bank at the expense of Arab farmers." There was, according to the study, "an expansion of the Israeli water control system, in order to serve the requirements of agricultural projects established by the Jewish settlements." The government "restricted the water consumption of the Palestinians in the West Bank and the Gaza Strip in order to make a larger amount of water available for Israeli consumption."[93]

In the West Bank and Gaza Strip ownership by Arabs of cooking ranges, motor vehicles, refrigerators, washing machines, and television sets increased after Israel began its occupation. Government figures showed an 11 percent increase in per capita income up to 1980, a 9 percent increase in private demand, and an annual average 13 percent increase in the gross national product.[94] The government cited these increases as showing that the occupation benefited the Arabs economically. These consumption gains did not come, however, from economic development in the West Bank or Gaza Strip. They resulted in large part from the employment of Gazans and West Bankers in the Persian Gulf and inside the 1949 armistice lines.[95] The purchases benefited Israel's economy but did not build up the economies of the West Bank or Gaza.

Israel's economic policies in the West Bank and Gaza Strip were similar, analysts charged, to those followed by European powers in their Third World colonies.[96] For the West Bank and Gaza Strip, one study concluded, Israel's economic policy led to a migratory labor situation, stagnated production, a lack of capital formation, minimal physical infrastructure, a near total dependence on Israel's economy, a brain drain of professionals, the emigration of entrepreneurs, the export of capital, and the proletarianization of the farm population.[97]

The argument that the consumption benefits justified the occupation carried a "strong element of the kind of economic bribery that was more or less the standard rationale for colonialism," said the analyst John Dunne.[98] A similar argument was used, noted the economist Sarah Graham-Brown, to justify economic policies in the white settler states of southern Africa.[99]

26

By the Sword: The Palestine Arabs'

Claim of a Right to Resist

But indeed if any do help
And defend themselves
After a wrong [done]
To them, against such
There is no cause
Of blame.
—*Holy Quran*, xlii, 41

Defense Minister Dayan said after the 1967 war that the Arabs do not "hate the Jews for personal, religious, or racial reasons. They consider us—and justly, from their point of view—as Westerners, foreigners, invaders who seized an Arab country to turn it into a Jewish state. Therefore, we are obliged to gain our objectives against the will of the Arabs, and we must live in a state of permanent war."[1]

The 1967 war provided an impetus for the growth of the Fatah organization. The defeat of the Arab states convinced many Palestine Arabs that reliance on the Arab states was fruitless. First, Fatah tried to organize a structure of resistance in the West Bank. But by late 1967 the government drove it out.[2] Fatah did, however, attract new recruits in Jordan and from there it raided into the West Bank against Israeli targets.

Most of Fatah's attacks were against military posts, but civilians were killed in these raids and some operations were aimed at civilian targets.[3] In response, Israel made reprisal attacks against Fatah camps in Jordan, often killing large numbers of people, most of them unconnected with Fatah. The Security Council, as before the 1967 war, condemned Israel for these attacks. Denouncing a 1968 Israeli attack on Karameh, Jordan, it deplored the "loss of life and heavy damage to property."[4] It condemned a 1968 raid by Israel on Fatah bases near the Jordanian town of Es-Salt, again deploring the "loss of life and heavy damage to property." It said that Israel's "premeditated and repeated military attacks endanger the maintenance of the peace."[5]

In the Security Council Pakistan said that Israel's 1967 aggression deprived it of the right to use any force against Fatah, since it was protecting the territory it had taken unlawfully. It denied that Israel, as "the perpetrator of an aggression," had a right to force "equal to that of the victim of that aggression."[6] France objected to Israel's claim of a need to use force in reprisal for "the security of the territory and population" under its jurisdiction because "we cannot recognise that jurisdiction, which was established through occupation."[7]

Fatah took the same position, justifying its raids as a manifestation of the resistance of a people to armed occupation of its territory. The occupier, it declared, has no right of reprisal.[8] France, in criticizing Israel for one reprisal raid, called the Fatah attacks into the West Bank the "almost inevitable consequence of military occupation."[9] Pakistan said that the "popular resistance" was part of the "legitimate struggle of the people of Palestine for a return in freedom to their own homeland."[10]

During these same years the Security Council was asked to address similar issues arising in Africa. Portugal still held the colonies of Angola, Mozambique, and Guinea-Bissau, and guerrilla groups in all three tried to overthrow it. Guerrillas were based in neighboring states, and Portuguese forces frequently mounted raids into those states in search of the guerrillas. In handling these cases the council in each instance found colonial states in Africa were acting unlawfully when they made cross-border reprisal raids against guerrillas seeking independence.[11] It condemned Portugal's attacks into Zambia,[12] Senegal,[13] and Guinea.[14] The council condemned Portugal in these cases, despite allegations of mutual violations of the territorial integrity of the parties concerned.[15] Therefore, it did not put the guerrilla forces and the colonial state on a footing of equality but recognized a superior right to force on the part of the guerrilla forces. It criticized Portugal not only for attacking but also for failing to respect the right to self-determination.[16] It rejected the claim of Portugal of a right to retaliate to keep its colonies under its control.[17]

In the 1980s South Africa mounted raids into Botswana in search of guerrillas seeking to overthrow the apartheid system of South

Africa. The Security Council condemned South Africa for an "un-provoked and unwarranted military attack" and affirmed Botswana's right to give sanctuary to victims of apartheid, the circumstance South Africa asserted justified the raids.[18] South Africa also made raids into Angola to fight forces of the South-West Africa (Namibia) People's Organization (SWAPO), which sought to drive South Africa out of Namibia. South Africa, it was generally recognized, held Namibia in violation of the self-determination right of the people of Namibia. The Security Council condemned South Africa's attacks into Angola.[19]

In considering reprisal attacks by Israel, the council did not con-demn the guerrilla organizations or the states from which they oper-ated. Its evident rationale was that the Arab refugees were justified because they sought self-determination. The Security Council, in finding the Fatah attacks lawful, dealt with them as attacks by a colonized people entitled to the right of self-determination.[20]

When self-determination is denied, the injured entity is the people affected.[21] The Security Council's practice in the cases just men-tioned suggests that when all else fails a people denied self-determi-nation may resort to forcible self-help to remove from its territory the state holding it in dependence. The Palestine National Covenant viewed the force that might be used to achieve Palestinian self-determination as self-defense. "The liberation of Palestine from an international viewpoint," it declared, "is a defensive act necessitated by the demands of self defense."[22] In an International Court of Jus-tice case involving Namibia, Judge Fouad Ammoun shared that view. Citing the French national movement under Nazi German occupa-tion, and the Polish, Czech, and Slovak peoples under the Austro-Hungarian Empire, he said that a people has a right to armed strug-gle to achieve self-determination. "In law, the legitimacy of the peoples' struggle cannot be in any doubt," he said, "for it follows from the right of self-defence, inherent in human nature, which is con-firmed by Article 51 of the United Nations Charter."[23] Ammoun found South Africa's presence in Namibia to constitute aggression since it was maintained against the will of the population, even though South Africa came into control by a mandate of the League of Nations.[24]

This theory that colonialism constitutes continuing aggression has been opposed by other authorities.[25] Julius Stone argued that colonialism is not "illegal per se,"[26] and Louis Henkin said that even if colonialism is illegal, the presence of a colonial administration is not an armed attack within the meaning of Article 51 of the UN Charter.[27] John Norton Moore suggested that, when asserted by the Palestine Arabs, the theory of continuing aggression is merely "a rhetorical substitution of an armed attack claim in place of an underlying self-determination claim" and that the charter's prohibition against force "does not contain an exception permitting unilateral determination of denial of self-determination as a basis for lawful use of major coercion."[28]

Moore's criticism casts light on a difficulty in the theory that a people denied self-determination may use force because, according to Moore, the people may "unilaterally" decide it has been denied self-determination. While that may be a problem in many instances, it would not seem to be so in the case of the Palestine Arabs. The community of states has repeatedly affirmed the right of the Palestine Arabs to self-determination, so their claim of a denial of self-determination cannot be said to be "unilateral."[29]

Another objection to the view that colonialism constitutes a continuing attack is that the taking was lawful at the time it occurred since until the twentieth century forcible seizure of territory as colonies was permitted.[30] While that may be true for some peoples denied the right to self-determination, it is not true of the Palestine Arabs. Their territory was taken from them, as already indicated, after international law prohibited acquisition of colonies by force. Thus, the taking was unlawful from the outset.

Another theory has been suggested that would legitimate anticolonial force. The UN Charter defined unlawful force as that used against "the territorial integrity or political independence of any state,"[31] which implied force against another state. When a dependent people uses force against a colonizer, argued Kadar Asmal, it is not using force against another state, but rather against an entity that occupies its own territory.[32]

In its 1960 Declaration on the Granting of Independence to Colonial Countries and Peoples, the General Assembly said that "all armed action or repressive measures of all kinds directed against dependent peoples shall cease in order to enable them to exercise peacefully and freely their right to complete independence, and the integrity of their national territory shall be respected."[33] That resolution, by referring to the territory of a dependent people as "their national territory," seemed to follow the theory that anticolonial force is not force against another state. The resolution implied that a dependent people may lawfully use force to displace a colonizer.

India relied on this theory in 1961 after it used force to remove Portugal from the enclave of Goa, on the Indian coast. Portugal had held Goa as a colony for four hundred years. India claimed the right to use force to take Goa. Portugal complained to the Security Council that India's action was aggression.[34] India replied that there was "no legal frontier" between India and Goa, and it said there could be "no question of aggression against your own frontier, or against your own people, whom you want to liberate."[35] In the Security Council discussion, socialist and Third World states sided with India, while Western states sided with Portugal.[36]

In later years the General Assembly took the position that a dependent people may lawfully use force to achieve independence, though it did not specify which theory it was following. In 1965 the General Assembly recognized "the legitimacy of the struggle by the peoples under colonial rule to exercise their right to self-determination and independence."[37] In 1970, in its Declaration on Friendly Relations, the General Assembly, while not explicitly asserting a right to use force to overthrow a colonizer,[38] strongly implied such a right by outlawing force that would deprive a people of self-determination. "Every state," it declared, "has the duty to refrain from any forcible action which deprives peoples . . . of their right to self-determination and freedom and independence." The assembly referred to their "resistance to such forcible action in pursuit of the exercise of their right to self-determination." The declaration authorized even action that might eliminate a state by saying that nothing in the declaration "shall be construed as authorizing or encouraging any action which would dismember or impair, totally or in part, the territorial integrity or political unity of sovereign and independent States conducting themselves in compliance with the principle of equal rights and self-determination of peoples" and "thus possessed of a government representing the whole people belonging to the territory without distinction as to race, creed or colour."[39] A state not "possessed of a government representing the whole people . . . without distinction as to race, creed or colour" is not protected. Later in 1970 the assembly affirmed the right of "colonial peoples and peoples under alien domination" to "exercise their right to self-determination and independence by all the necessary means at their disposal."[40]

When it defined the concept of aggression in 1974 the assembly made it clear that anticolonial force was not to be deemed aggression. In a special proviso it said that "nothing in this Definition" could "in any way prejudice the right to self-determination, freedom and independence, as derived from the Charter, of peoples forcibly deprived of that right." The proviso referred back to the 1970 Declaration on Friendly Relations to indicate it meant "particularly peoples under colonial and racist regimes or other forms of alien domination." It mentioned specifically "the right of these peoples to struggle" to end the domination, and to "seek and receive support" for that purpose, "in accordance with the principles of the Charter and in conformity with the above-mentioned Declaration."[41] Though Julius Stone argued that this proviso does not reflect customary law,[42] the General Assembly adopted the definition of aggression without a vote. Tom Farer called it a "global consensus,"[43] and it would seem to reflect the views of the overwhelming majority of states.

The assembly followed this approach in resolutions relating to Palestine. In one resolution it upheld "the legality of the peoples' struggle for self-determination and liberation from colonial and foreign domination and alien subjugation, notably in southern Africa and in particular that of the people of Zimbabwe, Namibia, Angola, Mozambique and Guinea (Bissau), as well as the Palestinian people, by all available means consistent with the Charter of the United Nations."[44] The General Assembly characterized Israel's occupation of the West Bank and Gaza Strip as a denial of self-determination and hence a "serious and increasing threat to international peace and security." It felt the Arabs there were under foreign domination and the struggle for independence by such peoples, including armed struggle, is legitimate.[45]

The Organization of African Unity found a "right of the people of Palestine to continue their struggle in all political and military forms as well as the use of all means to liberate their occupied territory and to recover their inalienable national rights, particularly, their right to return to their homeland, the exercise of their right to self-determination and to establish an independent State in their territory."[46]

Apart from the right of self-determination, the guerrilla raids were arguably justifiable on the ground that the guerrilla groups were attempting to retake territory gained by aggression. Force used for that purpose is considered by some authorities to be aggression.[47] If territory taken by aggression may be recaptured by force, argued Oscar Schachter, "self-defense would sanction armed attacks for countless prior acts of aggression and conquest. It would completely swallow up the basic rule against using force."[48] "Re-caption," said Derek Bowett, "is unlawful."[49]

But if a state recaptures its own territory by force, "this is not an employment of force contrary to the provisions of Article 2(4) of the Charter," argued R. Y. Jennings in reply. "It cannot be force used against the territorial integrity or political independence of another State because the actor State is merely occupying its own territory."[50] Jennings relied on the UN Charter definition of aggression as force used against the territorial integrity or political independence of a state. When Egypt and Syria attacked Israel in October 1973 to recover the Sinai Peninsula and Golan Heights, which Israel took from them in 1967, the Security Council did not condemn them.[51]

In the late 1960s the Popular Front for the Liberation of Palestine, one of the constituent groups of the Palestine Liberation Organization, undertook airplane hijacking as a method of bringing attention to the denial of self-determination to the Palestine Arabs.[52] After it destroyed an Israeli government airliner at the Athens airport, the IDF attacked the Beirut airport in response and destroyed thirteen civilian airliners. The Security Council condemned Israel for "premeditated military action."[53]

In its reprisal raids the IDF began to use air strikes rather than ground troops. These air attacks brought heavy civilian casualties in the villages and refugee camps where guerrillas were based.[54] The Security Council condemned a 1969 air attack on Fatah bases near El-Salt, condemning the "recent premeditated air attacks launched by Israel on Jordanian villages and populated areas."[55] Following a 1969 air attack into Lebanon, the council condemned the "premeditated air attack by Israel on villages in southern Lebanon in violation of its obligations under the Charter" as acts of "military reprisal."[56]

In airplane hijackings and other attacks in Israel and elsewhere various constituent groups of the Palestine Liberation Organization attacked civilians. Such use of force was unlawful, as recognized by the General Assembly in its 1985 resolution, "Measures to Prevent International Terrorism."[57] Under the rules of warfare, a state in waging war—even in self-defense—must refrain from attacking civilians. Similarly, a national liberation movement in conducting warfare to achieve self-determination must follow the same rule.

That rule has been viewed as harsh by many national liberation movements. They typically do not have at their command military resources equal to those of the state against which they are fighting. To hold them to the same rules of warfare works to their disadvantage. As viewed by many Palestine Arabs, violence against civilians, particularly against Israeli civilians, is justified by the violence Israel has used against Palestinian civilians, particularly its bombing raids on Palestinian refugee camps in Lebanon. Through these raids, the IDF killed far more civilians than did the Palestine Arabs. A poll taken among Palestine Arabs in the West Bank in 1986 showed 87.6 percent support for acts of violence against civilians by Palestinian commando teams inside the 1949 armistice lines.[58]

Terrorist acts are a product of frustration over inability to gain self-determination by other means. Terrorism is "not an aberration of demented personalities," according to David Shipler, writing about the Palestine Arabs, but "an integral part of an existing subculture, encouraged and supported and approved by the mainstream of the society that forms the terrorist's reference points."[59] While the frustration has a solid basis, violence against civilians is not justified by the denial of self-determination or by violence against civilians by the other side.

The General Assembly studied terrorist acts in the 1970s and concluded that they are often undertaken as a result of the inability of a dependent people to attain self-determination by political or legitimate military means.[60] In order to eliminate "the causes and the problem of international terrorism," the United Nations should "pay special attention to all situations, including, inter alia, colonialism, racism and situations involving alien occupation, that may give rise to international terrorism and may endanger international peace and security, with a view to the application, where feasible and necessary, of the relevant provisions of the Charter of the United Nations, including Chapter VII thereof."[61] Chapter 7 of the charter provides for economic and military sanctions to be imposed by the Security Council against a state that threatens the peace. By referring to Chapter 7 the assembly was suggesting that the Security Council mandate collective coercive measures to terminate the denial of self-determination.

27

Guns and Stones: Resistance by

the Palestine Arabs to Occupation

The first priority is to use force, might, beatings.
—Yitzhak Rabin, Minister of Defense, 1988

In 1970 Jordan expelled the Palestine Liberation Organization from its borders, and the PLO moved its base of operation to Lebanon. It operated primarily in southern Lebanon where many Palestine Arabs, expelled from northern Palestine in 1948, lived in refugee camps. From southern Lebanon the PLO mounted raids into Israel. Israel initiated reprisals, leading to more Security Council condemnations.[1] In 1970 Israel undertook a substantial invasion into Lebanese territory. The council demanded the "immediate withdrawal of all Israeli armed forces from Lebanese territory"[2] and condemned Israel for "its premeditated military action." It deplored the "loss of life and damage to property."[3] When the IDF remained in place, the council repeated its demand for withdrawal.[4]

In 1972, as raids by the PLO continued, Israel again sent troops into Lebanon. The Security Council demanded "that Israel immediately desist" from "any ground and air military action against Lebanon" and that it "forthwith withdraw all its military forces from Lebanese territory."[5] The council, "while profoundly deploring all acts of violence," condemned "the repeated attacks of Israeli forces on Lebanese territory and population."[6]

In May 1972 a group sent by the Popular Front for the Liberation of Palestine took a commercial flight to Tel Aviv and in the airport customs hall they opened fire, killing twenty-five persons and wounding seventy-two others.[7] The Black September organization, affiliated with the PLO, kidnapped eleven Israeli athletes in September at the Olympic Games in Munich. In trying to free the athletes, German police shot and killed them, along with four of the captors.[8] The IDF responded with air strikes into Syria, in which it killed several hundred civilians.[9] All of these events led to the formation of new guerrilla groups, and this in turn led to increased numbers of hijackings by them.[10]

In 1973 the Security Council condemned Israel's "repeated" attacks into Lebanon and its "violation of Lebanon's territorial integrity and sovereignty." It called on Israel to "desist forthwith from all military attacks on Lebanon."[11] In 1974 branches of the PLO raided the Israeli town of Qiryat Shmona where they took eighteen civilians as hostages, killing them and themselves when confronted.[12] They raided the town of Maalot as well where they took as hostages ninety high school students, twenty of whom were killed when government forces tried to free them.[13]

In March 1978, following a series of guerrilla raids into Israel from Lebanon, Israel invaded Lebanon in pursuit of the PLO. It occupied southern Lebanon, killing 2,000, mostly Lebanese and Palestinian civilians, and causing 200,000 to flee their homes. It established a seven-mile-wide "security belt," which it held for three months. When it withdrew, it left in charge a Lebanese force it had organized and financed.[14] The council called on Israel "immediately to cease its military action against Lebanese territorial integrity" and to "withdraw forthwith its forces from all Lebanese territory."[15]

In July 1981 Israel and the PLO concluded an agreement by which the PLO agreed not to launch an attack into Israel. As a result, the PLO did not attack Israel from mid-1981 to mid-1982.[16] But in June 1982 Israel again invaded Lebanon, and it used aerial bombardment to destroy entire camps of Palestine Arab refugees.[17] By these means Israel killed 20,000 persons, mostly civilians,[18] and while it occupied southern Lebanon it incarcerated 15,000 persons, according to the International Committee of the Red Cross. The IDF continued north to Beirut, where it forced the PLO out of Lebanon.

Israel claimed self-defense for its invasion, but the lack of PLO attacks into Israel during the previous year made that claim dubious. By invading Lebanon, Israel evidently sought to destroy the extensive Palestinian military and administrative infrastructure in Lebanon[19] and, by removing the PLO, to convince the Arabs of the Gaza Strip and West Bank that they would get no help from the PLO.[20] In the United States Harold Saunders, a former assistant secretary of state for Near Eastern and South Asian affairs, said that Israel aimed, by the invasion, "to destroy once and for all any hope among the people of the West Bank and Gaza that the process of shaping the Palestinian people into a nation could succeed." It was designed, he continued, "to break any final resistance to total Israeli control and to pave the way for making life so difficult for those who valued their freedom and political self-expression that they would eventually leave for Jordan."[21]

The Security Council demanded "that Israel withdraw all its military forces forthwith and unconditionally to the internationally recognized boundaries of Lebanon."[22] But the IDF continued its attacks in Beirut, destroying entire neighborhoods by aerial bombardment, and blocking food and medical supplies from reaching victims of the bombardment. The council demanded "that the Government of Israel lift immediately the blockade of the city of Beirut in order to permit the dispatch of supplies to meet the urgent needs of the civilian population."[23] In Beirut the IDF allowed militia of a Lebanese faction hostile to the PLO to enter the refugee camps of Sabra and Shatilla, where the militia killed a number of civilians variously estimated from 300 to 3500.[24] The Security Council and General Assembly condemned the killings as a "criminal massacre of Palestinian civilians," and the assembly called them "an act of genocide."[25] Israel subsequently withdrew from most of Lebanon but kept troops in a strip of southern Lebanon.

In 1985 Israel's air force attacked the headquarters of the PLO in a suburb of Tunis, Tunisia, resulting in the deaths of sixty-eight persons in the vicinity. The Security Council said the attack was directed against "an exclusively residential urban area which traditionally has been home to Tunisian families and a small number of Palestinian civilians who had to flee from Lebanon following the invasion of that country by the Israeli army."[26]

Inside the West Bank and Gaza Strip the IDF met civilian resistance to its occupation. The Palestine Arabs pressed for political rights. They held street demonstrations, often resulting in violence against the IDF troops and violent reaction from them. Despite Israel's ban on political activity, underground affiliates of the various PLO factions organized supporters in the two areas. Arrest on security-related charges became a rite of passage for youths.

Arabs detained on security-related charges frequently complained that interrogators used force to convince them to confess. In 1987 a government commission found that security officials had frequently used physical force to extract confessions. When called to testify in court about the confession, the interrogators would routinely deny having used force.[27] The commission reported interviewing "service personnel who felt that the judges were part of the game," meaning that judges were aware that security service interrogators were lying when they denied having used torture.[28] The commission criticized the interrogators for giving false testimony but ruled that in the interrogation of persons suspected of security-related offenses "the employment of moderate physical pressure cannot be avoided." The usual means of investigation was deemed inadequate because the public in the West Bank or Gaza Strip was unlikely to cooperate with authorities to report crime.[29] The commission did not define in public documents what "physical pressure" was to be permitted but drafted secret guidelines to set limits.[30] The cabinet endorsed the commission's report, thereby authorizing interrogators to use moderate physical force against suspects.[31]

To thwart resistance the government expelled hundreds of persons, primarily those it considered potential leaders.[32] From Jerusalem it expelled civic leaders who opposed the annexation of Jerusalem.[33] Ariel Sharon, as defense minister, threatened to expel large numbers of West Bank and Gaza Strip residents. He said that "the Palestinians should not forget 1948."[34]

The government used the Defense (Emergency) Regulations to detain persons without charge,[35] to impose curfews on towns, to demolish houses of persons suspected of offenses, and to prohibit public demonstrations, artwork, and other nationalist expression.[36] One Arab woman was put on trial in an IDF court for hanging a map of Palestine in her private office,[37] and an IDF court convicted Arabs for singing nationalist songs at a wedding.[38]

In addition to the regulations, the military governments of the Gaza Strip and the West Bank issued local orders to suppress nationalism. An order titled Prohibition of Incitement and Adverse Propaganda punished anyone who tried "whether verbally or in any other manner to influence public opinion . . . in a manner which might endanger public security or order." The order required a permit for "a march of ten or more people together; or the assembling for the purpose of marching together from one place to another for a political purpose; or for a matter which can be interpreted as a political matter whether or not they were in fact walking and whether or not they had congregated." Violation was punishable by a ten-year imprisonment.[39]

Arabs challenged some of the military orders in court. The Supreme Court of Israel gave military commanders great latitude by interpreting "military necessity" to include "strategic as well as tactical security considerations."[40] The Supreme Court upheld all challenged military orders, with one exception. In 1987 it ruled invalid Military Order 1164 of February 25, 1986, which gave the military governor power to appoint the executive board of a lawyers' union on the West Bank. The court said that the union had the right to elect its own board.[41]

Much of Israel's suppression activity violated the Geneva Convention Relative to the Treatment of Civilian Persons in Time of War. Article 49 stated: "Individual or mass forcible transfers, as well as deportations of protected persons from occupied territory to the territory of the Occupying Power or to that of any other country, occupied or not, are prohibited, regardless of their motive." As already indicated, Article 49 prohibits the transfer of population into occupied territory, but it also prohibits the expulsion of inhabitants from occupied territory. Israel's Supreme Court ruled, however, that Article 49 prohibits only mass deportations for purposes of forced labor or extermination and, therefore, does not prohibit Israel's deportations of individuals or small groups, done for punitive purposes.[42] The government of Israel took that view as well,[43] though it was rejected by other states.[44]

The convention also protects property and forbids penalties imposed on groups or communities as opposed to individual perpetrators. Thus, the punitive demolition of the houses occupied by persons suspected of violent acts violated the convention. The curfews also represented a penalty taken against a group for the acts of an individual. In addition, the detention of persons without charge violated the convention. From early in the occupation, the UN General Assembly regularly criticized Israel for these violations.[45]

As Israel's occupation of the West Bank and Gaza Strip began its third decade, the situation of the Palestine Arabs there became increasingly difficult. They had been deprived for twenty years of any political role. Their land was being taken at a rate that presaged a nearly total dispossession, as had occurred inside the 1949 armistice lines. Israel's virtual destruction of the West Bank and Gaza economies gave Arab youth little future. Young people who acquired an education were unable to find positions commensurate with their qualifications.

In December 1987 a demonstration in Gaza City developed into rioting through the Gaza Strip and the West Bank. Merchants closed their businesses in civil resistance against the occupation; local committees began to provide basic services, and West Bank and Gaza residents reduced their purchases of Israeli-made goods; many West Bank and Gaza residents who worked inside the armistice lines did not go to their jobs; and an underground leadership emerged to direct the campaign, which was called *intifada* (uprising).[46] Residents held street demonstrations, and these often developed into serious confrontations with the IDF. Youths threw stones at the soldiers, and the soldiers beat and shot at the youths.

The UN Human Rights Commission saw this use of force by the Palestine Arabs against Israel as lawful. The commission found a "right of the Palestinian people to regain their rights by all means in accordance with the purposes and principles of the Charter of the United Nations and with relevant United Nations resolutions" and said that "the uprising of the Palestinian people against the Israeli occupation since 8 December 1987 is a form of legitimate resistance."[47]

The government responded quickly and harshly to suppress the uprising. The IDF arrested several thousand Palestine Arabs, some on specific charges, but most under the administrative detention procedures that did not require a criminal charge. To house the prisoners, it opened a major new prison camp and expanded others. The IDF reacted to demonstrations with live fire from high-velocity military weapons, causing many deaths. The UN Security Council "strongly deplored" the "opening of fire by the Israeli army, resulting in the killing and wounding of defenseless Palestinian civilians."[48]

In reaction to the international criticism of the shootings—in particular from the United States[49]—the government announced a policy of summary physical beatings to be administered by the IDF at the site of demonstrations.[50] Defense Minister Itzhak Rabin said that the purpose was to instill fear in the population.[51] Implementing this policy, IDF soldiers broke the hands or arms of many demonstrators with methodically directed blows, according to reports by many physicians. In addition to beating persons at the site of demonstrations, the IDF rounded up at their homes youths living near the scene of confrontations, took them to remote areas, and beat them. The uprising continued into a second year, and shooting deaths of Arabs by the IDF continued, the number of fatalities exceeding five hundred.

In trying to suppress the uprising the IDF used many of the same tactics employed in the West Bank and Gaza Strip since 1967 to suppress resistance, but it applied them more rigorously. It imposed curfews on localities of demonstrations, extending at times for weeks. With some curfews it prevented residents from leaving their houses, while with others it let them circulate locally but prohibited them from leaving their towns. The curfews kept farmers in some areas from harvesting crops that were rotting in their fields and kept Palestine Arabs from getting basic provisions. The UN Relief and Works Agency reported that IDF soldiers were seen confiscating food from Palestine Arabs who broke the curfew to take food to others, and the soldiers then destroyed the food on the spot.[52]

Soon after the uprising started the government began to expel persons it considered uprising leaders. The United States protested these expulsions as a violation of Article 49 of the Geneva Convention,[53] as did the European Economic Community[54] and the UN Security Council.[55] The United States, explaining its vote in the Security Council, said that Article 49 prohibits all expulsions of residents of occupied territory.[56]

In response to the desire for independence that came out of the uprising, Jordan renounced its claim to the West Bank. The Palestine Arabs began to lay plans for establishing an independent West Bank – Gaza state. In reaction, Israel banned organizations deemed to be promoting the declaration of statehood. These were the same organizations that provided many basic services to the population during the uprising. It closed schools and universities, and when teachers and parents organized classes for children outside regular buildings, it prohibited them.

Many of the methods Israel used to suppress the uprising were criticized by UN bodies as contrary to the Palestinians' right to self-determination, to their rights under the law of belligerent occupation, and to human rights norms. The situation led the United States, which had in earlier years been mild in its criticism of Israel's occupation practices, to issue a strong condemnation of many of Israel's policies.[57] The UN Human Rights Commission, using the Geneva Convention's provision that certain violations of humanitarian law are "grave breaches" meriting criminal punishment for perpetrators, found a number of Israel's practices during the uprising to constitute "war crimes." It included physical and psychological torture of Palestinian detainees and their subjection to improper and inhuman treatment; the imposition of collective punishment on towns, villages, and camps; the administrative detention of thousands of Palestinians; the expulsion of Palestinian citizens; the confiscation of Palestinian property; and the raiding and demolition of Palestinian houses.[58]

Part Five

Resolution of the

Palestine-Israel Conflict

28

Statehood in the Making: Palestine Declares Independence

The Palestine National Council . . . hereby proclaims the establishment of the State of Palestine. —Declaration of Independence, 1988

Israel's occupation of Gaza and the West Bank led the Palestinians to alter their priorities. As it became clear that the occupation would not end quickly, the Palestinians made Israel's withdrawal from Gaza and the West Bank a central demand. The same dynamic was operating on Egypt. Israel's occupation of Sinai was prompting Egypt to focus on an Israeli withdrawal from that piece of territory and to deemphasize its earlier primary demand that related to self-determination for the Palestinians. In return for withdrawing from Sinai, Israel would be able, in 1978, to wrest diplomatic recognition from Egypt.

With the Palestinians, Israel's aim, similarly, was to gain recognition as a state, and of its hold over the territory it took in 1948. By holding the Gaza Strip and West Bank, Israel was forcing the Palestinians to focus on reversing that occupation, rather than occupation of the 1948 territory. On two basic issues, the Palestinian attitude evolved during the 1970s, as the Palestinians sought to salvage some national existence, even at the expense of their full aspirations. One issue was the Jews who had migrated to Palestine under British auspices.

The Palestine Arabs considered Jews whose families had long resided in Palestine to be Palestinians, but they did not so regard Jews who came as part of the project to establish a Jewish state. The Palestine National Covenant recited: "Jews who were living permanently in Palestine until the beginning of the Zionist invasion will be considered Palestinians."[1] The Balfour Declaration of 1917 was taken as the beginning of the "Zionist invasion," so Jews migrating to

Palestine after that time would have to leave. "How can one peacefully coexist," a Palestine Arab asked, "with people occupying one's own town and plowing one's own field?"[2]

By the early 1970s, however, Fatah was calling for a "democratic secular state" in a Palestine to be inhabited by all then residing there, plus those displaced Palestine Arabs who would choose to return.[3] Fatah did not in principle view the post-Balfour settlers as entitled to remain but offered the proposal as a compromise.[4] "We are willing," it was said in explanation, "to grant an equal right to those who have no right and we are willing to live on the basis of equality with those who made us exiled and dispersed us."[5] It was proposed at the time to amend the Palestine National Covenant to conform to this view, but the amendment failed because of differences over the nature of the "democratic secular state."[6]

In tandem with this concession on residency rights came the beginning of a concession on territory. In 1974 the Palestine National Council declared as its aim to liberate any portion of Palestinian soil it could wrest from Israel, and to administer that piece of territory under the "national authority of the people."[7] In 1977 the council clarified that this "national authority" was to be a state that would exist alongside Israel.[8] The council did not disavow its aim of a democratic secular state in all Palestine but relegated it to a future time. First a Palestine state would be set up alongside Israel, and if the two could coexist peacefully they might eventually be able to merge into a single state.[9]

The Palestinian concessions came as prospects emerged for United Nations involvement that might lead to a settlement. Augmented by states recently emerging from colonialism, the United Nations, and in particular its General Assembly, took the Palestine Arabs' claim of self-determination seriously.[10] In 1974 the General Assembly invited the PLO to "participate as an observer in the sessions and the work of all international conferences convened under the auspices of the General Assembly in the capacity of observer."[11] The assembly said that the Palestinian people were "a principal party in the establishment of a just and lasting peace in the Middle East."[12]

Recently independent states viewed Israel as part of the colonialism they had overthrown. They were angered by Israel's political and financial collaboration with South Africa, then under apartheid. In

1973 the UN General Assembly condemned "the unholy alliance between Portuguese colonialism, South African racism, zionism and Israeli imperialism."[13] In a resolution on racial discrimination in 1975, the assembly quoted a resolution of the Organization of African Unity "that the racist régime in occupied Palestine and the racist régimes in Zimbabwe and South Africa have a common imperialist origin, forming a whole and having the same racist structure and being organically linked in their policy aimed at repression of the dignity and integrity of the human being." The assembly referred as well to a statement by the Non-Aligned Countries that "condemned zionism as a threat to world peace and security and called upon all countries to oppose this racist and imperialist ideology." With those quotations as a preface, the General Assembly proclaimed "that zionism is a form of racism and racial discrimination."[14]

This characterization called Israel's formation and existence into question. Jeane Kirkpatrick, the former U.S. ambassador to the United Nations, commented: "It is a short step from the proposition that Zionism is racism to the proposition that the State of Israel is based on aggression." She said: "Adoption of this resolution was tantamount to declaring Israel an illegitimate state based on an illegitimate philosophy." Zionism, she said, "is the national movement on which Israel is based. When the UN majority declared Zionism is racism, it declared immoral the foundations of Israel."[15]

As it declared Zionism to be racist, the UN General Assembly established infrastructure within the UN to promote Palestinian self-determination. A Committee on the Exercise of the Inalienable Rights of the Palestinian People would pursue a political solution to the conflict.[16] A Special Unit on Palestinian Rights was set up in the UN Secretariat to assist the committee.[17] Later the unit was upgraded as a division of the secretariat.[18]

In 1983 the General Assembly concretized a proposal for an end to the conflict. It called for an international conference based on a Palestinian right of return to home areas inside Israel, a right to self-determination, and a right to establish a state in Palestine. Israel would withdraw from the territories it took in 1967, including Jerusalem, leaving two states in Palestine. The PLO would represent the Palestinian people in negotiations.[19]

After its expulsion from Beirut in 1982, the PLO saw that its chances of defeating Israel militarily were remote. The tactics of some PLO-affiliated groups of attacking Israeli civilians yielded no political dividend. The Palestine National Council welcomed the General Assembly's idea, which took an approach in line with the evolving Palestinian position.[20]

Most UN member states supported the idea of a conference. Israel did not, knowing it would be outnumbered by states insisting on proposals it sought to avoid. The United States sided with Israel. No conference was held, and no other steps toward a settlement followed. When in 1987 Palestinian frustration with the occupation erupted in the intifada, television cameras recorded brutality by the IDF. A Palestinian David was seen pitted against an Israeli Goliath. The Palestinians began to be regarded as the oppressed.

Buoyed by the goodwill generated by the intifada, the Palestine National Council in 1988 declared independence. The council called for a Palestine state.[21] Although the council did not specify borders, it said in a communiqué that multilateral negotiations, as contemplated by the UN General Assembly, should be based on UN Security Council Resolution 242. That reference suggested that the council contemplated a state in the Gaza Strip and West Bank, since Resolution 242 asks Israel to withdraw from those territories.

The PLO did what the logic of accepting Resolution 242 required. It said it no longer questioned Israel as a state. It also renounced the use of violence against Israeli civilians.[22] Modest rewards followed. Members of Israel's Knesset met publicly with Palestine National Council officials.[23] The United States opened communication with the PLO.[24]

Jordan made good on the promise it had made in 1950 not to stand in the way of Palestine. Renouncing sovereignty over the West Bank, in deference to the PLO, King Hussein said, "The independent Palestinian state will be established on the occupied Palestinian land after its liberation."[25] The PLO began to exercise limited governmental functions in the West Bank, even as Israel remained in occupation. The PLO took over from Jordan the paying of salaries of some civil servants. Local committees operating under the PLO began providing social services.[26]

Within months, eighty-nine states recognized Palestine as a

state.[27] The UN General Assembly enhanced the Palestinian presence at the UN. In line with the declaration of statehood, the assembly began referring to the entity enjoying observer status as "Palestine," rather than as the "Palestine Liberation Organization."[28]

The Palestinian Declaration of Independence cited two sources of legitimacy. It referred first to the Palestinian people's "inalienable rights in the land of its patrimony." It also referred to General Assembly Resolution 181 as providing "the conditions for international legitimacy that guarantees the right of the Palestinian Arab people to sovereignty on their homeland."

The reference to Resolution 181, relied upon as well by the Jewish Agency when it declared statehood in 1948, amounted to recognition of a Jewish state in Palestine. A political declaration issued by the council along with the Declaration of Independence referred to Israel, nonetheless, as "a fascist, racist, colonialist state based on the usurpation of the Palestinian land and on the annihilation of the Palestinian people."

As the Palestinian side moved in the direction of an accommodation with Israel, a contrary element entered the picture. In 1989 the United States clamped down on the migration of Soviet Jews to the United States, and by the thousands they began to enter Israel. The number soon reached half a million, substantially augmenting the Jewish component of Israel's population.

Israeli officials delighted at the political impact of having more Israelis. Mayor Teddy Kollek of Jerusalem proclaimed that Israel should "bring as many immigrants to the city as possible and make it an overwhelmingly Jewish city, so that [the Palestinians] will get it out of their heads that Jerusalem will not be Israel's capital."[29] In east Jerusalem, the Israeli development authority built apartment buildings to settle the new arrivals.[30]

Another negative development for the Palestinians was that the goodwill generated by the intifada was soon squandered. In 1990, when Iraq occupied Kuwait, the United States prepared to invade Iraq, proclaiming that the occupation of foreign territory could not stand. Palestinians, relating the Iraq-Kuwait situation to their own, viewed the United States as following a double standard, dealing with occupation only when its interests were at stake. Chairman Arafat did not join in the denunciation of Iraq that came from other world leaders.[31] The PLO was perceived as siding with Iraq. The PLO put itself at odds not only with the West, but with major Arab governments.

29

Oslo via Madrid:

A Turn to Peace?

It is time to put an end to decades of confrontation and conflict. — Declaration of Principles, 1993

The Iraq-Kuwait situation indirectly affected the dynamics of the Palestinian-Israeli conflict. The charges against the United States of a double standard put pressure on it to resolve the "other occupation." Still, the United States would not accede to a UN conference, because in such a context Israel might be pressured to respect the rights of the Palestinians. Instead, the United States promoted the idea of negotiation between the two parties alone, and without a prior understanding of rights to be protected. The United States organized a conference in Madrid to adopt this approach.[1] The result would be a Palestinian-Israeli agreement that presumably would be recognized by the international community.[2]

In a letter to the Palestinians, the United States made clear its view that the UN should keep hands off the anticipated bilateral process: "Since it is in the interest of all parties for this process to succeed, while this process is actively ongoing, the United States will not support a competing or parallel process in the United Nations Security Council."[3] The United States did not want the Security Council criticizing Israel for rights violations.

As part of its diplomatic offensive, the United States promoted repeal of the resolution passed in 1975 that called Zionism racist. Against the fears of Arab governments that nullifying the resolution would encourage Israel to become more intransigent, U.S. diplomats argued that repeal would encourage Israel to participate meaningfully in the bilateral process sponsored by the United States. With the USSR departing from the world scene, eastern European governments were amenable to the U.S. government's position.[4] The General Assembly voted, tersely, "to revoke the determination contained in its resolution 3379 . . . of 10 November 1975."[5]

Israel enjoyed a preponderance of power on the ground and the political and financial backing of the United States. The Palestinians had only youths hurling stones. With the international community sidelined, Israel might reject a Palestine state, keep Israeli settlers in place, and refuse to repatriate the displaced Palestinians. The Palestinians feared that the United States was giving Israel a free hand to force its entire agenda upon them.

Despite its enthusiasm for bilateral talks, the United States was unwilling to have the PLO as the interlocutor on the Palestinian side. Virtually the entire international community viewed the PLO as the representative of the Palestinian people, but Israel refused to deal with it, and the United States deferred to Israel's wishes. Only Palestinians participating as individuals would be allowed to negotiate.

It was not clear on what basis a group of individuals could make a commitment for the Palestinian people. From the political perspective, the exclusion of the PLO potentially set back the Palestinian cause. Nonetheless, the PLO did not try to prevent the talks. The Palestinians who participated said they would act under PLO direction. Proceeding on this basis, the Palestinian negotiators entered talks in Washington in 1991, under the auspices of the U.S. Department of State. As they formulated negotiating positions, the Palestinian negotiators conferred with the PLO leadership, then based in Tunis.

The Palestinian negotiators were concerned not only about what they might negotiate with Israel, but as well about what was occurring on the ground. The upsurge in settlement activity resulting from the Soviet immigration might preempt the outcome of the negotiations over settlements. The Palestinian negotiators took the position with Israel that before serious talks on any topic could begin, Israel must freeze the construction of settlements.[6] Israel was not willing to stop the settlement building. The talks languished. Settlement continued. The Labor Party government that came into office in Israel in 1992 said it would build less expansively, and it reduced the financial incentives given to settlers.[7] Nonetheless, it continued construction at significant levels.[8] A group of Israelis who opposed the settlements challenged them in the Supreme Court of Israel, but the court declined to rule on what it considered a political issue.[9]

While the Washington talks faltered, secret discussion began in Oslo between Israel and the PLO. Despite its oft-stated refusal to deal with the PLO, Israel had reasons to do so. If the PLO could be convinced to say that Israel had a right to exist, more Arab governments might recognize it. Acceptance in the region was a key Israeli objective. At the practical level, Israel was having trouble maintaining order in the Palestinian territories. If it could turn control over to the PLO, Israel could be relieved of policing and thus avoid the bad press and domestic criticism over its methods in suppressing the Palestinian intifada.[10]

For the PLO, a dialogue with Israel gave it a central role at a time when the organization's fortunes were low, its military option expended. Israel's willingness to talk with the PLO suggested that Israel might be prepared to compromise on major issues.

In contrast to the position taken by the Palestinian negotiators in Washington, the PLO did not insist that Israel agree to freeze settlements. Israel would turn over partial control in Gaza and the West Bank to the PLO, and the two parties would begin negotiating within three years about borders, Jerusalem, refugees, settlements, and security arrangements. These agreements were recorded in a Declaration of Principles, which the parties signed at a ceremony in Washington in September 1993.[11]

Simultaneously, each side recognized the other. Prime Minister Itzhak Rabin sent Chairman Yassir Arafat a letter reciting, "Israel has decided to recognize the PLO as the representative of the Palestinian people." Arafat sent Rabin a letter reciting, "The PLO recognizes the right of the State of Israel to exist in peace and security."[12]

The declaration recited that the parties would negotiate on the basis of UN Security Council Resolution 242. The PLO's concern that Resolution 242 regarded the Palestinians only as individuals, but not as an entity with territorial rights, was addressed by Rabin's recognition of the PLO, and by the declaration's reference to borders as a matter to be negotiated. Negotiating borders implied a Palestine state alongside Israel.

Settlement activity provided the first indication that the Declaration of Principles would not lead to an easy final agreement. Israel continued to expand its settlements. In 1995 it announced that it would expropriate new tracts of land in east Jerusalem to build housing for Jews. The UN Security Council met on the matter. The delegate from the United Kingdom said that Israel should "refrain from taking actions which seek to change the status quo on this most sensitive of all issues before the conclusion of the final-status negotiations."[13] Delegates of Russia, Indonesia, Italy, and France all expressed concern that the land seizures were intended to preempt the Palestinian claim to east Jerusalem.[14]

The PLO viewed this settlement activity as inconsistent with the Declaration of Principles for the same reason. It demanded "cessation of all actions that may preempt negotiations on the final settlement, including the termination of all colonial settlement activities, whether old or new."[15] Although the Declaration of Principles did not forbid new settlements, under international law parties must fulfill treaty obligations in good faith. A state that agrees to resolve a contentious issue may not take action that renders the issue more intractable.[16]

In 1997 Israel announced yet another major settlement initiative. It would construct 6,500 units of housing for Jews in a section of east Jerusalem called Jebel Abu Ghneim. The projected settlement, to be named Har Homa, was problematic not only for the land it would take and the new population it would bring into east Jerusalem but for its location. Har Homa would complete a string of settlements between east Jerusalem and the rest of the West Bank, thus cutting east Jerusalem's Arabs off from the rest of the West Bank.

Har Homa would also strengthen Israel's claim to sovereignty over east Jerusalem. Providing justification for the fear that settlements would preempt an agreement, Israel's minister of internal security, Avigdor Kahalani, said that an aim of the new construction was to "make unequivocally clear that Jerusalem is the Jewish capital, and we can build within its municipal boundaries."[17]

The UN Security Council met. A European-sponsored resolution was proposed to condemn Israel's settlement plan as illegal, and as a "major obstacle to peace." Fourteen of the Council's fifteen members voted in favor of the draft resolution, but the United States vetoed.[18] The General Assembly then took up the matter and adopted the failed Security Council resolution as its own. This resolution asked Israel "to refrain from all actions or measures, including settlement activities, which alter the facts on the ground, preempting the final status negotiations, and having negative implications for the Middle East Peace Process."[19]

When Israel began construction of Har Homa, yet another draft resolution was proposed in the Security Council, to demand that Israel "immediately cease construction of the Jebel Abu Ghneim settlement in East Jerusalem, as well as all other Israeli settlement activities in the occupied territories." Thirteen states voted in favor, but again the United States vetoed.[20]

In casting vetoes, the United States did not view the construction as lawful. Rather, in line with its emphasis on the bilateral negotiation process, it said that the UN was not the "proper forum." As viewed by other UN member states, however, the settlements threatened a peace arrangement and thus were very much the concern of the UN. The UN General Assembly condemned the Har Homa construction and asked states not to give aid to Israel that might be used for it.[21]

When by mid-1997 no action had been taken by Israel to stop construction of Har Homa, the General Assembly met again in special session. This time it asked states to prevent even private parties from involvement in Israel's settlement construction. It also called on Israel to provide information on goods produced in its settlements, so that other states might determine if their nationals were involved.[22]

To provide secure access to settlements, Israel began building connector roads, confiscating more of the Palestinians' land for the purpose. The Palestinians increasingly were boxed into small parcels of territory.

30

Talks Fail:

The Sword Replaces the Pen

the daily humiliation of Palestinians —UN Committee on the Rights of the
Child

Settlements were not the only issue on which Israel showed reluc-
tance. It stated a negative position on a repatriation of displaced Palestinians. Prime Minister Benjamin Netanyahu, speaking in anticipation of negotiations with the PLO, said that Israel would oppose
"the right of return of Arab populations to any part of the Land of
Israel west of the Jordan River."[1] Netanyahu thus opposed not only a
repatriation to Israel, but even Palestinian immigration to the projected Palestine state.

European states were alarmed at Israel's intransigence, which
was seen as being at odds with the commitment in the Declaration of
Principles to seek a peace settlement. Europe, a major export market
for Israel, pressured Israel in the economic realm. In 1995 the European Union concluded with Israel an agreement like others it has
with non-European states, to allow for reduced tariffs on their products entering Europe. Reduced tariffs would apply to products of Israeli origin.[2]

In identifying products, Israel included, as Israeli-produced, items
from its settlements in the Palestinian territories. The European
Commission, the executive arm of the European Union, interpreted
the agreement as excluding goods from Gaza and the West Bank, since
they are not territory of Israel. It asked Israel to specify which products had their origin in Israel, and which in the occupied territories.
Israel refused.[3] It said that the EU was trying "to prejudge Israel's
borders, before this problem is duly settled in Israel's talks with its
neighbours."[4] This reply suggested that Israel might be planning to

keep Gaza and the West Bank. The European Commission began to make its own determinations about the true origin of goods marked "made in Israel" and asked member states not to import products from Israeli settlements.[5]

Sympathy for the PLO grew at the United Nations as Israel showed itself unwilling to deal in good faith with the issues to be resolved. In 1998 the General Assembly upgraded Palestine's observer status, giving it additional privileges at the UN. The assembly recited that its aim was to contribute to "the achievement of the inalienable rights of the Palestinian people."[6]

In 1999 Israel and the PLO finally began the negotiations anticipated by the Declaration of Principles. Prospects for an agreement were not great. The PLO considered that it had made its compromise with Israel by agreeing to forgo a claim to territory in the portion of Palestine that the Jewish Agency took in 1948. Israel had taken not only the 53 percent proposed by the UN General Assembly, but additional land that gave it 78 percent of Palestine. Now the PLO was prepared to let Israel keep this land. From the PLO's perspective, all that remained for Israel was to agree to pull out of Gaza and the West Bank, including east Jerusalem, remove its settlers, and allow the Palestinians displaced in 1948 to return. The PLO would be settling for territory comprising only 22 percent of mandate Palestine.

Israel's expectations were less clear. Moreover, it was not obvious that there was a unified Israeli expectation. The left was more inclined than the right to withdraw from Gaza and the West Bank. Jerusalem was sought as appertaining to Israel, including east Jerusalem, which by then had a population of Jews equal to the population of Arabs. As for the displaced Palestinians, no significant political force in Israel was willing to consider a repatriation. It was hoped that the Palestinians, by taking territory for a state, would forgo their claim of a right to return to home areas within Israel. If Israel was to be a Jewish state, and Palestine a Palestinian state, then a repatriation of Arabs to Israel seemed to Israelis to be inconsistent.

After desultory negotiation in the winter of 1999–2000, Israel and the PLO accepted an invitation from President Bill Clinton to meet at the presidential retreat at Camp David, Maryland. The two parties talked, but to little end. Israel demanded that it be allowed to keep most settlers in place and retain control of the borders. On Jerusalem, it said the Palestinians could control Arab neighborhoods, a proposal that would leave Jerusalem in Israeli hands. Israel rejected a repatriation of the displaced.[7]

Israel's refusal to acknowledge Palestinian rights led the Palestinian public to despair over a negotiated peace. Rioting ensued when Israel sent police to accompany Ariel Sharon and others on a visit to the Muslim holy site Haram al-Sharif in Jerusalem, as a demonstration of Israel's claim to east Jerusalem. A new intifada followed. Oslo had brought the Palestinians only more Israeli settlers. This intifada involved not merely youths hurling stones but organized armed resistance. The situation on the ground deteriorated. Ariel Sharon, by now prime minister, declared the Oslo process "dead" and Arafat "irrelevant." A last attempt at negotiating was made in January 2001, but again without result.

Palestinian groups began suicide bombings against civilians inside Israel. Israel re-occupied West Bank towns it had allowed the PLO to administer. The UN Security Council asked Israel to withdraw but did nothing to enforce its call.[8] The IDF assassinated Palestinian resistance figures, firing missiles from helicopters that sometimes hit the intended target, and sometimes hit bystanders.

Daily life for the Palestinians in the occupied territories reached a new low. IDF checkpoints popped up all over, making it even less possible than before for Palestinians to get to their jobs, to market their products, or to have access to health care.

The United States backed Sharon's refusal to negotiate with Arafat, and in 2003 a Palestinian position of prime minister was created to bring a new figure into the picture for possible negotiations.

Although the United Nations did nothing to turn this situation around, its agencies that were not hamstrung by the veto power examined what was occurring and reported on it. As the intifada and reprisals proceeded, the UN Commission on Human Rights dispatched fact-finding missions that visited the Palestinian territories and castigated Israel for abusing the Palestinians.[9]

Treaty-monitoring committees also criticized Israel. In the 1990s Israel ratified human rights treaties that required it to report periodically to these committees. When Israel filed reports, it included information on its human rights performance only in its own territory, but not in Gaza or the West Bank. Israel took the position that provisions in these treaties that describe the scope of a state's obligations do not require a state to apply them outside its own sovereign territory. The committees, citing the same provisions, replied that Israel's obligations under these treaties extend to non-Israeli territory it occupies. Examining Israel, these committees pressed it for information about its practices in Gaza and the West Bank.[10]

The Human Rights Committee, which monitors the International Covenant on Civil and Political Rights, found Israel in violation for the assassination of opposition figures, for demolishing Palestinian houses as a punishment, for using physical force in interrogating suspects, and for building a security barrier that the committee said would disrupt access to health care and to water sources.[11]

The Committee on the Rights of the Child, which monitors the Convention on the Rights of the Child, addressed the issue of violence by Palestinians. It noted "continuing acts of terror on both sides, especially the deliberate and indiscriminate targeting and killing of Israeli civilians, including children, by Palestinian suicide bombers." But the committee found that Israel's own actions were at the root of this violence: "the committee recognizes that the illegal occupation of Palestinian territory, the bombing of civilian areas, extrajudicial killings, the disproportionate use of force by the Israeli Defence Forces, the demolition of homes, the destruction of infrastructure, mobility restrictions and the daily humiliation of Palestinians continue to contribute to the cycle of violence."[12] Evaluations by these committees did not lead to visible change, but they brought a new level of informed criticism of Israel.

When the intifada erupted in Gaza and the West Bank in 2000, many Israeli Arabs took to the streets in support. Israeli Arabs had remained on the sidelines during the intifada of 1987. Their new activism shocked the Israeli government. Prime Minister Ariel Sharon, calling them disloyal, suggested that if a Palestine state were established, the Israeli Arabs should go there. This hint at a new expulsion only soured further the prospects for negotiation.

Israel had taken steps in the 1990s to relieve discrimination against Israeli Arabs. Yet the basic pillars of inequality remained: the Law of Return, the Nationality Law, and the land tenure system.

The Committee on Economic, Social and Cultural Rights, which monitors the International Covenant on Economic, Social and Cultural Rights, noted in 2003 "the continuing difference in treatment between Jews and non-Jews, in particular Arab and Bedouin communities, with regard to their enjoyment of economic, social and cultural rights." It said that an "excessive emphasis upon the State as a 'Jewish State' encourages discrimination and accords a second-class status to its non-Jewish citizens."[13]

The situation of internally displaced Israeli Arabs remains unresolved. As we saw in chapter 13, Arabs who were forced out of their homes in 1948 but remained in Israel were not permitted to reoccupy their home areas. Many lived in squalid circumstances in new makeshift towns. They pressed the government to repatriate them, but Israel continued to refuse.

31

Jerusalem and the Settlements:

Who Should Stay?

Negotiations shall cover . . . Jerusalem. —Declaration of Principles, 1993

The issues identified in the Declaration of Principles of 1993 still cry out for resolution. Until that occurs, unrest is likely to flare from time to time. Palestinians will continue to live in impossible circumstances. Israelis will live in fear of violence against them.

In this conundrum no single territorial sector is more contested than Jerusalem, which both sides claim as their capital. "Jerusalem, complete and united" is "the capital of Israel," declares an Israeli statute.[1] The phrase "complete and united" means the western and eastern sectors, the eastern sector in the boundaries that Israel extended in 1967 farther into the West Bank. An Israeli court has read the statute as an assertion of sovereignty over both sectors.[2]

The Palestinian claim is asserted no less strongly. When the Palestine National Council issued its call for independence in 1988, it declared "the establishment of the State of Palestine in the land of Palestine with its capital in Jerusalem."[3] The claim for sovereignty in Jerusalem is part of the more general Palestinian claim to territory in Palestine, based on centuries-long occupation.[4]

The UN General Assembly's partition resolution of 1947 proposed that Jerusalem be placed under international administration.[5] Israel's prime legal claim to territory in Palestine was the partition resolution (see chapter 7), but since the resolution called for an internationalized Jerusalem, it provided Israel with no basis for sovereignty in west Jerusalem. West Jerusalem is almost entirely Jewish-populated, the absence of Arabs the result of their having been forced out in 1948 (see chapter 5).

Israel occupied west Jerusalem in 1948 and declared it Israel's capital in 1950 (see chapter 11).[6] Other states declined to move their embassies from Tel Aviv to west Jerusalem, however. They viewed sovereignty over Jerusalem as unresolved and feared that moving their embassies to west Jerusalem would bolster Israel's claim. Their refusal to move their embassies bespoke rejection of Israel's claim.

In 1967 the UN Security Council in Resolution 242 asked Israel to withdraw from territory that it occupied in that year. This call was read by some as an implicit recognition of Israeli sovereignty in the territory it held before June 1967 (see chapter 23), which of course includes west Jerusalem. There is no indication, however, that the Security Council implicitly recognized Israeli rights over west Jerusalem. Resolution 242, only a few paragraphs in length, made no attempt to deal with the many outstanding political and territorial issues. After 1967 other states kept their embassies in Tel Aviv, a fact that suggests that they did not view Resolution 242 as changing the picture.

While Israel has claimed all of Jerusalem as an Israeli city, the PLO, in the proposals it has made, has been more modest, even though it has the stronger legal claim to the city, in its entirety. It has proposed variously an east-west division of Jerusalem or shared sovereignty over the entire city. Moreover, as we will see in the next chapter, it insists on repatriation of the Palestine Arabs displaced in 1948, which includes the thousands displaced from west Jerusalem.

In the discussion leading to the adoption of Resolution 242, there was uncertainty over how to define the territory from which Israel must withdraw. The armistice line drawn in 1949 from which Israel started during the June 1967 war represented the positions of Israeli and Jordanian forces at the time the armistice was agreed. It was not intended at the time as an international border. Neither Jordan nor Israel viewed it as such. The diplomats in 1967 were reluctant to enshrine that line, for the first time, as a border. A border might be agreed upon in future that would involve trading villages on one side of the line for villages on the other. At the same time, the diplomats were clear that Israel could not lawfully retain the territory it took in June 1967.[7]

The United Nations viewed east Jerusalem as part of the territory under Israel's occupation. When Israel declared its legislation to apply in east Jerusalem, the United Nations condemned this measure as tantamount to annexation, saying that Israel held east Jerusalem only as a belligerent occupant.[8] When Israel declared the entirety of Jerusalem its capital,[9] the Security Council and General Assembly each pronounced the action unlawful.[10] The Security Council "reaffirm[ed] that acquisition of territory by force is inadmissible," and "reaffirm[ed] the overriding necessity to end the prolonged occupation of Arab territories occupied by Israel since 1967, including Jerusalem."[11] These two reaffirmations read as an interpretation by the Security Council of Resolution 242. They make clear that east Jerusalem is included in the territory from which Israel must withdraw.

The General Assembly has also been precise on Israel's obligation to withdraw from east Jerusalem. It stated "that the acquisition of territory by force is inadmissible under the Charter of the United Nations," and that "Israel must withdraw unconditionally from all the Palestinian and other Arab territories occupied by Israel since 1967, including Jerusalem."[12]

In 1990 Israel asserted its claim to east Jerusalem in the midst of a controversy with the UN. After a shooting incident in east Jerusalem in which Israeli police killed seventeen Palestinians, the UN Security Council asked the UN secretary-general to propose appropriate measures in response.[13] The secretary-general suggested sending investigators. Israel objected, on the grounds that east Jerusalem was part of its sovereign territory, and that the UN had no right to send investigators without its permission. It told the secretary-general: "Jerusalem is not, in any part, 'occupied territory'; it is the sovereign capital of the State of Israel. Therefore, there is no room for any involvement on the part of the United Nations in any matter relating to Jerusalem."[14] The Security Council backed off sending investigators but expressed "alarm" at Israel's refusal.[15]

East Jerusalem was almost entirely Arab-populated until 1967. By 2004, 175,000 Jews had moved into east Jerusalem. An Israeli civil rights organization charged that Israel sought "a demographic and geographic reality that will preempt every future effort to question Israeli sovereignty in East Jerusalem."[16]

As Israel brought in more Israelis to settle in east Jerusalem, it removed many Arabs by a process of attrition. Israel had offered Israeli citizenship to east Jerusalemites after 1967, but few accepted, because to do so would have given credence to Israel's claim of sovereignty. Israel devised a legal status for the east Jerusalem Arabs that allowed it to terminate their residency rights. It rationalized that since, by its view, east Jerusalem was part of Israel, and since the east Jerusalem Arabs did not opt for Israeli citizenship, they were "permanent residents" of Israel. By Israel's administrative regulations, such persons who transferred their "center of life" abroad would lose the status of "permanent resident" of Israel and thus forfeit the right to reside in east Jerusalem.[17]

These regulations violated the law of belligerent occupation, under which an occupant must respect the status of the inhabitants it finds. That includes their status as citizens of the territory. Israel is obligated to respect the status of east Jerusalem Arabs as lawful inhabitants, with rights that are not forfeited by temporary residence abroad. Nonetheless, thousands of east Jerusalem Arabs who after 1967 went abroad for work or study were deprived by Israel of their right to reside in the city. By the mid 1990s, as a result both of pushing Arabs out and bringing Israeli Jews in, the number of Jews living in east Jerusalem inched above the number of Arabs.

As for Israel's settlers in east Jerusalem, their presence violates Israel's obligations as a belligerent occupant. As we saw in chapter 24, transferring civilians into occupied territory is prohibited to an occupant. As a result, the Israelis have no right to reside in east Jerusalem, absent agreement by Palestine.

By 2004 settlers in Gaza and the West Bank, outside east Jerusalem, numbered 225,000. Like the settlers in east Jerusalem, they have no right to remain. They could, in principle, apply to the Palestine government for naturalization. Palestine would not be required to grant them the right to remain, however. By international practice, persons who settle during an occupation acquire no rights against the sovereign. In 1938 Germany occupied and annexed Austria, and Germans settled in Austria. When Austria in 1945 again began to function as a state, it adopted a nationality law that extended Austrian nationality only to those who held it in 1938, plus their descendants.[18]

Evacuation would presumably accompany a peace agreement. Israel arranged for evacuation of settlers once before, when it withdrew from the Sinai Peninsula. After Israel occupied Sinai during the 1967 war, Israeli civilians began to establish settlements there. In the Camp David treaty of 1979 with Egypt, Israel agreed to a "complete withdrawal of all its armed forces and civilians from the Sinai not later than three years from the date of exchange of instruments of ratification of this Treaty."[19]

Evacuation of the settlers is the appropriate solution. As a matter of human rights law, the settlers must be treated humanely.[20] Israel evacuated its settlers from the Sinai without violence, despite the objections of settlers to moving.[21] Israel compensated the Sinai settlers in amounts ranging from $132,000 to $437,500 per family.[22] The issue of compensating Gaza Strip and West Bank settlers for leaving has been publicly discussed in Israel.[23] Members of the Knesset have called on the government to allocate funds for this purpose.[24]

Israel's evacuation of settlers from the Sinai was consistent with international practice. Nationals of an occupying power who settle in occupied territory are not entitled to remain when the occupation ends. Italians who settled in territory occupied by Italy during World War II were not entitled to the nationality of the states in question, after Italy's withdrawal at the end of the war. The postwar peace treaty required states from whose territory Italy withdrew to extend nationality to resident Italians, but only to those who were domiciled there as of June 10, 1940, the date on which Italy declared war on France and Great Britain.[25] This limitation excluded Italians who entered under Italian occupation.

Upon a withdrawal, the rights of Palestinians whose land was taken for settlements must be addressed. Israel took not title to the land but possession. The taking of possession violated the rules of belligerent occupation, since an occupant may not use occupied land to settle civilians. Palestinian landowners are entitled both to restoration of their land and to compensation for the time they were excluded.

When an occupant withdraws, any land it has occupied typically reverts to its owner. The compensation issue was addressed by the European Court of Human Rights, when Turkey, after occupying northern Cyprus in 1974, took over land of displaced Greeks. A Greek Cypriot woman who was forbidden access to her land in northern Cyprus claimed compensation from Turkey for the profit she could have gained from her land. Turkey refused to pay. The court ruled in her favor and ordered Turkey to compensate her.[26]

32

The Displaced:

Where Will They Go?

Negotiations shall cover . . . refugees. —Declaration of Principles, 1993

Perhaps the most delicate issue to be negotiated is the status of the Palestinian Arabs displaced in 1948 out of the territory that the Jewish Agency occupied. The displaced and their descendants claim a right to return to their home areas. It is unclear how many would choose repatriation if it were offered.

Israel denies that a state in its situation is obliged to repatriate. In its view the displaced left voluntarily and thereby forfeited their rights. Moreover, Israel disputes that any right of repatriation for wartime displaced persons can be found in customary international law, in particular when a new state comes into being in the territory.

Palestine argues for a right of repatriation for the wartime displaced, a right it finds in customary international law, applicable to the displaced Palestinians regardless of their reason for departing, although the voluntariness of their departure is denied. Israel's appearance as a new state does not in the Palestinian view negate a right of repatriation.

In direct dialogue between the parties during 1999–2000, there was little movement from their polar-opposite positions. The Palestinian view starts from the generally accepted proposition that a state may not exclude nationals who are, for whatever reason, resident abroad but who seek to return.[1] Other states are under no obligation to accept a non-national permanently. As an incident of a state's control over its own territory, it may demand that the state of origin repatriate its own nationals.

Additionally, the displaced person has a claim for repatriation, as a matter of personal rights. "Everyone has the right to leave any country, including his own," proclaims the Universal Declaration of Human Rights, "and to return to his country."[2] When a treaty, the International Covenant on Civil and Political Rights, was drafted to implement the Universal Declaration, comparable language was used: "no one shall be arbitrarily deprived of the right to enter his own country."[3]

Israel defined Israeli nationality in a way that excluded the Palestinians displaced in 1948 (see chapter 17). An Israeli lawyer has argued that since Israel does not recognize the nationality of these persons, they have no right to return: "the right [of repatriation] probably belongs only to nationals of the State, and at most to permanent residents. The Palestinian Arab refugees have never been nationals or permanent residents of Israel."[4]

The Universal Declaration and International Covenant, however, both use the term "country" rather than "state of nationality," to make clear that the right of entry does not depend on whether the state holding the territory recognizes the person as a national. Anyone who was a national or habitually resident before a change in sovereignty is entitled to the nationality of the successor state.[5] A country's "population follows the change of sovereignty in matters of nationality."[6] Treaties of cession of territory routinely give inhabitants the nationality of the new sovereign, unless they refuse it.[7]

The right of individuals to reside in their home country was recognized in the law well before Israel came on the scene. In drafting a Convention on Nationality in 1930, a research team from Harvard Law School said: "those persons who were nationals of the first state become nationals of the successor state, unless in accordance with the provisions of its law they decline the nationality of the successor state."[8]

The rule requiring a new state to offer its nationality applies, said the research team, in particular when the new state acquires the territory through hostilities. The Harvard drafters said that this provision reflected customary law as of 1930.[9] A leading international lawyer wrote in 1941, to the same effect, that in customary international law: "The nationality of the predecessor state is lost and that of the successor state is acquired by such inhabitants of the ceded or annexed territory as were subjects of the superseded sovereign."[10]

A treaty between Greece and Turkey in 1923 is sometimes regarded as demonstrating that the will of inhabitants need not be
respected, and that it it is proper to move populations to avoid conflict between them. The treaty provided for an exchange of Greek
inhabitants of Turkey to Greece, and of Turkish inhabitants of Greece
to Turkey, without consideration of the desires of the individuals
involved.[11] The treaty was concluded, however, not on the basis of
the advisability of separating the two population groups but as a
matter of expediency. Turkey had unilaterally expelled Greeks who
were longtime residents of Turkey. Greece was unable to persuade
Turkey to repatriate them.

The treaty gave Greece a way of coping with this unlawful fait
accompli, by allowing Greece to expel Turks to free land on which
the expelled Greeks could make a living. The expulsion by Turkey
was regarded as unlawful.[12] Lord Curzon said of the treaty that the
compulsory transfer was "a thoroughly bad and vicious solution, for
which the world would pay a heavy penalty for a hundred years to
come."[13]

In 1948 the UN acted on the assumption that the displaced Palestinians had a right to return. The UN mediator for Palestine, Count
Folke Bernadotte (see chapter 10), recounted the horrors that befell
the Palestinians as they were forced out of their homes. Shortly before being assassinated, Bernadotte wrote in his progress report to the
UN that "it would be an offence against the principles of elemental
justice if these innocent victims of the conflict were denied the right
to return to their homes."[14]

A few months later, the UN General Assembly adopted a resolution reciting "that the refugees wishing to return to their homes and
live at peace with their neighbours should be permitted to do so at
the earliest practicable date" (see chapter 11).[15] The assembly set up a
Conciliation Commission for Palestine, to promote repatriation and
resolve other issues. The Commission pressed Israel for immediate
repatriation. When Israel balked, a commission member appointed
by the United States called Israel's refusal "morally reprehensible."[16]
The assembly thereafter repeated this demand on Israel year after
year.

Israel and Palestine spar about the meaning of this General Assembly resolution. Israel views it as a request only, since the General

Assembly does not have decision-making power. Palestine reads the resolution as a demand. It views the assembly's call for repatriation as a reflection of a customary norm of international law requiring repatriation of the wartime displaced. In the Palestinian view, the legal force of the call rests not on the call itself but on the underlying principle of law.

Israeli analysts point out that the resolution did not use the term "right" in regard to repatriation, but rather that it said that the refugees "should be permitted" to return. They cite this choice of terminology as meaning that repatriation was viewed merely as desirable.[17] By saying that the displaced "should" be permitted to return, however, the assembly was indicating what Israel should do to implement what the assembly viewed as a right. During the discussion in the General Assembly, China, for example, referred to "the rights of the Arab refugees to return to their homes."[18] Colombia said that "they should have the right to choose between receiving compensation or returning to their homes."[19] In resolutions in later years the General Assembly did use the term "right." In one resolution, it referred to "the inalienable right of the Palestinians to return to their homes and property from which they have been displaced and uprooted," and "call[ed] for their return."[20]

UN Security Council Resolution 242, which the parties took as a basis for the post-Oslo negotiations, calls for "a just settlement of the refugee problem," without using the term "right."[21] That phrasing is taken by Israeli analysts to mean that any settlement that is just will suffice, whether repatriation or some other resolution, perhaps resettlement in other countries.[22] "Just settlement," however, is more plausibly read to mean that which the United Nations had found since 1948 to be a just outcome for the displaced Palestinians, namely repatriation.[23]

Prime Minister Benjamin Netanyahu of Israel said that returning Palestinians might be a fifth column and a demographic threat to Israel as a Jewish state.[24] Whatever the validity of these concerns, they do not trump the right of return. Neither demographic balance nor military security justifies a refusal to repatriate. The states of temporary residence cannot be compelled to accept a new population because the state of origin desires a given ethnic balance or is experiencing security problems. Nor, on such grounds, can the human right of entry to one's country be limited. In UN practice calls on states to repatriate have been made, for example with regard to the territory of the former Yugoslavia in the 1990s, even where a military situation was tenuous, and where ethnic conflict was intense.[25] The UN High Commissioner for Refugees has promoted repatriation in the face of security concerns.[26]

When the repatriation clause was debated in the UN General Assembly in 1948, Guatemala moved to amend to require Israel to repatriate only "after the proclamation of peace by the contending parties in Palestine, including the Arab states."[27] Guatemala feared that Palestinians who returned before a peace agreement "would not obey the Government," and that "their return could only create new difficulties and bloodshed."[28] Israel applauded Guatemala's proposal.[29]

The proposal was rejected.[30] The United Kingdom replied, "There were minorities in many countries which disputed the rights of their Governments or indeed of their State to exist." The United Kingdom did not think "that such minorities should be driven out as refugees into other countries because of differences of political opinion with the Governments of the countries in which they lived."[31]

The United States "could not accept the proclamation of peace as a prerequisite for the return of refugees." "These unfortunate people," it said, meaning the displaced, "should not be made pawns in the negotiations for a final settlement."[32]

The view of the General Assembly thus was that under international law, Israel must repatriate the displaced Palestinians, and that repatriation could not be put off to the time of an eventual peace agreement. After Oslo, with a peace agreement to be negotiated, Israel continued to refuse to consider repatriation. No longer able to argue that the issue should be deferred until a peace agreement, it fell back on demographics and physical security.

As a legal matter, the repatriation issue involves both the individual rights of each displaced person and a collective right of the Palestinians as a people. The UN General Assembly has referred to the repatriation as a right in both senses.

Repatriation should, to be sure, be addressed by the governments, as contemplated by the Declaration of Principles of 1993. That is how the matter has been handled in other conflict situations. The agreement that ended the hostilities in Bosnia provides: "All refugees and displaced persons have the right freely to return to their homes of origin. . . . The Parties confirm that they will accept the return of such persons who have left their territory, including those who have been accorded temporary protection by third countries."[33] The right was that of individuals, but the negotiation was done at the governmental level.

The PLO has indicated that because the right of return is an individual right, it is constrained in what it can concede to Israel. Were the PLO to concede rights that adhere to individuals, the right of the individuals would not be extinguished but could still be pursued.

The absence of a role in the negotiations for the international community reduces the likelihood that a provision calling for the repatriation of the displaced will be written into a peace agreement. In other conflict situations, where there has been an outflow of persons, the international community typically views repatriation as a basic element of a peace arrangement. A peace settlement that excludes the displaced leaves a major issue unresolved.

Repatriation after the passage of time presents practical difficulty. However, it is not impossible. In 1995 Lennart Meri, president of Estonia, offered to repatriate Baltic Germans, including descendants, who had been forced out of Estonia and Latvia under Soviet-German agreements reached in 1939.[34] Thousands of Crimean Tatars forced out of Crimea in 1944 were repatriated in the 1990s, even though many of their towns no longer existed, and despite an influx of others during the intervening half-century.[35]

If the governments of Israel and Palestine were to fail to deal with the issue, it would remain open, and the disaffected could press their claims against the appropriate government, or before international human rights enforcement organs.

33

The Way Forward:

Peace or Confrontation?

. . . to practice tolerance and live together in peace with one another as good neighbors. —Preamble, UN Charter

From the days of the League of Nations, it was apparent that the Zionist project was taking Palestine in a direction incompatible with the rights of the population. The Jewish immigration permitted by Britain in fulfillment of that project set Palestine on a road to disaster. Britain let migration continue even as it became obvious that the migration threatened the aspirations of the population to an independent national existence.

The mandate system was a compromise between the nineteenth century and the twentieth. A Europe that was beginning to doubt colonialism had not fully embraced self-determination. From the perspective of colonialism, the insertion of an outside population was acceptable. From the perspective of self-determination, it was anathema. The Arabs of Palestine, like Arabs elsewhere in the region, sought immediate independence. Finding no way out of the dilemma it had created, Britain withdrew.

The United States emerged from World War II as the major world power and replaced Britain as a power broker in the Middle East. With oil as the attraction, the United States began to inject itself into domestic politics. In Palestine, it fostered the emergence of a Jewish state. Intent, like the European powers, on keeping displaced European Jews from thronging its borders, the United States pushed the partition proposal through the UN General Assembly, even though many non-European UN members viewed partition as inconsistent with the national rights of Palestine's Arab population.

Although the United States quickly dropped its support for partition and promoted a temporary UN trusteeship over Palestine, President Truman scuttled that approach when he told the Jewish Agency that he would recognize the Jewish state it was poised to declare. By removing the UN from the scene, Truman allowed the Jewish Agency to continue to depopulate Palestine of its Arabs.

The UN Security Council bears responsibility, under Chapter 7 of the UN Charter, for the international peace. Yet it did little to affect the situation in Palestine in 1948 as the Jewish Agency expelled the Arab population and extended its control. The UN General Assembly, which has no operational authority, did what it could by calling on Israel to repatriate the displaced Arabs.

When Israel occupied Gaza and the West Bank in 1967, the Security Council failed to identify Israel as the aggressor or take effective steps to force it to withdraw. In later years the Security Council and General Assembly criticized Israel for mistreatment of the Palestinians, putting itself more and more on the Palestinian side on the rhetorical level. Yet it did little to affect the situation on the ground.

The difficulties of the years 2002–2003 led some Palestinians to abandon the two-state idea. If the Palestinians were not to be able to establish a genuine state, even in a territory as limited as Gaza and the West Bank, they said, perhaps it would be better to let Israel absorb the two sectors. For the Palestinians, this would mean operating within the Israeli political structure, but with the prospect that eventually, they might outnumber the Jews.

That prospect was precisely the dilemma for Israel. If it annexed Gaza and the West Bank, Israel might not long have a Jewish-majority population. In some circles in Israel, the idea was bandied of forcing the Arabs out.

For the Palestinians, one danger of being absorbed into Israel was precisely that Israel might find ways to get rid of them. By keeping them in a subordinate status, Israel could make their existence sufficiently difficult that emigration would be attractive. That had been the experience of the occupation of Gaza and the West Bank. Many educated youths found little outlet for their skills and left.

In 2002 the League of Arab States offered to normalize relations with Israel if it would end its occupation of Palestinian territory. The league proposed a regional negotiating forum to get Israel back into talks. Israel declined the offer.

As the body delegated by the United Nations with the task of maintaining the international peace, the Security Council cannot permanently remove itself from the longest-standing conflict in the history of the United Nations. The Council's failure has only been highlighted by the period of heightened violence that began in late 2000. As negotiations were replaced by open hostilities, the Security Council sat helpless. With the Security Council marginalized, the General Assembly in theory could take up the slack. But if the General Assembly makes recommendations to states that are opposed by the United States, the chances for implementation are remote.

International involvement and an international forum offer better prospects for success. If applicable international norms inform the negotiations between Israel and the PLO, the parties might achieve a negotiated solution that could stand the test of time. The international community bears a responsibility to ensure an outcome consistent with the legal rights of the parties. If the matter is left exclusively to the parties, there is a serious risk of an inappropriate outcome. That would be unfortunate for the inhabitants of the region. It would also increase the likelihood that the international community, which has dealt with the Palestinian-Israeli conflict for half a century, will face many more years of turmoil in the region.

Notes

1 Zionist Settlement in Palestine: The British Connection

1 Michael Florinsky, *Russia: A History and an Interpretation*, vol. 2, pp. 1120–1121 (1953).

2 Raphael Patai (ed.), *The Complete Diaries of Theodor Herzl* (1960), p. 1195. Nathan Weinstock, *Zionism: False Messiah* (1979), p. 32.

3 Florinsky, *supra* note 1, p. 1121.

4 Ariel Hecht, "The Influence of Public Law on Private Ownership of Real Estate in Israel," in U. Yadin (ed.), *Israeli Reports to the Sixth International Congress of Comparative Law* (1962), p. 15, at p. 23.

5 Yigal Allon, "The Zionist Settlement Movement as a Military Factor in the Israel War of Liberation," in Dov Knohl (ed.), *Siege in the Hills of Hebron: The Battle of the Etzion Bloc* (1958), p. 374, at p. 375.

6 Abraham Granovsky, "The Struggle for Land," *Palestine Yearbook*, vol. 2, p. 423, at p. 424 (1946). Sami Hadawi, *Palestinian Rights and Losses in 1948* (1988), p. 7. Neville Mandel, *The Arabs and Zionism Before World War I* (1976), p. 231. Rosemary Sayigh, *Palestinians: From Peasants to Revolutionaries* (1979), pp. 44–46.

7 Arieh L. Avneri, *The Claim of Dispossession: Jewish Land-Settlement and the Arabs 1878–1948* (1984), p. 110.

8 Walter Lehn, *The Jewish National Fund* (1988), pp. 14–24.

9 Keren Kayemeth Leisrael Limited (Jewish National Fund), Memorandum of Association, art. 3(1), March 28, 1907, reprinted in *Palestine Yearbook of International Law*, vol. 2, p. 195 (1985), cited in *Keren Kayemeth Le Jisroel, Ltd. v. Inland Revenue Commissioners*, House of Lords, 1932 A.C. 650 (opinion of Lord Tomlin).

10 Morris Rothenberg, "Jewish National Fund," *Palestine Yearbook*, vol. 1, p. 425 (1945).

11 Granovsky, *supra* note 6, p. 424.

12 Memorandum of Association, *supra* note 9, art. 3.

13 Patai, *supra* note 2, p. 88.

14 Kenneth Stein, *The Land Question in Palestine, 1917–1939* (1984), p. 24.

15 Rashid Khalidi, "Palestinian Peasant Resistance to Zionism before World War I," in Edward Said and Christopher Hitchens (eds.), *Blaming the Victims: Spurious Scholarship and the Palestinian Question* (1988), p. 207, at pp. 214, 216–217.

16   Laurence Oliphant, *Haifa, or Life in Modern Palestine* (1887), reprinted as *Haifa, or Life in the Holy Land 1881–1885* (1976), pp. 73–77.

17   Yitzhak Epstein, "A Hidden Question" (lecture at Seventh Zionist Congress, Basle, 1905), reprinted in *New Outlook* (December 1985), p. 27, at p. 28.

18   Ahad Ha'am, Letter of November 18, 1913, to Moshe Smilansky, in Hans Kohn, "Zion and the Jewish National Idea," *Menorah Journal*, p. 18, at p. 34 (Autumn–Winter 1958).

19   Patai, *supra* note 2, p. 88.

20   Michael Palumbo, *The Palestinian Catastrophe* (1987), pp. 11–12.

21   Moshe Menuhin, *The Decadence of Judaism in Our Time* (1965), p. 52.

22   Lehn, *supra* note 8, p. 35.

23   Avneri, *supra* note 7, pp. 110–114. Hadawi, *supra* note 6, p. 8.

24   Khalidi, *supra* note 15, pp. 217, 220.

25   Mohammed Shadid, *The United States and the Palestinians* (1981), p. 15. Muhammad Y. Muslih, *The Origins of Palestinian Nationalism* (1988), p. 80.

26   Avneri, *supra* note 7, p. 113.

27   Simha Flapan, *Zionism and the Palestinians* (1979), p. 219.

28   Shadid, *supra* note 25, p. 15.

29   Yigal Allon, *The Making of Israel's Army* (1970), p. 4. Moshe Pearlman, *The Army of Israel* (1950), p. 19.

30   Weinstock, *supra* note 3, p. 146.

31   General Act of the Conference at Berlin, February 26, 1885, *British and Foreign State Papers*, vol. 76, p. 4. Also in Clive Parry (ed.), *Consolidated Treaty Series*, vol. 165, p. 485 (1978).

32   Benjamin Beit-Hallahmi, *The Israeli Connection: Who Israel Arms and Why* (1987), p. 226.

33   Theodor Herzl, *The Jewish State (Der Judenstaat)* (1970, Harry Zohn, trans.), p. 52.

34   Alan R. Taylor, *Prelude to Israel: An Analysis of Zionist Diplomacy, 1897–1947* (1959), p. 7.

35   Chaim Weizmann, "The Jewish People and Palestine" (Statement before the Palestine Royal Commission, Jerusalem, August 1936), in Paul Goodman (ed.), *Chaim Weizmann: A Tribute on his Seventieth Birthday* (1945), p. 246, at pp. 255–256. Nathan Feinberg, "The Recognition of the Jewish People in International Law," *Jewish Yearbook of International Law: 1948* (1949), p. 1, at pp. 12–13. Walter Laqueur, *A History of Zionism* (1976), pp. 126–129.

36   Patai, *supra* note 2, p. 1600.

37   Hannah Arendt, "Zionism Reconsidered," in Hannah Arendt, *The Jew as Pariah* (1978), p. 152. Laqueur, *supra* note 35, pp. 114–119.

38   Abdullah Schliefer, *The Fall of Jerusalem* (1972), p. 23.

39   Patai, *supra* note 2, p. 1194.

40   Frederick S. Rodkey, "Lord Palmerston and the Rejuvenation of Turkey, 1830–41—Part II, 1839–41," *Journal of Modern History*, vol. 2, p. 193, at pp. 214–215 (1930). Regina Sharif, *Non-Jewish Zionism: An Investigation into Its Roots and Origins in England in Relation to British Imperialism, 1600–1919* (Baghdad, Symposium on Zionism, November 8–12, 1976).

41 Norman Bentwich, *England in Palestine* (1932), pp. 2–12. Weizmann, *supra* note 35, pp. 254–255.

42 Charles Webster, *The Foreign Policy of Palmerston 1830–1841*, vol. 2, p. 761 (1969). Weinstock, *supra* note 3, p. 53.

43 Richard P. Stevens, "Zionism as a Phase of Western Imperialism," in Ibrahim Abu-Lughod (ed.), *The Transformation of Palestine: Essays on the Origin and Development of the Arab-Israeli Conflict* (1971), p. 27.

44 Herbert Adams Gibbons, "Zionism and the World Peace," *Century*, vol. 97, p. 368, at p. 371 (1919), reprinted in Richard P. Stevens, *Zionism and Palestine Before the Mandate: A Phase of Western Imperialism: An Essay with a Selection of Readings* (1972), p. 50, at pp. 56–57. Ilan Halevi, *Question juive: la Tribu, la Loi, l'Espace* (1981), pp. 11–12.

45 Leonard Stein, *The Balfour Declaration* (1983), p. 8.

46 Florinsky, *supra* note 1, pp. 861–869. Arthur L. Goodhart, *Israel, the United Nations and Aggression* (1968), pp. 7–8. Gibbons, *supra* note 44, p. 371 (in Stevens reprint at pp. 11–12).

47 Taylor, *supra* note 34, pp. 9–25.

48 Sydney H. Zebel, *Balfour: A Political Biography* (1973), p. 241.

49 Chaim Weizmann, *Trial and Error: the Autobiography of Chaim Weizmann* (1949), p. 149.

50 Zebel, *supra* note 48, p. 244.

51 Stein, *supra* note 45, pp. 548–549. W. Thomas Mallison, "The Balfour Declaration: An Appraisal in International Law," in Ibrahim Abu-Lughod, *The Transformation of Palestine: Essays on the Origin and Development of the Arab-Israeli Conflict* (1971), pp. 61–111.

52 Marion Mushkat, "Some Legal and Political Problems of the Arab War Against Israel," *International Problems*, vol. 6, nos. 4–5, p. 47, at p. 57 (1967).

53 Stein, *supra* note 45, pp. 625–626.

54 Louis Brandeis, "Palestine Has Developed Jewish Character," in Zionist Organization of America, *Brandeis on Zionism: A Collection of Addresses and Statements by Louis D. Brandeis* (1942), p. 144, at p. 147.

55 Ronald Storrs, *Memoirs* (1937), p. 364.

56 Weinstock, *supra* note 3, p. 91.

57 Zebel, *supra* note 48, p. 243. Max Egremont, *Balfour: A Life of Arthur James Balfour* (1980), p. 292.

58 Weinstock *supra* note 3, p. 94.

59 Zebel, *supra* note 48, p. 242.

60 Egremont, *supra* note 57, p. 294.

61 Quincy Wright, "Legal Aspects of the Middle East Situation," *Law and Contemporary Problems*, vol. 33, p. 5, at p. 12 (1968).

62 Zebel, *supra* note 48, p. 240.

63 Chaim Weizmann, "The Political Situation in 1931: Seventeenth Zionist Congress, Basle, July 1st, 1931," in Goodman, *supra* note 35, p. 205, at p. 206.

64 Frank Hardie and Irwin Herrmann, *Britain and Zion: The Fateful Entanglement* (1980), p. 75.

65 Egremont, *supra* note 57, p. 294. Zebel, *supra* note 48, p. 247. Maxine Rodinson,

Israel: A Colonial-Settler State? (1973), p. 47. Paul Fauchille, *Traité de droit international public* (1st part), vol. 1, p. 315 (1922).

66 Ernst Frankenstein, "The Meaning of the Term 'National Home for the Jewish People,'" *Jewish Yearbook of International Law: 1948* (1949), p. 27, at p. 30. Weinstock, *supra* note 3, p. 99.

67 Weizmann, *supra* note 63, p. 206.

68 *Report of the Palestine Royal Commission* (Peel Commission), July 1937, Command Paper 5479, p. 23.

69 Weinstock, *supra* note 3, p. 106.

70 Arendt, *supra* note 37, p. 152.

71 Nathan Feinberg, "The Arab-Israeli Conflict in International Law (A Critical Analysis of the Colloquium of Arab Jurists in Algiers)," in Nathan Feinberg, *Studies in International Law with Special Reference to the Arab-Israel Conflict* (1979), p. 433, at pp. 500–501.

72 Frankenstein, *supra* note 66, pp. 28–29.

73 Weizmann, *supra* note 35, p. 258.

74 *Foreign Relations of the United States: Paris Peace Conference 1919*, vol. 4, p. 169 (1943).

75 Ritchie Ovendale, *The Origins of the Arab-Israeli Wars* (1984), p. 47.

76 *Id.*, p. 45.

77 *Foreign Relations of the United States: Paris Peace Conference 1919*, vol. 4, pp. 161–162 (1943).

78 Israel Cohn (ed.), *Speeches on Zionism by the Right Hon. the Earl of Balfour* (1928), pp. 25–26.

79 *Documents on British Foreign Policy 1919–1939*, 1st series, vol. 4, p. 345 (memorandum by Balfour to Curzon, August 11, 1919).

80 Hugh O'Beirne, in Hardie and Herrmann, *supra* note 64, p. 97.

81 Shadid, *supra* note 25, p. 25.

82 Chadwick F. Alger, "The Quest for Peace," *Ohio State University, Mershon Center, Quarterly Report*, vol. 11, no. 2, p. 1, at p. 3 (1986). W. Ofuatey-Kodjoe, *The Principle of Self-Determination in International Law* (1977), p. 70.

83 Gibbons, *supra* note 44, p. 374 (in Stevens reprint at p. 63).

84 Secretary of State Robert Lansing, 1918, in Leften Stavrianos, *Global Rift: The Third World Comes of Age* (1981), p. 513.

85 Muslih, *supra* note 25, pp. 178–190.

86 Report of the King-Crane Commission, in *Foreign Relations of the United States: Paris Peace Conference 1919*, vol. 12, p. 747, at pp. 792–793 (1947).

87 *Foreign Relations of the United States: Paris Peace Conference 1919*, vol. 4, p. 165 (1943).

88 Albert Hyamson, *Palestine: a Policy* (1942), pp. 129–130.

89 Telegram, June 20, 1919, C. R. Crane and H. C. King to President Wilson, *Foreign Relations of the United States: Paris Peace Conference 1919*, vol. 12, p. 748 (1947).

90 Anstruther MacKay, "Zionist Aspirations in Palestine," *Atlantic* (July 1920), p. 122, at p. 124.

91 Morris R. Cohen, "Zionism: Tribalism or Liberalism?" in Morris R. Cohen, The Faith of a Liberal (1946), pp. 329–330, originally published in *New Republic*, vol.

18, p. 182 (March 8, 1919).

92 *Foreign Relations of the United States: Paris Peace Conference 1919*, vol. 4, p. 170, (1943).

93 *Id.*, p. 165.

94 Chaim Weizmann, "Address" (Czernowitz, Rumania, December 12, 1927), in Goodman, *supra* note 35, p. 199.

95 Letter of Representative Julius Kahn to President Woodrow Wilson, *New York Times*, March 5, 1919, p. 7.

96 Statement of N. Sokolow, *Foreign Relations of the United States: Paris Peace Conference 1919*, vol, 4, p. 161, (1943).

97 Gibbons, *supra* note 44, p. 374 (in Stevens reprint at p. 63).

2   Zionist-Arab Conflict under the British Mandate: The Struggle for Land

* *Christian Science Monitor*, March 3, 1939, p. 3. Mahatma K. Gandhi, "The Jews in Palestine, 1938," in Walid Khalidi, *From Haven to Conquest: Readings in Zionism and the Palestine Problem until 1948* (1971), pp. 367–368.

1 General Syrian Congress, Resolution, Damascus, July 2, 1919, in George Antonius, *The Arab Awakening: The Story of the Arab National Movement* (1946), p. 440.

2 James Brown Scott, "The Two Institutes of International Law," *American Journal of International Law*, vol. 23, p. 91 (1932).

3 Report of the United Nations Special Committee on Palestine, *General Assembly Official Records*, 2d sess., Supplement No. 11, September 3, 1947. UN Doc. A/364, vol. 1, p. 29.

4 Legal Consequences for States of the Continued Presence of South Africa in Namibia (South-West Africa) Notwithstanding Security Council Resolution 276 (1970), International Court of Justice, *Reports of Judgments, Advisory Opinions and Orders* (1971), p. 1, at p. 30, para. 50. Sally V. Mallison and W. Thomas Mallison, "The Juridical Bases for Palestinian Self-Determination," *Palestine Yearbook of International Law*, vol 1, p. 36, at p. 38 (1984).

5 Duncan Hall, *Mandates, Dependencies, and Trusteeships* (1948), p. 81.

6 Aaron Margalith, *The International Mandates* (1930), p. 46. International Status of South-West Africa (Advisory Opinion), International Court of Justice, *Reports of Judgments, Advisory Opinions and Orders* (1950), p. 131.

7 Quincy Wright, *Mandates Under the League of Nations* (1930), p. 530.

8 Legal Consequences for States, *supra* note 4, p. 31, para. 53.

9 Michael Akehurst, "The Arab-Israeli Conflict in International Law," *New Zealand Universities Law Review*, vol. 5, p. 231, at p. 235 (1973).

10 Covenant of the League of Nations, art. 22, para. 4.

11 Report of the Committee of Jurists Entrusted by the Council of the League of Nations with the Task of Giving an Advisory Opinion upon the Legal Aspects of the Aaland Islands Question, League of Nations, *Official Journal*, Special Supplement No. 3, pp. 5–6, (October 1920). Nathaniel Berman, "Sovereignty in Abeyance: Self-Determination and International Law," *Wisconsin International Law Journal*, vol. 7, p. 51, at pp. 72–76 (1988).

12 Mandate for Palestine, art. 2, League of Nations, *Official Journal*, vol. 8, p. 1007 (1922); also in *Terms of League of Nations Mandates: Republished by the United Nations*, UN Doc. A/70 (1946), reprinted from Permanent Mandates Commission No. 466, League of Nations Doc. C.529.M.314.1992.VI and C.667.M.396.1992.VI; also in Convention between the United States and Great Britain Concerning Palestine, December 3, 1924, *United States Statutes at Large*, vol. 44, p. 2184.

13 Berriedale Keith, "Mandates," *Journal of Comparative Legislation and International Law*, 3d series, vol. 4, p. 71, at p. 78 (1922).

14 *Parliamentary Debates* (House of Lords), 5th series, vol. 50, col. 1034 (1922).

15 Nathan Feinberg, "The Arab-Israel Conflict in International Law (A Critical Analysis of the Colloquium of Arab Jurists in Algiers," in Nathan Feinberg, *Studies in International Law with Special Reference to the Arab-Israel Conflict* (1979), p. 433, at pp. 445, 452–453.

16 Chaim Weizmann, "Palestine in 1936: Address given at Chatham House, London, on June 9th, 1936," in Paul Goodman (ed.), *Chaim Weizmann: A Tribute on his Seventieth Birthday* (1945), p. 235, at p. 243.

17 W. Thomas Mallison and Sally V. Mallison, *The Palestine Problem in International Law and World Order* (1986), pp. 64–65, 172.

18 Mandate for Palestine, *supra* note 12, art. 4. W. Thomas Mallison, "The Legal Problems Concerning the Juridical Status and Political Activities of the Zionist Organization/Jewish Agency," *William and Mary Law Review*, vol. 9, p. 556, at pp. 566–578 (1968).

19 Chaim Weizmann, "The Mandatory Power" (Speech at Fourteenth Zionist Congress, Vienna, August 19, 1925), in Goodman, *supra* note 16, p. 183, at p. 184.

20 Chaim Weizmann, "Zionism a Political Reality" (Speech at Zionist Conference, Carlsbad, August 25, 1922), in Goodman, *supra* note 16, p. 175, at p. 178.

21 *Id.*, p. 188.

22 Norman Bentwich, "Mandated Territories: Palestine and Mesopotamia (Iraq)," *British Year Book of International Law*, vol. 2, p. 48, at p. 49 (1921–22).

23 *Id.*, p. 56.

24 Kenneth Stein, *The Land Question in Palestine, 1917–1939* (1984), p. 39. John Ruedy, "Dynamics of Land Alienation," in Ibrahim Abu-Lughod (ed.), *The Transformation of Palestine: Essays on the Origin and Development of the Arab-Israeli Conflict* (1971), p. 119, at pp. 124–129. Nathan Weinstock, *Zionism: False Messiah* (1979), p. 141. Walter Lehn, "The Jewish National Fund," *Journal of Palestine Studies*, vol. 3, no. 4, p. 74, at pp. 88–96 (1973). Arieh L. Avneri, *The Claim of Dispossession: Jewish Land-Settlement and the Arabs 1878–1948* (1984), p. 111. Rony Gabbay, *A Political Study of the Arab-Jewish Conflict: The Arab Refugee Problem (A Case Study)* (1959), pp. 26–27.

25 Yigal Allon, *The Making of Israel's Army* (1970), p. 6. Moshe Pearlman, *The Army of Israel* (1950), p. 23.

26 Louis Brandeis, "Palestine Has Developed Jewish Character," in Zionist Organization of America, *Brandeis on Zionism* (1942), pp. 144–148.

27 Yigal Allon, "The Zionist Settlement Movement as a Military Factor in the Israel War of Liberation," in Dov Knohl (ed.), *Siege in the Hills of Hebron: The Battle of*

the Etzion Bloc (1958), p. 374, at p. 375.

28 Michael Bar-Zohar, *Ben-Gurion: the Armed Prophet* (1968), p. 33.

29 Anglo-American Committee of Inquiry, *Report to the United States Government and His Majesty's Government in the United Kingdom*, Lausanne, April 20, 1946, Command Paper 6808, p. 24, para. 9, also published by U.S. Dept. of State, 1946. Weinstock, *supra* note 24, pp. 183–186.

30 Haim Hanegbi, "The Histadrut: Union and Boss," in Arie Bober, *The Other Israel* (1972), p. 123, at p. 125.

31 Moshe Menuhin, *The Decadence of Judaism in Our Time* (1965), p. 64.

32 Walid Khalidi, "The Arab Perspective," in W. Roger Louis and Robert W. Stookey (eds.), *The End of the Palestine Mandate* (1986), p. 104.

33 Quincy Wright, "The Palestine Problem," *Political Science Quarterly*, vol. 41, p. 382, at p. 392 (1926).

34 *Id.*, p. 403.

35 Quincy Wright, "The Palestine Conflict in International Law," in M. Khadduri (ed.), *Major Middle Eastern Problems in International Law* (1972), p. 13, at p. 26.

36 Walter Lehn, *The Jewish National Fund* (1988), p. 54, pp. 77–78.

37 Palestine Land Development Company v. Arab Tenants at Jinujar, and JNF Purchases at Wadi Hawarith, 1929, eviction of tenants, Judgment of the Court, 11 June 1930, CO 733/190/77182, in Stein, *supra* note 24, p. 77. Saleh Ibrahim Oufi et al. v. Chief Execution Officer, Nablus, Bishara Tayan's Heirs, Department of Lands, and Keren Kayemeth Le-Israel, High Court No. 25 of 1930, June 4, 1930, in M. McDonnell, *Law Reports of Palestine. Vol. 1, 1920–1933*, pp. 471–473.

38 *Report of the Palestine Royal Commission* (Peel Commission), July 1937, Command Paper 5479, p. 223.

39 Avneri, *supra* note 24, p. 124. Shabtai Teveth, *Ben-Gurion and the Palestinian Arabs: From Peace to War* (1985), pp. 76–77.

40 *Report of the Commission on the Palestine Disturbances of August 1929* (Shaw Commission), March 1930, Command Paper 3530, pp. 163–164. *The Times*, April 1, 1930.

41 Avneri, *supra* note 24, p. 130.

42 Weizmann to Marshall, January 17, 1930, in Simha Flapan, *Zionism and the Palestinians* (1979), p. 71.

43 Lehn, *supra* note 36, p. 85.

44 Sally Morphet, "The Palestinians and Their Right to Self-Determination," in R. J. Vincent (ed.), *Foreign Policy and Human Rights: Issues and Responses* (1986), p. 85, at p. 89. Stein, *supra* note 24, p. 36.

45 Edward Rizk (trans.), *The Palestine Question: Seminar of Arab Jurists on Palestine, Algiers, 22–27 July, 1967* (1968), p. 51. Maxime Rodinson, *Israel: A Colonial-Settler State?* (1973), p. 87.

46 Shaw Commission, *supra* note 40, p. 165.

47 *Id.*, pp. 123–124.

48 *Id.*, pp. 124, 166.

49 *Id.*, pp. 112, 165.

50 John Chancellor to Lord Passfield (colonial secretary), January 17, 1930, in Stein, *supra* note 24, pp. 84–86.

51 *Report on Immigration, Land Settlement and Development* (Hope Simpson Commission), October 1930, Command Paper 3686, p. 51.

52 *Id.*, p. 141.

53 Teveth, *supra* note 39, p. 112.

54 Stein, *supra* note 24, pp. 142–172. Weinstock, *supra* note 24, pp. 162–163.

55 Letter to Hans Kohn, May 30, 1930, in Susan Lee Hattis, *The Bi-National Idea in Palestine during Mandatory Times* (1970), p. 49.

56 Uri Davis, *Israel: Utopia Incorporated: A Study of Class, State, and Corporate Kin Control* (1977), p. 56.

57 David Ben-Gurion, Lecture, Berlin, 1931, in Eric Rouleau, "The Palestinian Quest," *Foreign Affairs*, vol. 53, p. 264, at p. 266 (1975).

58 Teveth, *supra* note 39, p. 125.

59 Stein, *supra* note 24, pp. 173–211.

60 Flapan, *supra* note 42, p. 206.

61 David Hirst, *The Gun and the Olive Branch: The Roots of Violence in the Middle East* (1984), p. 63.

62 Abraham Granott (Granovsky), *The Land System in Palestine: History and Structure* (1952), p. 272.

63 Peel Commission, *supra* note 38, p. 241.

64 Stein, *supra* note 24, p. 171.

65 Constitution of the Jewish Agency, Zurich, August 14, 1929, art. 3(e), in Hope Simpson Commission, *supra* note 51, p. 53.

66 Lease Contract, art. 25, in Lehn, *supra* note 36, p. 192; and in *Palestine Yearbook of International Law*, vol. 2, p. 221 (1985). The language quoted in the text is from the English translation. Hope Simpson Commission, *supra* note 51, p. 53.

67 Norman Bentwich and Helen Bentwich, *Mandate Memories 1918–1948* (1965), p. 53.

68 Arnold Toynbee, "The Present Situation in Palestine," *International Affairs: Journal of the Royal Institute of International Affairs*, vol. 10, no. 1, p. 38, at p. 53 (January 1931).

69 Hope Simpson Commission, *supra* note 51, p. 54.

70 Anglo-American Committee of Inquiry, *supra* note 29, p. 39, para. 3.

71 Hope Simpson Commission, *supra* note 51, p. 55.

72 Noam Chomsky, *Peace in the Middle East? Reflections on Justice and Nationhood* (1974), p. 12.

73 Rodinson, *supra* note 45, p.88.

74 Stein, *supra* note 24, p. 175. Ariel Hecht, "The Influence of Public Law on Private Ownership of Real Estate in Israel," in U. Yadin (ed.), *Israeli Reports to the Sixth International Congress of Comparative Law* (1962), p. 15, at p. 24.

75 Stein, *supra* note 24, p. 208.

76 Flapan, *supra* note 42, p. 250.

77 Raanan Weitz, "Settlement," in Israel Pocket Library, *Immigration and Settlement in Israel* (1973), p. 87, at pp. 92–93.

78 Constitution of the Jewish Agency, Zurich, August 14, 1929, art. 3(d), in Hope Simpson Commission, *supra* note 51, p. 53.

79 Jewish National Fund, Lease Contract, art. 17, in Lehn, *supra* note 36, p. 192; and

in *Palestine Yearbook of International Law*, vol. 2, p. 221 (1985).

80   Lehn, *supra* note 36, p. 60.

81   Lease Contract, arts. 17, 34, in Lehn, *supra* note 36, p. 192. Hope Simpson Commission, *supra* note 51, p. 53.

82   Keren Kayemeth Leisrael Limited, Memorandum of Association, art. 3, March 28, 1907, in *Palestine Yearbook of International Law*, vol. 2, p. 195 (1985).

83   Avi Shlaim, *Collusion Across the Jordan: King Abdullah, the Zionist Movement, and the Partition of Palestine* (1988), pp. 51–56.

3 Things Fall Apart: The Collapse of the British Mandate

1   Rony Gabbay, *A Political Study of the Arab-Jewish Conflict* (1959), p. 32.

2   Anglo-American Committee of Inquiry, *Report to the United States Government and His Majesty's Government in the United Kingdom*, Lausanne, April 20, 1946, Command Paper 6808, p. 21, para. 12, p. 24, para. 9, also published by U.S. Dept. of State, 1946.

3   Walid Khalidi in "The Arab Perspective," in W. Roger Louis and Robert W. Stookey (eds.), *The End of the Palestine Mandate* (1986), p. 104, at p. 106.

4   David Hirst, *The Gun and the Olive Branch: The Roots of Violence in the Middle East* (1984), pp. 82–83.

5   Simha Flapan, *The Birth of Israel: Myths and Realities* (1987), pp. 62–63. Hirst, *supra* note 4, pp. 80–81.

6   Munya M. Mardor, *Haganah* (1964), pp. 3–16. Ilan Halevi, *Israël de la Terreur au Massacre d'Etat* (1984), pp. 97–104. Yoram Peri, "Bread, Circuses, and Reprisal Raids," *New Outlook* (October–November 1985), p. 7.

7   Simha Flapan, *Zionism and the Palestinians* (1979), p. 116. Hirst, *supra* note 4, p. 101.

8   Defense (Emergency) Regulations, Palestine (Defense) Order in Council, March 18, 1937, *Palestine Gazette*, extraordinary no. 675, supplement no. 2, March 24, 1937.

9   *Report of the Palestine Royal Commission* (Peel Commission), July 1937, Command Paper 5479, p. 240.

10   *Id.*, pp. 224–225.

11   *Id.*, p. 241.

12   *Id.*, p. 235.

13   *Id.*, pp. 225, 251. Kenneth Stein, *The Land Question in Palestine, 1917–1939* (1984), pp. 217–218.

14   Richard Crossman, *Palestine Mission: A Personal Record* (1947), p. 159.

15   Peel Commission, *supra* note 9, p. 381. Avi Shlaim, *Collusion Across the Jordan: King Abdullah, the Zionist Movement, and the Partition of Palestine* (1988), p. 62.

16   Peel Commission, *supra* note 9, pp. 390–391.

17   Cable, Arab Higher Committee to League of Nations, September 13, 1937, League of Nations Doc. C.P.M. 1944, October 13, 1937.

18   Letter to Moshe Sneh, July 20, 1937, in Shabtai Teveth, *Ben-Gurion and the Pal-*

estinian Arabs: From Peace to War (1985), p. 188.

19 Letters by Ben-Gurion to his children, 1937–38, in Teveth, *supra* note 18, p. 188.

20 Flapan, *supra* note 5, p. 22.

21 Flapan, *supra* note 7, p. 144.

22 Ilan Halevi, *Sous Israël la Palestine* (1978), p. 145.

23 Judah L. Magnes, "A Solution Through Force?" in Martin Buber, Judah L. Magnes, and El Simon (eds.). *Towards Union in Palestine: Essays on Zionism and Jewish-Arab Cooperation* (1947, reprinted 1972), p. 14, at p. 16. Hirst, *supra* note 4, p. 36.

24 Ilan Halevi, *Question juive: la Tribu, la Loi, l'Espace* (1981), p. 226.

25 Michael Palumbo, *The Palestinian Catastrophe* (1987), p. 4.

26 Stein, *supra* note 13, p. 91. David Gilmour, *The Dispossessed: the Ordeal of the Palestinians* (1980), pp. 40–41. Flapan, *supra* note 7, pp. 69, 246.

27 Halevi, *supra* note 22, p. 138, Palumbo, *supra* note 25, pp. 23, 32.

28 Letter to Amos Ben-Gurion, October 5, 1937, in Benny Morris, *The Birth of the Palestinian Refugee Problem, 1947–1949* (1987), p. 25.

29 Flapan, *supra* note 7, pp. 263–264.

30 Joseph Weitz, "A Solution to the Refugee Problem: An Israeli State with a Small Arab Minority," Davar, September 29, 1967, p. 3. Weitz gives the quoted language as written by him in 1940.

31 Flapan, *supra* note 7, pp. 141–142.

32 *Christian Science Monitor*, March 3, 1939, p. 3. Mahatma K. Gandhi, "The Jews in Palestine, 1938," in Walid Khalidi, *From Haven to Conquest: Readings in Zionism and the Palestine Problem until 1948* (1971), pp. 367–368.

33 Teveth, *supra* note 18, pp. 175–176, 187. Elias Sanbar, *Palestine 1948: L'Expulsion* (1984), p. 85. Mardor, *supra* note 6, p. 24.

34 Klaus Polkehn, "The Secret Contacts: Zionism and Nazi Germany, 1933–1941," *Journal of Palestine Studies*, vol. 5, nos. 3–4, p. 54, at p. 56 (1976).

35 Nathan Weinstock, *Zionism: False Messiah* (1979), p. 204.

36 Uri Davis, *Zionism: Utopia Incorporated* (1977), pp. 24–25. Bernard Avishai, *The Tragedy of Zionism: Revolution and Democracy in the Land of Israel* (1985), p. 152.

37 Francis R. Nicosia, *The Third Reich and the Palestine Question* (1985), p. 63.

38 Davis, *supra* note 36, p. 25.

39 *Palestine: Statement by His Majesty's Government in the United Kingdom*, art. 4, November 1938, Command Paper 5893.

40 *Palestine: Statement of Policy*, arts. 10, 14, 16, May 1939, Command Paper 6019.

41 *New York Times*, May 18, 1939, p. A4.

42 *Id.*, p. A2.

43 *Id.*, May 19, 1939, p. A1. J. Bowyer Bell, *Terror Out of Zion: Irgun Zvai Leumi, LEHI, and the Palestine Underground, 1929–1949* (1977), p. 48. Hirst, *supra* note 4, pp. 96–97.

44 Nevill Barbour, *Palestine: Star or Crescent?* (1947), pp. 236–237.

45 *New York Times*, May 30, 1939, p. A11; June 1, 1939, p. A17; June 3, 1939, p. A3; July 4, 1939, p. A4.

46 *Id.*, June 20, 1939, p. A9.

47 Hirst, *supra* note 4, p. 105.

48 Bell, *supra* note 43, p. 62.
49 Kermit Roosevelt, "The Partition of Palestine: A Lesson in Pressure Politics," *Middle East Journal*, vol. 2, pp. 1–16 (1948). Ritchie Ovendale, *The Origins of the Arab-Israeli Wars* (1984), p. 74.
50 Weinstock, *supra* note 35, p. 208.
51 David Ben-Gurion, *Israel: Years of Challenge* (1963), pp. 17–18.
52 Abraham Granovsky, "The Struggle for Land," *Palestine Yearbook*, vol. 2, p. 423, at pp. 428–429 (1946).
53 *New York Times*, September 24, 1943, p. A14; September 28, 1943, p. A7. Government of Palestine, *A Survey of Palestine*, vol. 2, pp. 594–595 (1946).
54 *New York Times*, August 1, 1943, p. A23. Government of Palestine, *supra* note 53, pp. 593–594.
55 *New York Times*, May 12, 1942, p. A12. George Kirk, *The Middle East 1945–1950* (1954), pp. 189–190.
56 Shlaim, *supra* note 15, p. 72.
57 *New York Times*, October 18, 1944, p. A14. Hannah Arendt, *The Jew as Pariah: Jewish Identity and Politics in the Modern Age* (1978), p. 131.
58 *New York Times*, August 14, 1945, p. A15. Arendt, *supra* note 57, p. 131.
59 Bell, *supra* note 43, pp. 89–100.
60 Arnold Toynbee, "Two Aspects of the Palestine Question," in Arnold Toynbee, *Importance of the Arab World* (1962), p. 63.
61 Weinstock, *supra* note 35, pp. 202–204, 220, 226. Lenni Brenner, *The Iron Wall: Zionist Revisionism from Jabotinsky to Shamir* (1984), p. 136.
62 Earl Harrison, Report to the President of the United States, *New York Times*, September 30, 1945, p. A38.
63 Hirst, *supra* note 4, pp. 108–115. Noam Chomsky, *The Fateful Triangle: The United States, Israel, and the Palestinians* (1983), p. 93.
64 Alfred M. Lilienthal, *What Price Israel?* (1953), p. 36.
65 Moshe Menuhin, *The Decadence of Judaism in Our Time* (1965), pp. 95–96.
66 *New York Times*, October 9, 1944, p. A6.
67 *The Times*, October 9, 1944, p. 3. B. Y. Boutros-Ghali, "The Arab League: Ten Years of Struggle," *International Conciliation*, no. 498, p. 385, at p. 406 (May 1954).
68 Michael Akehurst, "The Arab-Israeli Conflict in International Law," *New Zealand Universities Law Review*, vol. 5, p. 231, at p. 232 (1973).
69 Dan Kurzman, *Genesis 1948: The First Arab-Israeli War* (1970), pp. 107–113.
70 Joseph C. Harsch, "Terrorism—Past, Present, and Future," *Christian Science Monitor*, June 20, 1985, p. 16. Kirk, *supra* note 55, pp. 187–251. Ovendale, *supra* note 49, pp. 104–106, 198.
71 Anglo-American Committee of Inquiry, *supra* note 2, pp. 45–46, paras. 4–5.
72 Kirk, *supra* note 55, pp. 195, 203. Menachem Begin, *The Revolt* (1951), p. 195.
73 Colonial Office, *Statement of Information Relating to Acts of Violence*, July 1946, Command Paper 6873, pp. 3–9.
74 Kirk, *supra* note 55, p. 221. Begin, *supra* note 72, p. 226.
75 Shlaim, *supra* note 15, pp. 73, 76–77.
76 *Id.*, pp. 81–82.

77 *Id.*, p. 89.
78 *New York Times*, October 8, 1946. p. A2.
79 Government of Palestine, *A Survey of Palestine*, vol. 1, p. 75 (1946).
80 *Id.*, January 19, 1948, p. A2.
81 Sabri Jiryis, *The Arabs in Israel* (1976), pp. 11–12.
82 *Id.*, p. 12.
83 *Id.*, p. 11.
84 *Id.*, p. 13.
85 Anglo-American Committee of Inquiry, *supra* note 2, pp. 3–5.
86 Flapan, *supra* note 7, p. 195.
87 I. F. Stone, "Holy War," *New York Review of Books* (August 3, 1967), p. 6, at p. 10.
88 Crossman, *supra* note 14, p. 158.
89 Report of conversation involving Ben-Gurion and Bevin, in "The Charge in the United Kingdom (Gallman) to the Secretary of State: Secret, Urgent," February 4, 1947. *Foreign Relations of the United States 1947*, vol. 5, p. 1024, at p. 1025 (1971).
90 "The Chargé in the United Kingdom (Gallman) to the Secretary of State: Secret," Feb. 7, 1947, *Foreign Relations of the United States 1947*, vol 5, p. 1024, at p. 1031 (1971).
91 UN Doc. A/286, April 3, 1947. *Yearbook of the United Nations 1946–47* (1947), p. 276.

4   A Portrait by Picasso: The United Nations Recommendation of Partition

1 UN Docs. A/287–91, April 21–23, 1947; A/294, April 25, 1947.
2 G. A. Res. 106, May 15, 1947.
3 Nabil Elaraby, "Some Legal Implications of the 1947 Partition Resolution and the 1949 Armistice Agreements," *Law and Contemporary Problems*, vol. 33, p. 97, at p. 100 (1968).
4 G. A. Res. 104, May 5, 1947.
5 Statement of Warren Austin, May 2, 1947, *Foreign Relations of the United States 1947*, vol. 5, p. 1079 (1971).
6 "The Under Secretary of State (Acheson) to the Director of the Office of Near Eastern and African Affairs (Henderson): Secret," February 15, 1947, *Foreign Relations of the United States 1947*, vol. 5, p. 1048, at p. 1049 (1971).
7 "Memorandum of Conversation, by the Secretary of State," June 19, 1947, *Foreign Relations of the United States 1947*, vol. 5, p. 1105, at p. 1106 (1971).
8 *Yearbook of the United Nations 1947–48* (1949), p. 227.
9 Report of the UN Special Committee on Palestine, *General Assembly Official Records*, 2d sess., Supplement No. 11, September 3, 1947, UN Doc. A/364, vol. 1, p. 35, para. 176.
10 Chaim Weizmann, letter to U.S. President Truman, June 24, 1949, *Foreign Relations of the United States 1949*, vol. 6, p. 1172 (1977).
11 Morris L. Ernst, *So Far So Good* (1948), p. 175.
12 Nathan Weinstock, *Zionism: False Messiah* (1979), pp. 226–227.
13 Arnold Toynbee, *A Study of History* (1954), vol. 8, p. 259.

14   Arnold Toynbee, "Two Aspects of the Palestine Question," in Arnold Toynbee, *Importance of the Arab World* (1962), pp. 57–59.

15   Kermit Roosevelt, "The Partition of Palestine: A Lesson in Pressure Politics," *Middle East Journal*, vol. 2, p. 1, at p. 10 (1948).

16   "The Consul General at Jerusalem (Macatee) to the Secretary of State," September 2, 1947, *Foreign Relations of the United States 1947*, vol. 5, p. 1143 (1971).

17   Hal Lehrman, *Israel: The Beginning and Tomorrow* (1948), p. 47. Walid Khalidi, "The Arab Perspective," in W. Roger Louis and Robert W. Stookey (eds.), *The End of the Palestine Mandate* (1986), p. 104, at p. 118. Christopher Sykes, *Crossroads to Israel* (1973), p. 336.

18   Netanel Lorch, *The Edge of the Sword: Israel's War of Independence, 1947–1949* (1961), p. 44.

19   *Id.*, p. 55.

20   George Kirk, *The Middle East 1945–1950* (1954), p. 247. B. Y. Boutros-Ghali, "The Arab League: Ten Years of Struggle," *International Conciliation*, no. 498, p. 385, at p. 411 (May 1954).

21   Izzat Tannous, *The Palestinians* (1988), p. 411.

22   Avi Shlaim, *Collusion Across the Jordan: King Abdullah, the Zionist Movement, and the Partition of Palestine* (1988), p. 98.

23   Maxime Rodinson, *Israel: A Colonial-Settler State?* (1973), p. 67. Judah L. Magnes, "A Solution Through Force?" in Martin Buber, Judah L. Magnes, and El Simon (eds.), *Towards Union in Palestine: Essays on Zionism and Jewish-Arab Cooperation* (1947, reprint 1972), p. 14, at p. 15.

24   "The Director of the Office of Near Eastern and African Affairs ([Loy W.] Henderson) to the Secretary of State," September 22, 1947, *Foreign Relations of the United States 1947*, vol. 5, p. 1153, at p. 1157 (1971).

25   Simha Flapan, *The Birth of Israel: Myths and Realities* (1987), pp. 38–39, 135–139. Shlaim, *supra* note 22, pp. 105, 107.

26   Golda Meir, *My Life* (1975), p. 207. Shlaim, *supra* note 22, pp. 112–116. Lorch, *supra* note 18, p. 143. Alec Kirkbride, *From the Wings: Amman Memoirs 1947–1951* (1976), p. 4.

27   Shlaim, *supra* note 22, p. 116.

28   *Id.*, pp. 108, 150–151.

29   *Yearbook of the United Nations 1947–48* (1949), p. 227.

30   *Id.*, p. 237.

31   Report of Sub-Committee 2 to the Ad Hoc Committee on the Palestinian Question, November 11, 1947. *General Assembly Official Records*, 2d sess., UN Doc. A/AC.14/32, pp. 299–301 (1947).

32   *Yearbook of the United Nations 1947–48* (1949), p. 241. Syria: Draft Resolution Concerning Reference of Certain Legal Questions to the International Court of Justice, *General Assembly Official Records*, 2d sess., UN Doc. A/AC.14/25, p. 241, Annex 17 (1947). Egypt: Draft Resolution Concerning Reference of a Legal Question to the International Court of Justice, *General Assembly Official Records*, 2d sess., UN Doc. A/AC.14/24, p. 240, Annex 16 (1947). *General Assembly Official Records*, 2d sess., UN Doc. A/AC.14/32, p. 273 (1947).

33   Shabtai Rosenne, "Directions for a Middle East Settlement—Some Underlying

Legal Problems," *Law and Contemporary Problems*, vol. 33, p. 44, at p. 46 (1968).

34 Ad Hoc Committee on the Palestinian Question, *General Assembly Official Records*, 2d sess., UN Doc. A/AC.14/32, p. 203 (1947). *Yearbook of the United Nations 1947–48* (1949), p. 245.

35 *General Assembly Official Records*, 2d sess., UN Doc. A/AC.14/32, p. 272 (1947).

36 Edwin Samuel, "Israel and Its Problems," *Middle East Journal* (January 1949), p. 1, at p. 7.

37 "Memorandum by Mr. Robert M. McClintock [Special Assistant to Dean Rusk]: Top Secret," June 23, 1948, *Foreign Relations of the United States 1948*, vol. 5, p. 1134, at p. 1135 (1976).

38 Report of Sub-Committee 2 to the Ad Hoc Committee on the Palestinian Question, *General Assembly Official Records*, 2d sess., UN Doc. A/AC.14/32, November 11, 1947, Appendix I, "Estimated Population of Palestine as at 31 December 1946," p. 304.

39 "The British Secretary of State for Foreign Affairs (Bevin) to the Secretary of State," February 9, 1947, *Foreign Relations of the United States 1947*, vol. 5, p. 1035, at p. 1037 (1976). "The Chargé in the United Kingdom (Gallman) to the Secretary of State: Secret," February 11, 1947, *Foreign Relations of the United States 1947*, vol. 5, p. 1042, at pp. 1042–1043 (1971).

40 *General Assembly Official Records*, 2d sess., November 11, 1947, UN Doc. A/AC.14/32, p. 304, Annex I.

41 *Id.* Michael Akehurst, "The Arab-Israeli Conflict in International Law," *New Zealand Universities Law Review*, vol. 5, p. 231, at p. 236 (1973).

42 *Yearbook of the United Nations 1947–48* (1949), p. 245. Sally Morphet, "The Palestinians and Their Right to Self-Determination," in R. J. Vincent (ed.), *Foreign Policy and Human Rights: Issues and Responses* (1986), p. 85, at pp. 86–87.

43 *New York Times*, November 30, 1947, p. A64.

44 Sumner Welles, *We Need Not Fail* (1948), p. 63.

45 Alistair Cooke, "Final UN Vote on Palestine Postponed," *Manchester Guardian*, November 27, 1947, p. 5. Alistair Cooke, "More Complaints on Pressure," *Manchester Guardian*, November 29, 1947, p. 5. Mohammed K. Shadid, *The United States and the Palestinians* (1981), p. 35. Alan R. Taylor, *Prelude to Israel: An Analysis of Zionist Diplomacy, 1897–1947* (1959), pp. 103–104. J. R. Gainsborough, *the Arab-Israeli Conflict: A Politico-Legal Analysis* (1986), p. 34. W. Roger Louis, *The British Empire in the Middle East 1945–1951: Arab Nationalism, the United States, and Postwar Imperialism* (1984), pp. 485–486. Henry Cattan, *Palestine and International Law: The Legal Aspects of the Arab-Israeli Conflict* (2d ed. 1976), pp. 82–87.

46 *New York Times*, November 30, 1948, p. A1.

47 *Yearbook of the United Nations 1947–48* (1949), p. 245.

48 Michael Palumbo, *The Palestinian Catastrophe* (1987), p. 31.

49 Millar Burrows, *Palestine Is Our Business* (1949), p. 71.

50 Editorial, "The Partition Gamble," *Christian Century*, vol. 64, p. 1541 (December 17, 1947).

51 "Report by the Policy Planning Staff on Position of the United States With Respect to Palestine: Top Secret," January 19, 1948, *Foreign Relations of the United States*

1948, vol. 5, p. 546, at p. 553 (1976).

52 Alistair Cooke report, *Manchester Guardian*, November 28, 1947, p. 8.

53 *The Times*, December 1, 1947, p. 4.

54 Benjamin Akzin, "The United Nations and Palestine," *Jewish Yearbook of International Law: 1948* (1949), p. 87, at p. 113.

55 Elaraby, *supra* note 3, p. 97.

56 International Status of South-West Africa, International Court of Justice, *Reports of Judgments, Advisory Opinions and Orders* (1950), p. 128. Legal Consequences for States of the Continued Presence of South Africa in Namibia (South-West Africa) Notwithstanding Security Council Resolution 276 (1970), International Court of Justice, *Reports of Judgments, Advisory Opinions and Orders* (1971), p. 1. Western Sahara, *id.* (1975), pp. 3–176.

57 Mohammed Bedjaoui, "Inaugural Address," in Edward Rizk (trans.), *The Palestine Question: Seminar of Arab Jurists*, Algiers, 22–27 July 1967 (1968), p. 3, at p. 7.

58 Konstantin Obradović, *The Palestinian Question from the Standpoint of Human Rights—A Review of Existing Problems*, UN Seminar on Violation of Human Rights in the Palestinian and Other Arab Territories Occupied by Israel, 29 November–3 December 1982, UN Doc. HR/GENEVA/1982/BP.3, p. 19.

59 E. H. Hutchison, *Violent Truce: A Military Observer Looks at the Arab-Israeli Conflict 1951–1955* (1956), p. 95.

60 Flapan, *supra* note 25, pp. 30–33.

61 *Keesing's Contemporary Archives*, vol. 6, p. 8979 (1946–48).

62 Flapan, *supra* note 25, pp. 122–123. Shlaim, *supra* note 22, pp. 108, 123.

63 Shlaim, *supra* note 22, pp. 123–124.

64 *Id.*, p. 109.

65 *Id.*, p. 98.

66 *Id.*, pp. 128–129. New York Times, January 18, 1948, p. E6.

67 Benny Morris, *The Birth of the Palestinian Refugee Problem, 1947–1949* (1987), pp. 19–21.

68 David Hirst, *The Gun and the Olive Branch: The Roots of Violence in the Middle East* (1984), pp. 133–134. Khalidi, *supra* note 17, p. 106.

69 Lorch, *supra* note 18, p. 39.

70 *Id.*, p. 43.

71 Richard Crossman, *Palestine Mission: A Personal Record* (1947), p. 158.

72 Flapan, *supra* note 25, p. 34.

73 *New York Times*, January 11, 1948, p. A1.

74 Harry Sacher, *Israel: the Establishment of a State* (1952), p. 217.

75 *New York Times*, December 1, 1947, p. A1.

5 Chaos on the Ground: Palestine in a Power Vacuum

1 *New York Times*, December 3, 1947, p. A1; December 4, 1947, p. A1; December 5, 1947, p. A1.

2 *New York Times*, December 3, 1947, p. A1; December 5, 1947, p. A1.

3 *Id.*, December 3, 1947, p. A1.

4   *Id.*, December 5, 1947, p. A1.

5   "Report by the Central Intelligence Agency: Secret: Possible Developments in Palestine," February 28, 1948, *Foreign Relations of the United States 1948*, vol. 5, p. 666, at p. 671 (1976).

6   *New York Times*, December 5, 1947, p. A1. *The Times*, December 12, 1947, p. 4; December 13, 1947, p. 4.

7   R. D. Wilson, *Cordon and Search: With 6th Airborne Division in Palestine* (1949), p. 156. For a chronology of hostilities, November 1947 to May 1948, see *Keesing's Contemporary Archives*, pp. 9237–9241 (1946–48).

8   Netanel Lorch, *The Edge of the Sword: Israel's War of Independence, 1947–1949* (1961), p. 57. Michael Palumbo, *The Palestinian Catastrophe* (1987), p. 35.

9   *New York Times*, December 13, 1947, p. A1.

10 *Id.*, December 14, 1947, p. A1.

11 Palumbo, *supra* note 8, p. 36. "Report by the Central Intelligence Agency," *supra* note 5, p. 672.

12 Menachem Begin, *The Revolt* (1951), pp. 337–338.

13 *New York Times*, December 13, 1947, p. A1. *The Times*, December 13, 1947, p. 4.

14 Wilson, *supra* note 7, p. 156.

15 *New York Times*, December 15, 1947, p. A1.

16 Simha Flapan, *The Birth of Israel: Myths and Realities* (1987), pp. 90–91.

17 *New York Times*, December 9, 1947, p. A16.

18 *Id.*, December 18, 1947, p. A3.

19 *Id.*, December 20, 1947, p. A8; December 22, 1947, p. A1. Jon and David Kimche, *Both Sides of the Hill: Britain and the Palestine War* (1960), p. 83.

20 *New York Times*, December 22, 1947, p. A1.

21 Christopher Sykes, *Crossroads to Israel* (1973), p. 337.

22 *New York Times*, December 21, 1947, p. A1.

23 *Id.*, December 22, 1947, p. A1. Lorch, *supra* note 8, p. 59. Sydney D. Bailey, *The Making of Resolution 242* (1985), pp. 153–154.

24 "Report by the Central Intelligence Agency," *supra* note 5, p. 672.

25 *The Times*, December 22, 1947, p. 4.

26 Michael Bar-Zohar, *Ben Gurion: The Armed Prophet* (1967), p. 103.

27 "The Consul General at Jerusalem (Macatee) to the Secretary of State, Jerusalem," February 9, 1948, *Foreign Relations of the United States 1948*, vol. 5, p. 607 (1976).

28 *New York Times*, January 4, 1948, p. A1.

29 *Id.*, January 7, 1948, p. A1.

30 *Id.*, December 31, 1947, p. A1.

31 Benny Morris, *The Birth of the Palestinian Refugee Problem, 1947–1949* (1987), pp. 41–42.

32 *New York Times*, January 10, 1948, p. A1; January 18, 1948, p. E6. Report of the UN Palestine Commission, *Security Council Official Records*, Special Supplement No. 2, p. 13, UN Doc. S/676 (February 16, 1948).

33 Morris, *supra* note 31, pp. 38, 42–43.

34 Benny Morris, "The Harvest of 1948 and the Creation of the Palestinian Refugee Problem," *Middle East Journal*, vol. 40, p. 671, at p. 672 (1986).

35 *New York Times*, January 5, 1948, p. A1; January 6, 1948, p. A6. Palumbo, *supra* note 8, pp. 83–84. Morris, *supra* note 31, p. 46. Lorch, *supra* note 8, p. 59.

36 *New York Times*, January 7, 1948, p. A1. Morris, *supra* note 31, p. 50.

37 *New York Times*, January 7, 1948, p. A1.

38 Begin, *supra* note 12, p. 348.

39 *New York Times*, January 15, 1948, p. A6.

40 *Id.*, January 16, 1948, p. A4.

41 Alec Kirkbride, *From the Wings: Amman Memoirs 1947–1951* (1976), p. 5.

42 Avi Shlaim, *Collusion Across the Jordan: King Abdullah, the Zionist Movement, and the Partition of Palestine* (1988), pp. 130, 136–137.

43 *Id.*, p. 151.

44 George Kirk, *The Middle East 1945–1950* (1954), p. 260.

45 Hal Lehrman, *Israel, the Beginning and Tomorrow* (1948), p. 47. Ben Yechiel, "On the Eve of Statehood," *New Judaea* (May 1948), p. 125.

46 Morris *supra* note 31, pp. 50–52.

47 Larry L. Leonard, "The United Nations and Palestine," *International Conciliation* (1949), p. 607, at p. 650.

48 Tom Segev, *1949: The First Israelis* (1986), p. 25. Morris, *supra* note 31, p. 52.

49 Noam Chomsky, *Turning the Tide: U.S. Intervention in Central America and the Struggle for Peace* (1985), p. 77.

50 Morris, *supra* note 31, p. 52.

51 S. C. Res. 42, March 5, 1948.

52 "Report by the Policy Planning Staff on Position of the United States With Respect to Palestine," January 19, 1948, *Foreign Relations of the United States 1948*, vol. 5, p. 546, at pp. 549, 553 (1976).

53 *Foreign Relations of the United States 1948*, vol. 5, p. 801 (1976). *Security Council Official Records*, 3d year, 271st mtg., March 19, 1948, UN Doc. S/PV.271, p. 31. *New York Times*, March 20, 1948, p. A2.

54 S. C. Res. 44, April 1, 1948. Bailey, *supra* note 23, p. 165. Kirk, *supra* note 44, p. 257.

55 "Power of the UN Security Council to Aid Political Settlement with Force," *Stanford Intramural Law Review* (June 1948), pp. 105–118.

56 Pitman B. Potter, "The Palestine Problem Before the United Nations," *American Journal of International Law*, vol. 42, p. 858, at p. 860 (1948). Jacques Dehaussy, "La crise du moyen-orient et l'ONU," *Journal du droit international*, vol. 95, p. 853, at p. 855 (1968).

57 G. A. Res. 181, paras. 3, 5, November 29, 1947.

58 Letter from the United Kingdom Delegation, *General Assembly Official Records*, 1st spec. sess., vol. 1, Plenary Meetings, April 2, 1947, UN Doc.A/286, reprinted as "The British Representative at the United Nations (Cadogan) to the Assistant Secretary General of the United States (Hoo)," April 2, 1947, *Foreign Relations of the United States 1947*, vol. 5, p. 1067 (1976).

59 G. A. Res. 181, Part A, operative para. 1, November 29, 1947.

60 Hans Kelsen, *The Law of the United Nations: A Critical Analysis of Its Fundamental Problems* (1950), p. 195.

61 *Security Council Official Records*, February 24, 1948, 3d year, 253d mtg., p. 265,

UN Doc. S/PV.253 (1948); also in *Department of State Bulletin*, vol. 18, p. 294 (1948).

62 Statement of Mr. Creech Jones, U.K., *Security Council Official Records*, 3d yr., 253d mtg., pp. 271–272, UN Doc. S/PV.253 (1948).

63 Statement of Mr. El-Khouri, Syria, *Security Council Official Records*, 3d yr., 254th mtg., p. 280, February 24, 1948, UN Doc. S/PV.254 (1948).

64 Statement of Mr. Fawzi Bey, Egypt, *Security Council Official Records*, 3d year, 255th mtg., p. 299, February 25, 1948, UN Doc. S/PV.255 (1948).

65 Statement of Amir Faisal Al Saud, *General Assembly Official Records*, 2d sess., 128th mtg., p. 1425, November 29, 1947, UN Doc. A/PV.128 (1947).

66 Statement of Prince Seif El Islam Abdullah, Yemen, *General Assembly Official Records*, *supra* note 65, p. 1427.

67 Statement of Mr. Ayub, Pakistan, *General Assembly Official Records*, *supra* note 65, p. 1426.

68 Statement of Mr. Jamali, Iraq, *General Assembly Official Records*, *supra* note 65, pp. 1426–1427.

69 G. A. Res. 181, para. 4, November 29, 1947.

70 James Crawford, *The Creation of States in International Law* (1979), p. 331.

71 G. A. Res. 181, Part A, November 29, 1947.

72 Edward Rizk (trans.), *The Palestine Question: Seminar of Arab Jurists on Palestine, Algiers, 22–27 July 1967* (1968), p. 85.

73 Kelsen, *supra* note 60, p. 197.

74 Pierre-Marie Martin, *Le conflit Israëlo-Arabe: Recherches sur l'Emploi de la force en droit international public positif* (1973), p. 53.

75 *Security Council Official Records*, 3d year, 253d mtg., p. 267, February 24, 1948, UN Doc. S/PV.253 (1948).

76 *Security Council Official Records*, *supra* note 75, p. 265; also in *Department of State Bulletin*, vol. 18, pp. 294–297 (1948).

77 Julius Stone, *Israel and Palestine: Assault on the Law of Nations* (1981), p. 60.

78 Antonio Cassese, "Legal Considerations on the International Status of Jerusalem," in Hans Köchler (ed.), *The Legal Aspects of the Palestine Problem with Special Regard to the Question of Jerusalem* (1981), p. 144, at pp. 145–146.

79 Crawford, *supra* note 70, p. 426. Stone, *supra* note 77, p. 62. Elihu Lauterpacht, "The Contemporary Practice of the United Kingdom in the Field of International Law—Survey and Comment, IV, January 1–June 30, 1957," *International and Comparative Law Quarterly*, vol. 6, p. 506, at p. 515 (1957).

80 Cassese, *supra* note 78, p. 146.

6 Whose Land to Give? The UN's Power over Palestine

* Raphael Patai (ed.), *The Complete Diaries of Theodor Herzl* (1960), p. 1600.

1 Statement of Moshe Shertok, Jewish Agency for Palestine, *General Assembly Official Records*, April 27, 1948, UN Doc. A/C.1/SR.127 (1948).

2 Statute of the International Court of Justice, Statutes at Large of the United States, vol. 59, p. 1055, Treaty Series (U.S.A.) No. 993, *Yearbook of the United Nations*

1976, p. 1052. UN Charter, art. 17. Julius Stone, *Israel and Palestine: Assault on the Law of Nations* (1981), p. 60.

3 Hans Kelsen, *The Law of the United Nations: A Critical Analysis of Its Fundamental Problems* (1950), pp. 195–196.

4 Leland Goodrich and Edvard Hambro, *The Charter of the United Nations: Commentary and Documents* (1949), pp. 151–152.

5 Clyde Eagleton, "Palestine and the Constitutional Law of the United Nations," *American Journal of International Law*, vol. 42, p. 397 (1948).

6 "Remarks by Ambassador Herschel V. Johnson at his Press Conference of October 31, 1947," *Foreign Relations of the United States 1947*, vol. 5, p. 1219, at p. 1221 (1971).

7 F. Blaine Sloane, "The Binding Force of a 'Recommendation' of the General Assembly of the United Nations," *British Year Book of International Law*, vol. 25, p. 1, at p. 24 (1948).

8 D. H. N. Johnson, "The Effect of Resolutions of the General Assembly of the United Nations," *British Year Book of International Law*, vol. 32, p. 97, at p. 109 (1955–56). Pitman B. Potter, "The Palestine Problem Before the United Nations," *American Journal of International Law*, vol. 42, p. 858, at p. 860 (1948).

9 Ian Brownlie, *Principles of Public International Law* (1979), p. 175.

10 Elihu Lauterpacht, *Jerusalem and the Holy Places* (1968), p. 16.

11 Emile Giraud, "Le droit international public et la politique," *Recueil des cours*, vol. 110, p. 419, at p. 732 (no. 3, 1963).

12 Allan Gerson, "Trustee-Occupant: The Legal Status of Israel's Presence in the West Bank," *Harvard International Law Journal*, vol. 14, p. 1, at p. 33 (1973).

13 Nathan Feinberg, "The Arab-Israel Conflict in International Law, A Critical Analysis of the Colloquium of Arab Jurists in Algiers," in Nathan Feinberg, *Studies in International Law with Special Reference to the Arab-Israel Conflict* (1979), p. 433, at pp. 473–474.

14 International Status of South-West Africa (Advisory Opinion), International Court of Justice, *Reports of Judgments, Advisory Opinions and Orders* (1950), p. 144.

15 Feinberg, *supra* note 13, p. 474.

16 G. A. Res. 2145, October 27, 1966.

17 South-West Africa, *supra* note 14, p. 49.

18 Gerson, *supra* note 12, pp. 33–34.

19 Legal Consequences for States of the Continued Presence of South Africa in Namibia (South-West Africa) Notwithstanding Security Council Resolution 276 (1970), International Court of Justice, *Reports of Judgments, Advisory Opinions and Orders* (1971), p. 37, para. 71, citing identical language from South-West Africa, *supra* note 14, p. 137.

20 Judge Fitzmaurice, dissenting opinion, in Legal Consequences, *supra* note 19, p. 226.

21 Kelsen, *supra* note 3, p. 593. Isaak Dore, *The International Mandate System and Namibia* (1985), pp. 9–10. Moshe Avidán (Israeli ambassador to Chile), "Aspectos legales del conflicto del medio oriente," *Revista chilena de derecho*, vol. 5, p. 244, at p. 247 (1978).

22 South-West Africa, *supra* note 14, p. 143.

23 Judge McNair, separate opinion, *id.*, p. 158. Judge Read, separate opinion, *id.*, p. 166.

24 Legal Consequences, *supra* note 19, p. 49, para. 103. W. Thomas Mallison and Sally V. Mallison, *The Palestine Problem: International Law and World Order* (1986), p. 170.

25 UN Charter, art. 73(e).

26 South-West Africa, *supra* note 14, p. 136.

27 *Id.*, p. 144.

28 *Id.*, p. 159.

29 Kelsen, *supra* note 4, pp. 596–597.

30 Statement of Mr. Austin, U.S.A., *Security Council Official Records*, 3d year, p. 164, March 19, 1948, UN Doc. S/PV.271, quoted approvingly in Judge Van Wyk, dissenting opinion, South-West Africa Cases (Ethiopia v. South Africa; Liberia v. South Africa) (preliminary objections), International Court of Justice, *Reports of Judgments, Advisory Opinions and Orders* (1962), p. 638.

31 Report of Sub-Committee 2 to the *Ad Hoc* Committee on the Palestinian Question, *General Assembly Official Records*, 2d sess., November 11, 1947, UN Doc. A/AC. 14/32, p. 276.

32 Covenant of the League of Nations, art. 5.

33 South-West Africa Cases (Ethiopia v. South Africa, Liberia v. South Africa), second phase, International Court of Justice, *Reports of Judgments, Advisory Opinions and Orders* (1966), p. 31.

34 UN Charter, art. 18, para. 2.

35 Judge Lauterpacht, separate opinion, Voting Procedure on Questions Relating to Reports and Petitions Concerning the Territory of South-West Africa, Advisory Opinion, International Court of Justice, *Reports on Judgments, Advisory Opinions and Orders* (1955), p. 115.

36 André Cocâtre-Zilgien, "L'imbroglio moyen-oriental et le droit," *Revue générale de droit international public*, vol. 73, p. 52, at p. 57 (1969).

37 Voting Procedure, *supra* note 35, p. 116.

38 Benjamin Akzin, "The United Nations and Palestine," *Jewish Yearbook of International Law: 1948* (1949), p. 87, at p. 102.

39 J. Halderman, "Some International Constitutional Aspects of the Palestine Case," *Law and Contemporary Problems*, vol. 33, p. 78, at p. 88 (1968). M. Cherif Bassiouni, "The 'Middle East': the Misunderstood Crisis," *Kansas Law Review*, vol. 19, p. 373, at p. 387 (1971).

40 Palestine National Covenant (1968), art. 19, in *New York University Journal of International Law and Politics*, vol. 3, p. 239 (1970).

41 UN Charter, art. 80. Quincy Wright, "The Palestine Conflict in International Law," in Majdia Khadduri (ed.), *Major Middle Eastern Problems in International Law* (1972), p. 13, at p. 26.

42 J. L., "The International Status of Palestine," *Journal du droit international*, vol. 90, p. 964, at p. 966 (1963).

43 Report of Sub-Committee 2 to the Ad Hoc Committee on the Palestinian Question, *General Assembly Official Records*, 2d sess., November 11, 1947, UN Doc. A/AC. 14/32, pp. 278–279 (1947).

44 Covenant of the League of Nations, art. 22.

45 Michael Akehurst, "The Arab-Israeli Conflict in International Law," *New Zealand Universities Law Review*, vol. 5, p. 231, at p. 235 (1973).

46 Frank L. M. Van de Craen, "The Territorial Title of the State of Israel to 'Palestine': An Appraisal in International Law," *Revue belge de droit international*, vol. 14, p. 500, at p. 508 (1978–79). Shabtai Rosenne, "Directions for a Middle East Settlement—Some Underlying Legal Problems." *Law and Contemporary Problems*, vol. 33, p. 44, at p. 51 (1968).

47 Rodolfo Rotman, "Conflicto de títulos territoriales sobre Palestina," *Revista Jurídica Argentina La Ley*, vol. 135, p. 1507, at p. 1520 (1969).

48 UN Charter, art. 25.

49 Rotman, *supra* note 47, p. 1520.

50 *Id.*

51 *Id.*

52 See *supra* chapter 5.

7 Sten Guns and Barrel Bombs: The Realization of the Zionist Dream

1   Golda Meir, *My Life* (1975), pp. 203, 206.

2   George Kirk, *The Middle East 1945–1950* (1954), p. 317.

3   Edgar O'Ballance, *The Arab-Israeli War, 1948* (1956, reprinted 1981), pp. 31–67.

4   Netanel Lorch, *The Edge of the Sword: Israel's War of Independence, 1947–1949* (1961), p. 87. Walid Khalidi, "Plan Dalet: The Zionist Master Plan for the Conquest of Palestine," *Middle East Forum* (November 1961), p. 22, at p. 27. David Hirst, *The Gun and the Olive Branch: The Roots of Violence in the Middle East* (1984), p. 139.

5   "Report by the Central Intelligence Agency: Possible Developments in Palestine," February 28, 1948, *Foreign Relations of the United States 1948*, vol. 5, p. 666, at p. 672 (1976).

6   Simha Flapan, *The Birth of Israel: Myths and Realities* (1987), p. 42. Benny Morris, *The Birth of the Palestinian Refugee Problem, 1947–1949* (1987), p. 63.

7   Morris, *supra* note 6, p. 40.

8   *Id.*, p. 41.

9   *Id.*, p. 52.

10 *Id.*, p. 59.

11 David Ben-Gurion, *Rebirth and Destiny of Israel* (1954), p. 237.

12 Avi Shlaim, *Collusion Across the Jordan: King Abdullah, the Zionist Movement, and the Partition of Palestine* (1988), pp. 155, 158–159.

13 Lorch, *supra* note 4, pp. 89–90. Hirst, *supra* note 4, p. 139.

14 *New York Times*, April 10, 1948, p. A6.

15 *Id.*, p. A6. Menachem Begin, *The Revolt* (1951), pp. 162–165. Jacques de Reynier, *1948 à Jérusalem* (1969), pp. 69–76.

16 Arnold Toynbee, *A Study of History*, vol. 8, p. 290 (1954).

17 O'Ballance, *supra* note 3, p. 58.

18 Harry Levin, *I Saw the Battle of Jerusalem* (1950), p. 37.

19 Michael Palumbo, *The Palestinian Catastrophe* (1987), p. 52. Shlaim, *supra* note

12, p. 164.

20 Erskine Childers, "The Wordless Wish: From Citizens to Refugees," in Ibrahim Abu-Lughod, *The Transformation of Palestine: Essays on the Origin and Development of the Arab-Israeli Conflict* (1971), pp. 165, 186.

21 Joseph C. Harsch, "Terrorism—Past, Present, and Future," *Christian Science Monitor*, June 20, 1985, p. 16.

22 Toynbee, *supra* note 16, p. 290. Nafez Nazzal, *The Palestinian Exodus from Galilee 1948* (1978), pp. 34, 44, 52, 90. Michael Akehurst, "The Arab-Israeli Conflict and International Law," *New Zealand Universities Law Review*, vol. 5, p. 231, at p. 233 (1973).

23 Statement of Mr. Austin, *General Assembly Official Records*, 2d spec. sess., vol. 2, Main Committees, April 16–May 14, 1948, p. 7, UN Doc. A/C.1/SR.117 (1948).

24 Ritchie Ovendale, *The Origins of the Arab-Israeli Wars* (1984), p. 121. George Kirk, *A Short History of the Middle East from the Rise of Islam to Modern Times* (1949), pp. 210–214.

25 *Palestine Post*, April 28, 1948, p. 1. *New York Times*, April 28, 1948, p. A14. Kirk, *supra* note 2, p. 261. Yitshaq Ben-Ami, *Years of Wrath, Days of Glory: Memoirs from the Irgun* (1982), p. 446.

26 Begin, *supra* note 15, pp. 198, 202.

27 *Id.*, p. 188.

28 Morris, *supra* note 6, p. 123.

29 Childers, *supra* note 20, p. 183. Walid Khalidi, "Why Did the Palestinians Leave? An Examination of the Zionist Version of the Exodus of '48," *Middle East Forum*, vol. 35, p. 21, at p. 35 (July 1959).

30 Khalidi, *supra* note 29, p. 24. Palumbo, *supra* note 19, p. 62.

31 IDF, Intelligence Branch, "The Emigration of the Arabs of Palestine in the Period 1/12/1947–1/6/1948," June 30, 1948, in Benny Morris, "The Causes and Character of the Arab Exodus from Palestine: the Israel Defence Forces Intelligence Branch Analysis of June 1948," *Middle Eastern Studies*, vol. 22, p. 5, at p. 10 (1986).

32 R. D. Wilson, *Cordon and Search: With 6th Airborne Division in Palestine* (1949), pp. 144–147.

33 Leo Heiman, "All's Fair . . .," *Marine Corps Gazette* (June 1964), p. 37, at p. 39.

34 S. C. Res. 46, April 17, 1948.

35 Palumbo, *supra* note 19, p. 107.

36 *Palestine Post*, April 19, 1948, p. 1; April 21, 1948, p. 3. Dan Kurzman, *Genesis 1948: The First Arab-Israeli War* (1970), p. 150.

37 *Palestine Post*, April 21, 1948, p. 1.

38 *Id.*, April 23, 1948, p. 2.

39 Arthur Koestler, *Promise and Fulfillment: Palestine 1917–1949* (1949), p. 207.

40 Childers, *supra* note 20, p. 189.

41 Morris, *supra* note 31, p. 6.

42 Jon Kimche, *Seven Fallen Pillars: The Middle East, 1945–1952* (1953), p. 229.

43 *Palestine Post*, April 23, 1948, p. 1. Kurzman, *supra* note 36, p. 156.

44 Begin, *supra* note 15, p. 165.

45 Wilson, *supra* note 32, p. 193.

46 Morris, *supra* note 6, pp. 85–86.

47 Lynne Reid Banks, *Torn Country: An Oral History of the Israeli War of Independence* (1982), p. 116.

48 Kurt René Radley, "The Palestinian Refugees: the Right to Return in International Law," *American Journal of International Law*, vol. 72, p. 586, at p. 589 (1978). Rony Gabbay, *A Political Study of the Arab-Jewish Conflict* (1959), pp. 94–95.

49 Morris, *supra* note 6, pp. 79, 85.

50 Walid Khalidi, "The Fall of Haifa," *Middle East Forum*, vol. 35, p. 22, at pp. 24–25, 32 (December 1959). Palumbo, *supra* note 19, pp. 69–70.

51 *New York Times*, April 28, 1948, p. A14; April 29, 1948, p. A1. Palumbo, *supra* note 19, p. 93.

52 Morris, *supra* note 6, pp. 96–97.

53 *Palestine Post*, May 4, 1948, p. 1.

54 Begin, *supra* note 15, p. 363.

55 Banks, *supra* note 47, p. 124.

56 Palumbo, *supra* note 19, pp. 89–90.

57 Noam Chomsky, *Turning the Tide: U.S. Intervention in Central America and the Struggle for Peace* (1985). p. 77.

58 Nazzal, *supra* note 22, p. 32.

59 *Id.*, pp. 34–35.

60 Lorch, *supra* note 4, pp. 118–120.

61 *Palestine Post*, May 3, 1948, p. 1. Harry Levin, *Jerusalem Embattled: A Diary of the City under Siege, March 25th, 1948 to July 18th, 1948* (1950), p. 137. Palumbo, *supra* note 19, p. 113. Morris, *supra* note 6, pp. 107–108.

62 Uri Avnery, *My Friend, the Enemy* (1986), p. 264.

63 *Palestine Post*, May 11, 1948, p. 1. Morris, *supra* note 6, p. 107. Palumbo, *supra* note 19, p. 116.

64 Childers, *supra* note 20, pp. 192–193.

65 Nazzal, *supra* note 22, p. 58.

66 "Dr. Chaim Weizmann to President Truman," April 9, 1948, *Foreign Relations of the United States 1948*, vol. 5, p. 807 (1976).

67 *General Assembly Official Records*, April 27, 1948, UN Doc. A/C.1/SR.127, p. 108 (1948).

68 Statement of Moshe Shertok, *General Assembly Official Records*, April 27, 1948, UN Doc. A/C.1/SR.127, pp. 113–115 (1948).

69 *New York Times*, April 27, 1948, p. A1.

70 Levin, *supra* note 61, p. 104.

71 *Palestine Post*, May 9, 1948, p. 1.

72 *Id.*, May 6, 1948, p. 1.

73 Akehurst, *supra* note 22, p. 233. Childers, *supra* note 20, p. 193. Morris, *supra* note 31, pp. 6–7.

74 *Id.*, p. 9.

75 Shlaim, *supra* note 12, p. 168. Lorch, *supra* note 4, p. 141.

76 Kurzman, *supra* note 36, p. 157. Childers, *supra* note 20, p. 181. Palumbo, *supra* note 19, p. 66.

77 *Palestine Post*, May 12, 1948, p. 3. Erskine B. Childers, "The Other Exodus,"

Spectator, May 12, 1961, p. 672. Khalidi, *supra* note 29, p. 23.

78 Childers, *supra* note 77, p. 672.

79 Levin, *supra* note 61, p. 104.

80 *Palestine Post*, May 3, 1948, p. 3.

81 Khalidi, *supra* note 50, pp. 24–25.

82 Childers, *supra* note 77, p. 672. Morris, *supra* note 6, p. 69.

83 Morris, *supra* note 31, p. 11.

84 IDF intelligence branch, in Morris, *supra* note 31, p. 11.

85 Khalidi, *supra* note 29, pp. 23–24.

86 *Palestine Post*, May 6, 1948, p. 2. Khalidi, *supra* note 29, p. 24.

87 *Palestine Post*, May 9, 1948, p. 3.

88 "Draft memorandum by the Director of the Office of United Nations Affairs (Rusk) to the Under Secretary of State (Lovett)" (secret; drafted by Mr. McClintock), May 4, 1948, *Foreign Relations of the United States 1948*, vol. 5, pp. 894–895 (1976).

89 G. A. Res. 186, May 14, 1948.

90 Declaration of the Establishment of the State of Israel, *Laws of the State of Israel*, vol. 1, p. 3 (1948).

91 Cablegram from foreign secretary of provisional government of Israel to secretary-general, May 15, 1948, *Security Council Official Records*, 3d year, Supplement for May 1948, pp. 88–89, UN Doc. S/747 (1948).

92 Statement of Abba Eban, Jewish Agency for Palestine, *Security Council Official Records*, 3d year, No. 72, 302d mtg., p. 32, May 22, 1948, UN Doc. S/PV.302 (1948). Rodolfo Rotman, "Conflicto de títulos territoriales sobre Palestina," *Revista Jurídica Argentina La Ley*, vol. 135, pp. 1507–1521 (1969). Nabil Elaraby, "Some Legal Implications of the 1947 Partition Resolution and the 1949 Armistice Agreements," *Law and Contemporary Problems*, vol. 33, p. 97, at p. 103 (1968).

93 Nathan Feinberg and J. Stoyanovsky, "Israel's Declaration of Independence," *Jewish Yearbook of International Law: 1948* (1949), p. ix, at p. x.

94 "The Agent of the Provisional Government of Israel (Epstein) to President Truman," *Foreign Relations of the United States 1948*, vol. 5, p. 989 (1976).

95 *Id.*, pp. 992–993.

8 Kaftans and Yarmulkes: The Claim of Ancient Title to Palestine

1 Julius Stone, *Israel and Palestine: Assault on the Law of Nations* (1981), p. 22.

2 *Laws of the State of Israel*, vol. 1, p. 3 (1948).

3 David Ben-Gurion, "The Only Solution of the Jewish Problem," *Palestine Yearbook* (Zionist Organization of America), vol. 1, p. 11, at p. 19 (1945).

4 Moshe Avidán, "Aspectos legales del conflicto del medio oriente," *Revista chilena de derecho*, vol. 5, p. 244, at p. 245 (1978).

5 Nathan Feinberg and J. Stoyanovsky, "Israel's Declaration of Independence," *Jewish Yearbook of International Law: 1948* (1949), p. ix.

6 Statement of Abba Eban, Jewish Agency for Palestine, *Security Council Official Records*, 3d year, No. 72, 302d mtg., May 22, 1948, UN Doc. S/PV.302.

7   UN Charter, art. 73.

8   UN Charter, art. 1, para. 2.

9   Eugene V. Rostow, "Palestinian Self-Determination: Possible Futures for the Unallo-cated Territories of the Palestine Mandate," *Yale Studies in World Public Order*, vol. 5, p. 147, at pp. 153–154 (1978). Marilyn J. Berliner, "Palestinian Arab Self-Determination and Israeli Settlements on the West Bank: An Analysis of Their Legality Under International Law," *Loyola of Los Angeles International and Comparative Law Journal*, vol. 8, p. 551, at p. 555 (1986).

10   Wolfgang Benedek, "Progressive Development of the Principles and Norms of International Law Relating to the NIEO: The UNITAR Exercise," Österreichische Zeitschrift für Öffentliches Recht und Völkerrecht, vol. 36, p. 289, at pp. 307–311 (1986).

11   Vienna Convention on the Law of Treaties, art. 33, para. 3, UN Doc. A/CONF.39/27 (1969).

12   G. A. Res. 421(D), December 4, 1950, *General Assembly Official Records*, 5th sess., Supplement No. 20, p. 43, UN Doc. A/1775 (1950). Vote: 30–9–13.

13   G. A. Res. 545, *General Assembly Official Records*, vol. 6, Supplement No. 20, pp. 36–37, UN Doc. A/2119 (1952). The vote on this paragraph of Res. 545 was 40–4–10.

14   R. Y. Jennings, *The Acquisition of Territory in International Law* (1963), pp. 16–35. Island of Palmas, *United Nations Reports of International Arbitral Awards*, vol. 2, p. 829 (1928). Minquiers and Ecrehos (France v. United Kingdom), *International Court of Justice, Reports of Judgments, Advisory Opinions and Orders* (1953), p. 57. Western Sahara, *id.* (1975), pp. 40–68.

15   Sabatino Moscati, *The Semites in Ancient History* (1959), p. 82.

16   Anthony Nutting, *The Arabs: A Narrative History from Mohammed to the Present* (1964), p. 5. Sabatino Moscati, *Ancient Semitic Civilizations* (1957), p. 108.

17   Ilan Halevi, *Question juive: la Tribu, la Loi, l'Espace* (1981), pp. 196–197.

18   Stephen H. Longrigg, *The Middle East: A Social Geography* (1963), p. 35.

19   Edward Rizk (trans.), *The Palestine Question: Seminar of Arab Jurists on Palestine, Algiers, 22–27 July 1967* (1968), p. 17.

20   Moscati, *supra* note 16, p. 111.

21   Quincy Wright, "The Palestine Problem," *Political Science Quarterly*, vol. 41, p. 384, at pp. 393–394 (1926).

22   Cecil Roth, *A History of the Jews from Earliest Times through the Six Day War* (1970), p. 11.

23   Ray L. Cleveland, "The Palestinians and the Diminution of Historical Legitimacy," in Glenn Perry (ed.), *Palestine: Continuing Dispossession* (1986), p. 95, at p. 104.

24   Longrigg, *note* 18, p. 36. Roth, *supra* note 22, p. 13.

25   Roth, *supra* note 22, p. 78.

26   *Id.*, p. 62.

27   *Id.*, p. 87. Frank H. Epp, *Whose Land Is Palestine: The Middle East Problem in Historical Perspective* (1970), pp. 44–67.

28   Roth, *supra* note 22, p. 115.

29   Michael Akehurst, "The Arab-Israeli Conflict and International Law," *New Zea-*

land Universities Law Review, vol. 5, p. 231 (1973). Maps in Stone's *Israel and Palestine: Assault on the Law of Nations* (1981), p. 137, exaggerate the time and area of Hebrew predominance. The boundaries he shows represent only the maximum temporary extent of the Israelite and Judean empires. They incorrectly suggest Hebrew predominance until A.D. 636, the time of the Arab conquest. For criticism of Stone's maps, see Perry, *supra* note 23, p. 14.

30 Ilene Beatty, *Arab and Jew in the Land of Canaan* (1957), p. 40.

31 Edward F. Henderson, *Maps and Mythology: What Israeli Records Reveal About the Land and People of Palestine* (1982), p. 4.

32 Raphael Patai, *The Seed of Abraham: Jews and Arabs in Contact and Conflict* (1986), p. 300. Alexander Schölch, "The Demographic Development of Palestine, 1850–1882," *International Journal of Middle East Studies* (1985), p. 485, at p. 504.

33 *Parliamentary Debates* (House of Lords), 5th series, vol. 50, col. 1021 (1922).

34 King-Crane Commission Report, *Foreign Relations of the United States: Paris Peace Conference 1919*, vol. 12, p. 748, at p. 794 (1947).

35 Stone, *supra* note 29, p. 255.

36 Minquiers and Ecrehos, *supra* note 14, p. 56.

37 Konstantin Obradovič, *The Palestinian Question from the Standpoint of Human Rights—A Review of Existing Problems*, UN Seminar on Violations of Human Rights in the Palestinian and Other Arab Territories Occupied by Israel, p. 18, UN Doc. HR/GENEVA/1982/BP.3 (1982). Mohammed Bedjaoui, "Inaugural Address," in Rizk, *supra* note 19, p. 3, at p. 7. John Collins, "Self-Determination in International Law: The Palestinians," *Case Western Reserve Journal of International Law*, vol. 12, p. 137, at pp. 156–157 (1980). Frank L. M. Van de Craen, "The Territorial Title of the State of Israel to 'Palestine': An Appraisal in International Law," *Revue belge de droit international*, vol. 14, p. 500, at p. 527 (1978–79).

38 Stone, *supra* note 29, p. 254.

39 Statement of N. Sokolow, February 27, 1919, *Foreign Relations of the United States: Paris Peace Conference 1919*, vol. 4, p. 163 (1943).

40 Joseph Reinach, "Sur le sionisme," *Journal des débats politiques et littéraires* (March 30, 1919), pp. 1–2.

41 Western Sahara, International Court of Justice, *Reports of Judgments, Advisory Opinions and Orders* (1975), p. 41, para. 86. Minquiers and Ecrehos, *supra* note 14, p. 56.

42 Philippe de Saint Robert, *Le Jeu de la France en Méditerranée* (1970), p. 182.

43 Louis Brandeis, "The Jewish Problem," in Zionist Organization of America, *Brandeis on Zionism: A Collection of Statements and Addresses by Louis D. Brandeis* (1942), p. 12, at p. 21.

44 Cleveland, *supra* note 23, p. 105.

45 Raphael Patai and Jennifer Patai Wing, *The Myth of the Jewish Race* (1975), p. 116.

46 Jean-Pierre Alem, *Juifs et Arabes: 3000 Ans d'Histoire* (1968), pp. 31–32.

47 Raymond Aron, *DeGaulle, Israel and the Jews* (1969), p. 124. Patai and Patai Wing, *supra* note 45, p. 52.

48 Patai and Patai Wing, *supra* note 45, pp. 53, 73, 75, 80. W. F. Abboushi, *The Angry Arabs* (1974), p. 145.

49   Arnold Toynbee, *A Study of History* (1947), p. 138.
50   Maxime Rodinson, *Israel: A Colonial-Settler State?* (1973), pp. 79–80. Patai and Patai Wing, *supra* note 45, pp. 69–70.
51   Patai and Patai Wing, *supra* note 45, p. 53.
52   Arthur Koestler, *The Thirteenth Tribe: The Khazar Empire and Its Heritage* (1976), p. 187.
53   Roth, *supra* note 22, p. 264. Koestler, *supra* note 52, pp. 13–14. D. M. Dunlop, *The History of the Jewish Khazars* (1954), pp. ix–x, 89–170. D. M. Dunlop, "Khazars," in *Encyclopedia Judaica*, vol. 10, pp. 950–951 (1972). L. N. Gumilev, *Otkrytie Khazarii: istorichesko-geograficheskii etiud* (The Discovery of Khazaria: An Historical-Geographic Study, 1966). Mikhail Artamonov, *Istoriia khazar (History of the Khazars,* 1962), p. 265.
54   Norman Golb and Omeljan Pritsak, *Khazarian Hebrew Documents of the Tenth Century* (1982), pp. xii–xiv. Salo Baron, *The Social and Religious History of the Jews*, vol. 3, p. 196 (1952). Max L. Margolis and Alexander Marx, *A History of the Jewish People* (1927), p. 526. Hugo Kutschera, *Die Chasaren* (1910), p. 209. Alem, *supra* note 46, p. 33. S. M. Dubnow, *History of the Jews in Russia and Poland from the Earliest Times Until the Present Day*, vol. 1, p. 20 (1975, orig. pub. 1916). Alfred M. Lilienthal, "The Right of Self-Determination: Why Not the Palestinians?" in Hans Köchler (ed.), *The Legal Aspects of the Palestine Problem with Special Regard to the Question of Jerusalem* (1981), p. 50, at p. 51.
55   Ananiasz Zajaczkowski, "Khazarian Culture and Its Inheritors," *Acta Orientalia Academiae Scientarium Hungaricae*, vol. 12, p. 299, at p. 306 (1961).
56   Baron, *supra* note 54, p. 206. Louis Greenberg, *The Jews in Russia*, vol. 1, p. 4 (1944). D. M. Dunlop, "The Khazars," in Cecil Roth (ed.), *World History of the Jewish People*, vol. 11, p. 325, at pp. 355–356 (1966).
57   Patai and Patai Wing, *supra* note 45, p. 71.
58   Alfred H. Posselt, *Geschichte des Chazarisch-Judischen Staates* (1982), p. 204. Koestler, *supra* note 52, p. 145. Joshua Starr, "Khazars," in *Universal Jewish Encyclopedia*, vol. 6, p. 375, at pp. 377–378 (1942). Patai and Patai Wing, *supra* note 45, p. 72.
59   Dunlop, *History, supra* note 53, p. 262. Dunlop, *supra* note 56, p. 355. Koestler, *supra* note 52, pp. 142–143.
60   Baron, *supra* note 54, p. 206. Josef Meisl, *Geschichte des Juden in Polen und Russland* (1921), p. 39. Adam Vetulani, "The Jews in Medieval Poland," *Jewish Journal of Sociology* (December 1962), p. 274.
61   Dunlop, *History, supra* note 53, p. 262.
62   Koestler, *supra* note 52, pp. 156–157.
63   Margolis and Marx, *supra* note 54, pp. 527–528. James Parkes, *The Jew and His Neighbor: A Study of the Causes of Anti-Semitism* (1930), p. 16. Bernard D. Weinryb, *The Jews of Poland: A Social and Economic History of the Jewish Community in Poland from 1100 to 1800* (1973), p. 27.
64   Meisl, *supra* note 60, p. 39. J. Marcus, *Social and Political History of the Jews in Poland, 1919–1939* (1983), p. 3.
65   Koestler, *supra* note 52, pp. 164–167. M. Cherif Bassiouni and Eugene Fisher, "The Arab-Israeli Conflict—Real and Apparent Issues: An Insight into Its Future

from the Lessons of the Past," *St. John's Law Review*, vol. 44, p. 399, at p. 413 (1970).

66 Kutschera, *supra* note 54, p. 235.

67 Thomas Kiernan, *The Arabs: Their History, Aims and Challenge to the Industrialized World* (1975), p. 236. A. N. Poliak, *Khazaria—The History of a Jewish Kingdom in Europe* (in Hebrew, 1951), pp. 246–275. Koestler, *supra* note 52, pp. 141, 151. Kutschera, *supra* note 54, pp. 16–17. Aron, *supra* note 47, p. 124. Patai and Patai Wing, *supra* note 45, p. 90. Saint Robert, *supra* note 42, p. 181.

68 Avidán, *supra* note 4, p. 245.

69 *Laws of the State of Israel*, Declaration, *supra* note 2, para. 2.

70 *Holy Bible*, Numbers 33:50–56. Norton Mezvinsky, "The Palestinian People and the Right of Self-Determination," in Köchler, *supra* note 54, p. 34, at pp. 42–45.

71 Klaus Herrmann, "Politics and the 'Divine Promise,'" in *Judaism or Zionism: What Difference for the Middle East?* (1986), pp. 18–39.

72 Alan R. Taylor, "Vision and Intent in Zionist Thought," in Ibrahim Abu-Lughod (ed.), *The Transformation of Palestine: Essays on the Origin and Development of the Arab-Israeli Conflict* (1971), p. 9, at pp. 10–13.

73 Ilan Halevi, *Sous Israël la Palestine* (1978), p. 145.

74 Speech, Knesset, *Jerusalem Post*, June 13, 1967, p. 2.

75 Benjamin Shalit and Others v. Minister of the Interior and Another (dissent), High Court 58/68, Supreme Court sitting as High Court of Justice, January 23, 1970, in Asher Felix Landau (ed.), *Selected Judgments of the Supreme Court of Israel: Special Volume* (1971), p. 35, at p. 56.

76 *Knesset Debates*, vol. 6, pp. 2035–2036 (July 3, 1950).

77 Hugh R. Trevor-Roper, "Jewish and Other Nationalisms," *Commentary* (January 1963), p. 15, at pp. 16–17.

78 Tom Segev, *1949: the First Israelis* (1986), p. 115.

79 Trevor-Roper, *supra* note 77, pp. 16–17. Ben Halpern, *The Idea of the Jewish State* (1961), p. 105.

9 Arab vs. Zionist: War of Independence or War of Aggression?

1 Amos Elon, *The Israelis: Founders and Sons* (1983), pp. 158–159.

2 Dov Ronen, *The Quest for Self-Determination* (1979), pp. 86–89. Moshe Avidán, "Aspectos legales del conflicto del medio oriente," *Revista chilena de derecho*, vol. 5, p. 244, at p. 251 (1978).

3 Julius Stone, "Peace and the Palestinians," *New York University Journal of International Law and Politics*, vol. 3, p. 247, at pp. 248–251 (1970).

4 Golda Meir, Interview, *Sunday Times*, June 15, 1969, p. 12.

5 George Antonius, *The Arab Awakening: The Story of the Arab National Movement* (1946), pp. 292–294. Simha Flapan, *Zionism and the Palestinians* (1979), pp. 79–80.

6 Letter from Mr. (Herbert) Samuel to Earl Curzon, April 2, 1920, *Documents on British Foreign Policy*, 1919–1939 (1st series), vol. 13, p. 241 (1963). Raphael Patai, *The Seed of Abraham: Jews and Arabs in Contact and Conflict* (1986), p. 314.

7   Flapan, *supra* note 5, pp. 79–80.

8   Rosemary Radford Ruether and Herman J. Ruether, *The Wrath of Jonah: The Crisis of Religious Nationalism in the Israeli-Palestinian Conflict* (1989), p. 103.

9   Flapan, *supra* note 5, p. 80. Muhammad Muslih, *The Origins of Palestinian Nationalism* (1988), pp. 207–210.

10 Moshe Gabai, "Israeli Arabs: Problems of Identity and Integration," *New Outlook* (October-November, 1984), p. 18.

11 "Comments by W. Michael Reisman," in "Self-Determination and Settlement of the Arab-Israeli Conflict," *Proceedings of the American Society of International Law*, vol. 65, p. 31, at p. 50 (1971).

12 Stone, *supra* note 3, p. 259.

13 Statement of Issa Nakhleh, Arab Higher Committee, *Security Council Official Records*, 3d year, No. 66, 292d mtg., pp. 8–9, May 15, 1948, UN Doc. S/PV.292 (1948).

14 Mohammed Bedjaoui, "Inaugural Address," in Edward Rizk, (trans.), *The Palestine Question: Seminar of Arab Jurists on Palestine, Algiers, 22–27 July 1967* (1968), p. 3, at p. 6.

15 Institute of International Law, Resolution, 1931, para. 6. Text of Resolution in James Brown Scott, "The Two Institutes of International Law," *American Journal of International Law*, vol. 23, p. 91 (1932).

16 Mandate for Palestine, art. 5, League of Nations, *Official Journal*, vol. 8, p. 1007 (1922); also in *Terms of League of Nations Mandates: Republished by the United Nations*, UN Doc. A/70 (1946), reprinted from Permanent Mandates Commission No. 466, League of Nations Docs. C.529.M.314.1922.VI and C.667.M.396.1922.VI; also in Convention between the United States and Great Britain Concerning Palestine, December 3, 1924, *United States Statutes at Large*, vol. 44, p. 2184.

17 Mandate for Palestine, *supra* note 16, art. 7. Palestinian Citizenship Order in Council, July 24, 1925, *Statutory Rules and Orders*, No. 777, p. 474 (1925). Norman Bentwich, "Nationality in Mandated Territories Detached from Turkey," *British Year Book of International Law*, vol. 7, p. 97, at p. 102 (1926). J. L., "The International Status of Palestine," *Journal du droit international*, vol. 90, p. 964, at p. 966 (1963).

18 J. L., *supra* note 17, p. 966.

19 *Id.*, p. 964.

20 M. Cherif Bassiouni, "The 'Middle East': the Misunderstood Conflict," *Kansas Law Review*, vol. 19, p. 373, at p. 390 (1971).

21 Edward Miller, "Self-Defense, International Law, and the Six Day War," *Israel Law Review*, vol. 20, p. 49, at pp. 57–58 (1985).

22 Ian Brownlie, *International Law and the Use of Force by States* (1963), p. 279.

23 Definition of Aggression, G. A. Res. 3314, December 14, 1974.

24 Brownlie, *supra* note 22, p. 279. Derek Bowett, *Self-Defence in International Law* (1958), p. 56. Oscar Schachter, "The Right of States to Use Armed Force," *Michigan Law Review*, vol. 82, p. 1620, at p. 1626 (1984).

25 Bassiouni, *supra* note 20, p. 389.

26 Myres McDougal and Florentino Feliciano, *Law and Minimum World Public Order: The Legal Regulation of International Coercion* (1961), p. 221.

27 Nathan Feinberg, "On an Arab Jurist's Approach to Zionism and the State of Israel," in Nathan Feinberg, *Studies in International Law with Special Reference to the Arab-Israel Conflict* (1979) p. 433, at p. 462. W. Ofuatey-Kodjoe, *The Principle of Self-Determination in International Law* (1977), pp. 99–103. André Mathiot, "Le status des territoires dépendants d'après la Charte des Nations Unies," *Revue générale de droit international public*, vol. 50, pp. 159–209 (1946).

28 Harry Sacher, "The Jewish State," *New Judaea* (May 1948), p. 125.

29 Statement of Mr. Eliash, Jewish Agency for Palestine, *Security Council Official Records*, 3d year, No. 66, 292d mtg., p. 7, May 15, 1948, UN Doc. S/PV.292 (1948).

30 A. L. W. Munkman, review of *Jerusalem and the Holy Places*, by Elihu Lauterpacht, *British Year Book of International Law*, vol. 43, p. 306, at p. 309 (1968–69).

31 *Yearbook of the United Nations 1947–48* (1949), pp. 417–422.

32 S. C. Res. 49, art. 1, May 22, 1948.

33 S. C. Res. 54, July 15, 1948.

34 Cablegram of Egypt to Security Council, *Security Council Official Records, supra* note 29, p. 3.

35 Statement of Mr. Fawzi, Egypt, *Security Council Official Records*, 3d year, No. 72, 301st mtg., p. 21, May 22, 1948, UN Doc. S/PV.301 (1948).

36 Cablegram of Egyptian Minister of Foreign Affairs to President of Security Council, *Security Council Official Records, supra* note 29, p. 3.

37 UN Doc. S/748, May 15, 1948, *Yearbook of the United Nations 1947–48* (1949), p. 416.

38 Statement of Issa Nakhleh, Arab Higher Committee, *Security Council Official Records, supra* note 29, p. 8.

39 Statement of Mr. Fawzi, *supra* note 35.

40 Statement of Mr. El-Khouri, Syria, *Security Council Official Records, supra* note 29, p. 18.

41 Statement of Saudi foreign minister to secretary-general, May 21, 1948, *Security Council Official Records*, 3d year, Supplement for May 1948, UN Doc. S/772, p. 96.

42 Netanel Lorch, *The Edge of the Sword: Israel's War of Independence, 1947–1949* (1961), pp. 141–142.

43 *Palestine Post*, May 17, 1948, p. 1; May 19, 1948, p. 1; May 20, 1948, p. 1.

44 Lorch, *supra* note 42, pp. 227–229. Avi Shlaim, *Collusion Across the Jordan: King Abdullah, the Zionist Movement, and the Partition of Palestine* (1988), p. 239.

45 Shlaim, *supra* note 44, pp. 203, 235, 244. Alan Bullock, *Ernest Bevin, Foreign Secretary, 1945–1951* (1983), p. 509.

46 *New York Times*, May 17, 1948, p. A1.

47 Sydney N. Fisher, *The Middle East* (1966), p. 585.

48 Shlaim, *supra* note 44, p. 247.

49 Bullock, *supra* note 45, p. 595. Alec Kirkbride, *From the Wings: Amman Memoirs 1947–1951* (1976), p. 34.

50 *International Legal Materials*, vol. 15, p. 1224 (1976).

51 *Yearbook of the United Nations 1947–48* (1949), p. 418.

52 Urs Schwarz, *Confrontation and Intervention in the Modern World* (1970), pp. 103–108.

53 Brownlie, *supra* note 22, p. 327.

54 *Id.*, p. 325.

55 Michael Akehurst, "The Arab-Israeli Conflict and International Law," *New Zealand Universities Law Review*, vol. 5, p. 231, at p. 237 (1973).

56 Frank L. M. Van de Craen, "The Territorial Title of the State of Israel to 'Palestine': An Appraisal in International Law," *Revue belge de droit international*, vol. 14, p. 513 (1978–79). J. R. Gainsborough, *The Arab-Israeli Conflict: A Politico-Legal Analysis* (1986), p. 53.

57 Munkman, *supra* note 30, p. 308.

58 George Kirk, *The Middle East 1945–1950* (1954), pp. 280–281. Uri Avnery, *My Friend, the Enemy* (1986), p. 85. Simha Flapan, *The Birth of Israel: Myths and Realities* (1987), pp. 39, 128–129.

59 John Quigley, "The United States Invasion of Grenada: Stranger than Fiction," *Inter-American Law Review*, vol. 18, p. 271, at pp. 345–346 (1987).

60 Feinberg, *supra* note 27, p. 499. Yehuda Z. Blum, "The Missing Reversioner: Reflections on the Status of Judea and Samaria," *Israel Law Review*, vol. 3, p. 279, at p. 287 (1968). Pierre-Marie Martin, *Le conflit Israëlo-Arabe: Recherches sur L'Emploi de la Force en Droit International Public Positif* (1973), p. 57.

61 *New York Times*, December 9, 1947, p. A14.

62 *Yearbook of the United Nations 1947–48* (1949), p. 418.

63 Pact of the League of Arab States, March 22, 1945, *United Nations Treaty Series*, vol. 70, p. 237 (1950).

10 Exodus: The Departure of the Palestine Arabs

1 IDF intelligence branch, "The Emigration of the Arabs of Palestine in the Period 1/12/1947–1/6/1948," June 30, 1948, in Benny Morris, "The Causes and Character of the Arab Exodus from Palestine: the Israel Defence Forces Intelligence Branch Analysis of June 1948," *Middle Eastern Studies*, vol. 22, p. 5, at p. 9 (1986).

2 Harry Levin, *Jerusalem Embattled: A Diary of the City under Siege, March 25th, 1948 to July 18th, 1948* (1950), p. 160.

3 Uri Avnery, "Les réfugiés arabes, obstacle à la paix," *Le Monde*, May 9, 1964, p. 1, at p. 2.

4 *Palestine Post*, May 16, 1948, p. 1. Michael Palumbo, *The Palestinian Catastrophe* (1987), p. 119. Benny Morris, *The Birth of the Palestininan Refugee Problem, 1947–1949* (1987), pp. 107–108.

5 Netanel Lorch, *The Edge of the Sword: Israel's War of Independence, 1947–1949* (1961), p. 188.

6 Yigal Allon, *The Making of Israel's Army* (1970), p. 3. Simha Flapan, *The Birth of Israel: Myths and Realities* (1987), p. 190.

7 Flapan, *supra* note 6, pp. 195–197.

8 *Id.*, p. 196. Yitzhak Greenberg, "Financing the War of Independence," *Studies in Zionism*, vol. 9, p. 63, at p. 78 (1988). Maxime Rodinson, *Israel: A Colonial-Settler State?* (1973), p. 75. George Kirk, *The Middle East 1945–1950* (1954), p. 277.

9 Golda Meir, *My Life* (1975), p. 222.

10 Edgar O'Ballance, *The Arab-Israeli War, 1948* (1956, reprinted 1981), pp. 64, 172.

11 Avnery, *supra* note 3, p. 2.

12 Palumbo, *supra* note 4, pp. 116–117. Morris, *supra* note 1, pp. 15–16.

13 *New York Times*, October 23, 1979, p. A23. Morris, *supra* note 4, p. 207. Benny Morris, "Operation Dani and the Palestinian Exodus from Lydda and Ramle in 1948," *Middle East Journal*, vol. 40, p. 82, at p. 96 (1986). Reja-e Busailah, "The Fall of Lydda, 1948: Impressions and Reminiscences," *Arab Studies Quarterly*, vol. 3, p. 123, at p. 128 (1981). Kirk, *supra* note 8, p. 281. Fouzi El-Asmar, *To Be an Arab in Israel* (1978), pp. 4–13. Jon and David Kimche, *Both Sides of the Hill: Britain and the Palestine War* (1960), pp. 227–228. O'Ballance, *supra* note 10, p. 147.

14 O'Ballance, *supra* note 10, p. 147.

15 El-Asmar, *supra* note 13, p. 7.

16 O'Ballance, *supra* note 10, p. 147.

17 Lorch, *supra* note 5, pp. 275–276.

18 Nafez Nazzal, *The Palestinian Exodus from Galilee 1948* (1978), p. 79. Palumbo, *supra* note 4, p. 123.

19 Peretz Kidron, "Truth Whereby Nations Live," in Edward Said and Christopher Hutchins, *Blaming the Victims: Spurious Scholarship and the Palestinian Question* (1988), p. 86. Palumbo, *supra* note 4, p. 123. Nazzal, *supra* note 18, p. 79.

20 Michael Bar Zohar, interview, Israel Radio, October 22, 1986, reported in Didi Yizraeli, "Ben-Gurion Supported the Expulsion of Arabs," *Hadashot*, October 19, 1986, in Israel Shahak, *Collection: The Kufr Kassem Massacre of 1956 and the "Ideals" of Ben-Gurion* (1987), p. 13. Morris, *supra* note 4, p. 202.

21 Kidron, *supra* note 19, p. 87.

22 Morris, *supra* note 4, p. 201.

23 Palumbo, *supra* note 4, pp. 123–125.

24 Interview by author, December 1984, Jerusalem, with 1948 Arab residents of Nazareth.

25 Kurt René Radley, "The Palestinian Refugees: the Right to Return in International Law," *American Journal of International Law*, vol. 72, p. 586, at p. 594 (1978).

26 Arnold Toynbee, *A Study of History*, vol. 8, p. 290 (1954). Michael Akehurst, "The Arab-Israel Conflict and International Law," *New Zealand Universities Law Review*, vol. 5, p. 231, at p. 233 (1973). Rony Gabbay, *A Political Study of the Arab-Jewish Conflict* (1959), p. 108. Nadav Safran, *From War to War: The Arab-Israeli Confrontation, 1948–1967* (1969), p. 35. Morris, *supra* note 13, p. 104. Benny Morris, "The Crystallization of Israeli Policy Against a Return of the Arab Refugees: April–December, 1948," *Studies in Zionism*, vol. 6, p. 85, at pp. 91–93, 104 (1985). I. F. Stone, "Holy War," *New York Review of Books* (August 3, 1967), p. 6, at p. 10.

27 Lorch, *supra* note 5, pp. 294–296.

28 Palumbo, *supra* note 4, p. 140.

29 Kirk, *supra* note 12, p. 8. Nafez Nazzal, "The Zionist Occupation of Western Galilee, 1948," *Journal of Palestine Studies*, vol. 3, no. 3, pp. 58–76 (1974).

30 Nazzal, *supra* note 18, p. 75. Morris, *supra* note 4, p. 200.

31 Rosemary Sayigh, *Palestinians: From Peasants to Revolutionaries* (1979), p. 83.

32 Count Folke Bernadotte, progress report of the UN mediator on Palestine, *General Assembly Official Records*, 3d sess., Supplement No. 11, UN Doc. A/648 (1948), p. 14, para. 7.

33 Morris, *supra* note 13, pp. 103–104. Benny Morris, "Yosef Weitz and the Transfer Committees, 1948–49," *Middle Eastern Studies*, vol. 22, p. 522, at pp. 536–537 (1986).

34 Tom Segev, *1949: The First Israelis* (1986), pp. 27–28.

35 Morris, *supra* note 4, pp. 160–169.

36 Morris, *supra* note 33, pp. 530–531. Morris, *supra* note 26, pp. 103, 109. Morris, *supra* note 4, p. 148.

37 Palumbo, *supra* note 4, p. viii.

38 Morris, *supra* note 33, pp. 532–533, 543–544. Morris, *supra* note 26, pp. 106, 109.

39 Palumbo, *supra* note 4, p. 147. Morris, *supra* note 4, pp. 145–147. Avi Shlaim, *Collusion Across the Jordan: King Abdullah, the Zionist Movement, and the Partition of Palestine* (1988), pp. 283–284.

40 Letter from the foreign minister of Israel to the mediator, July 30, 1948, *Security Council Officials Records*, 3d year, Supplement for August 1948, UN Doc. S/949, p. 106, at p. 108.

41 Progress report, *supra* note 32, p. 14, para. 6.

42 "Troubled Truce," *Economist*, August 21, 1948, p. 289.

43 Segev, *supra* note 34, p. 70. Palumbo, *supra* note 4, p. 90.

44 Jon Kimche, *Seven Fallen Pillars* (1953), p. 234.

45 Progress report, *supra* note 32, p. 14, para. 7.

46 *New York Times*, September 12, 1988, p. A3.

47 Palumbo, *supra* note 4, p. 164.

48 Segev, *supra* note 34, p. 28.

49 Nazzal, *supra* note 18, p. 95.

50 Noam Chomsky, "Introduction," in Sayigh, *supra* note 31, p. 3.

51 Segev, *supra* note 34, p. 57. Rafik Halabi, *The West Bank Story* (1981), p. 235.

52 *Knesset Debates*, vol. 3, p. 37 (November 14, 1949) (MK Tawfiq Toubi).

53 Palumbo, *supra* note 4, pp. 169–172.

54 *Id.*, p. 173.

55 Walter Schwarz, *The Arabs in Israel* (1959), p. 158. Palumbo, *supra* note 4, pp. ix–xii, 173.

56 Lorch, *supra* note 5, pp. 357–359. Palumbo, *supra* note 4, p. xi. Morris, *supra* note 4, p. 221.

57 Morris, *supra* note 4, p. 224.

58 "Paper Reports Slaying of Palestinians in '48," *Boston Globe*, August 26, 1984, p. 14.

59 Palumbo, *supra* note 4, p. xiv. Noam Chomsky, *Turning the Tide: U.S. Intervention in Central America and the Struggle for Peace*, p. 76 (1985).

60 Palumbo, *supra* note 4, p. xii. Morris, *supra* note 4, p. 222.

61 Segev, *supra* note 34, p. 58.

62 Charles S. Kamen, "The Arab Population in Palestine and Israel, 1946–1951," *New Outlook* (October–November 1984), p. 36, at p. 38.

63 Progress report, *supra* note 32, p. 47.

64 *Palestine Post*, May 11, 1948, p. 1; May 4, 1948. Ian Lustick, "The Quiescent Palestinians: the System of Control over Arabs in Israel," in Khalil Nakhleh and Elia Zureik (eds.)., *The Sociology of the Palestinians* (1980), p. 66.

65 *Palestine Post*, May 13, 1948, p. 1. Basheer K. Nijim (ed.), *Toward the De-Arabization of Palestine/Israel* (1984), p. 108.

66 Kirk, *supra* note 8, at 249.

67 Ori Stendel, *The Minorities in Israel: Trends in the Development of the Arab and Druze Communities, 1948–1973* (1973), p. 77.

68 David Shipler, *Arab and Jew: Wounded Spirits in a Promised Land* (1986), pp. 35–36.

69 Segev, *supra* note 34, p. 30.

70 Janet Abu-Lughod, "The Demographic Transformation of Palestine," in Ibrahim Abu-Lughod (ed.), *The Transformation of Palestine: Essays on the Origin and Development of the Arab-Israeli Conflict* (1971), p. 139, at p. 161.

71 Zeev Schiff, "The Pros and Cons of the Military Government," *New Outlook* (March–April 1962), p. 64, at pp. 66–67. Kamen, *supra* note 62, p. 38.

72 Rupert Emerson, *From Empire to Nation: The Rise to Self-Assertion of Asian and African Peoples* (1962), p. 314.

11 To Justify A State: Israel as a Fact

1 Simha Flapan, *The Birth of Israel: Myths and Realities* (1987), p. 48. "Troubled Truce," *Economist*, August 21, 1948, pp. 289–290. Avi Shlaim, *Collusion Across the Jordan: King Abdullah, the Zionist Movement, and the Partition of Palestine* (1988), pp. 308–311.

2 Shlaim, *supra* note 1, pp. 341, 380.

3 *Id.*, p. 382.

4 Jon and David Kimche, *Both Sides of the Hill: Britain and the Palestine War* (1960), pp. 267–268.

5 Shlaim, *supra* note 1, p. 406.

6 *Id.*, p. 387.

7 UN Doc. S/1093 (1948), *Yearbook of the United Nations 1948–49* (1950), p. 395.

8 *Yearbook of the United Nations 1948–49* (1950), pp. 396–397.

9 G. A. Res 194, December 11, 1948.

10 "The Consul at Jerusalem (Burdett) to the Secretary of State," Apr. 9, 1949, *Foreign Relations of the United States 1949*, vol. 6, p. 903 (1977).

11 Knesset speech, May 17, 1961, in *The Times*, May 18, 1961, p. 12.

12 Uri Avnery, "Les réfugiés arabes, obstacle à la paix," *Le Monde*, May 9, 1964, p. 1, at p. 2. Dan Kurzman, *Genesis 1948: The First Arab-Israeli War* (1970), p. 157.

13 Benny Morris, "The Causes and Character of the Arab Exodus from Palestine: the Israel Defence Forces Intelligence Branch Analysis of June 1948," *Middle Eastern Studies*, vol. 22, p. 5, at pp. 16–17. Kurzman, *supra* note 12, pp. 157–158. John Davis, *The Evasive Peace* (1968), p. 56. John Davis, "Why and How the Palestin-

ians Fled from Palestine," *Middle East International* (May 1971), p. 35, at p. 37. Simha Flapan, *Zionism and the Palestinians* (1979), p. 301. Erskine Childers, "The Wordless Wish: From Citizens to Refugees," in Ibrahim Abu-Lughod, *The Transformation of Palestine: Essays on the Origin and Development of the Arab-Israeli Conflict* (1971), pp. 165, 196–201. Avnery, *supra* note 12, p. 2. J. L. Taulbee and David P. Forsythe, "International Law and Conflict Resolution: Palestinian Claims and the Arab States," *Vanderbilt Journal of Transnational Law*, vol. 6, p. 121, at p. 129 (1972).

14   See *supra* chapter 7.

15   Nathan Feinberg, "On an Arab Jurist's Approach to Zionism and the State of Israel," in Nathan Feinberg, *Studies in International Law with Special Reference to the Arab-Israel Conflict* (1979), p. 515, at p. 573.

16   Childers, *supra* note 13, p. 197.

17   Kenneth W. Bilby, *New Star in the Near East* (1950), p. 60. Shlaim, *supra* note 1, p. 368.

18   Edgar O'Ballance, *The Arab-Israeli War 1948* (1956), pp. 198–201. Netanel Lorch, *The Edge of the Sword: Israel's War of Independence, 1947–1949* (1961), pp. 404–433.

19   Tom Segev, *1949: The First Israelis* (1986), p. 3. James McDonald, *My Mission in Israel, 1948–1951* (1951), pp. 116–117. "The Special Representative of the United States in Israel (McDonald) to the Acting Secretary of State," December 31, 1948, *Foreign Relations of the United States 1948*, vol. 5, p. 1705 (1976).

20   "Message from Acting Secretary of State to U.S. Representative (McDonald) in Israel," December 30, 1948, *Foreign Relations of the United States 1948*, vol. 5, p. 1704 (1976). McDonald, *supra* note 19, pp. 107–108.

21   O'Ballance, *supra* note 18, p. 201. Abba Eban, *An Autobiography* (1977), p. 137.

22   *New York Times*, March 9, 1964, p. A7.

23   Israel-Egypt, General Armistice Agreement, *United Nations Treaty Series*, vol. 42, p. 251 (1949). Israel-Jordan, General Armistice Agreement, *id.*, p. 303. Israel-Syria, General Armistice Agreement, *id.*, p. 327. Israel-Lebanon, General Armistice Agreement, *id.*, p. 287. Shlaim, *supra* note 1, pp. 386–433. Lorch, *supra* note 18, pp. 439–449.

24   Shlaim, *supra* note 1, pp. 409–425.

25   Lorch, *supra* note 18, pp. 448–449.

26   Israel-Egypt, *supra* note 23, art. 5, para. 2. Israel-Jordan, *supra* note 23, art. 6, para. 9. Israel-Syria, *supra* note 23, art. 5, para. 1.

27   Israel-Lebanon, *supra* note 23, art. 5, para. 1.

28   S. C. Res. 69, March 4, 1949.

29   Eban, *supra* note 21, pp. 138–140.

30   *Yearbook of the United Nations 1948–49* (1950), pp. 399–401. Eban, *supra* note 21, pp. 140–142.

31   G. A. Res. 273, May 11, 1949.

32   Philip Baum, "Full Recognition of Israel," *Lawyer's Guild Review*, vol. 8, p. 441 (1948). Philip Marshall Brown, "The Recognition of Israel," *American Journal of International Law*, vol. 42, pp. 620–627 (1948). Eban, *supra* note 21, p. 136.

33   L. C. Green, in "Self-Determination and Settlement of the Arab-Israeli Conflict,"

Proceedings of the American Society of International Law, vol. 65, p. 31, at p. 57 (1971). Elihu Lauterpacht, *Jerusalem and the Holy Places* (1968), p. 19.

34 Ian Brownlie, *Principles of Public International Law* (1966), p. 159.

35 Daniel P. O'Connell, *International Law*, vol. 1, p. 496 (1965).

36 Quincy Wright, "The Palestine Conflict in International Law," in Majdia Khadduri (ed.), *Major Middle Eastern Problems in International Law* (1972), p. 13, at p. 26.

37 Brownlie, *supra* note 34, pp. 85–90. Henry Cattan, *Palestine and International Law* (1976), p. 103.

38 Brownlie, *supra* note 34, p. 99.

39 O'Connell, *supra* note 35, p. 140.

40 Frank L. M. Van de Craen, "The Territorial Title of the State of Israel to 'Palestine': An Appraisal in International Law," *Revue belge de droit international*, vol. 14, p. 500, at p. 503 (1978–79).

41 Erich Röper, "Rechtsfragen bei der Entstehung Israels," *Das Parlament* (supplement), vol. 18, p. 3, at p. 20 (1978).

42 Van de Craen, *supra* note 40, p. 502. Friedrich Berber, *Lehrbuch des Völkerrechts*, vol. 1, p. 337 (1960).

43 O'Connell, *supra* note 35, p. 140.

44 A. L. W. Munkman, review of *Jerusalem and the Holy Places*, by Elihu Lauterpacht, *British Year Book of International Law*, vol. 43, p. 306, at p. 309 (1968–69).

45 Michael Akehurst, "The Arab-Israeli Conflict in International Law," *New Zealand Universities Law Review*, vol. 5, p. 231, at p. 238 (1973). Lauterpacht, *supra* note 33, pp. 41–42.

46 Brownlie, *supra* note 34, p. 596.

47 Yehuda Blum, "The Missing Reversioner: Reflections on the Status of Judea and Samaria," *Israel Law Review*, vol. 3, p. 279, at p. 283 (1968).

48 Western Sahara, International Court of Justice, *Reports of Judgments, Advisory Opinions and Orders* (1975), p. 69, para. 163.

49 André Cocâtre-Zilgien, "L'imbroglio moyen-oriental et le droit," *Revue générale de droit international public*, vol. 73, p. 52, at p. 56 (1969).

50 J. L., "The International Status of Palestine," *Journal du droit international*, vol. 90, p. 964, at p. 972 (1963).

51 Sanford R. Silverburg, "Uti Possidetis and a Pax Palestiniana: A Proposal," *Duquesne Law Review*, vol. 16, p. 757, at p. 775 (1977–78).

52 Ian Brownlie, "Recognition in Theory and Practice," *British Year Book of International Law*, vol. 53, p. 197, at p. 206 (1982).

53 D. H. N. Johnson, "Acquisitive Prescription in International Law," *British Year Book of International Law*, vol. 27, p. 332, at p. 345 (1950).

54 The Chamizal Arbitration Between the United States and Mexico: Minutes of Meeting of the Joint Commission, June 10, 1911, *American Journal of International Law*, vol. 5, p. 782, at p. 806 (1911).

55 Rosalyn Higgins, "The June War: The United Nations and Legal Background," in John Norton Moore, *The Arab-Israeli Conflict: Readings and Documents* (1977), p. 535, at p. 536.

56 Shlaim, *supra* note 1, p. 450.

57 Stephen Schwebel, "What Weight to Conquest?" *American Journal of Interna-*

tional Law (1970), p. 344, at p. 346. Lauterpacht, *supra* note 33, pp. 44–45.

58 See *supra* chapter 9.

59 Akehurst, *supra* note 45, p. 238. Antonio Cassese, "Legal Considerations on the International Status of Jerusalem," in Hans Köchler (ed.), *The Legal Aspects of the Palestine Problem with Special Regard to the Question of Jerusalem*, p. 144, at p. 146. R. Y. Jennings, *The Acquisition of Territory in International Law* (1963), p. 55. Munkman, *supra* note 44, p. 310.

60 Letter of October 27, 1949, of Israeli delegation to conciliation commission, in General Progress Report and Supplementary Report of the UN Conciliation Commission for Palestine covering the period from 11 December 1949 to 23 October 1950, *General Assembly Official Records*, 5th sess., Supplement No. 18, UN Doc. A/1367/Rev.1, p. 20 (1950).

61 *Supra* note 26. Wright, *supra* note 36, p. 26. Akehurst, *supra* note 45, p. 239.

62 Quincy Wright, "Legal Aspects of the Middle East Situation," *Law and Contemporary Problems*, vol. 33, p. 5, at pp. 17–18 (1968). Lidia Modzhorian, *Mezhdunarodnyi sionizm na sluzhbe imperialisticheskoi reaktsii: pravovoi aspekt* (International Zionism in the Service of Imperialist Reactionary Forces: The Legal Aspect, 1984), p. 70.

63 Akehurst, *supra* note 45, p. 239.

64 G. I. A. D. Draper, "The Status of Jerusalem as a Question of International Law," in Köchler, *supra* note 59, p. 154, at p. 160.

65 Statement of U.S. secretary of state, John F. Dulles, *Department of State Bulletin*, vol. 30, p. 329 (March 1, 1954). J. L., *supra* note 50, p. 976. Shlomo Slonim, "The United States and the Status of Jerusalem 1947–1984," *Israel Law Review*, vol. 19, pp. 179–252 (1984).

66 G. A. Res. 303, December 9, 1949.

67 *New York Times*, January 24, 1950, p. A1.

68 Cassese, *supra* note 59, pp. 148–149.

12 The Real Conquest: The Repopulation of Palestine

1 Alec Kirkbride, *From the Wings: Amman Memoirs 1947–1951* (1976), pp. 105–106, 118.

2 Prevention of Infiltration (Offences and Jurisdiction) Law, *Laws of the State of Israel*, vol. 8, p. 133 (1954).

3 Tom Segev, *1949: The First Israelis* (1986), p. 61.

4 *Id.*, p. 59. Charles S. Kamen, "The Arab Population in Palestine and Israel, 1946–1951," *New Outlook* (October–November 1984), p. 36, at p. 38.

5 Rosemary Sayigh, *Palestinians: From Peasants to Revolutionaries* (1979), pp. 85, 88–89, 103. Kamen, *supra* note 4, p. 38.

6 Segev, *supra* note 3, p. 52.

7 Benny Morris, *The Birth of the Palestinian Refugee Problem, 1947–1949* (1987), pp. 239–242.

8 *Knesset Debates*, vol. 1, p. 85 (March 9, 1949) (MK Tawfiq Toubi). Sabri Jiryis, *The Arabs in Israel* (1976), p. 81. M. Cherif Bassiouni and Eugene Fisher, "The

Arab-Israeli Conflict—Real and Apparent Issues: An Insight into Its Future from the Lessons of the Past," *St. John's Law Review*, vol. 44, p. 399, at p. 453 (1970).

9   Jiryis, *supra* note 8, p. 81.

10   Elias Chacour, *Blood Brothers* (1984), p. 52.

11   Bassiouni and Fisher, *supra* note 8, p. 453.

12   "The Consul at Jerusalem (Burdett) to the Secretary of State," August 15, 1949, *Foreign Relations of the United States 1949*, vol. 6, p. 1314 (1977). Avi Shlaim, *Collusion Across the Jordan: King Abdullah, the Zionist Movement, and the Partition of Palestine* (1988), p. 456.

13   *Palestine Post*, November 14, 1949, p. 1.

14   Jiryis, *supra* note 8, p. 82. Bassiouni and Fisher, *supra* note 8, p. 453. Segev, *supra* note 3, p. 62.

15   Ilan Halevi, *Question juive: la Tribu, la Loi, l'Espace* (1981), p. 244.

16   Segev, *supra* note 3, p. 62.

17   Jiryis, *supra* note 8, p. 82. Bassiouni and Fisher, *supra* note 8, p.453.

18   Bassiouni and Fisher, *supra* note 8, p. 453.

19   Jiryis, *supra* note 8, p. 82.

20   Rafik Halabi, *The West Bank Story* (1982), p. 204.

21   Bassiouni and Fisher, *supra* note 8, p. 453.

22   Halabi, *supra* note 20, p. 235.

23   Walter Schwarz, *The Arabs in Israel* (1959), pp. 158–159. Ghazi Falah, "How Israel Controls the Bedouin," *Journal of Palestine Studies*, vol. 19, no.2, p. 35, at p. 41 (1985). *Al-Fajr*, December 20, 1985, p. 8. Sayigh, *supra* note 5, p. 99.

24   Segev, *supra* note 3, p. 96.

25   "Troubled Truce," *Economist*, August 21, 1948, p. 289, at pp. 289–290.

26   Segev, *supra* note 3, p. 97.

27   Shlaim, *supra* note 12, p. 365. Segev, *supra* note 3, p. 97.

28   James G. McDonald, *My Mission in Israel* (1951), p. 277.

29   Moshe Menuhin, *The Decadence of Judaism in Our Time* (1965), p. 132.

30   Halevi, *supra* note 15, p. 234.

31   Abbas Shiblak, *The Lure of Zion: The Case of the Iraqi Jews* (1986), p. 101.

32   Segev, *supra* note 3, p. 97.

33   David Ben-Gurion, *Rebirth and Destiny of Israel* (1954), p. 404.

34   *Id.*, pp. 276–277.

35   Segev, *supra* note 3, p. 101.

36   Declaration of the Establishment of the State of Israel, *Laws of the State of Israel*, vol. 1, p. 3 (1948).

37   Ben-Gurion, *supra* note 33, pp. 276–277.

38   Halevi, *supra* note 15, p. 235.

39   *New York Times*, January 19, 1948, p. A2.

40   Halevi, *supra* note 15, p. 234.

41   *Palestine Post*, May 6, 1948, p. 3.

42   *New York Times*, February 21, 1959, p. A6.

43   Segev, *supra* note 3, p. 108.

44   *Id.*, p. 109.

45   *Id.*, p. 107.

46 Ilan Halevi, *Israël de la Terreur au Massacre d'Etat* (1984), p. 113. Menuhin, *supra* note 29, p. 144.

47 Amos Elon, *The Israelis: Founders and Sons* (1983), p. 24.

48 *Department of State Bulletin*, vol. 30, p. 708, at p. 712 (May 10, 1954).

49 Rony Gabbay, *A Political Study of the Arab-Jewish Conflict* (1959), p. 305. Segev, *supra* note 3, p. 110.

50 *New York Times*, December 6, 1947, p. A1; December 7, 1947, p. A1.

51 *The Times*, December 1, 1947, p. 3.

52 *New York Times*, January 6, 1948, p. A6; January 11, 1948, pp. A2, A3.

53 Elon, *supra* note 47, p. 24. Raphael Patai, *The Seed of Abraham: Jews and Arabs in Contact and Conflict*, pp. 295–296.

54 Shiblak, *supra* note 31, p. 157.

55 Halevi, *supra* note 15, p. 28. Joseph Schechtman, *On Wings of Eagles: The Plight, Exodus and Homecoming of Oriental Jewry* (1961), p. 62.

56 Marion Woolfson, *Prophets in Babylon: Jews in the Arab World* (1980), pp. 182–201. David Hirst, *The Gun and the Olive Branch: The Roots of Violence in the Middle East* (1984), pp. 155–164. Halevi, *supra* note 46, pp. 112–113. Kokhavi Shemesh, "The Iraqi Jews and Their Coming to Israel," *The Black Panther*, November 9, 1972, in Uri Davis, Norton Mezvinsky, *Documents from Israel 1967–1973: Readings for a Critique of Zionism* (1975), pp. 126–133. Uri Avnery, *My Friend, the Enemy* (1986), pp. 135–136.

57 Wilbur Crane Eveland, *Ropes of Sand: America's Failure in the Middle East* (1980), p. 48.

58 Hirst, *supra* note 56, p. 159.

59 Eveland, *supra* note 57, pp. 48–49. Shiblak, *supra* note 31, p. 121.

60 Shlomo Hillel, *Operation Babylon* (1987), p. 284.

61 Woolfson, *supra* note 56, p. 199.

62 "Memorandum of Conversation, by the Assistant Secretary of State for Near Eastern, South Asian, and African Affairs (McGhee)," June 11, 1951, *Foreign Relations of the United States 1951*, vol. 5, p. 707, at p. 710 (1982).

63 "Memorandum of Conversation by the Director of the Office of Near Eastern Affairs (Jones)," August 2, 1951, *Foreign Relations of the United States 1951*, vol. 6 p. 813, at p. 815 (1982).

64 Shiblak, *supra* note 31, pp. 106, 112.

65 Ian Lustick, *Arabs in the Jewish State* (1980), p. 44.

66 Moshe Avidán, "Aspectos legales del conflicto del medio oriente," *Revista chilena de derecho*, vol. 5, p. 244, at p. 251 (1978).

67 World Zionist Organization—Jewish Agency (Status) Law, art. 5, *Laws of the State of Israel*, vol. 7, p. 3 (1952).

68 Patai, *supra* note 53, p. 122.

69 *New York Times*, October 21, 1957, p. A5.

70 Patai, *supra* note 53, p. 146.

71 Segev, *supra* note 3, p. 117.

72 *New York Times*, February 11, 1962, p. A6.

73 Defense (Emergency) Regulations, *Palestine Gazette*, no. 1442, supplement no. 2, September 27, 1945, pp. 1055–1098; also published as Government of Palestine,

The Defence (Emergency) Regulations, 1945 (as amended until 2d March, 1947) (1947). Michael Saltman, "The Use of Mandatory Emergency Laws by the Israeli Government," *International Journal of the Sociology of Law*, vol. 10, p. 385, at p. 387 (1982).

74 Defense (Emergency) Regulations, *supra* note 73, art. 112.

75 *Id.*, art. 111. Jiryis, *supra* note 8, p. 30.

76 Defense (Emergency) Regulations, *supra* note 73, arts. 109–110.

77 *Id.*, art. 125. Saltman, *supra* note 73, pp. 390–392.

78 Defense (Emergency) Regulations, *supra* note 73, arts. 86–101.

79 *Id.*, arts. 84–85.

80 *Id.*, art. 142.

81 *Id.*, art. 124.

82 Law and Administration Ordinance, art. 11, *Laws of the State of Israel*, vol. 1, p. 7 (1948).

83 Palestine (Revocations) Order in Council, sec. 2, para. 2, May 12, 1948, Statutory Instrument No. 1004 (1948). André Rosenthal, "The 1945 Defence Regulations: Valid Law in the West Bank?" (1986, unpublished).

84 Letter of Tim Renton, minister of foreign and commonwealth office, to Al-Haq (West Bank affiliate of the International Commission of Jurists), April 22, 1987.

85 *Laws of the State of Israel*, vol. 3, p. 73 (1949).

86 Rosenthal, *supra* note 83, p. 2.

87 Law and Administration Ordinance, art. 9(a), *Laws of the State of Israel*, vol. 1, p. 7 (1948).

88 *Al-Awdeh Weekly*, December 22, 1985, in Joost R. Hiltermann, *Israel's Deportation Policy in the Occupied West Bank and Gaza* (1986), p. 18.

89 David Kretzmer, *The Legal Status of the Arabs in Israel*, pp. 116, 128. Jiryis, *supra* note 8, p. 26.

90 Kretzmer, *supra* note 89, p. 116.

91 State Controller's Report No. 9 on the Defence Ministry for the Year 1957/58 (1959), p. 78, in Michael Adams, *Israel's Treatment of the Arabs in the Occupied Areas*, Symposium on Zionism, Baghdad, November 8–12, 1976, pp. 13–14.

13 The Present Are Absent: The Fate of the Arabs

1 Zvi Zinger (Yaron), "State of Israel (1948–72)," in Israel Pocket Library, *Immigration and Settlement in Israel* (1973), p. 50, at p. 57. David Tanne, "Housing," *id.*, p. 122, at p. 129. Rony Gabbay, *A Political Study of the Arab-Jewish Conflict: the Arab Refugee Problem (A Case Study)* (1959), p. 284. Don Peretz, *Israel and the Palestine Arabs* (1958), p. 156. Benny Morris, *The Birth of the Palestinian Refugee Problem, 1947–1949* (1987), pp. 190–194.

2 Ben-Gurion, *Knesset Debates*, vol. 1, p. 399 (April 26, 1949).

3 Tom Segev, *1949: The First Israelis* (1986), p. 78.

4 *Id.*, pp. 74–76. Morris, *supra* note 1, p. 191.

5 Segev, *supra* note 3, pp. 52–56.

6 Michael Palumbo, *The Palestinian Catastrophe* (1987), pp. 151–152.

7   Maxim Ghilan, *How Israel Lost Its Soul* (1974), p. 233.

8   Aziz Haidar, *Social Welfare Services for Israel's Arab Population* (1987), p. 14.

9   Walter Schwarz, *The Arabs in Israel* (1959), p. 76.

10 Haidar, *supra* note 8, pp. 140–143.

11 Hanna Dib Nakkara, "Israeli Land Seizure Under Various Defense and Emergency Regulations," *Journal of Palestine Studies*, vol. 14, no. 2, p. 13, at pp. 28–30 (1985).

12 Mubadda Hanna Daoud et al. v. Minister of Defence et al., High Court of Justice 64/51, *Piskei Din*, vol. 5, part 2, pp. 1117–1123 (1951), in *Palestine Yearbook of International Law*, vol. 2, p. 119 (1985).

13 Segev, *supra* note 3, p. 59.

14 *Id.* Ghilan, *supra* note 7, pp. 236–237. Uri Davis and Norton Mezvinsky, *Documents from Israel, 1967–1973: Readings for a Critique of Zionism* (1975), pp. 32–33. Elias Chacour, *Blood Brothers* (1984), pp. 73–81.

15 *New York Times*, July 24, 1972, p. A2.

16 Emergency Regulations (Security Zones) (Extension of Validity) (No. 2) Law, *Laws of the State of Israel*, vol. 3, p. 56 (1949). Daoud v. Minister of Defence, *supra* note 12.

17 Defense (Emergency) Reguations, art. 125, *Palestine Gazette*, no. 1442, supplement no. 2, September 27, 1945, pp. 1055–1098; also published as Government of Palestine, *The Defence (Emergency) Regulations, 1945 (as amended until 2d March, 1947)* (1947). Committee of Displaced Persons from Ikrit, Rama and Others v. Government of Israel et al., High Court of Justice 141/81, *Piskei Din*, vol. 36, part 1, pp. 129–133 (1982), in *Palestine Yearbook of International Law*, vol. 2, p. 129 (1985) (noting that art. 125 was applied to Ikrit in 1963 and 1972).

18 Committee of Displaced Persons v. Government, *supra* note 17.

19 U.S. Dept. of State, *Country Reports on Human Rights Practices for 1981* (1982), p. 997. David Gilmour, *Dispossessed: The Ordeal of the Palestinians* (1982), pp. 102–103. Segev, *supra* note 2, p. 59." "Iqrit and Biram Residents Demonstrate," *Al-Fajr*, September 12, 1986, p. 4. Elaine Ruth Fletcher, "People Who Never Lost Hope," *Jerusalem Post*, international edition, week ending February 14, 1987, p. 11.

20 Davis and Mezvinsky, *supra* note 14, p. 34. *Al-Fajr*, November 8, 1987, p. 4.

21 "Statutory Martial Law," Defense (Emergency) Regulations, *supra* note 17, part 15 (arts. 148–162).

22 David Kretzmer, *The Legal Status of the Arabs in Israel* (1987), p. 116.

23 Schwarz, *supra* note 9, pp. 64–65, 82–83. Gabbay, *supra* note 1, p. 287. Edward Rizk (trans.), *The Palestine Question: Seminar of Arab Jurists*, Algiers, 22–27 July 1967 (1968), p. 56.

24 Aharon Cohen, *Israel and the Arab World* (1970), p. 493. H. Baruch, "Facing the 180,000: How the Military Government Rules," *Ner* (December 1958–January 1959), p. 37, at p. 50. Ze'ev Schiff, "The Pros and Cons of the Military Government," *New Outlook* (March–April 1962), p. 64, at p. 66.

25 Gabbay, *supra* note 1, p. 53.

26 Schwarz, *supra* note 9, p. 65. Sabri Jiryis, *The Arabs in Israel* (1976), p. 30.

27 Elia T. Zureik, *The Palestinians in Israel: A Study in Internal Colonialism* (1979), p. 120. Gabbay, *supra* note 1, p. 288. Michael Saltman, "The Use of Mandatory Emergency Laws by the Israeli Government," *International Journal of the Sociol-*

ogy of Law, vol. 10, p. 385, at p. 387 (1982).

28 Gabbay, *supra* note 1, p. 288. Baruch, *supra* note 24, p. 46.

29 Schwarz, *supra* note 9, p. 85.

30 Jiryis, *supra* note 26, p. 28. Schwarz, *supra* note 9, p. 85.

31 Ghilan, *supra* note 7, p. 196.

32 *Knesset Debates*, vol. 1, pp. 753–754 (June 30, 1949) (MK Amin Jarjoura).

33 Schwarz, *supra* note 9, p. 64.

34 Segev, *supra* note 3, pp. 49, 65.

35 Gabbay, *supra* note 1, p. 287.

36 Uri Avnery, "Government Suppressing Free Speech," *New Outlook* (September 1964), p. 50.

37 Segev, *supra* note 3, p. 63.

38 Schwarz, *supra* note 9, pp. 61–63. Nakkara, *supra* note 11, pp. 28–30.

39 Emergency Land Requisition (Regulation) Law, art. 3, *Laws of the State of Israel*, vol. 4, p. 3 (1949).

40 Emergency Regulations (Cultivation of Waste [Uncultivated] Lands), *Laws of the State of Israel*, vol. 2, pp. 71–77 (1948–1949). Sabri Jiryis, "The Legal Structure for the Expropriation and Absorption of Arab Lands in Israel," *Journal of Palestine Studies* vol. 2, no. 4, p. 98 (1973).

41 Absentees' Property Law, art. 1(b), *Laws of the State of Israel*, vol. 4, p. 68 (1950).

42 Segev, *supra* note 3, p. 80.

43 *Id.*

44 Hasan Amun, Uri Davis, and Nasr San'allah, "Deir Al-Asad: The Destiny of an Arab Village in Galilee: A Case Study Towards a Social and Political Analysis of the Palestinian-Arab Society in Israel," in Hasan Amun (ed.), *Palestinian Arabs in Israel: Two Case Studies* (1977), p. 5.

45 Kretzmer *supra* note 22, p. 102.

46 Amnon Rubinstein, *Constitutional Law of the State of Israel* (in Hebrew, 1980), p. 187. Kretzmer, *supra* note 22, p. 115.

47 *Jerusalem Post*, January 18, 1953, p. 3. Ian Lustick, *Arabs in the Jewish State* (1980), p. 57.

48 Segev, *supra* note 3, p. 82.

49 *Laws of the State of Israel*, vol. 7, p. 43 (1953). A new statute was adopted in 1973 on procedures for compensation for property taken as absentee, the Absentees' Property (Compensation) Law, *Laws of the State of Israel*, vol. 27, p. 176 (1973).

50 Kretzmer, *supra* note 22, pp. 102, 115. Rubinstein, note 46, pp. 185–186.

51 Peretz, *supra* note 1, p. 126.

52 Schwarz, *supra* note 9, p. 102.

53 *Id.*, p. 103.

54 Jiryis, *supra* note 26, p. 127.

55 Defense (Emergency) Regulations, *supra* note 17.

56 Segev, *supra* note 3, p. 81.

57 Shimon Peres, "Military Law Is the Fruit of Military Governance," Davar, January 26, 1962, p. 2.

58 *Knesset Debates*, vol. 36, p. 1217 (February 20, 1963).

59 Zureik, *supra* note 27, p. 120.

60 Amun, Davis, and San'allah, *supra* note 44, p. 13.

61 Abner Cohen, *Arab Border Villages in Israel: A Study of Continuity and Change in Social Organization* (1965), p. 19.

62 Segev, *supra* note 3, pp. 73–74.

63 *Id.*, p. 74.

64 Schwarz, *supra* note 9, p. 160. Yitzhak Oded, "Bedouin Lands Threatened by Takeover," *New Outlook* (November–December 1964), pp. 45–52.

65 Schwarz, *supra* note 9, p. 159.

66 *Id.*

67 *Id.*

68 Absentees' Property (Amendment No. 3) (Release and Use of Endowment Property) Law, art. 29B, *Laws of the State of Israel*, vol. 19, p. 55 (1965). Sabri Jiryis, *Democratic Freedoms in Israel* (1972), p. 12.

69 Segev, *supra* note 3, p. 81.

70 Lustick, *supra* note 47, p. 179. Amun, Davis, and San'allah, *supra* note 44, p. 39.

71 Progress Report of the UN Conciliation Commission for Palestine, *General Assembly Official Records*, 6th sess., Supplement No. 18, UN Doc. A/1985, p. 5, para. 36 (1951).

72 Don Peretz, "Problems of Arab Refugee Compensation," *Middle East Journal*, vol. 8, p. 403, at pp. 404–408 (1954).

73 Statement of Mordechai Schattner, custodian of absentee property, *Jerusalem Post*, January 18, 1953, p. 3.

74 Arnold Toynbee, *A Study of History*, vol. 8, p. 289 (1954).

75 Charles S. Kamen, "The Arab Population in Palestine and Israel, 1946–1951," *New Outlook* (October–November 1984), p. 36, at p. 37. Israel Shahak, "Arab Villages Destroyed in Israel," in Davis and Mezvinsky, *supra* note 14, p. 43, at p. 47. Amun, Davis, and San'allah, *supra* note 44, p. 38.

76 Schwarz, *supra* note 9, p. 69.

77 Moshe Dayan, "My Standing in the Labor Party," lecture, Haifa Technical Institute, *Ha'aretz*, April 4, 1969, p. 15.

78 Amun, Davis, and San'allah, *supra* note 44, p. 32. Davis and Mezvinsky, *supra* note 14, pp. 27–28.

79 Negev Land Acquisition (Peace Treaty with Egypt) Law, *Laws of the State of Israel*, vol. 34, p. 190 (1980). U.S. Dept. of State, *Country Reports on Human Rights Practices for 1980* (1981), p. 997. Negev group for human rights, letter to "In These Times" (Chicago), August 13, 1980.

80 Rafik Halabi, *The West Bank Story* (1982), pp. 245, 249.

81 Meir Shamir, director of Israel Land Registration Office (meeting of committee appointed by minister of agriculture to study land policy), in Moshe Lichtman, "An Arab Kept Separately Is a Good Arab," *Monitin* (March 1983), p. 110, at p. 112.

82 Halabi, *supra* note 80, p. 255.

14 Hewers of Wood: Arab Commerce Agriculture, and Labor

* St. Augustine, *The City of God* (Marcus Dods, ed. and trans., 1948) book 4, vol. 1, p. 139.

1 Charles S. Kamen, "The Arab Population in Palestine and Israel, 1946–1951," *New Outlook* (October–November 1984), p. 36, at p. 39.

2 Tom Segev, *1949: The First Israelis* (1986), pp. 69–79.

3 Henry Cattan, *The Palestine Question* (1988), p. 84.

4 George Kirk, *The Middle East 1945–1950* (1954), p. 316.

5 Sami Hadawi, *Palestinian Rights and Losses in 1948* (1988), pp. 102, 130–131, 155–156. Palestine Conciliation Commission, progress report (for period 1 May 1964 to 22 December 1965), December 28, 1965, UN Doc. A/6225.

6 Avraham Cohen, "The Arab Population of Israel, 1950–1980," *New Outlook* (October–November 1984), p. 43.

7 Interview by author with Tawfiq Zayyad, member of Knesset and mayor of Nazareth, in Jerusalem, May 21, 1986.

8 Yossi Amitay, "A Question of Identity: Like an Uprooted Tree," *New Outlook* (October–November 1984), p. 12, at p. 15.

9 Nawaf Masalhah, "Israeli Arabs: Equal Economic Development," *New Outlook* (May–June 1985), p. 35.

10 Jacob Dash, "Planning and Development," in Israel Pocket Library, *Immigration and Settlement in Israel* (1973), pp. 117–121.

11 Gabriel Ben-Dor, *The Druzes in Israel: A Political Study* (1979), pp. 134–135. Uri Davis and Norton Mezvinsky, *Documents from Israel 1967–1973: Readings for a Critique of Zionism* (1975), p. 28.

12 Ian Lustick, *Arabs in the Jewish State* (1980), p. 164.

13 David Kretzmer, *The Legal Status of the Arabs in Israel* (1987), p. 106. Elia Zureik, *The Palestinians in Israel: A Study in Internal Colonialism* (1979), pp. 133–136. David Gilmour, *Dispossessed: The Ordeal of the Palestinians* (1982), pp. 100–101. Lustick, *supra* note 12, pp. 188–189. Henry Rosenfeld, *The Condition and Status of the Arabs in Israel* (1985), p. 54.

14 David Shipler, "Israeli Arabs: Scorned, Ashamed, and '20th Class'," *New York Times*, December 29, 1983, p. A2.

15 Lustick, *supra* note 12, p. 168. David Shipler, *Arab and Jew: Wounded Spirits in a Promised Land* (1986), pp. 443–444. Kretzmer, *supra* note 13, pp. 109–111. Ibrahim Nimr Hussein, mayor of Shfaram, "Profile," *New Outlook* (October–November 1984), p. 60.

16 U.S. Dept. of State, *Country Reports on Human Rights Practices for 1979* (1980), p. 757.

17 *Jerusalem Post*, international edition, week ending February 7, 1987, supplement, p. XII.

18 "The Histadrut Elections and Other Activities," *The Other Israel: Newsletter of the Israeli Council for Israeli-Palestinian Peace*, no. 15, p. 6 (June 1985). Zureik, *supra* note 13, p. 128.

19 Yosef Goell, "Where Israel's Union Fails," *Jerusalem Post*, international edition,

week ending February 14, 1987, p. 10.

20 *Laws of the State of Israel*, vol. 13, p. 258 (1959).

21 5738 *Yalkut HaPirsumim* (Public Notices), p. 1249; 5739 *Yalkut HaPirsumim*, p. 1193. The towns are listed in *Information for Investors*, issued by A. Sason, director of development areas, ministry of industry and commerce, October 1984. Kretzmer, *supra* note 13, p. 100. Lustick, *supra* note 12, p. 186. Yitzhak Oked, "The Survival Factor," *Jerusalem Post*, international edition, week ending March 26, 1988, supplement, p. II.

22 Goell, *supra* note 19, p. 10.

23 Oked, *supra* note 21, p. II.

24 Kamen, *supra* note 1, p. 39.

25 *Jerusalem Post*, February 8, 1971, p. 7.

26 Kretzmer, *supra* note 13, p. 121.

27 Peanut Production and Marketing Board Law, art. 5, *Laws of the State of Israel*, vol. 13, p. 77 (1959).

28 Vegetable Production and Marketing Board Law, art. 5, *Laws of the State of Israel*, vol. 13, p. 245 (1959).

29 Egg and Poultry Board (Production and Marketing) Law, art. 5, *Laws of the State of Israel*, vol. 18, p. 10 (1963).

30 Fruit Production and Marketing Board Law, art. 4, *Laws of the State of Israel*, vol. 27, p. 370 (1973).

31 Walter Lehn, *The Jewish National Fund* (1988), p. 149–150.

32 Sabri Jiryis, *The Arabs in Israel* (1976), pp. 215–217.

33 Maxim Ghilan, *How Israel Lost Its Soul* (1974), p. 240.

34 Lustick, *supra* note 12, pp. 166–167.

35 Uri Davis, *Israel: An Apartheid State* (1987), pp. 50–55.

36 Walter Law, arts. 1, 36, *Laws of the State of Israel*, vol. 13, p. 173 (1959).

37 Kretzmer, *supra* note 13, p. 118.

38 Central Bureau of Statistics, *Statistical Abstract of Israel 1983* (no. 34), p. 484.

39 Lustick, *supra* note 12, p. 167.

40 Kretzmer, *supra* note 13, p. 120.

41 Lehn, *supra* note 31, pp. 68, 161.

42 Walter Law, *supra* note 36, art. 46. Hasan Amun, Uri Davis, and Nasr San'allah, "Deir Al-Asad: The Destiny of an Arab Village in Galilee: A Case Study Towards a Social and Political Analysis of the Palestinian-Arab Society in Israel," in Hasan Amun (ed.), *Palestinian Arabs in Israel: Two Case Studies* (1977), p. 58.

43 Walter Law, *supra* note 36, art. 126.

44 Amun, Davis, and San'allah, *supra* note 42, p. 45.

45 Uri Davis, "Israel's Zionist Society: Consequences for Internal Opposition and the Necessity for External Intervention," in Committee for the Elimination of All Forms of Racial Discrimination and American Jewish Alternatives to Zionism, *Judaism or Zionism: What Difference for the Middle East?* (1986), p. 176, at p. 179.

46 Abner Cohen, *Arab Border Villages in Israel: A Study of Continuity and Change in Social Organization* (1965), p. 19.

47 Zureik, *supra* note 13, pp. 122–129.

48 Sarah Graham-Brown, "The Economic Consequences of the Occupation," in

Naseer Aruri, *Occupation: Israel over Palestine* (1983), p. 167, at pp. 209–210.

49 Zureik, *supra* note 13, p. 131. Amun, Davis, and San'allah, *supra* note 42, p. 44. Cohen, *supra* note 46, p. 24.

50 Michael Saltman, "The Use of the Mandatory Emergency Laws in Israel," *International Journal of the Sociology of Law*, vol. 10, p. 385, at p. 391 (1982).

51 Zureik, *supra* note 13, p. 132.

52 Cohen, *supra* note 46, p. 19.

53 Sabri Jiryis, *Democratic Freedoms in Israel* (1972), p. 82.

54 Saltman, *supra* note 50, p. 391.

55 Jiryis, *supra* note 32, pp. 33–34.

56 Rosenfeld, *supra* note 13, p. 51.

57 Rafik Halabi, *The West Bank Story* (1982), p. 235. Saltman, *supra* note 50, p. 392.

58 Kretzmer, *supra* note 13, p. 116. Amnon Rubinstein, *Constitutional Law of the State of Israel* (in Hebrew, 1980), p. 186.

59 Severance Pay Law, arts. 1, 30, *Laws of the State of Israel*, vol. 17, p. 161 (1963).

60 *Id.*, art. 8, para. 2.

61 *Id.*, para. 22.

62 Minister of Labor, *Severance Pay Regulations, Calculation of Compensation and Resignation That Is Deemed Dismissal* (in Hebrew, 1964), Regulation 12(b).

63 *Jerusalem Post*, May 12, 1953, p. 4.

64 Ori Stendel, *The Minorities in Israel: Trends in the Development of the Arab and Druze Communities, 1948–1973* (1973), p. 153. Jacob M. Landau, *The Arabs in Israel: A Political Study* (1969), p. 178.

65 Zureik, *supra* note 13, p. 128. Landau, *supra* note 65, pp. 178–183.

66 *Jerusalem Post*, May 23, 1986, pp. 17–18. Gilmour, *supra* note 13, p. 99.

67 "The Palestinian Working Class," *Democratic Palestine* (May 1986), p. 10, at p. 12.

68 Yosef Goell, *supra* note 19, p. 10.

69 Zureik, *supra* note 13, pp. 128–129.

70 Goell, *supra* note 19, p. 10.

71 *Id.*

15 The National Institutions: The Legislation That Makes Israel Jewish

1 Declaration of the Establishment of the State of Israel, paras. 10–11, *Laws of the State of Israel*, vol. 1, p. 3 (1948). Yehuda Savir, "The Definition of a Jew under Israel's Law of Return," *Southwestern Law Journal*, vol. 17, p. 123, at p. 124 (1963). Claude Klein, *Le caractère juif de l'état d'Israël* (1977), p. 14.

2 Izhak England, "Law and Religion in Israel," *American Journal of Comparative Law*, vol. 35, p. 185, at p. 187 (1987).

3 World Zionist Organization—Jewish Agency (Status) Law, *Laws of the State of Israel*, vol. 7, p. 3 (1952). W. Thomas Mallison, "The Zionist-Israel Juridical Claims to Constitute 'the Jewish People' Nationality Entity and to Confer Membership in It: An Appraisal in International Law," *George Washington Law Review*, vol. 32, p. 983, at pp. 1036–1039 (1964).

4 Basic Law: The Knesset (Amendment No. 9), *Sefer Ha-Hukim* (Primary Legisla-

tion), No. 1155, August 7, 1985, p. 196. *Israel and Palestine Political Report*, March 1986, p. 5. Sammy Smooha, "Political Intolerance: Threatening Israel's Democracy," *New Outlook* (July 1986), p. 27, at p. 29.

5 Adopted as amendment to art. 134 of Knesset Rules, 5746 *Yalkut HaPirsumim* (Public Notices), p. 772, in David Kretzmer, *The Legal Status of the Arabs in Israel* (1987), p. 42. Aryeh Rubinstein, "Knesset Forbids Racist and Anti-Zionist Bills," *Jerusalem Post*, November 14, 1985, p. 2. Asher Wallfish, "Knesset Expected to Bar Racist Bills," *Jerusalem Post*, November 13, 1985, p. 1.

6 Prime Minister's Office, *Government Yearbook (1953–54)*, p. 57, in W. Thomas Mallison, "The Legal Problems Concerning the Juridical Status and Political Activities of the Zionist Organization/Jewish Agency," *William and Mary Law Review*, vol. 9, p. 556, at p. 586 (1968).

7 Resolution of the 23d Zionist Congress, 1951, in Mallison, *supra* note 6, p. 581.

8 Flag and Emblem Law, *Laws of the State of Israel*, vol. 3, p. 26 (1949).

9 Klein, *supra* note 1, p. 25.

10 Flag and Emblem law, *Laws of the State of Israel*, vol. 3, p. 26 (1949).

11 Klein, *supra* note 1, p. 25.

12 *Id.*

13 Fouzi El-Asmar, *To Be an Arab in Israel* (1978), p. 137.

14 Law of Return, *Laws of the State of Israel*, vol. 4, p. 114 (1950).

15 Kretzmer, *supra* note 5, p. 43.

16 David Shipler, "Israeli Arabs: Scorned, Ashamed, and '20th Class'," *New York Times*, December 29, 1983, p. A2.

17 Haim H. Cohn, in *International Lawyers Convention in Israel 1958* (1959), p. 20.

18 Haim H. Cohn, *Human Rights in Jewish Law* (1984), p. 17.

19 Foundations of Law, *Laws of the State of Israel*, vol. 34, p. 181 (1980).

20 Kretzmer, *supra* note 5, p. 28.

21 Haim Shapiro, "Rabbis Put Judge in Dock," *Jerusalem Post*, international edition, week ending July 2, 1988, p. 8.

22 Shabtai Rosenne, *The Constitutional and Legal System of Israel* (1957), p. 12.

23 Izhak Englard, "The Problem of Jewish Law in a Jewish State," *Israel Law Review*, vol. 3, p. 254, at p. 272 (1968).

24 *Id.*, pp. 273–274.

25 Dan Gordon, "Limits on Extremist Political Parties: A Comparison of Israeli Jurisprudence with that of the United States and West Germany," *Hastings International and Comparative Law Review*, vol. 10, p. 347, at p. 361 (1987).

26 Rosenne, *supra* note 22, p. 11.

27 *International Lawyers Convention, supra* note 17, pp. 13–14.

28 Englard, *supra* note 23, p. 268.

29 Menachem Elon, "The Sources and Nature of Jewish Law and Its Application in the State of Israel," *Israel Law Review*, vol. 4, p. 80, at p. 82 (November 1969).

30 *Knesset Debates*, vol. 41, p. 463 (November 1964).

31 Elon, *supra* note 29, p. 84.

32 Chamber of Advocates Law, art. 3, para. 6, *Laws of the State of Israel*, vol. 15, p. 196 (1961).

33 Rabbinical Courts Jurisdiction (Marriage and Divorce) Law, art. 1, *Laws of the*

State of Israel, vol. 7, p. 139 (1953).

34 Rosenne, *supra* note 22, p. 11.

35 Nancy Jo Nelson, "The Zionist Organizational Structure," *Journal of Palestine Studies*, vol. 10, no. 1, pp. 80–93 (1980). Lee O'Brien, *American Jewish Organizations and Israel* (1986), pp. 19–28.

36 Information Department of the Jewish Agency and World Zionist Organization, *The Jewish Agency's Digest of Press and Events*, Jerusalem, May 16, 1952, pp. 1067–1070, in Elmer Berger, "The Unauthenticity of 'Jewish People' Zionism," in *Judaism or Zionism: What Difference for the Middle East?* (1986), p. 133, at p. 141.

37 World Zionist Organization—Jewish Agency (Status) Law, arts. 3, 11, *Laws of the State of Israel*, vol. 7, p. 3 (1952). Mallison, *supra* note 3, pp. 1039–1043. Mallison, *supra* note 6, pp. 580–591.

38 Sally V. Mallison and W. Thomas Mallison, "Zionism, Freedom of Information, and the Law," in Roselle Tekiner, Samir Abed-Rabbo and Norton Mezvinsky (eds.), *Anti-Zionism: Analytical Reflections* (1988), p. 153, at p. 159.

39 Walter Lehn, *The Jewish National Fund* (1988), p. 97.

40 Aryeh Rubinstein, "Working for Zion: Moshe Rivlin/Profile," *Jerusalem Post*, international edition, week ending February 14, 1987, p. 16.

41 Resolution: "Status for the Zionist Organization," para. c, in Organization Department of the Zionist Executive, *Fundamental Issues of Zionist at the 23d Zionist Congress*, pp. 135–136 (1952), in Mallison, *supra* note 6, p. 583.

42 "Status for the Zionist Organization," *supra* note 41, para. b.

43 *Id.*, para. e(2). William Wilson Harris, *Taking Root: Israeli Settlement in the West Bank, the Golan and Gaza-Sinai, 1967–1980* (1980), p. 46.

44 Agreement for the reconstitution of the Jewish Agency for Israel, June 21, 1971, reported in *Jerusalem Post*, June 21, 1971, p. 8. "Special Supplement—Founding Assembly: The Reconstituted Jewish Agency," *Jerusalem Post*, June 21, 1971. Charles Hoffman, "A WZO-Jewish Agency Shell Game," *Jerusalem Post*, international edition, week ending July 12, 1986, p. 8. W. Thomas Mallison and Sally V. Mallison, *The Palestine Problem in International Law and World Order* (1986), p. 131.

45 Harry Rosen and Shlomo Tadmor, "In Defence of the Agency," *Jerusalem Post*, international edition, week ending July 12, 1986, p. 9.

46 World Zionist Organization—Jewish Agency for Israel (Status) (Amendment) Law, art. 7, *Laws of the State of Israel*, vol. 30, p. 43 (1975).

47 Prime Minister's Office, *Israel Government Year Book 5729 (1968/69)* (1969), p. 255.

48 Hasan Amun, Uri Davis, and Nasr Dakhlallah San'allah, "Deir Al-Asad: The Destiny of an Arab Village in Galilee: A Case Study toward a Social and Political Analysis of the Palestinian-Arab Society in Israel," in Hasan Amun et al. (eds.), *Palestinian Arabs in Israel: Two Case Studies* (1977), p. 1, at p. 59.

49 Planning and Building Law, art. 1, sec. 2(b)(11), *Laws of the State of Israel*, vol. 19, p. 330 (1965).

50 Planning and Building Law, First Schedule, sec. 2(5), *Laws of the State of Israel*, vol. 19, p. 330, at p. 390 (1965).

51 See *supra* chapter 14.
52 Aziz Haidar, *Social Welfare Services for Israel's Arab Population* (1987), p. 54. Kretzmer, *supra* note 5, p. 97.
53 Kretzmer, *supra* note 5, pp. 108–109.
54 Charles Hoffman, "Steps to Renewal," *Jerusalem Post*, international edition, week ending April 30, 1988, p. 3 (magazine section). Joshua Brilliant, "Project Renewal Money Now Helps Arabs Too," *Jerusalem Post*, international edition, week ending April 1, 1989, p. 5

16   Holding the Soil: Arab Access to Land

1   Development Authority Law, art. 3, para 4(a), *Laws of the State of Israel*, vol. 4, p. 151 (1950).
2   Lee O'Brien, *American Jewish Organizations and Israel* (1986), pp. 130–134.
3   Keren Kayemeth Le-Israel Law, art. 2, *Laws of the State of Israel*, vol. 8, p. 35 (1953).
4   Walter Lehn, *The Jewish National Fund* (1988), pp. 99–100, 120–130.
5   Covenant, November 28, 1961, executive reports, 26th Zionist Congress (December 1964), p. 345, at pp. 345–355, in W. Thomas Mallison, "The Legal Problems Concerning the Juridical Status and Political Activities of the Zionist Organization/Jewish Agency," *William and Mary Law Review*, vol. 9, p. 556, at p. 594 (1968); and in *Palestine Yearbook of International Law*, vol. 2, pp. 214–217 (1985).
6   Keren Hayesod Law, art. 2, *Laws of the State of Israel*, vol. 10, p. 24 (1956).
7   Keren Kayemeth Le-Israel Head Office, *Report on the Legal Structure, Activities, Assets, Income and Liabilities of the Keren Kayemeth Leisrael* (1973), in Noam Chomsky, *Towards a New Cold War: Essays on the Current Crisis and How We Got There* (1982), pp. 247–248.
8   Ian Lustick, *Arabs in the Jewish State: Israel's Control of a National Minority* (1980), p. 100.
9   Lehn, *supra* note 4, pp. 147–148.
10 Lustick, *supra* note 8, p. 99. Noam Chomsky, "Israelis and Palestinians," in Uri Davis (ed.), *Israelis and Palestinians* (1975), p. 386. Joseph Weitz, "Land Ownership," in Israel Pocket Library, *Immigration and Settlement in Israel* (1973), p. 103, at p. 108. Israel Lands Administration report, 1961–62, in Lehn, *supra* note 4, p. 114.
11 U.S. Dept. of State, *Country Reports on Human Rights Practices for 1984* (1985), p. 1266.
12 Uri Davis and Walter Lehn, "And the Fund Still Lives: The Role of the Jewish National Fund in the Determination of Israel's Land Policies," *Journal of Palestine Studies*, vol. 7, no. 4, p. 3, at pp. 23–25 (1978).
13 Lehn, *supra* note 4, p. 135.
14 Ian Lustick, "The Quiescent Palestinians: the System of Control over Arabs in Israel," in Khalil Nakhleh and Elia Zureik (eds.), *The Sociology of the Palestinians* (1980), p. 68.
15 Development Authority Law, *Laws of the State of Israel*, vol. 4, p. 151 (1950).
16 Basic Law: Israel Lands, art. 1, *Laws of the State of Israel*, vol. 14, p. 48 (1960).

17 Keren Kayemeth Le-Israel, Memorandum of Association, art. 3(h), May 20, 1954, approved by minister of justice, in *Palestine Yearbook of International Law*, vol. 2, p. 206 (1985).

18 Abraham Granott (Granovsky), *Agrarian Reform and the Record of Israel* (1956), p. 104.

19 David Tanne, "Housing," in Israel Pocket Library, *supra* note 10, p. 122, at p. 125.

20 J. Weisman, "The Kibbutz: Israel's Collective Settlement," *Israel Law Review*, vol. 1, p. 99, at p. 101 (1966). Israel Shahak, "The Racist Nature of Zionism and of the Zionistic State of Israel," in *Pi-Ha'aton* (student newspaper, Hebrew University), November 5, 1975, in Israel Shahak, *The Non-Jew in the Jewish State: A Collection of Documents* (1975), p. 131, at p. 133.

21 Keren Kayemeth Le-Israel, Memorandum of Association, arts. 3(a), 3(g), in *Palestine Yearbook*, *supra* note 17, p. 206.

22 See *supra* chapter 1.

23 Keren Kayemeth Le-Israel, Memorandum of Association, art. 3(e), in *Palestine Yearbook*, *supra* note 17, p. 206.

24 *Id.*, art. 3(b).

25 *The JNF, Association Limited by Guarantee and Not Having a Capital Divided into Shares* (Jerusalem, 1952), in Davis and Lehn, *supra* note 12, p. 9.

26 David Kretzmer, *The Legal Status of the Arabs in Israel* (1987), p. 74.

27 Lease Contract, art. 25, in Lehn, *supra* note 4, p. 192; and in *Palestine Yearbook of International Law*, vol. 2, p. 221 (1985).

28 Editorial, "Struck Off the Israeli List," *The Times*, June 20, 1984, p. 11.

29 Israel Lands Administration Law, art. 2(a), *Laws of the State of Israel*, vol. 14, p. 50 (1960).

30 Covenant *supra* note 5, art. 2.

31 Israel Lands Administration Law, art. 3, *Laws of the State of Israel*, vol. 14, p. 50 (1960).

32 Covenant, *supra* note 5, art. 9. Weitz, *supra* note 10, p. 108. Jacob Tsur, "The Jewish National Fund," in Israel Pocket Library, *supra* note 10, p. 112, at p. 115.

33 Kretzmer, *supra* note 26, p. 76. Lehn, *supra* note 4, p. 116.

34 Covenant, *supra* note 5, art. 10. Lustick, *supra* note 8, p. 99. Davis and Lehn, *supra* note 12, pp. 16–21. Hasan Amun, Uri Davis, and Nasr San'allah, "Deir Al-Asad: The Destiny of an Arab Village in Galilee: A Case Study Towards a Social and Political Analysis of the Palestinian-Arab Society in Israel," in Hasan Amun (ed.), *Palestinian Arabs in Israel: Two Case Studies* (1977), pp. 58–59.

35 Covenant, *supra* note 5, art. 10. Lustick, *supra* note 8, p. 99.

36 Uzi Ornan, "'Who is a Jew?' and the Rights of the Jews," *Ma'ariv*, January 30, 1974, in Shahak, *supra* note 20, p. 53, at pp. 54–55. Uzi Ornan, "The Regime of Privileges," *Ha'aretz*, March 26, 1975, *id.*, p. 56, at p. 59.

37 Keren Kayemeth Le-Israel Head Office, Jerusalem, *Report on the Legal Structure, Activities, Assets, Income and Liabilities of the Keren Kayemeth Leisrael* (1973), p. 6, in Chomsky, *supra* note 7, p. 249; and in Lehn, *supra* note 4, p. 115.

38 Chomsky, *supra* note 7, p. 248.

39 Keren Kayemeth Le-Israel, Memorandum of Association, art. 3(3), in *Palestine Yearbook*, *supra* note 17, p. 206. Kretzmer, *supra* note 26, p. 76.

40 Amun, Davis, and San'allah, *supra* note 34, p. 46.

41 Agricultural Settlement (Restrictions on Use of Agricultural Land and of Water) Law, arts. 1–2, First Schedule, *Laws of the State of Israel*, vol. 21, p. 105 (1967).

42 *Knesset Debates*, vol. 47, p. 165 (October 31, 1966) (MK Avnery). *Id.*, p. 168 (MK Toubi). Lehn, *supra* note 5, pp. 118–119.

43 Roman Prister, "Ishmael National Fund," *Ha'aretz*, October 14, 1966, magazine section, pp. 5–7. The title of the article—in Hebrew, "Keren Kayemeth Israel"—is a take-off from Keren Kayemeth Israel (Jewish National Fund), Ishmael being the biblical ancestor of the Arabs. The implication was that the Fund was serving Arabs.

44 Agricultural Settlement (Restrictions on Use of Agricultural Land and of Water) Law, arts. 7–8, *Laws of the State of Israel*, vol. 21, p. 105 (1967).

45 Uri Davis, "Palestine into Israel," *Journal of Palestine Studies*, vol. 3, no. 1, p. 88, at pp. 97–98 (1973).

46 Meir Hareuveni, "The Israeli Settlement Authorities are taking action against the leasing of lands to Arabs," *Ma'ariv*, July 3, 1975, p. 4.

47 Lustick, *supra* note 8, p. 100.

48 Bantu Land Act, no. 27 (1913), *Statutes of the Republic of South Africa*, vol. 9, p. 21.

49 Bantu Trust and Land Act, no. 18 (1936), *Statutes of the Republic of South Africa*, vol. 9, p. 371.

50 Penal Law, art. 2, *Laws of the State of Israel: Special Volume, 5737–1977*, p. 9.

51 *Id.*, arts. 277–297.

52 W. Thomas Mallison and Sally V. Mallison, *The Palestine Problem in International Law and World Order* (1986), p. 160.

53 Claude Klein, *Le caractère juif de l'état d'Israël* (1977), p. 22.

54 Kretzmer, *supra* note 26, p. 71

55 Lustick, *supra* note 8, p. 106.

56 Jiryis, *supra* note 42. p. 58.

57 Roselle Tekiner, *Jewish Nationality Status as the Basis for Institutionalized Racism in Israel*, Paper no. 40, International Organization for the Elimination of All Forms of Racial Discrimination (1985), p. 12.

17 The Law of Ingathering: Nationality and Citizenship

1 Law of Return, art. 1, *Laws of the State of Israel*, vol. 4, p. 114 (1950).

2 Nationality Law, art. 2, *Laws of the State of Israel*, vol. 6, p. 50 (1952). M. D. Gouldman, *Israel Nationality Law* (1970). L. Warsoff, "Citizenship in Israel—A Comment," *New York University Law Review*, vol. 33, pp. 857–861 (1958). Haim Margalith, "Enactment of a Nationality Law in Israel," *American Journal of Comparative Law*, vol. 2, pp. 63–66 (1953).

3 Roselle Tekiner, *Jewish Nationality Status as the Basis for Institutionalized Racism in Israel* (1985, Paper No. 40, International Organization for the Elimination of All Forms of Racial Discrimination), p. 9.

4 Shabtai Rosenne, "The Israel Nationality Law 5712–1952 and the Law of Return

5710–1950," *Journal du droit international*, vol. 81, p. 5, at p. 7 (1954).

5 *Knesset Debates*, vol. 6, p. 2035 (July 3, 1950).

6 *Department of State Bulletin*, vol. 30, p. 628, at p. 632 (April 26, 1954).

7 Dorflinger v. Minister of the Interior, H.C. 563/77, *Piskei Din*, vol. 33, part 2, p. 97 (1977), in *Israel Yearbook on Human Rights*, vol. 12, p. 318 (1982). Rufeisen v. Minister of the Interior, H.C. 72/62, *Piskei Din*, vol. 16, p. 2428 (1962), in *Selected Judgments of the Supreme Court of Israel: Special Volume* (1971), pp. 1–34, summarized in Doris Lankin, *Biennial Survey of Israel Law 1962–1963* (1964), pp. 57–63.

8 Akiva Orr, *The Unjewish State: the Politics of Jewish Identity in Israel* (1983), p. 15. Uri Davis and Walter Lehn, "And the Fund Still Lives: The Role of the Jewish National Fund in the Determination of Israel's Land Policies," *Journal of Palestine Studies*, vol. 7, no. 4, p. 3, at pp. 4–6 (1978).

9 Nationality (Amendment No. 3) Law, *Laws of the State of Israel*, vol. 25, p. 117 (1971).

10 Claude Klein, *Le caractère juif de l'état d'Israël* (1977), p. 96.

11 Lidia Modzhorian, *Mezhdunarodnyi sionizm na sluzhbe imperialisticheskoi reaktsii: pravovoi aspekt* (International Zionism in the Service of Imperialist Reactionary Forces: The Legal Aspect, 1984), p. 15.

12 Nationality Law, art. 3, *Laws of the State of Israel*, vol. 6, p. 50 (1952).

13 Rosenne, *supra* note 4, p. 9, Klein, *supra* note 10, p. 93.

14 Rosenne, *supra* note 4, p. 9.

15 Margalith, *supra* note 2, pp. 63–66.

16 Israeli League for Human and Civil Rights, "Citizenship in the State of Israel Today" (August 1971), in Uri Davis and Norton Mezvinsky, *Documents from Israel, 1967–1973: Readings for a Critique of Zionism* (1975), p. 88.

17 Nationality (Amendment No. 2) Law, art. 3, *Laws of the State of Israel*, vol. 22, p. 241 (1968).

18 Nationality (Amendment No. 4) Law, *Laws of the State of Israel*, vol. 34, p. 254 (1980). David Kretzmer, *The Legal Status of the Arabs in Israel* (1987), pp. 54–55.

19 Kretzmer, *supra* note 18, p. 55.

20 Nationality (Amendment No. 4) Law, art. 2 (adding a new art. 3A to the original law), *Laws of the State of Israel*, vol. 34, p. 254 (1980). Kretzmer, *supra* note 18, p. 55.

21 Uri Davis, *Israel: An Apartheid State* (1987), pp. 37–38.

22 U.S. Dept. of State, *Country Reports on Human Rights Practices for 1983* (1984), p. 1286. Roselle Tekiner, "On the Inequality of Israeli Citizens," *Without Prejudice*, vol. 1, p. 48, at pp. 51–54 (1987).

23 Uri Davis, *Israel: Utopia Incorporated* (1977), p. 96.

24 Bantu Homelands Citizenship Act, Act No. 26 (1970), explained in *Annual Survey of South African Law 1970* (1971), p. 58. Maxim Ghilan, *How Israel Lost Its Soul* (1974), p. 174.

25 Klein, *supra* note 10, p. 34.

26 Asa Kasher, "Justice and Affirmative Action: Naturalization and the Law of Return," *Israel Yearbook on Human Rights*, vol. 15, pp. 101–112 (1985). Ruth Lapidoth, "The Right of Return in International Law with Special Reference to

the Palestinian Refugees," *id.*, vol. 16, p. 103, at p. 121 (1986).

27 F. de Castro, "La Nationalité, la Double Nationalité et la Supra-Nationalité," in Hague Academy of International Law, *Recueil des cours*, vol. 1, p. 515, at pp. 566–568 (1961).

28 International Convention on the Elimination of All Forms of Racial Discrimination, art. 1(3), March 7, 1966, entered into force January 4, 1969, *United Nations Treaty Series*, vol. 660, p. 195 (1969), reprinted in *International Legal Materials*, vol. 5, p. 352 (1966).

29 J. Lador-Lederer, "Jewry's Nationals," *Israel Law Review*, vol. 16, pp. 75–102 (1981).

30 Marc Galanter, "A Dissent on Brother Daniel," *Commentary* (July 1963), pp. 10–17.

31 Heinz Wagner, *Der Arabisch-Israelische Konflikt im Völkerrecht* (1971), p. 39. Nathan Feinberg, "The Arab-Israel Conflict in International Law (A Critical Analysis of the Colloquium of Arab Jurists in Algiers)," in Nathan Feinberg, *Studies in International Law With Special Reference to the Arab-Israel Conflict* (1979), p. 433, at pp. 443–451.

32 Benjamin Shalit and Others v. Minister of the Interior and Another (dissent), H.C. 58/68, Supreme Court sitting as High Court of Justice, January 23, 1970, in Felix Asher Landau (ed.), *Selected Judgments of the Supreme Court of Israel: Special Volume* (1971), p. 35, at p. 51, para. 6.

33 W. Thomas Mallison, "The Zionist-Israel Juridical Claims to Constitute 'the Jewish People' Nationality Entity and to Confer Membership in It: An Appraisal in International Law," *George Washington Law Review*, vol. 32, p. 983, at p. 987 (1964). F. Yahia, *The Palestine Question and International Law* (1970), p. 18.

34 *New York Times*, December 7, 1962, p. A15.

35 Oswald Rufeisen v. Minister of the Interior (Case of Brother Daniel), H.C. 72/62, *Piskei Din*, vol. 16, p. 2428 (1962), Felix Landau and Peter Elman (eds.), *Selected Judgments of the Supreme Court of Israel: Special Volume* (1971), pp. 1–34, esp. p. 11, para. 5; also (translation varies) in *New York Times*, December 7, 1962, p. 15. Decision summarized in Doris Lankin, *Biennial Survey of Israel Law 1962–1963* (1964), pp. 56–63, analyzed in Yehuda Savir, "The Definition of a Jew under Israel's Law of Return," *Southwestern Law Journal*, vol. 17, p. 123 (1963), and in Oscar Kraines, *The Impossible Dilemma: Who Is a Jew in the State of Israel?* (1976), pp. 22–28.

36 Case of Rufeisen, *supra* note 35.

37 Law of Return (Amendment No. 2), sec. 1, inserted into the Law of Return as sec. 4B, *Laws of the State of Israel*, vol. 24, p. 28 (1970).

38 Dorflinger v. Minister of the Interior, *supra* note 7.

39 Letter to Rabbi Elmer Berger, in Whiteman, *Digest of International Law*, vol. 8, p. 35 (1967); and in Mallison, *supra* note 33, p. 1075.

40 M. Cherif Bassiouni and Eugene Fisher, "The Arab-Israeli Conflict: Real and Apparent Issues: An Insight into Its Future from the Lessons of the Past," *St. John's Law Review*, vol. 44, p. 399, at pp. 419–421 (1970). Ilan Halevi, *Question juive: la Tribu, la Loi, l'Espace* (1981), p. 199.

41 Tekiner, *supra* note 3, p. 13.

42 Emergency Regulations (Possession and Presentation of Identity Certificate) (Extension of Validity) Law, *Laws of the State of Israel*, vol. 25, p. 108 (1971); vol.

27, p. 59 (1973) (lowering age at which card required from 17 to 16).

43 George Raphael Tamarin v. State of Israel (1972) C.A. 630/70, *Piskei Din*, vol. 26, part 1, p. 197. *New York Times*, January 21, 1972, p. A14; analyzed in Klein, *supra* note 10, pp. 61–65.

44 Moshe Gabai, "Israeli Arabs: Problems of Identity and Integration," *New Outlook* (October–November 1984), p. 18, at pp. 22–23.

45 Abba Eban, *Voice of Israel* (1969), p. 76.

18 Divide and Conquer: Arabs in Israel's Political System

1 Alfred Witkon, "Elections in Israel," *Israel Law Review*, vol. 5, pp. 42–52 (1970).

2 Ori Stendel, *The Minorities in Israel: Trends in the Development of the Arab and Druze Communities, 1948–1973* (1973), pp. 116–148.

3 Ian Lustick, *Arabs in the Jewish State: Israel's Control of a National Minority* (1980), p. 115.

4 *Government Year Book 5741 (1980–81)*, in Simha Flapan, "Integration or Alienation," *New Outlook* (October–November 1984), p. 33, at p. 34.

5 David H. Rosenbloom, "Israel's Administrative Culture, Israeli Arabs, and Arab Subjects," *Syracuse Journal of International Law and Commerce*, vol. 13, p. 435, at pp. 446–454 (1987).

6 Walter Schwarz, *The Arabs in Israel* (1959), p. 118.

7 Lustick, *supra* note 3, p. 91.

8 George Jabbour, *Settler Colonialism in Southern Africa and the Middle East* (1970), p. 81. Mohammed Aly El Ewainy, "Racial Ideology in Israel and Southern Africa," *Revue Egyptienne de droit international*, vol. 29, p. 279, at p. 282 (1973).

9 Jacob M. Landau, *The Arabs in Israel: A Political Study* (1969), p. 191. Stendel, *supra* note 2, p. 190. U.S. Dept. of State, *Country Reports on Human Rights Practices for 1984* (1985), p. 1266. "Israel's New Parliament: Distribution of Seats in Israel's 120-member Parliament," *New York Times*, November 3, 1988, p. A6.

10 Elia Zureik, *The Palestinians in Israel: A Study in Internal Colonialism* (1979), p. 120. Atallah Mansour, "Israel's Arabs Go to the Polls," *New Outlook* (January 1960), p. 23, at pp. 23–24.

11 Rafik Halabi, *The West Bank Story* (1982), p. 237. Sabri Jiryis, *The Arabs in Israel* (1976), pp. 50–51.

12 Teddy Kollek, *For Jerusalem* (1978), p. 121.

13 Tom Segev, *1949: The First Israelis* (1986), p. 66.

14 *Id.*

15 Schwarz, *supra* note 6, p. 67. Maxim Ghilan, *How Israel Lost Its Soul* (1974), pp. 197–198.

16 Moshe Menuhin, *The Decadence of Judaism in Our Time* (1965), p. 194. Landau, *supra* note 9, pp. 108–155.

17 Jiryis, *supra* note 11, p. 248. Landau, *supra* note 9, pp. 156–178.

18 Lustick, *supra* note 3, pp. 142–143.

19 H. Baruch, "Facing the 180,000: How the Military Government Rules," *Ner* (December 1958–January 1959), p. 37, at pp. 44–45.

20 Segev, *supra* note 13, p. 64.

21 *Id.*, p. 67.

22 Lustick, *supra* note 3, pp. 126–129. Schwarz, *supra* note 6, p. 68. Akiva Orr, *The Unjewish State: The Politics of Jewish Identity in Israel* (1983), p. 17. Ghilan, *supra* note 15, p. 215.

23 Baruch, *supra* note 19, p. 42.

24 Landau, *supra* note 9, p. 94. Michael Saltman, "The Use of the Mandatory Emergency Laws in Israel," *International Journal of the Sociology of Law*, vol. 10, p. 385, at p. 392 (1982).

25 Lustick, *supra* note 3, pp. 192–193.

26 Baruch, *supra* note 19, p. 42.

27 Zureik, *supra* note 10, p. 173.

28 Sabri Jiryis v. Haifa District Commissioner, High Court Case No. 253/64, November 11, 1964, *Piskei Din*, vol. 18, part 4, p. 673; paraphrased in *Jerusalem Post*, November 17, 1964, p. 4. Stendel, *supra* note 2, p. 142.

29 Saltman, *supra* note 24, p. 392.

30 Jiryis V. Haifa District Commissioner, *supra* note 28. Landau, *supra* note 9, pp. 228–230. Saltman, *supra* note 24, pp. 392–393. David Kretzmer, *The Legal Status of the Arabs in Israel* (1987), pp. 31–33.

31 Jiryis, *supra* note 11, p. 192.

32 Zureik, *supra* note 10, p. 174. Halabi, *supra* note 11, p. 237.

33 Stendel, *supra* note 2, pp. 143–144.

34 Kretzmer, *supra* note 30, p. 34.

35 Yaridor v. Central Elections Committee, *Piskei Din*, vol. 19, part 3, p. 369 (1965); paraphrased in *Jerusalem Post*, November 14, 1965, p. 4. Kretzmer, *supra* note 30, p. 34.

36 Dan Gordon, "Limits on Extremist Political Parties: A Comparison of Israeli Jurisprudence with that of the United States and West Germany," *Hastings International and Comparative Law Review*, vol. 10, p. 347, at p. 352 (1987).

37 Yaridor v. Central Elections Committee, *supra* note 35. Stendel, *supra* note 2, p. 144. Landau, *supra* note 9, pp. 92–108. Gordon, *supra* note 36, pp. 350–353.

38 Yaridor v. Central Elections Committee, *supra* note 35, p. 386.

39 *Id.*, p. 389.

40 *Id.*, pp. 381–382.

41 5741 *Yalkut HaPirsumim* (Public Notices), p. 700; 5741 *Yalkut HaPirsumim*, p. 1375, both in Kretzmer, *supra* note 30, p. 131. U.S. Dept. of State, *Country Reports on Human Rights Practices for 1980* (1981), p. 998. Saltman, *supra* note 24, p. 393. Halabi, *supra* note 11, p. 257.

42 *The Times*, June 20, 1984, p. 6.

43 Naiman v. Central Elections Committee, *Piskei Din*, vol. 39, part 2, p. 233 (1984); reported in *New York Times*, June 29, 1984, p. A3. U.S. Dept. of State, *Country Reports on Human Rights Practices for 1984* (1985), p. 1266. Simha Flapan, "Integration or Alienation," *New Outlook* (October–November 1984), p. 33. Gordon, *supra* note 36, pp. 353–364.

44 Naiman v. Central Elections Committee, *supra* note 43, pp. 243, 275–276 (Judge Shamgar), pp. 304, 307 (Judge Barak).

45 Naiman v. Central Elections Committee, *supra* note 43, p. 288 (Judge Elon), p.

324 (Judge Beiski).

46 Basic Law: The Knesset (Amendment No. 9), *Sefer Ha-Hukim* (Primary Legislation), No. 1155, August 7, 1985, p. 196.

47 Uri Avnery, *My Friend, the Enemy* (1986), p. 334.

48 Kretzmer, *supra* note 30, p. 41.

49 Segev, *supra* note 13, p. 65.

50 Meron Benvenisti, *West Bank Data Project: A Survey of Israel's Policies* (1984), p. 44.

51 Michael Palumbo, *The Palestinian Catastrophe* (1987), p. 150.

52 David Gilmour, *Dispossessed: The Ordeal of the Palestinians* (1982), p. 112. Ann Elizabeth Mayer, book review of Aharon Layish, *Marriage, Divorce and Succession in the Druze Family*, in *American Journal of Comparative Law*, vol. 33, p. 111, at p. 114 (1985). Osama Halabi, "From a Group to a Nation?" in *Al-Jadid* (Jerusalem, in Arabic, June 1987), pp. 31–44.

53 Schwarz, *supra* note 6, pp. 148–149.

54 "The Palestinian Working Class," *Democratic Palestine* (May 1986), p. 10, at p. 12. Jiryis, *supra* note 11, p. 201.

55 *Al-Fajr*, December 20, 1985, p. 15. Rony Gabbay, *A Political Study of the Arab-Jewish Conflict: The Arab Refugee Problem (A Case Study)* (1959), pp. 111–112. Nafez Nazzal, *The Palestinian Exodus from Galilee 1948* (1978), pp. 32–33. Benny Morris, *The Birth of the Palestinian Refugee Problem, 1947–1949* (1987), p. 225.

56 Nathan Weinstock, *Zionism: False Messiah* (1979), p. 239. Jiryis, *supra* note 11, p. 199. Gabriel Ben-Dor, *The Druzes in Israel: A Political Study* (1979), pp. 129–130.

57 Nazzal, *supra* note 55, pp. 65–66.

58 Lustick, *supra* note 3, p. 133.

59 Jiryis, *supra* note 11, p. 48.

60 Ben-Dor, *supra* note 56, p. 131. U.S. Dept. of State, *Country Reports on Human Rights Practices for 1983* (1984), p. 1289.

61 U.S. Dept. of State, *Country Reports on Human Rights Practices for 1983* (1984), p. 1289.

62 Ben-Dor, *supra* note 56, p. 131.

63 "To Serve or Not to Serve: Palestinian Druze Caught in Controversy over Israeli Army Draft," *Al-Fajr*, December 20, 1985, p. 8.

64 Yossi Amitay, "A Question of Identity: Like an Uprooted Tree," *New Outlook* (October–November 1984), p. 12, at p. 14.

65 *Al-Fajr*, December 20, 1985, p. 15. "Yale Kan, first-year student of physics, interviews a Druse conscientious objector," in Israel Shahak, *The Non-Jew in the Jewish State: A Collection of Documents* (1975), pp. 118–120.

66 See *infra* chapter 19.

67 Lustick, *supra* note 3, pp. 133, 210. Zureik, *supra* note 10, p. 138.

68 Elaine Ruth Fletcher, "Aim Is Complete Equality for Druse," *Jerusalem Post*, international edition, week ending February 7, 1987, p. 5.

69 Schwarz, *supra* note 6, p. 65.

70 Stendel, *supra* note 2, p. 42. *Kovetz Hatakanot* (Collected Regulations), no. 695,

p. 1280, April 21, 1957, in Sabri Jiryis, *Democratic Freedoms in Israel* (1971), p. 13.

71 Norman Bentwich, "The Legal System of Palestine under the Mandate," *Middle East Journal*, vol. 2, pp. 33–46 (1948). Salman H. Falah, "Druze Communal Organization in Israel," *New Outlook* (March–April 1967), pp. 40–44.

72 Jiryis, *supra* note 11, p. 200.

73 Rabbinical Courts Jurisdiction (Marriage and Divorce) Law, *Laws of the State of Israel*, vol. 7, p. 139 (1953). Dayanim (Rabbinical Judges) Law, *Laws of the State of Israel*, vol. 9, p. 74 (1955). Qadis (Shari'a Judges) Law, *Laws of the State of Israel*, vol. 15, p. 123 (1961).

74 Druze Religious Courts Law, *Laws of the State of Israel*, vol. 17, p. 27 (1962), analyzed in Doris Lankin, *Biennial Survey of Israel Law 1962–1963* (1964), pp. 14–16. *Al-Fajr*, December 20, 1985, p. 15. Ben-Dor, *supra* note 56, p. 101.

75 Lustick, *supra* note 3, p. 210.

76 *Id.*, p. 133.

77 Segev, *supra* note 13, p. 66.

78 *Jerusalem Post*, September 1, 1970, p. 2. Stendel, *supra* note 2, p. 46. Ben-Dor, *supra* note 56, pp. 101–102.

79 Lustick, note 3, p. 133. Schwarz, note 6, p. 148. Jiryis, note 11, p. 200.

80 Sarah Graham-Brown, *Education, Repression and Liberation: Palestinians* (1984), p. 42.

81 *Al-Fajr*, December 20, 1985, p. 15.

82 "Young Druse Charge Discrimination," *Jerusalem Post*, February 8, 1971, p. 7. Ben-Dor, *supra* note 56, pp. 110–111. *Al-Fajr*, December 20, 1985, p. 15. Jiryis, *supra* note 11, p. 201.

83 "To Serve or Not to Serve: Palestinian Druze Caught in Controversy over Israeli Army Draft," *Al-Fajr*, December 20, 1985, p. 8. See *infra* chapter 19.

84 Fletcher, *supra* note 68, p. 5. See *supra* chapter 14.

85 Yehuda Litani, "New Stage," *Jerusalem Post*, international edition, week ending July 4, 1987, p. 7.

86 Sheikh Amin Tarif (spiritual head of Israeli Druze community), "The Druze Community," *New Outlook* (March–April 1962), pp. 84–85. Salman Falah, "The Druze Community in Israel," *New Outlook* (June 1962), pp. 30–35, 53.

87 Schwarz, *supra* note 6, p. 156.

88 Jiryis, *supra* note 11, p. 202.

19 Protecting Privilege: Arabs and Governmental Services

1 Israel Shaham, "Public Housing in Israel," in J. S. Fuerst (ed.), *Public Housing in Europe and America* (1974), p. 52.

2 David Kretzmer, *The Legal Status of the Arabs in Israel* (1987), pp. 67–70.

3 Jacob Dash, "Planning and Development," in Israel Pocket Library, *Immigration and Settlement in Israel* (1973), p. 117.

4 David Tanne, "Housing," in Israel Pocket Library, *supra* note 3, p. 122, at p. 128.

5   Jewish Agency, *Proposal for a General Development Program in the Galilee Hills* (Safad, August 1973), in Noam Chomsky, *Towards a New Cold War: Essays on the Current Crisis and How We Got There* (1982), p. 436.

6   Israel Shaham, "Public Housing in Israel," in J. S. Fuerst (ed.), *Public Housing in Europe and America* (1974), p. 52, at p. 53.

7   Kretzmer, *supra* note 2, p. 113.

8   Tanne, *supra* note 4, p. 125.

9   Atallah Mantzur, "Equality and the Fear of Precedent," *Ha'aretz*, January 19, 1986, p. 9.

10 Abraham Rabinovich, "The Two Nazareths: Too Close for Comfort," *Jerusalem Post*, international edition, week ending March 5, 1988, p. 12, at p. 13.

11 Akiva Orr, "Socialism and the Nation-State," in Fouzi el-Asmar, Uri Davis, and Naim Khader (eds.), *Debate on Palestine* (1981), p. 40, at p. 41.

12 Kretzmer, *supra* note 2, pp. 83–85. David Shipler, "Israeli Arabs: Scorned, Ashamed and '20th Class'," *New York Times*, December 29, 1983, p. 2.

13 *Knesset Debates* (December 2, 1964), vol. 41, p. 486.

14 Ya'acov Friedler, "Upper Nazareth—A Mixed Town," *Jerusalem Post*, international edition, week ending August 16, 1986, p. 20.

15 Yeuda Goren, "Carmiel," *Ma'ariv*, January 20, 1986, in Israel Shahak, *Collection: Between Equality and Apartheid* (1986), p. 8.

16 Ian Lustick, *Arabs in the Jewish State: Israel's Control of a National Minority* (1980), p. 291. Ray L. Cleveland, *Palestine and Israel: The Civil Rights Configuration* (1983), p. 18. Sharon Bray, "Jaffa's Arabs," *New Outlook* (October–November 1984), pp. 47–49. Kretzmer, *supra* note 1, p. 113. Aziz Haidar, *Social Welfare Services for Israel's Arab Population*, p. 52.

17 Donald Neff, *Warriors for Jerusalem* (1984), pp. 289, 324.

18 Muhammad Said Bourkan v. Minister of Finance, Company for the Restoration and Development of the Jewish Quarter in the Old City of Jerusalem, Ltd., and Minister of Housing, Supreme Court (sitting as High Court of Justice), June 14, 1978, Judges Cohn, Shamgar, and Bechor, *Piskei Din*, vol. 32, part 2, pp. 800–808 (1978); criticized in Kretzmer, *supra* note 2, pp. 12–13; and in Allan E. Shapiro, "Jewish Quarter Case Revisited," *Jerusalem Post*, August 9, 1978, p. 8.

19 Moshe Lichtman, "An Arab Kept Separately Is a Good Arab," *Monitin* (March 1983), in Israel Shahak, *The Official Racism in Operation with Regard to the Land in Israel* (1983), p. 1, at p. 3.

20 Michael Adams, "Israel's Treatment of the Arabs in the Occupied Areas," Symposium on Zionism, Baghdad, November 8–12, 1976, pp. 22–23. Sarah Graham-Brown, "The Economic Consequences of the Occupation," in Naseer Aruri, *Occupation: Israel Over Palestine* (1983), p. 167, at p. 205.

21 Rafik Halabi, *The West Bank Story* (1982), p. 42.

22 Aryeh Rubinstein, "MK Warns of Political Danger; Calls for Development Law: More Jews Leave Galilee than Move In," *Jerusalem Post*, May 23, 1986, p. 3.

23 Randijo Land, "Changing Its Role," *Jerusalem Post*, international edition—Keren Kayemeth supplement, week ending January 31, 1987, p. 4.

24 Regulations, ministry of housing, March 31, 1985, in Henry Rosenfeld, *The Condition and Status of the Arabs in Israel* (1985), p. 53.

25 Prime Minister, *Israel Government Year Book 5729 (1968/69)* (1969), p. 250. *Id.,* *(1971–72)* (1972), p. 222.

26 *Jerusalem Post*, November 21, 1962, p. 2.

27 Sarah Graham-Brown, *Education, Repression and Liberation: Palestinians* (1984), p. 39. Kretzmer, *supra* note 2, p. 95. David Shipler, *Arab and Jew: Wounded Spirits in a Promised Land* (1986), p. 442.

28 Sabra Chartrand, "Israeli Draft: Sore Subject for Strict Orthodox," *New York Times*, October 29, 1988, p. A4.

29 Brochure, ministry of housing, May 1983, in Kretzmer, *supra* note 2, pp. 95–96.

30 Kretzmer, *supra* note 2, p. 95.

31 See *supra* chapter 14.

32 Lichtman, *supra* note 19, p. 110.

33 Haidar, *supra* note 16, p. 157.

34 *Palestine Perspectives* (November–December 1986), p. 12.

35 Hubert Law-Yone, Technion, Haifa, in *Jerusalem Post*, international edition, week ending November 1, 1986, p. 6.

36 *Kol Ha'ir*, February 15, 1985, in *Palestine/Israel Bulletin* (February 1986), pp. 5–6.

37 Kretzmer, *supra* note 2, pp. 45–46.

38 Dayanim Law, *Laws of the State of Israel*, vol. 9, p. 74 (1955) (dayan is a rabbinical court judge). Chief Rabbinate of Israel Law, *Laws of the State of Israel*, vol. 34, p. 97 (1980). Izhak England, "Law and Religion in Israel," *American Journal of Comparative Law*, vol. 35, p. 185, at p. 187 (1987).

39 Dina Goren, "Rumblings from the Temple Mount," *New Outlook* (January–February 1986), p. 7.

40 Shipler, *supra* note 27, p. 275.

41 Lotte Salzberger and Dan Schnitt, "Social Welfare Legislation in Israel," *Israel Law Review*, vol. 8, pp. 550–579 (1973).

42 U.S. Dept. of State, *Country Reports on Human Rights Practices for 1983* (1984), p. 1289.

43 National Insurance Law (Consolidated Version), arts. 104–105, *Laws of the State of Israel*, vol. 22, p. 114 (1968), as amended. *National Insurance Law (Consolidated Version) 5728—1968 in English Translation Incorporating All Amendments, Up to and Including Amendment No. 60* (1986).

44 *Laws of the State of Israel*, vol. 3, p. 10 (1949).

45 Discharged Soldiers (Reinstatement in Employment) (Amendment No. 4) Law, art. 1, *Laws of the State of Israel*, vol. 24, p. 126 (1970). Kretzmer, *supra* note 2, p. 86.

46 *Knesset Debates*, vol. 58, pp. 2493–2494 (July 14, 1970).

47 Kretzmer, *supra* note 2, p. 87. *New York Times*, December 29, 1983, p. A2. Sabri Jiryis, "Israeli Law and the UN Universal Declaration of Human Rights," in Hans Köchler (ed.), *The Legal Aspects of the Palestine Problem with Special Regard to the Question of Jerusalem* (1981), pp. 258–259.

48 Rosenfeld, *supra* note 24, p. 53. Graham-Brown, *supra* note 27, p. 39.

49 Regulations on Grants for Soldiers and Their Families, art. 1, 1970, in Kretzmer, *supra* note 2, p. 86.

50 Kretzmer, *supra* note 2, pp. 98–99.

51 *Id.*, pp. 88–89.

52 Council for Higher Education (Recognition of Institutions) Rules (1964), Rule 9, in Kretzmer, *supra* note 2, p. 163.

53 Elia Zureik, *The Palestinians in Israel: A Study in Internal Colonialism* (1979), p. 155. Adnan Abed Elrazik, Riyad Amin, Uri Davis, "The Destiny of Arab Students in Institutions of Higher Education in Israel: An Outline towards a Discussion of the Prospects for an Arabic University in Galilee," in Hasan Amun et al. (eds.), *Palestinian Arabs in Israel: Two Case Studies* (1977), p. 91, at p. 103. Graham-Brown, *supra* note 27, p. 57.

54 Rosenfeld, *supra* note 24, pp. 53–54.

55 "Arab Students in Israeli Universities," *Al-Awdeh English Weekly*, July 20, 1986, p. 11.

56 Kretzmer, *supra* note 2, p. 96.

57 Katzav Commission Guidelines, art. 2(e)(1), in Kretzmer, *supra* note 2, p. 97.

58 Kretzmer, *supra* note 2, p. 97.

59 *New York Times*, May 25, 1987, p. A3.

60 "'Racist' Tuition Ruling Sparks Uproar," *Jerusalem Post*, international edition, week ending May 30, 1987, p. 1.

61 State Education Law, arts. 2, 4, *Laws of the State of Israel*, vol. 7, p. 113 (1953).

62 England, *supra* note 38, p. 201.

63 Jewish Religious Services Budgets Law, arts. 1–2, *Laws of the State of Israel*, vol. 3, p. 66 (1949). Jewish Religious Services (consolidated version) Law, *Laws of the State of Israel*, vol. 25, p. 125 (1971).

64 Kretzmer, *supra* note 2, pp. 81–82.

65 Claude Klein, *Le caractère juif de l'état d'Israël* (1977), p. 117.

66 Kretzmer, *supra* note 2, p. 107. Klein, *supra* note 65, p. 117.

67 Chief Rabbinate of Israel law, art. 2(2), *Laws of the State of Israel*, vol. 34, p. 97 (1980).

68 Kretzmer, *supra* note 2, p. 30.

69 Central Office of Information, Ministry of Education and Culture, *Israel Government Year Book 5732 (1971–72)* (1972), pp. 220–224.

70 *Israel Government Year Book 5732 (1971–72)*, *supra* note 69, p. 222.

71 Charles Hoffman, "You Don't Have to Be Jewish to Get Rights," *Jerusalem Post*, international edition, week ending September 12, 1987, p. 8.

72 Specified Goods Tax and Luxury Tax Law, art. 26, *Laws of the State of Israel*, vol. 6, p. 150 (1952).

73 *Kovetz Hatakanot* (Collected Regulations, in Hebrew, 1975), p. 36, in Kretzmer, *supra* note 2, p. 59.

74 Purchase Tax Order (Exemption) 1975, Definition 15 (returning resident), Definition 20 (returning national), Collected Regulations, *supra* note 73.

75 Kretzmer, *supra* note 2, p. 59.

76 Purchase Tax Order (Exemption) 1975, art. 7 (duties assessed on a returning resident), art. 7A (duties assessed on a returning citizen), Collected Regulations, *supra* note 73.

20   Some Are More Equal: Ethnic Distinctions in the Law of Israel

1   David Kretzmer, *The Legal Status of the Arabs in Israel* (1987), p. 117.

2   Amnesty International, *Town Arrest Orders in Israel and the Occupied Territories*, October 2, 1984.

3   Kretzmer, *supra* note 1, p. 116.

4   Emergency Powers (Detention) Law, art. 12, *Laws of the State of Israel*, vol. 33, p. 89 (1979).

5   Najwa Makhoul v. District Commissioner of Jerusalem (1982), *Piskei Din*, vol. 37, part 1, p. 789. Kretzmer, *supra* note 1, p. 132. Described in Nat Hentoff, "Makhoul v. District Commissioner of Jerusalem," *Village Voice*, March 13, 1984, p. 6.

6   Order by minister of the interior to Canon Riah Abu al-Assal, rector of Christ Evangelical Anglican Church, Nazareth, August 1, 1986 (supplied by Fr. Abu al-Assal to Palestine Human Rights Campaign, Chicago).

7   Prevention of Terrorism Ordinance (Amendment) Law, arts. 1, 8, *Laws of the State of Israel*, vol. 34, p. 211 (1980).

8   David Kretzmer, "National Security and Draconian Law," *Jerusalem Post*, July 1, 1988, p. 10.

9   U.S. Dept. of State, *Country Reports on Human Rights Practices for 1981* (1982), p. 996.

10   U.S. Dept. of State, *Country Reports on Human Rights Practices for 1982* (1983), p. 1159.

11   *Jerusalem Post*, international edition, week ending February 14, 1987, p. 3.

12   *Id.*, week ending February 7, 1987, p. 13.

13   Nationality (Amendment No. 4) Law, art. 10, *Laws of the State of Israel*, vol. 34, p. 254 (1980), inserting the quoted language in the original law as a new sec. 11(b).

14   *AMUTOT Law, Laws of the State of Israel*, vol. 34, p. 239 (1980).

15   Uri Davis, *Israel: An Apartheid State* (1987), pp. 69–71.

16   Prevention of Terrorism (Amendment No. 2) Act, August 6, 1986, amending art. 4, *Sefer Ha-Hukim* (Primary Legislation), No. 1191, August 13, 1986, p. 219. *The Times*, August 7, 1986, p. 9. *Washington Post*, August 7, 1986, p. 27. *Al-Fajr*, August 14, 1986, p. 1. Asher Wallfish, "The Knesset's Big Double Fiasco," *Jerusalem Post*, international edition, week ending August 16, 1986, p. 6.

17   Amnon Zichroni, "A Totalitarian Society?" *Israel and Palestine Report* (December 1986), p. 13.

18   "4 Guilty of Contact with PLO Abroad," *Jerusalem Post*, international edition, week ending June 11, 1988, p. 6. "Four Get 6-Month Terms for Meetings with PLO," *Jerusalem Post*, international edition, week ending July 9, 1988, p. 1. "Prosecution of Hassan Jabareen," *Jerusalem*, no. 29–30, p. 13 (August–September 1987).

19   Hillel Schenker, "The Anti-Peace Amendment," *New Outlook* (March 1987), p. 7.

20   Eliahu S. Likhovski, *Israel's Parliament: The Law of the Knesset* (1971), pp. 13–14. Kretzmer, *supra* note 1, pp. 5–7. Izhak England, "Law and Religion in Israel," *American Journal of Comparative Law*, vol. 35, p. 185, at p. 190 (1987).

21 Likhovski, *supra* note 20, pp. 74, 78–79. Kretzmer, *supra* note 1, p. 12.

22 David Kretzmer, "A Bill of Rights That Spells Fewer Rights," *Jerusalem Post*, international edition, week ending January 2, 1988, p. 11.

23 Basic Law: Judicature, art. 15, *Laws of the State of Israel*, vol. 38, p. 101 (1984).

24 Avishai Ehrlich, "'Bagatzim': Petitions to the High Court—A Statistical Portrait," *Israeli Democracy* (May 1987), pp. 33–35.

25 Judges Law, *Laws of the State of Israel*, vol. 7, p. 124 (1953). Henry Baker, *The Legal System of Israel* (1968), pp. 204–207. Sabri Jiryis, *Democratic Freedoms in Israel* (1972), pp. 20–25.

26 "Press Can Criticize Mossad, Court Rules," *Jerusalem Post*, international edition, week ending January 12, 1989, p. 5.

27 Kretzmer, *supra* note 1, pp. 123, 134. Sabri Jiryis, *The Arabs in Israel* (1976), pp. 20–23, 33.

28 Emergency Powers (Detention) Law, arts. 6, 9, *Laws of the State of Israel*, vol. 33, p. 89 (1979).

29 Rafik Halabi, *The West Bank Story* (1982), pp. 235–236.

30 Maxim Ghilan, *How Israel Lost Its Soul* (1974), p. 165. Shawky Zeidan, "A Human Rights Settlement: The West Bank and Gaza," in George W. Sheperd and Ved P. Nanda, *Human Rights and Third World Development* (1985), p. 170. Sydney D. Bailey, *The Making of Resolution 242* (1985), p. 189.

31 Bernard Avishai, "Israel—the Forty Years' Crisis," *Nation*, p. 568, at p. 572, April 23, 1988.

32 American Law Institute, *Restatement of the Law: Foreign Relations Law of the United States (Revised)*, sec. 702 (1987). Max Planck Institute, "Apartheid," *Encyclopedia of Public International Law*, vol. 8, p. 37, at p. 39 (1985). South-West Africa cases (Ethiopia v. South Africa; Liberia v. South Africa), second phase, International Court of Justice, *Reports of Judgments, Advisory Opinions and Orders* (1966), p. 293 (Judge Tanaka, dissent).

33 UN Charter, arts. 1, 55, Legal Consequences for States of the Continued Presence of South Africa in Namibia (South-West Africa) Notwithstanding Security Council Resolution 276 (1970), International Court of Justice, *Reports of Judgments, Advisory Opinions and Orders* (1971), p. 57, para. 131.

34 International Convention on the Elimination of All Forms of Racial Discrimination, art. 1, *General Assembly Official Records*, 20th sess., Supplement No. 14, UN Doc. A/6014 (1966), *United Nations Treaty Series*, vol. 660, p. 195 (1969), reprinted in *International Legal Materials*, vol. 5, p. 352 (1966).

35 Yehuda Savir, "The Definition of a Jew under Israel's Law of Return," *Southwestern Law Journal*, vol. 17, p. 123, at pp. 124–125 (1963).

36 G. A. Res. 181, sec. 10(d), November 29, 1947.

37 W. Thomas Mallison and Sally V. Mallison, "An International Law Analysis of the Major United Nations Resolutions Concerning the Palestine Question," pp. 18–21, UN Doc. ST/SG/SER.F/4 (1979). Mümtaz Soysal, "Israeli Law and the General Principles of Human Rights," in Hans Köchler (ed.), *The Legal Aspects of the Palestine Problem with Special Regard to the Question of Jerusalem* (1981), p. 231, at p. 232. F. Yahia, *The Palestine Question and International Law* (1970), pp. 41–42.

38 G. A. Res. 3379, November 10, 1975.

39 Tom Franck, *Nation Against Nation: What Happened to the U.N. Dream and What the U.S. Can Do About It* (1985), p. 210.

40 Conference of Ministers for Foreign Affairs of Non-Aligned Countries, Lima, August 25–30, 1975, Doc. A/10217 and Corr. 1, annex, p. 3, in G. A. Res. 3379, November 10, 1975.

41 Assembly of Heads of State and Government, Organization of African Unity, Res. 77 (XII), Doc. A/10297, annex II, in G. A. Res. 3379, November 10, 1975.

42 *International Legal Materials*, vol. 21, p. 58 (1982).

43 *Jerusalem Post*, November 8, 1961, p. 2.

44 Brice Harris, "The South Africanization of Israel," *Arab Studies Quarterly*, vol. 6, pp. 169–189 (1984). Zeidan, *supra* note 30, p. 170. Thomas M. Ricks, "Palestine and the 19th–20th Century World History: A Case Study in Imperialism, Racism and Zionism," in Fouzi El-Asmar, Uri Davis, and Naim Khader (eds.), *Debate on Palestine* (1981) p. 126, at p. 127.

45 Myres S. McDougal, Harold D. Laswell, and Lung-chu Chen, *Human Rights and World Public Order: The Basic Policies of an International Law of Human Dignity* (1980), p. 523.

46 International Convention on the Suppression and Punishment of the Crime of Apartheid, art. 2, *International Legal Materials*, vol. 13, p. 50 (1974).

47 *Restatement, supra* note 32, sec. 702. Max Planck Institute, *supra* note 32, p. 39.

48 Statement of Abdeen M. Jabara, "On Behalf of the Committee to Challenge the Abuse of the Charitable Contribution Exemption and Deduction," in *General Tax Reform: Public Hearings before the Committee on Ways and Means, House of Representatives, Ninety-Third Congress, First Session*, (1973), p. 1758, at p. 1783.

49 Fayez A. Sayegh, *Zionist Colonialism in Palestine* (1965), p. 21.

50 Maxime Rodinson, *Israel: A Colonial-Settler State?* (1973), p. 77.

51 Res. 77 (XII), Assembly of the Heads of State and Government of the Organization of African Unity, July 28–August 1, 1975, quoted in Miguel A. D'Estéfano Pisani, "Connivencia de Estados Unidos con el sionismo en los órganos principales de las Naciones Unidas," *Revista de Africa y Medio Oriente*, vol. 2, no. 1, p. 55, at pp. 84–85 (1985).

52 Leften Stavrianos, *Global Rift: The Third World Comes of Age* (1981), p. 784.

53 Ali Mazrui, "Zionism and Apartheid: Strange Bedfellows or Natural Allies?" *Alternatives*, vol. 9, no. 1, p. 73, at p. 92 (1983).

54 Franck, *supra* note 39, p. 218–219.

55 John Norton Moore, "The Arab-Israeli Conflict and the Obligation to Pursue Peaceful Settlement of International Disputes," *University of Kansas Law Review*, vol. 19, p. 403, at p. 429 (1971).

56 Benjamin Beit-Hallahmi, "South Africa as Analogy and Inspiration," *New Outlook* (November–December 1988), p. 34, at p. 35.

57 *New York Times*, April 30, 1971, p. A39.

58 C. L. Sulzberger, in *New York Times*, April 30, 1971, p. A39. James Michener, *The Covenant* (1980), p. 266.

59 Richard P. Stevens, "Israel and South Africa: A Comparative Study in Racism and

Settler Colonialism," Symposium on Zionism, Baghdad, November 8–12, 1976,. pp. 5–6. Doc. ORIG/E/25.
60 Alfred T. Moleah, "Violations of Palestinian Human Rights: South African Parallels," in Köchler, *supra* note 37, p. 263, at p. 269.
61 "Arnold Toynbee on the Arab-Israeli Conflict: Interview," *Journal of Palestine Studies*, vol. 2, no. 3, p. 3, at pp. 11–12 (1973).

21   No Peace: War Always on the Horizon

1 J. L., "The International Status of Palestine," *Journal du droit international*, vol. 90, p. 964, at pp. 980–982 (1963). Yehuda Blum, "The Missing Reversioner: Reflections on the Status of Judea and Samaria," *Israel Law Review*, vol. 3, p. 279, at p. 289 (1968).
2 *New York Times*, April 25, 1950, p. A1.
3 Allan Gerson, *Israel, the West Bank and International Law* (1978), p. 78. Blum, *supra* note 1, p. 290.
4 Constitution of Palestine, art. 24, March 5, 1962, *Palestine Gazette*, March 29, 1962, in J. L., *supra* note 1, p. 984.
5 *Id.*, art. 54.
6 *Id.*, art. 47.
7 *Id.*, art. 44.
8 Richard Locke and Antony Stewart, *Bantustan Gaza* (1985), p. 7.
9 Alec Kirkbride, *From the Wings: Amman Memoirs 1947–1951* (1976), p. 106.
10 S. C. Res. 89, November 17, 1950. S. C. Res. 92, May 8, 1951. S. C. Res. 93, May 18, 1951.
11 S. C. Res. 95, September 1, 1951.
12 Avi Shlaim, *Collusion Across the Jordan: King Abdullah, the Zionist Movement, and the Partition of Palestine* (1988), p. 456.
13 Fred J. Khouri, "The Policy of Retaliation in Arab-Israeli Relations," *Middle East Journal*, vol. 20, pp. 435–455 (1966). Cheryl Rubenberg, *Israel and the American National Interest* (1986), p. 56.
14 Shlaim, *supra* note 12, pp. 570–574.
15 Sydney D. Bailey, *The Making of Resolution 242* (1985), p. 163. Rubenberg, *supra* note 13, p. 56. J. B. Glubb, "Violence on the Jordan-Israel Border," *Foreign Affairs*, vol. 32, pp. 552–562 (1954).
16 Barry Levenfeld, "Israel's Counter-*Fedayeen* Tactics in Lebanon: Self-Defense and Reprisal Under Modern International Law," *Columbia Journal of Transnational Law*, vol. 21, p. 1, at pp. 45–48 (1982). Pierre-Marie Martin, *Le conflit Israëlo-Arabe: Recherches sur l'emploi de la force en droit international public positif* (1973), pp. 199–227.
17 Derek Bowett, "Reprisals Involving Recourse to Armed Force," *American Journal of International Law*, vol. 66, p. 1, at p. 17 (1972).
18 Barry M. Blechman, "The Impact of Israel's Reprisals on the Behavior of Bordering Arab Nations Directed at Israel," *Journal of Conflict Resolution*, vol. 16, pp. 155–181 (June 1972). Quincy Wright, "The Palestine Conflict in International Law," in M. Khadduri (ed.), *Major Middle Eastern Problems in International Law*

(1972), pp. 23–24.

19 Ilan Halevi, *Question Juive: la Tribu, la Loi, l'Espace* (1981), pp. 253–254.

20 Bowett, *supra* note 17, p. 17.

21 *Id.*, p. 32.

22 Dan Horwitz and Shlomo Aronson, Hebrew University, in Yoram Peri, "Bread, Circuses, and Reprisal Raids," *New Outlook* (October–November 1985), p. 7.

23 Bowett, *supra* note 17, pp. 33–36.

24 Ritchie Ovendale, *The Origins of the Arab-Israeli Wars* (1984), p. 133.

25 Livia Rokach, *Israel's Sacred Terrorism: A Study Based on Moshe Sharett's Personal Diary and Other Documents* (1981), pp. 15–16.

26 Report by the Chief of Staff of the Truce Supervision Organization, Maj. Gen. Bennike, *Security Council Official Records*, 8th year, 630th mtg., UN Doc. S/PV.630, paras. 21, 24 (1953).

27 Rokach, *supra* note 25, pp. 16–17.

28 *Id.*

29 *Id.*, p. 15.

30 S. C. Res. 101, November 24, 1953.

31 S. C. Res. 106, March 29, 1955. Ovendale, *supra* note 24, p. 134.

32 *New York Times*, January 20, 1956, p. A1.

33 S. C. Res. 111, art. 2, January 19, 1956.

34 *Department of State Bulletin*, vol. 30, p. 628, at p. 632 (April 26, 1954).

35 Rokach, *supra* note 25, p. 46.

36 Uri Avnery, *My Friend, the Enemy* (1986), p. 86.

37 Roakch, *supra* note 25, p. 18.

38 Shlaim, *supra* note 12, pp. 611–612.

39 Rokach, *supra* note 25, p. 18.

40 *Id.*, pp. 40–41.

41 Ovendale, *supra* note 24, pp. 149–163.

42 Noam Chomsky, *The Fateful Triangle* (1983), p. 97.

43 S. C. Res. 119, October 31, 1956. Vote: 7–2 (France, U.K.).

44 *New York Times*, November 11, 1956, p. A1.

45 Secretary-General, "Aide-mémoire on the Israel Position on the Sharm el-Sheikh Area and the Gaza Strip," p. 5, *General Assembly Official Records*, 11th sess., UN Doc. A/3511, January 24, 1957. Report by the Secretary-General in Pursuance of the Resolution of the General Assembly of 19 January 1957 (A/RES/453), part 2, para. 5(a), UN Doc. A/3512, January 24, 1957.

46 Aide-mémoire to Ambassador Abba Eban by Secretary John Foster Dulles, February 11, 1957, *Department of State Bulletin*, vol. 36, p. 392 (March 11, 1957). Donald Neff, *Warriors at Suez* (1981), pp. 431–435. Rubenberg, *supra* note 13, pp. 80–87. Benny Morris, "Creeping Withdrawal," *Jerusalem Post*, international edition, week ending December 10, 1988, p. 9.

47 Tom Segev, *1949: The First Israelis* (1986), p. 108.

48 Joseph Schechtman, *On Wings of Eagles: The Plight, Exodus and Homecoming of Oriental Jewry* (1961), pp. 197–201.

49 Ovendale, *supra* note 24, p. 133. Rubenberg, *supra* note 13, p. 59.

50 David Hirst, *The Gun and the Olive Branch: The Roots of Violence in the Middle*

East (1984), pp. 164–170.

51   S. C. Res. 171, art. 3, April 9, 1962.

52   Rubenberg, *supra* note 13, p. 101.

53   S. C. Res. 228, November 25, 1966. Vote: 14–0–1. William V. O'Brien, "International Law and the Outbreak of War in the Middle East, 1967," *Orbis*, vol. 11, p. 692, at pp. 698–699 (1967). Martin, *supra* note 16, p. 209.

54   Helena Cobban, *The Palestine Liberation Organization: People, Power and Politics* (1984), p. 30.

55   Izzat Tannous, Palestine Liberation Organization, *General Assembly Official Records*, 20th sess., Special Political Committee, 437th mtg., UN Doc. A/SPC/SR.437, p. 3, para. 14 (1966).

56   Cobban, *supra* note 54, pp. 23–24.

57   Hirst, *supra* note 50, p. 277.

58   *Id.*, pp. 279–280.

59   Israel-Syria, General Armistice Agreement, art. 5, *United Nations Treaty Series*, vol. 42, p. 327 (1949).

60   S. C. Res. 93, May 18, 1951.

61   *New York Times*, April 8, 1967, p. A1. *Le Monde*, June 7, 1967, p. 3.

62   *Keesing's Contemporary Archives*, vol. 16, pp. 22063–22068 (1967). Henry Cattan, *Palestine and International Law: The Legal Aspects of the Arab-Israeli Conflict* (1976), pp. 167–176.

63   Ovendale, *supra* note 24, p. 178. Charles Yost, "How the Arab-Israeli War Began," *Foreign Affairs*, vol. 46, p. 304, at p. 307 (1967). Martin, *supra* note 16, p. 155.

64   Yost, *supra* note 63, p. 307. *New York Times*, May 13, 1967, p. A1.

65   Yost, *supra* note 63, p. 307. *Weekly News Bulletin* (government of Israel), May 9–15, 1967, p. 20, in Amos Shapira, "The Six-Day War and the Right of Self-Defence," *Israel Law Review*, vol. 6, p. 65, at p. 66 (1971).

66   Letter of Representative of Syria to President of Security Council, May 15, 1967, *Security Council Official Records*, 22d year, Supplement for April, May, and June 1967, p. 90, UN Doc. S/7885.

67   *New York Times*, May 17, 1967, p. A8.

68   Michael Akehurst, "The Arab-Israeli Conflict in International Law," *New Zealand Universities Law Review*, vol. 5, p. 231, at p. 240 (1973).

69   Nadav Safran, *From War to War: The Arab-Israeli Confrontation, 1948–1967* (1969), p. 306.

70   Rubenberg, *supra* note 13, p. 133.

71   Lyndon Johnson, *The Vantage Point: Perspectives of the Presidency 1963–1969* (1971), p. 289.

72   Report of the Secretary-General on the Situation in the Near East, May 19, 1967, *Security Council Official Records*, 22d yr., Supplement for April, May, and June 1967, p. 109, UN Doc. S/7896. *New York Times*, May 21, 1967, p. A2. Fred J. Khouri, *the Arab-Israeli Dilemma* (1976), p. 246.

73   David Kimche and Dan Bawly, *The Sandstorm: The Arab-Israeli War of June 1967: Prelude and Aftermath* (1968), p. 91. Arthur Lall, *The UN and the Middle East Crisis, 1967* (1970), pp. 7–8.

74   *New York Times*, May 16, 1967, p. A15.

75 Ovendale, *supra* note 24, p. 178.

76 *Pravda*, May 24, 1967, p. 1.

77 Ovendale, *supra* note 24, p. 178.

78 Indar Jit Rikhye, *The Sinai Blunder: Withdrawal of the United Nations Emergency Force Leading to the Six-Day War of June 1967* (1980), p. 16.

79 U Thant, *View from the UN* (1977), p. 232.

80 Report of the Secretary-General on the Withdrawal of the UNEF, June 26, 1967, p. 5, *General Assembly Official Records*, 22d sess., 5th emerg. spec. sess., UN Doc. A/6730/Add.3.

81 Thant, *supra* note 79, p. 222.

82 Interview with Nasser, *Le Monde*, February 19, 1970, p. 1. Kimche and Bawly, *supra* note 73, p. 92.

83 *Le Monde*, February 29, 1968, p. 4.

84 Ovendale, *supra* note 24, p. 178.

85 *Le Monde*, February 19, 1970, p. 1.

86 Rubenberg, *supra* note 13, pp. 107–108.

87 Rikhye, *supra* note 78, p. 16.

88 Ovendale, *supra* note 24, p. 178.

89 Report of the Secretary-General on the Withdrawal of the UNEF, June 26, 1967, para. 21, *General Assembly Official Records*, 22d sess., 5th emerg. spec. sess., UN Doc. A/6730/Add.2.

90 Thant, *supra* note 79, p. 223.

91 Ruth Lapidoth, "The Security Council in the May 1967 Crisis: A Study in Frustration," *Israel Law Review*, vol. 4, p. 534, at p. 536 (1969).

92 Remarks of Quincy Wright, in *Proceedings of the American Society of International Law*, vol. 64, p. 80 (1970).

93 Akehurst, *supra* note 68, p. 240.

22 Mortal Danger? The 1967 Israel-Arab War

1 Cheryl Rubenberg, *Israel and the American National Interest* (1986), p. 109.

2 Kenneth M. Lewan, "Justifications for the Opening of Hostilities in the Middle East," *Revue Egyptienne de droit international*, vol. 26, p. 88 (1970).

3 *Keesing's Contemporary Archives*, vol. 16, p. 22065 (1967).

4 David Kimche and Dan Bawly, *The Sandstorm: The Arab-Israeli War of June 1967: Prelude and Aftermath* (1968), p. 95.

5 Lewan, *supra* note 2, p. 88.

6 Donald Neff, *Warriors for Jerusalem: The Six Days that Changed the Middle East* (1984), p. 87. Lewan, *supra* note 2, p. 88. Arthur Lall, *The UN and the Middle East Crisis, 1967* (1970), p. 37.

7 David Mandel, "The 1967 Arab-Israel War in Retrospect: A Case Against 'Anticipatory Self-Defense'" (unpubl. 1988), p. 31.

8 Lewan, *supra* note 2, p. 89.

9 *New York Times*, May 26, 1967, p. A16. Michael Akehurst, "The Arab-Israeli Conflict in International Law," *New Zealand Universities Law Review*, vol. 5, p. 231, at p. 240 (1973).

10   Neff, *supra* note 6, p. 93.
11   Nadav Safran, *From War to War: The Arab-Israeli Confrontation, 1948–1967* (1969), p. 307.
12   Lyndon Johnson, *The Vantage Point: Perspectives of the Presidency 1963–1969* (1971), p. 293. Alfred J. Hotz, "Legal Dilemmas: The Arab-Israeli Conflict," *South Dakota Law Review*, vol. 19, p. 242, at p. 264 (1974).
13   Mandel, *supra* note 7, p. 35.
14   Quincy Wright, "Legal Aspects of the Middle East Situation," *Law and Contemporary Problems*, vol. 33, p. 5, at p. 8 (1968). Hisham Sharabi, "Prelude to War: the Crisis of May-June 1967," in Ibrahim Abu-Lughod (ed.), *The Arab-Israeli Confrontation of June 1967: An Arab Perspective* (1970), p. 49, at pp. 53–57. Hisham Sharabi, *Palestine and Israel: the Lethal Dilemma* (1969), pp. 110–111. F. Yahia, *The Palestine Question and International Law* (1970), pp. 152–154.
15   Asher Wallfish, "Meir Reveals Text of War Decision," *Jerusalem Post*, June 5, 1972, p. 1. Edgar O'Ballance, *The Third Arab-Israeli War* (1972), p. 35. Janice Stein and Raymond Tanter, *Rational Decision-Making: Israel's Security Choices, 1967* (1980), p. 241. Howard Koch, "June 1967: The Question of Aggression," *Arab World*, vol. 15, pp. 10–13 (June 1969). Kimche and Bawly, *supra* note 4, pp. 134–156.
16   Sydney D. Bailey, *The Making of Resolution 242* (1985), p. 68. Safran, *supra* note 11, pp. 320–330. O'Ballance, *supra* note 15, pp. 62–66.
17   Pierre-Marie Martin, *Le Conflit Israëlo-Arabe: Recherches sur l'Emploi de la Force en Droit International Public Positif* (1973), pp. 153–154. Tom J. Farer, "Law and War," in Charles Black and Richard Falk (eds.), *The Future of the International Legal Order: Vol. III: Conflict Management* (1971), p. 15, at p. 41.
18   Akehurst, *supra* note 9, p. 241. O'Ballance, *supra* note 15, p. 49. Hotz, *supra* note 12, pp. 254–255. Kimche and Bawly, *supra* note 4, p. 179.
19   Howard Koch, *Six Hundred Days: A Reappraisal of the Arab-Israeli Confrontation since June, 1967* (1969) p. 21.
20   O'Ballance, *supra* note 15, p. 181.
21   *Id.*, p. 70.
22   William O'Brien, "International Law and the Outbreak of War in the Middle East, 1967," *Orbis*, vol. 11, p. 692, at p. 703 (1967).
23   Neff, *supra* note 6, p. 216.
24   Stephen Green, *Taking Sides: America's Secret Relations with a Militant Israel* (1984), pp. 204–211. Daniel Southerland, "Ex-Pilot Says US Jets Spied for Israel in '67," *Christian Science Monitor*, March 15, 1984, p. 4.
25   Neff, *supra* note 6, pp. 223–224.
26   Safran, *supra* note 11, pp. 348–349, 351.
27   *Id.*, p. 328. Neff, *supra* note 6, p. 203.
28   Wilbur Crane Eveland, *Ropes of Sand: America's Failure in the Middle East* (1980), p. 325.
29   *Id.*
30   Neff, *supra* note 6, p. 205.
31   *Yearbook of the United Nations 1967* (1969), p. 178.
32   Bailey, *supra* note 16, pp. 84–85.

33 *Security Council Official Records*, 22d year, 1347th mtg., pp. 1–2, para. 6, June 5, 1967, UN Doc. S/PV.1347.

34 "Statement of the Soviet Government," *Pravda*, June 6, 1967, p. 1. *Security Council Official Records*, 22d year, 1348th mtg., p. 5, para. 49, June 6, 1967, UN Doc. S/PV.1348.

35 Communication of Permanent Representative of Israel to President of Security Council, *Security Council Official Records*, 22d year, 1347th mtg., p. 1, para. 4, p. 4, para. 30, June 5, 1967, UN Doc. S/PV.1347.

36 *Security Council Official Records*, 22d year, 1348th mtg., p. 15, June 6, 1967, UN Doc. S/PV.1348.

37 *Jerusalem Post*, June 13, 1967, p. 2.

38 Johnson, *supra* note 12, p. 296. Neff, *supra* note 6, pp. 216–217, 220.

39 *Yearbook of the United Nations 1967* (1969), p. 209.

40 *The Times*, July 8, 1967, p. 3. *New York Times*, July 8, 1967, p. A4.

41 Moshe Avidán, "Aspectos legales del conflicto del medio oriente," *Revista chileña de derecho*, vol. 5, p. 244, at p. 252 (1978).

42 Allan Gerson, *Israel, the West Bank and International Law* (1978), p. 71. *Yearbook of the United Nations 1967*, pp. 195–196. Stephen Schwebel, "What Weight to Conquest?" *American Journal of International Law*, vol. 64, p. 344, at p. 346 (1970). Amos Shapira, "The Six-Day War and the Right of Self-Defence," *Israel Law Review*, vol. 6, p. 65, at p. 76 (1971).

43 Akehurst, *supra* note 9, p. 241.

44 Edward Miller, "Self-Defence, International Law and the Six Day War," *Israel Law Review*, vol. 20, p. 49, at p. 60 (1985). John Norton Moore, "The Arab-Israeli Conflict and the Obligation to Pursue Peaceful Settlement of International Disputes," *University of Kansas Law Review*, vol. 19, p. 403, at p. 425 (1971). Barry Feinstein, "Self-Defence and Israel in International Law: An Appraisal," *Israel Law Review*, vol. 11, p. 516, at p. 554 (1976). Martin, *supra* note 17, p. 167. Shapira, *supra* note 42, pp. 67–68. Arthur Goodhart, *Israel, the United Nations and Aggression* (1968), p. 24. Yoram Dinstein, "The Legal Issues of 'Para-War' and Peace in the Middle East," *St. John's Law Review*, vol. 44, p. 466, at p. 469 (1970). Richard Falk, "Reply to Professor Julius Stone," *American Journal of International Law*, vol. 64, p. 162, at p. 163 (1970).

45 Heinz Wagner, *Der Arabisch-Israelische Konflikt im Völkerrecht* (1971), p. 434. Joseph L. Ryan, "The Myth of Annihilation and the Six-Day War," *Worldview* (September 1973), pp. 38–42.

46 *Le Monde*, February 29, 1968, p. 4.

47 *Id.*

48 *Id.*, June 3, 1972, p. 4.

49 *Id.*

50 Ezer Weizman, "Without Complications: A Formula to Minimize the Chances for a New War," *Ha'aretz*, March 29, 1972, p. 9.

51 *Id.*

52 "Excerpts from Begin Speech at National Defense College," *New York Times*, August 21, 1982, p. A6.

53 Akehurst, *supra* note 9, p. 241.

54 John L. Hargrove, "Abating the Middle East Crisis Through the United Nations (And Vice Versa)," *University of Kansas Law Review*, vol. 19, p. 365, at p. 367 (1971).

55 Akehurst, *supra* note 9, p. 241.

56 Hans Kelsen, *The Law of the United Nations: A Critical Analysis of Its Fundamental Problems* (1950), p. 792. Oscar Schachter, "In Defense of International Rules on the Use of Force," *University of Chicago Law Review*, vol. 53, no. 1, p. 113, at p. 133 (1986). Louis Henkin, *How Nations Behave: Law and Foreign Policy* (1979), pp. 141–143. Ian Brownlie, *International Law and the Use of Force by States* (1963), pp. 366–368. Judge Morozov, dissent, in Case Concerning Diplomatic and Consular staff in Tehran (U.S.A. v. Iran), International Court of Justice, *Reports of Judgments, Advisory Opinions and Orders* (1970), pp. 56–57.

57 U.S. secretary of state, Daniel Webster, 1842, in Moore, *Digest of International Law*, vol. 2, p. 412 (1906). Derek Bowett, *Self-Defence in International Law* (1958), pp. 188–193.

58 Martin, *supra* note 17, p. 163.

59 Statement of Mr. Eban, Israel, *Security Council Official Records*, 1348th mtg., p. 17, June 6, 1967, UN Doc. S/PV.1348.

60 Definition of aggression, G. A. Res. 3314, art. 3, para (c), December 14, 1974.

61 Roger Fisher, "Legality of Arab Position," *New York Times*, June 11, 1967, p. E13.

62 Abdel Latif Zeidan, "The Emergence of the Gulf of Aqaba Problem," *Revue Egyptienne de droit international*, vol. 35, pp. 1–65 (1979).

63 Majid Khadduri, "Some Legal Aspects of the Arab-Israeli Conflict of 1967," in Albert Lepawsky, Edward H. Buehrig, and Harold D. Lasswell (eds.), *The Search for World Order: Studies by Students and Colleagues of Quincy Wright* (1971), p. 238, at pp. 241–250. Charles Selak, "A Consideration of the Legal Status of the Gulf of Aqaba," *American Journal of International Law*, vol. 52, p. 660, at pp. 667–668 (1958). Lewan, *supra* note 2, pp. 95–99. "The Aqaba Question and International Law" (no author), *Revue Egyptienne de droit international*, vol. 13, p. 86, at pp. 91–93 (1957).

64 Selak, *supra* note 63, pp. 669–670.

65 Howard Levie, "The Nature and Scope of the Armistice Agreement," *American Journal of International Law*, vol. 50, p. 880, at p. 884 (1956). L. Oppenheim, *International Law* (H. Lauterpacht, ed., 7th ed., 1952), vol. 2, p. 547.

66 Levie, *supra* note 65, p. 886.

67 Richard R. Baxter, *The Law of Internal Waterways With Particular Regard to Interoceanic Canals* (1964), p. 215.

68 Letter from the permanent representative of Israel to secretary-general, January 25, 1957, *General Assembly Official Records*, 11th sess., UN Doc. A/3527, February 11, 1957, Annex V, p. 1. Shabtai Rosenne, *Israel's Armistice Agreements with the Arab States: A Juridical Interpretation* (1951), p. 85. Ruth Lapidoth, "Le passage par le détroit de Tiran," *Revue générale de droit international*, vol. 73, p. 29, at p. 47 (1969). Khadduri, *supra* note 63, pp. 248–250.

69 Richard R. Baxter, "The Definition of War," *Revue Egyptienne de droit international*, vol. 16, p. 1, at p. 8 (1960).

70 "The Aqaba Question," *supra* note 63, pp. 88–91. Lapidoth, *supra* note 68,

pp. 38–40.

71 Momtaz Djamchid, "Du droit de passage dans le détroit de Tiran," *Revue Egyptienne de droit international*, vol. 30, p. 27 (1974).

72 Convention on the Territorial Sea and the Contiguous Zone, art. 16, para. 4, *United Nations Treaty Series*, vol. 516, p. 205 (1964). *United States Treaties and Other International Agreements*, vol. 15, p. 1606 (1964).

73 Leo Gross, "The Geneva Conference on the Law of the Sea and the Right of Innocent Passage Through the Gulf of Aqaba," *American Journal of International Law*, vol. 53, p. 564, at pp. 574–580, 594 (1959).

74 *Department of State Bulletin*, vol. 37, p. 228, at p. 232 (August 5, 1957).

75 Arthur H. Dean, "The Geneva Conference on the Law of the Sea: What Was Accomplished," *American Journal of International Law*, vol. 52, p. 607, at p. 623 (1958).

76 Gross, *supra* note 73, p. 593.

77 Khadduri, *supra* note 63, p. 253. M. Burhan W. Hammad, "The Right of Passage in the Gulf of Aqaba," *Revue Egyptienne de droit international*, vol. 15, pp. 118–151 (1959). Zaki Hashem, "Rationale of the Theory of Historic Bays with Special Reference to the International Status of the Gulf of Aqaba," *Revue Egyptienne de droit international*, vol. 25, pp. 1–65 (1969).

78 Gross, *supra* note 73, pp. 566–572. Lapidoth, *supra* note 68, pp. 41–46.

79 Quincy Wright, "The Middle East Problem," *American Journal of International Law*, vol. 64, p. 270 (1970). Leo Gross, "Passage through the Strait of Tiran and in the Gulf of Aqaba," *Law and Contemporary Problems*, vol. 33, p. 125, at p. 144 (1968).

80 Fisher, *supra* note 61. Lewan, *supra* note 2, pp. 88–106.

81 UN Charter, art. 33.

23 Déjà Vu: Israel's Control of the West Bank and Gaza

1 "Palestinian Emigration and Israeli Land Expropriation in the Occupied Territories," *Journal of Palestine Studies*, vol. 3, no. 1, p. 106, at pp. 106–107 (1973). Sydney D. Bailey, *The Making of Resolution 242* (1985), p. 172. Janet Abu-Lughod, "The Continuing Expulsions from Palestine: 1948–1985," in *Palestine: Continuing Dispossession* (1986), p. 17, at pp. 20, 32. *New York Times*, June 12, 1967, p. A19.

2 Jacques Lefort, "Israël et les Palestiniens: l'Occupation," *Le Monde*, August 19, 1967, p. 2. Peter Dodd and Halim Barakat, *River Without Bridges: A Study of the Exodus of the 1967 Palestinian Arab Refugees* (1969), p. 40.

3 William Wilson Harris, *Taking Root: Israeli Settlement in the West Bank, the Golan and Gaza-Sinai, 1967–1980* (1980), p. 21. Noam Chomsky, *The Fateful Triangle: The United States, Israel and the Palestinians* (1983), p. 97.

4 "Palestinian Emigration," *supra* note 1, p. 106. Chomsky, *supra* note 3, p. 97.

5 Donald Neff, *Warriors for Jerusalem: The Six Days that Changed the Middle East* (1984), pp. 228–229.

6 Dodd and Barakat, *supra* note 2, p. 40. Fred J. Khouri, *The Arab-Israeli Dilemma*

(1976), p. 150. *New York Times*, June 12, 1967, p. A19.

7 Dodd and Barakat, *supra* note 2, p. 46.

8 Neff, *supra* note 5, p. 228.

9 Dodd and Barakat, *supra* note 2, pp. 41–42. Arthur C. Forrest, *The Unholy Land* (1972), pp. 16–17.

10 Neff, *supra* note 5, p. 292. John P. Richardson, *The West Bank: A Portrait* (1984), p. 66. N. G. Gussing, in *Report of the Secretary-General under General Assembly Resolution 2252 (ES-V) and Security Council Resolution 237 (1967)*, 5th emerg. spec. sess., p. 14, September 15, 1967, UN Doc. A/6797. Michael Akehurst, "The Arab-Israeli Conflict and International Law," *New Zealand Universities Law Review*, vol. 5, p. 231, at p. 242 (1973).

11 Amos Kenan, "Report on the Razing of Villages and the Expulsion of Refugees," June 1967, in Amos Kenan, *Israel: A Wasted Victory* (1970), pp. 18–21, reproduced in Fouzi El-Asmar, *To Be an Arab in Israel* (1978), pp. 140–142. Gussing, *supra* note 10, pp. 16–17. Akehurst, *supra* note 10, p. 242.

12 Neff, *supra* note 5, pp. 290–292. Dodd and Barakat, *supra* note 2, p. 47.

13 Harris, *supra* note 3, p. 22. Dodd and Barakat, *supra* note 2, p. 40.

14 Dodd and Barakat, *supra* note 2, p. 40.

15 *New York Times*, June 12, 1967, p. A19. Neff, *supra* note 5, p. 293.

16 Gussing, *supra* note 10, p. 13.

17 Dodd and Barakat, *supra* note 2, p. 46.

18 Khouri, *supra* note 6, p. 150. Dodd and Barakat, *supra* note 2, p. 47. Gussing, *supra* note 10, p. 13.

19 Report by the Secretary-General to the Security Council in pursuance of operative paragraph 3 of the Council's resolution 237 (1967), Annex I, *Security Council Official Records*, 22d year, Supplement for April, May, June 1967, p. 301, UN Doc. S/8021.

20 Bailey, *supra* note 1, p. 129.

21 *Jerusalem Post*, June 13, 1967, p. 2. *New York Times*, June 13, 1967, p. A1.

22 Misha Louvish, "The Spectre of the Green Line," *Jerusalem Post*, international edition, week ending October 25, 1986, p. 15.

23 *General Assembly Official Records*, 22d sess., 5th emerg. spec. sess., UN Doc. A/PV.1526, p. 15, para 165 (1967).

24 *New York Times*, June 11, 1967, p. A1.

25 Neff, *supra* note 5, p. 299.

26 Cheryl Rubenberg, *Israel and the American National Interest* (1986), pp. 104, 122, 131.

27 Ezer Weizman, "Without Complications: A Formula to Minimize the Chances for a New War," *Ha'aretz*, March 29, 1972, p. 9.

28 Abba Eban, *An Autobiography* (1977), p. 381.

29 *Washington Post*, June 5, 1967, p. A10.

30 Eban, *supra* note 28, p. 400.

31 *Le Monde*, June 3, 1972, p. 4.

32 Bailey, *supra* note 1, p. 173.

33 Joel Greenberg, "Shamir: Our Rule as Long as Jordan's," *Jerusalem Post*, international edition, week ending June 14, 1986, p. 3.

34 Benjamin Shalit and Others v. Minister of the Interior and Another (dissent), H.C. 58/68, Supreme Court sitting as High Court of Justice, January 23, 1970, in Asher Felix Landau (ed.), *Selected Judgments of the Supreme Court of Israel: Special Volume* (1971), p. 35, at p. 55.

35 *New York Times*, September 27, 1967, pp. A1, A15. Neff, *supra* note 5, p. 323.

36 Statement of the Zionist Executive, in *Reports submitted to the Twenty-Seventh Zionist Congress in Jerusalem for the period April, 1964-December, 1967* (June 1968), p. 53, in Abdeen M. Jabara, "On Behalf of the Committee to Challenge the Abuse of the Charitable Contribution Exemption and Deduction," in *General Tax Reform: Public Hearings before the Committee on Ways and Means, House of Representatives, Ninety-Third Congress, First Session* (1973), p. 1758, at p. 1773.

37 Bailey, *supra* note 1, p. 156. Ritchie Ovendale, *The Origins of the Arab-Israeli Wars* (1984), p. 185. John L. Hargrove, "Abating the Middle East Crisis Through the United Nations (And Vice Versa)," *University of Kansas Law Review*, vol. 19, p. 365, at p. 367 (1971).

38 S. C. Res. 242, November 22, 1967. Henry Cattan, "The Arab-Israeli Conflict and the Principles of Justice," *Revue Egyptienne de droit international*, vol. 28, p. 44, at pp. 50–55 (1972).

39 Bailey, *supra* note 1, pp. 112–113. Neff, *supra* note 5, p. 345.

40 Bailey, *supra* note 1, p. 153.

41 Conditions of Admission of a State to Membership in the United Nations (Article 4 of the Charter), International Court of Justice, *Reports of Judgments, Advisory Opinions and Orders* (1948), p. 65.

42 F. Yahia, *The Palestine Question and International Law* (1970), p. 189.

43 Bailey, *supra* note 1, p. 152.

44 Resolution on the Palestinian Question, para. 9, Council of Ministers of the Organization of African Unity, Forty-Fourth Ordinary Session, Addis Ababa, Ethiopia, July 21–26, 1986, Doc. CM/Res.1061 (XLIV), in United Nations, Division for Palestinian Rights, *Bulletin*, vol. 9, nos. 9–10, p. 20, at p. 23 (September–October 1986).

45 Konstantin Obradović, *The Palestinian Question from the Standpoint of Human Rights—A Review of Existing Problems*, UN Seminar on Violation of Human Rights in the Palestinian and Other Arab Territories Occupied by Israel, 29 November–3 December 1982, UN Doc. HR/GENEVA/1982/BP.3, p. 26.

46 UN Charter, art. 36.

47 UN Charter, arts. 41–42. Bailey, *supra* note 1, p. 151. Pierre-Marie Martin, *Le Conflit Israëlo-Arabe: Recherches sur l'Emploi de la Force en Droit International Public Positif* (1973), pp. 232–233.

48 S. C. Res. 476, June 30, 1980.

49 G. A. Res. 37/123(F) December 20, 1982.

50 UN Commission on Human Rights, Res. 1987/2, "Question of the Violation of Human Rights in the Occupied Arab Territories, Including Palestine," art. 1, 27th mtg., February 19, 1987, *Economic and Social Council Official Records*, 43d sess., Supplement No. 5, UN Doc. E/1987/18, Chapter 2, sec. A (1987).

51 Law and Administration Ordinance (Amendment No. 11) Law, *Laws of the State of Israel*, vol. 21, p. 75 (1967).

52 *Kovetz Hatakanot* (Collected Regulations), no. 2065, June 28, 1967, pp. 2690–2691, in Sabri Jiryis, "Israeli Laws as Regards Jerusalem," in Hans Köchler (ed.), *The Legal Aspects of the Palestine Problem with Special Regard to the Question of Jerusalem* (1981), p. 181, at p. 182. David Kimche and Dan Bawly, *The Sandstorm: The Arab-Israeli War of June 1967: Prelude and Aftermath* (1968), p. 215.

53 Minister of the Interior, "Proclamation of Enlargement of the Municipal Area of Jerusalem," *Kovetz Hatakanot* (Collected Regulations), no. 2065, June 28, 1967, pp. 2694–2695, in Jiryis, *supra* note 52, p. 183.

54 *New York Times*, July 10, 1967, p. A16.

55 S. C. Res. 252, May 21, 1968. S. C. Res. 267, July 3, 1969. G. A. Res. 2253, July 4, 1967. Vote: 110–0–2.

56 Bailey, *supra* note 1, pp. 115–116. John Dugard, *Recognition and the United Nations* (1987), pp. 111–115. Antonio Cassese, "Legal Considerations on the International Status of Jerusalem," *Palestine Yearbook of International Law*, vol. 3, p. 13, at pp. 28–32 (1986).

57 Basic Law: Jerusalem, Capital of Israel, *Laws of the State of Israel*, vol. 34, p. 209 (1980).

58 S. C. Res. 478, art. 2, August 20, 1980. G. A. Res. 35/169, December 15, 1980.

59 Martin, *supra* note 47, pp. 261–265.

60 See *supra* chapter 11.

61 J. R. Gainsborough, *The Arab-Israeli Conflict: A Politico-Legal Analysis* (1986), pp. 149, 158.

62 Quincy Wright, "The Palestine Conflict in International Law," in M. Khadduri, *Major Middle East Problems in International Law* (1972), p. 13, at p. 27. Quincy Wright, "The Middle East Problem," *American Journal of International Law*, vol. 64, p. 270 (1970). Obradovič, *supra* note 45, p. 31.

63 Dugard, *supra* note 56, p. 113. A. L. W. Munkman, review of *Jerusalem and the Holy Places*, by Elihu Lauterpacht, *British Year Book of International Law*, vol. 43, p. 306, at p. 310 (1968–69).

64 John Norton Moore, "The Arab-Israeli Conflict and the Obligation to Pursue Peaceful Settlement of International Disputes," *University of Kansas Law Review*, vol. 19, p. 403, at p. 425 (1971).

65 Hargrove, *supra* note 37, p. 367.

66 Akehurst, *supra* note 10, p. 242.

67 Yehuda Blum, "The Missing Reversioner: Reflections on the Status of Judea and Samaria," *Israel Law Review*, vol. 3, p. 279, at p. 294 (1968). Stephen Schwebel, "What Weight to Conquest?" *American Journal of International Law*, vol. 64, p. 344, at p. 346 (1970). Schwebel, remarks, *Israel Yearbook on Human Rights*, vol. 1, p. 374 (1971). Julius Stone, *Israel and Palestine: Assault on the Law of Nations* (1981), p. 52.

68 Cassese, *supra* note 56, p. 24.

24 More Land: Confiscation and Settlements

1 Meron Benvenisti, *The West Bank Data Project: A Survey of Israel's Policies* (1984), pp. 30–36. Antoine Mansour, *Palestine: Une Economie de Résistance en Cis-*

jordanie et à Gaza (1983), pp. 34–37. Sara Roy, *The Gaza Strip: A Demographic, Economic, Social and Legal Survey* (1986), pp. 134–135.

2   *Treatment of Palestinians in Israeli-Occupied West Bank and Gaza: Report of the National Lawyers Guild 1977 Middle East Delegation* (1978), pp. 4–8. Raja Shehadeh, *Occupier's Law: Israel and the West Bank* (1985), pp. 15–49. Raja Shehadeh and Jonathan Kuttab, *The West Bank and the Rule of Law* (1980), pp. 107–112.

3   Walter Lehn, *The Jewish National Fund* (1988) p. 165.

4   Geoffrey Aronson, *Creating Facts: Israel, Palestinians and the West Bank* (1987), p. 191. Meron Benvenisti, *West Bank Data Base Project 1986 Report: Demographic, Economic, Legal, Social and Political Developments in the West Bank* (1986), p. 35.

5   Benvenisti, *supra* note 4, p. 26. Walter Lehn, *The Jewish National Fund* (1988), p. 183. Benvenisti, *supra* note 1, p. 19.

6   Benvenisti, *supra* note 1, p. 64.

7   Emergency Regulations Law, *Laws of the State of Israel*, vol. 32, p. 58 (1977).

8   Benvenisti, *supra* note 1, pp. 19–28.

9   Misha Louvish, "The Spectre of the Green Line," *Jerusalem Post*, international edition, week ending October 25, 1986, p. 15. Gershom Gorenberg, "Shamir's Party Plans Huge Settlement Drive," *id.*, p. 5. Charles Hoffman, "U.S. Ban on Spending in Areas 'Has No Legal Basis,'" *id.*, week ending December 19, 1987, p. 8. William Wilson Harris, *Taking Root: Israeli Settlement in the West Bank, the Golan and Gaza-Sinai, 1967–1980* (1980), p. 44.

10 Lehn, *supra* note 3, p. 148.

11 Benvenisti, *supra* note 1, p. 27.

12 17 Residents of the Village of Rujeib v. Government of Israel et al., High Court of Justice 390/79, *Piskei Din*, vol. 34, part 1, pp. 1–31 (1980), in *Palestine Yearbook of International Law*, vol. 1, p. 134, at p. 145 (1984).

13 Roy, *supra* note 1, p. 137. Benvenisti, *supra* note 1, pp. 49–63.

14 Roy, *supra* note 1, p. 137. Aronson, *supra* note 4, p. 97.

15 Aronson, *supra* note 4, p. 268.

16 Ayoub v. Minister of Defence, High Court No. 302/72, *Piskei Din*, vol. 27, part 2 (1972), in Shehadeh, *supra* note 2, p. 109.

17 Ayoub v. Minister of Defence, High Court of Justice 606/78, *Piskei Din*, vol. 33, part 2, p. 113 (1978), summarized in *Israel Yearbook on Human Rights*, vol. 9, p. 337, at p. 340 (1979).

18 Amira et al. v. Minister of Defence et al., High Court of Justice 258/79, *Piskei Din*, vol. 34, part 1, p. 90 (1980), summarized in *Israel Yearbook on Human Rights*, vol. 10, p. 331, at p. 332 (1980).

19 Mustafa Dweikat et al. v. Government of Israel et al. (Elon Moreh Case), High Court No. 390/79, *Piskei Din*, vol. 34, part 1, p. 1 (1980), in Meir Shamgar (ed.), *Military Government in the Territories Administered by Israel 1967–1980: The Legal Aspects*, vol. 1, pp. 404–441 (1982); excerpted in *Israel Yearbook on Human Rights*, vol. 9, pp. 345–350 (1979).

20 David Hirst, *The Gun and the Olive Branch: The Roots of Violence in the Middle East* (1984), p. 371.

21 *Washington Post*, April 26, 1982, p. A1.

22 Hirst, *supra* note 20, p. 453.

23 Ian Lustick, "Israel and the West Bank after Elon Moreh: The Mechanics of De Facto Annexation," *Middle East Journal*, vol. 35, p. 557, at p. 558 (1981).

24 "Israeli Settlements in Occupied Territories," *Review of the International Commission of Jurists*, no. 19, p. 27, at pp. 30–32 (1977).

25 Yehoshafat Harkabi, *The Arab-Israeli Conflict: Future Perspective* (1985), p. 3.

26 *United Nations Treaty Series*, vol. 75, p. 287 (1950).

27 UN Commission on Human Rights, Res. 1987/2, "Question of the Violation of Human Rights in the Occupied Arab Territories, Including Palestine," art. 8(e), *Economic and Social Council Official Records*, 43d sess., UN Doc. E/1987/18, chapter 2, sec. A (1987).

28 Ambassador Netanel Lorch, Ministry for Foreign Affairs, Statement at Symposium on Human Rights, Faculty of Law, Tel Aviv University, July 1–4, 1971, in *Israel Yearbook on Human Rights*, vol. 1, p. 366 (1971). Yehuda Z. Blum, "The Missing Reversioner: Reflections on the Status of Judea and Samaria," *Israel Law Review*, vol. 3, p. 279 (1968). Cheryl V. Reicin, "Preventive Detention, Curfews, Demolition of Houses, and Deportations: An Analysis of Measures Employed by Israel in the Administered Territories," *Cardozo Law Review*, vol. 8, p. 515, at pp. 518–519 (1987).

29 Military Prosecutor v. Halil Muhamad Mahmud Halil Bakhis et al., Israel, Military Court Sitting in Ramallah, June 10, 1968, *International Law Reports*, vol. 47, p. 484 (1974).

30 *Department of State Bulletin*, vol. 61, p. 76 (1969). U.S. Dept. of State, *Country Reports on Human Rights Practices for 1983* (1984), p. 1292. S. C. Res. 237, June 14, 1967. G. A. Res. 2443, preambular para. 2, December 19, 1967. Wendy Olson, UN Security Council Resolutions Regarding Deportations from Israeli Administered Territories: The Applicability of the Fourth Geneva Convention Relative to the Protection of Civilian Persons in Time of War," *Stanford Journal of International Law*, vol. 24, p. 611, at p. 620 (1988).

31 Convention Respecting the Laws and Customs of War on Land, October 18, 1907, Annex: Regulations Respecting the Laws and Customs of War on Land, art. 43, *Statutes at Large*, vol. 36, p. 2277 (1910); and in Bevans, *Treaties and Other International Agreements of the United States of America 1776–1949*, vol. 1, p. 631 (1968).

32 Esther Cohen, *Human Rights in the Israeli-Occupied Territories 1967–1982* (1985), p. 43.

33 Shehadeh, *supra* note 2, p. 22.

34 Israel-Egypt, Framework for Peace in the Middle East, September 17, 1978, in *Department of State Bulletin* (October 1978), pp. 7–9.

35 William B. Quandt, "Camp David and Peacemaking in the Middle East," *Political Science Quarterly*, no. 3, p. 357, at p. 363 (1986). David H. Ott, *Palestine in Perspective: Politics, Human Rights and the West Bank* (1980), pp. 115–138. Frank L. M. Van de Craen, "The Territorial Title of the State of Israel to 'Palestine': An Appraisal in International Law," *Revue belge de droit international*, vol. 14, p. 500, at p. 536 (1978–1979).

36 *New York Times*, May 1, 1980, pp. A3, A31. Cheryl Rubenberg, *Israel and the American National Interest* (1986), pp. 217–219, 237.

37 G. A. Res. 34/65(B), para. 2, November 29, 1979.

38 Miguel A. d'Estéfano Pisani, "Connivencia de Estados Unidos con el sionismo en los órganos principales de las Naciones Unidas," *Revista de Africa y Medio Oriente*, vol. 2, no. 1, p. 55, at p. 66 (1985). Uri Davis, "Israel's Zionist Society: Consequences for Internal Opposition and the Necessity for External Intervention," in *Judaism or Zionism: What Difference for the Middle East?* (1986), p. 176, at p. 185.

39 Israel Shahak, "The Continuing Aims of Zionist Policies in the Middle East," *American-Arab Affairs*, no. 16, p. 68, at p. 70 (1986). Aronson, *supra* note 4, p. 93.

40 Richard Locke and Antony Stewart, *Bantustan Gaza* (1985), p. 17.

41 *New York Times*, March 27, 1981, p. A13.

42 S. C. Res. 484, December 19, 1980. U.S. Dept. of State, *Country Reports on Human Rights Practices for 1982* (1983), p. 1175. Aronson, *supra* note 4, pp. 278–282.

43 Local Authorities (Elections)/(Amendment No. 6) Law, *Laws of the State of Israel*, vol. 27, p. 170 (1973).

44 Henry Kamm, "Most Arabs Boycott Jerusalem Election," *New York Times*, January 1, 1974, p. A2. Ori Stendel, *The Minorities in Israel* (1973), pp. 135–136.

45 David Shipler, *Arab and Jew: Wounded Spirits in a Promised Land* (1986), p. 177.

46 Aronson, *supra* note 4, p. 295.

47 *Id.*, pp. 248–253.

48 U.S. Dept. of State, *Country Reports on Human Rights Practices for 1982* (1983), pp. 1165–1166.

49 *Id.*, p. 1175.

50 Meron Benvenisti, *1987 Report: Demographic, Economic, Legal, Social and Political Developments in the West Bank* (1987), p. 52. "Jews in Areas Nearing 58,000," *Jerusalem Post*, international edition, week ending November 14, 1987, p. 6.

51 Benvenisti, *supra* note 50, p. 37.

52 *Id.*, pp. 38–39.

53 Emergency Regulations (Judea and Samaria, Gaza Region, Sinai and Southern Sinai—Criminal Jurisdiction and Legal Assistance) (Amendment and Extension of Validity) Law, art. 4, *Laws of the State of Israel*, vol. 38, p. 43 (1984).

54 Emergency Regulation (Offences Committed in Israel-Held Areas—Jurisdiction and Legal Assistance) (Extension of Validity) Law, Schedule (Sec. 1), art. 7, *Laws of the State of Israel*, vol. 22, p. 20 (1967).

55 Shehadeh, *supra* note 2, pp. 93–94. Eli Nathan, "Israeli Civil Jurisdiction in the Administered Territories," *Israel Yearbook on Human Rights*, vol. 13, p. 90 (1983).

56 Meir Shamgar, "Legal Concepts and Problems of the Israeli Military Government —the Initial Stage," in Shamgar, *supra* note 19, p. 13, at pp. 49–57. Shehadeh and Kuttab, *supra* note 2, pp. 15–44. Shehadeh, *supra* note 2, pp. 76–100. T. Kuttner, "Israel and the West Bank: Aspects of the Law of Belligerent Occupation," *Israel Yearbook on Human Rights*, vol. 7, p. 166, at pp. 186–202 (1977). Moshe Drori, "The Legal System in Judea and Samaria: A Review of the Previous Decade with a Glance at the Future," *Israel Yearbook on Human Rights*, vol. 8, p. 144, at pp. 150–159 (1978).

57 Shehadeh, *supra* note 2, p. 94. Israel Shahak, "A Summary of the System of Legal Apartheid Which Is in Force in the Occupied Territories," *Palestine Human Rights Newsletter* (November–December 1986), p. 9.

58 Shipler, *supra* note 45, p. 129.

59 Emergency Regulations (Offences Committed in Israel-Held Areas—Jurisdiction and Legal Assistance) (Extension of Validity) Law, Schedule (Sec. 1), art. 2(a), *Laws of the State of Israel*, vol. 22, p. 20 (1967). Roy, *supra* note 1, p. 126.

60 Shehadeh, *supra* note 2, pp. 91–93. Military Order No. 783 (as amended by Military Order No. 1058) and Military Order No. 892, *id.*, p. 102. Raja Shehadeh, "The Legal System of the Israeli Settlements in the West Bank," *Review of the International Commission of Jurists*, no. 27, p. 59, at pp. 66–67 (1981). Raja Shehadeh, "An Analysis of the Legal Structure of Israeli Settlements in the West Bank," in Ibrahim Abu-Lughod (ed.), *Palestinian Rights: Affirmation and Denial* (1982), p. 79, at pp. 88–89.

61 Arie Pach, "Human Rights in West Bank Military Courts," *Israel Yearbook on Human Rights*, vol. 7, pp. 222–267 (1977). Zvi Hadar, "The Military Courts," in Shamgar, *supra* note 19, pp. 171–216. Amnesty International, *Report and Recommendations of an Amnesty International Mission to the Government of the State of Israel 3–7 June 1979* (1980).

62 Israel National Section, International Commission of Jurists, *The Rule of Law in the Areas Administered by Israel* (1981), p. 26. Shahak, *supra* note 57, p. 9.

63 Officer in Charge of the Judiciary, West Bank, Circular 49/1350, December 6, 1984, in Shehadeh, *supra* note 2, p. 93.

64 Aronson, *supra* note 4, pp. 103–107, 206–211, 286–290.

65 Ministry of Justice, *Investigation of Suspicions Against Israelis in Judea and Samaria: Report of the Inquiry Team (Karp Report)*, May 25, 1982, in Palestine Yearbook of International Law, vol. 1, pp. 185–215 (1984).

66 Shahak, *supra* note 57, p. 9.

67 International Convention on the Suppression and Punishment of the Crime of Apartheid, art. 2, *International Legal Materials*, vol. 13, p. 50 1974).

25 More Hewers of Wood: Commerce, Agriculture, and Labor

1 Sara Roy, *The Gaza Strip: A Demographic, Economic, Social and Legal Survey* (1986), p. 19.

2 U.S. Dept. of State, *Country Reports on Human Rights Practices for 1983* (1984), p. 1303.

3 Entrance to Israel Order (Exemption from Certain Provisions for Inhabitants of Judea and Samaria, Gaza Strip and North Sinai, Central Sinai, Solomon District and Golan Heights), *Kovetz Hatakanot* (Collected Regulations), no. 2190, p. 910 (1968), in Ruth Ben-Israel, "On Social Human Rights for Workers of the Administered Areas," *Israel Yearbook on Human Rights*, vol. 12, p. 141, at p. 143 (1982).

4 Meron Benvenisti, *West Bank Data Base Project: 1987 Report Demographic, Economic, Legal, Social and Political Developments in the West Bank* (1987), p. 8. Moshe Semyonov and Noah Lewin-Epstein, *Hewers of Wood and Drawers of Water:*

Noncitizen Arabs in the Israeli Labor Market (1987), p. 9. Joel Greenberg, "The Gaza Strip's Population Explosion," *Jerusalem Post*, international edition, week ending November 14, 1987, p. 6. Ben-Israel, *supra* note 3, pp. 142–143.

5   Semyonov, *supra* note 4, pp. 12, 87–88.

6   Roy, *supra* note 1, p. 35. Semyonov, *supra* note 4, p. 81.

7   Benvenisti, *supra* note 4, p. 31. Michael Shwartz, "The Apparatus Behind the Exploitation of the Workers from the Territories," Derekh Hanitzotz, February 17, 1986, in Israel Shahak, *Collection: The Treatment of the Palestinian Workers from the Occupied Territories Who Work in Israel* (1986), p. 1. Kenneth M. Lewan, "The Palestinian Migratory Workers in Israel," in Hans Köchler (ed.), *The Legal Aspects of the Palestine Problem with Special Regard to the Question of Jerusalem* (1981), p. 224, at p. 225.

8   Roy, *supra* note 1, p. 35.

9   General Exit Permit, No. 5, sec. 1, July 1972, *Collection of Proclamations and Orders by the Military Government in the Region of Judea and Samaria,*, vol. 31, p. 1228 (1973), in Ben-Israel, *supra* note 3, p. 144. International Labor Organization, *Report of the Director-General* (1983), p. 16. U.S. Dept. of State, *Country Reports on Human Rights Practices for 1982* (1983), p. 1173.

10   Semyonov and Lewin-Epstein, *supra* note 4, p. 14.

11   National Insurance Law (Consolidated Version), art. 31, *Laws of the State of Israel*, vol. 22, p. 114 (1968), reprinted as *National Insurance Law (Consolidated Version) 5728—1968: In English Translation Incorporating All Amendments Up to and Including Amendment No. 60* (1986); also in National Insurance Institute, Perla Werner (ed.), *National Insurance Programs in Israel April 1984* (1984), pp. 14–15.

12   National Insurance Law, *supra* note 11, arts. 127AAA, 127BBB. Werner, *supra* note 11, pp. 22–23.

13   National Insurance Law, *supra* note 11, art. 92(a)(2). Werner, *supra* note 11, pp. 12–13.

14   International Center for Peace in the Middle East, *Research on Human Rights in the Occupied Territories 1979–1983* (1985), p. 96.

15   National Insurance Law, *supra* note 11, art. 127A. Werner, *supra* note 11, pp. 22–23.

16   National Insurance Law, *supra* note 11, art. 90B. Werner, *supra* note 11, pp. 16–17.

17   National Insurance Law, *supra* note 11, art. 127EEEE. Werner, *supra* note 11, pp. 6–7.

18   National Insurance Law, *supra* note 11, art. 127V. Werner, *supra* note 11, pp. 8–9.

19   National Insurance Law, *supra* note 11, arts. 7, 21. Werner, *supra* note 11, pp. 4–5.

20   Werner, *supra* note 11, pp. 10–11.

21   International Center, *supra* note 14, p. 89.

22   National Insurance Law, *supra* note 11, art. 7. International Center, *supra* note 14, pp. 90–91. Ben-Israel, *supra* note 3, p. 150.

23   International Center, *supra* note 14, p. 90.

24   *Id.*, p. 92.

25   Director-General, International Labor Organization, Geneva, *Report on the Situation of Workers of the Occupied Arab Territories*, April 15, 1983. Schwartz, *supra* note 7, p. 2.

26 Salim Tamari, "The Palestinians in the West Bank and Gaza: The Sociology of Dependency," in Khalil Nakhleh and Elia Zureik (eds.), *The Sociology of the Palestinians* (1980), p. 84, at p. 91.

27 Shwartz, *supra* note 7, p. 4.

28 E. Rekhess, "The Employment in Israel of Arab Laborers from the Administered Areas," *Israel Yearbook on Human Rights*, vol. 5, p. 389, at p. 407 (1975). International Labor Organization, *supra* note 9, p. 18.

29 International Center, *supra* note 14, p. 96.

30 Benny Morris, "The 'Quality of Life' Fallacy," *Jerusalem Post*, international edition, week ending March 26, 1988, p. 9.

31 Semyonov and Lewin-Epstein, *supra* note 4, pp. 14, 88. Hisham M. Awartani, *A Survey of Industries in the West Bank and the Gaza Strip* (1979), p. 41. Roy, *supra* note 1, p. 32.

32 Emergency Regulations (Judea and Samaria, Gaza Region, Sinai and Southern Sinai—Criminal Jurisdiction and Legal Assistance) (Amendment and Extension of Validity) Law, art. 4, *Laws of the State of Israel*, vol. 38, p. 43 (1984).

33 Military Order No. 45, "An Order Concerning Banking Law," July 9, 1967, in Al Haq, West Bank Affiliate of the International Commission of Jurists, *Newsletter*, no. 15, p. 7 (September–October 1986). U.S. Dept. of State, *Country Reports on Human Rights Practices for 1979* (1980), p. 764. *Id., for 1980* (1981), p. 1006. Roy, *supra* note 1, p. 79. Interview of Crown Prince Hassan (Jordan), "Preserving Arab Identity on the Occupied Territories," *Jordan Times*, April 22, 1987, p. 4.

34 Don Peretz, *The West Bank: History, Politics, Society, and Economy* (1986), p. 117.

35 U.S. Dept. of State, *Country Reports on Human Rights Practices for 1983* (1984), p. 1303.

36 Sarah Graham-Brown, "The Economic Consequences of the Occupation," in Naseer Aruri (ed.), *Occupation: Israel over Palestine* (1983), p. 167, at p. 198. Joel Greenberg, "Bank of Palestine Branch for Gaza," *Jerusalem Post*, international edition, week ending June 14, 1986, p. 11. Roy, *supra* note 1, p. 79.

37 Greenberg, *supra* note 36, p. 11.

38 Military Order No. 1180, September 26, 1986, in Al-Haq, West Bank Affiliate of the International Commission of Jurists, *Newsletter*, no. 15, p. 7 (September–October 1986). "Jordanian Bank Opens in Nablus," *Al-Fajr*, November 7, 1986, p. 3. Benvenisti, *supra* note 4, pp. 27, 33.

39 Military Order No. 418, 1971, West Bank, in Benvenisti, *supra* note 4, p. 36.

40 Roy, *supra* note 1, p. 65.

41 Simcha Bahiri, *Industrialization in the West Bank and Gaza* (1987), p. 40.

42 Peretz, *supra* note 34, p. 118.

43 Meron Benvenisti, *The West Bank Data Project: A Survey of Israel's Policies* (1984), pp. 22–23. Geoffrey Aronson, *Creating Facts: Israel, Palestinians and the West Bank* (1987), p. 269.

44 International Labor Organization, *supra* note 9, p. 20. U.S. Dept. of State, *Country Reports on Human Rights Practices for 1979* (1980), p. 764. Roy, *supra* note 1, p. 76. Peretz, *supra* note 34, p. 118. Susan Hattis Rolef, "Partners in a Dialogue," *Jerusalem Post*, international edition, October 1, 1984, p. 8.

45 Graham-Brown, *supra* note 36, p. 219. Rolef, *supra* note 44, p. 8.

46 Graham-Brown, *supra* note 36, p. 198.

47 Benvenisti, *supra* note 43, p. 11. Bahiri, *supra* note 41, p. 40.

48 Quoted by James Mire, political officer, U.S. consulate, West Jerusalem, in Anthony T. Sullivan, "What Outlook for Peace: Conversations with Prominent Palestinians and Israelis Discourage Optimism that Any Political Settlement of the Israeli-Palestinian Conflict Is Likely Soon," *Americans for Justice in the Middle East News*, vol. 11, no. 3, p. 1, at p. 3 (December 1985–January 1986).

49 Antoine Mansour, *Palestine: Une Economie de Résistance en Cisjordanie et à Gaza* (1983), pp. 85–86.

50 *Id.*, p. 91. Awartani, *supra* note 31, p. 49. Roy, *supra* note 1, pp. 54, 58.

51 Mansour, *supra* note 49, p. 92.

52 Benvenisti, *supra* note 43, p. 10. Mansour, *supra* note 49, p. 81.

53 Awartani, *supra* note 31, p. 45. Roy, *supra* note 1, p. 67. Benvenisti *supra* note 4, p. 10.

54 Roy, *supra* note 1, pp. 63, 73. Tamari, *supra* note 26, p. 91. Bahiri, *supra* note 41, p. 39.

55 Roy, *supra* note 1, p. 46.

56 Benvenisti, *supra* note 43, p. 16.

57 Jan Metzger, Martin Orth, and Christian Sterzing, *This Land is Our Land: The West Bank under Israeli Occupation* (1983), pp. 112–113. Roy, *supra* note 1, p. 63.

58 Benvenisti, *supra* note 43, p. 17.

59 Roy, *supra* note 1, p. 82.

60 Sullivan, *supra* note 48, p. 3.

61 Thomas L. Friedman, "Palestinians Under Israel: Bitter Politics," *New York Times*, January 12, 1987, p. A1, at p. A6.

62 U.S. Dept. of State, *Country Reports on Human Rights Practices for 1983* (1984), p. 1303.

63 Raja Shehadeh, *Occupier's Law: Israel and the West Bank* (1985), p. 113. Mansour, *supra* note 49, pp. 105–106. Roy, *supra* note 1, p. 49.

64 Res. 1985/58, "Economic Development Projects in the Occupied Palestinian Territories," art. 4, *Economic and Social Council Official Records*, 2d regular session, Supplement No. 1a (1985), p. 12.

65 Shehadeh, *supra* note 63, p. 113. Israeli officials gave this reason for the denial. Interview by author with Mustafa Natshe, mayor of Hebron, in Hebron, May 25, 1986.

66 U.S. Dept. of State, *Country Reports on Human Rights Practices for 1984* (1985), p. 1282. Roy, *supra* note 1, p. 52. Richard Locke and Antony Stewart, *Bantustan Gaza* (1985), p. 21.

67 A. Agmon, former agriculture ministry staff officer for Gaza and northern Sinai, quoted in Dani Tzidkoni, "Colonial Policy in the Territories?" *New Outlook* (July–August 1975), p. 41.

68 "Gaza Project Revitalizes Fishing Industry," *Al-Fajr*, April 12, 1987, p. 9. Interview by author with Gaza fishermen, Gaza City, May 24, 1986.

69 Mansour, *supra* note 49, pp. 85–86.

70 *Id.*, p. 88. Roy, *supra* note 1, p. 45.

71 U.S. Dept. of State, *Country Reports on Human Rights Practices for 1983* (1984),

p. 1303.

72 Mansour, *supra* note 49, p. 87. Agmon, in Tzidkoni, *supra* note 67, p. 41. Roy, *supra* note 1, p. 49. Benvenisti, *supra* note 43, p. 15.

73 Tzidkoni, *supra* note 67, p. 41. Roy, *supra* note 1, p. 50.

74 *Al-Fajr*, October 25, 1987, p. 4.

75 Tzidkoni, *supra* note 67, p. 41.

76 U.S. Dept. of State, *Country Reports on Human Rights Practices for 1984* (1985), p. 1282.

77 Roy, *supra* note 1, p. 47. Bahiri, *supra* note 41, p. 34.

78 Roy, *supra* note 1, pp. 45–46.

79 Ibrahim Matar, "The New Sultans," *Israel and Palestine Political Report*, no. 126, p. 11, at p. 14 (August 1986). Locke and Stewart, *supra* note 66, p. 25.

80 Tzidkoni, *supra* note 67, p. 41. Roy, *supra* note 1, p. 50.

81 Tzidkoni, *supra* note 67, p. 42.

82 "Jericho Farmers Demand Better Markets," *Al-Fajr*, March 6, 1987, p. 1.

83 United Nations, *Israel's Policy on the West Bank Water Resources* (1980), p. 12.

84 *Id.*, p. 11.

85 *Id.*, p. 12.

86 *Id.*, pp. 13–14. Benvenisti, *supra* note 43, p. 14. Mansour, *supra* note 49, pp. 45–46.

87 U.S. Dept. of State, *Country Reports on Human Rights Practices for 1982* (1983), p. 1176. International Labor Organization, *supra* note 9, p. 25.

88 *Israel's Policy on the West Bank Water Resources, supra* note 83, p. 14.

89 *Id.*, p. 15. Peretz, *supra* note 34, p. 65.

90 G. A. Res. 36/147(C), para. 7(m), December 16, 1981.

91 Roy, *supra* note 1, p. 51.

92 Locke and Stewart, *supra* note 66, p. 26.

93 *Israel's Policy on the West Bank Water Resources, supra* note 83, p. 10.

94 Meir Shamgar (ed.), *Military Government in the Territories Administered by Israel 1967–1980: The Legal Aspects*, vol. 1 pp. 448–449. Raphael Meron, *Economic Development in Judea-Samaria and the Gaza District: Economic Growth and Structural Change, 1970–80* (1983), p. 24. *Coordination of Government Operations in Judaea, Samaria, Gaza District, Sinai, Golan Heights: A Thirteen-Year Survey (1967–1980)* (1981), in International Commission of Jurists, Israel National Section, *The Rule of Law in the Areas Administered by Israel* (1981), p. 59.

95 Aronson, *supra* note 43, p. 219.

96 Metzger, Orth, and Sterzing, *supra* note 57, p. 114.

97 Benvenisti, *supra* note 43, p. 11.

98 John Gregory Dunne, "This Year in Jerusalem," *Esquire* (December 1987), p. 237, at p. 245.

99 Graham-Brown, *supra* note 36, pp. 200–201.

26 By The Sword: The Palestine Arabs Claim of a Right to Resist

1 *Le Monde*, July 3, 1969, p. 4.

2 Helena Cobban, *The Palestine Liberation Organisation* (1984), p. 38.

3 David Hirst, *The Gun and the Olive Branch: The Roots of Violence in the Middle East* (1984), pp. 302–303.

4 S. C. Res. 248, March 24, 1968.

5 S. C. Res. 256, August 16, 1968.

6 Statement of Mr. Shahi, Pakistan, *Security Council Official Records*, 23d year, 1435th mtg., p. 7, UN Doc. S/PV.1435 (1968).

7 Statement of Mr. Berard, France, *Security Council Official Records*, 23d year., 1402d mtg., p. 5, UN Doc. S/PV.1402 (1968).

8 F. Yahia, *The Palestine Question and International Law* (1970), pp. 69–70.

9 Statement of Mr. Berard, France, *Security Council Official Records*, 23d yr., 1402d mtg., p. 5, UN Doc. S/PV.1402 (1968).

10 Statement of Mr. Shahi, Pakistan, *Security Council Official Records*, 24th yr., 1468th mtg., p. 5, UN Doc. S/PV.1468 (1969).

11 Derek Bowett, "Reprisals Involving Recourse to Armed Force," *American Journal of International Law*, vol. 66, p. 1, at p. 36 (1972).

12 S. C. Res. 268, July 28, 1969.

13 S. C. Res. 273, December 9, 1969.

14 S. C. Res. 290, December 8, 1970.

15 A. Rigo Sureda, *The Evolution of the Right of Self-Determination: A Study of United Nations Practice* (1973), p. 338.

16 S. C. Res. 302, paras. 6–7, November 24, 1971.

17 Kader Asmal, "Hot Pursuit and the Wars of National Liberation," p. 7, Conference of African International Lawyers, Lusaka, Zambia, April 2–5, 1986.

18 S. C. Res. 568, June 21, 1985.

19 S. C. Res. 571, September 20, 1985. S. C. Res. 574, October 7, 1985.

20 Rigo Sureda, *supra* note 15, p. 345.

21 Legal Consequences for States of the Continued Presence of South Africa in Namibia (South-West Africa) Notwithstanding Security Council Resolution 276 (1970), International Court of Justice, *Reports of Judgments, Advisory Opinions and Orders* (1971), p. 16, at p. 56, para. 27. G. I. Tunkin, *Theory of International Law* (1974), p. 419.

22 Palestine National Covenant, art. 16, in *New York University Journal of International Law and Politics*, vol. 3, no. 1, p. 199, at p. 202 (1970). Anis Kassim, *Claims to the Right of Self Defence in Public International Law: A Juridical Analysis of the Palestine War of 1947–1948 and World Minimum Order* (1973, Ph.D. diss., George Washington University), pp. 23–41.

23 Legal Consequences, *supra* note 21, p. 70 (separate opinion).

24 Legal Consequences, *supra* note 21, p. 92.

25 C. J. R. Dugard, "The Organisation of African Unity and Colonialism: An Inquiry into the Plea of Self-Defence as a Justification for the Use of Force in the Eradication of Colonialism," *International and Comparative Law Quarterly*, vol. 16 pp. 157–190 (1967).

26 Julius Stone, *Conflict Through Consensus: United Nations Approaches to Aggression* (1977), p. 67.

27 Louis Henkin, *How Nations Behave: Law and Foreign Policy* (1979), p. 144.

28 John N. Moore, "The Arab-Israeli Conflict and the Obligation to Pursue Peaceful

Settlement of International Disputes," *University of Kansas Law Review*, vol. 19, p. 403, at p. 422 (1971).

29 G. A. Res. 3236, art. 1, November 22, 1974.

30 Heather A. Wilson, *International Law and the Use of Force by National Liberation Movements* (1988), p. 131.

31 UN Charter, art. 2, para. 4.

32 Asmal, *supra* note 17, p. 24.

33 Declaration on the Granting of Independence to Colonial Countries and Peoples, G. A. Res. 1514, para. 4, December 14, 1960.

34 Michla Pomerance, *Self-Determination in Law and Practice* (1982), pp. 49–50.

35 Statement of Mr. Jha, India, *Security Council Official Records*, 16th year, 987th mtg., pp. 10–11, UN Doc. S/PV.987 (1961).

36 Quincy Wright, "The Goa Incident," *American Journal of International Law*, vol. 56, p. 617, at p. 629 (1962).

37 G. A. Res. 2105, December 20, 1965.

38 Stephen M. Schwebel, "Wars of Liberation—as Fought in UN Organs," in John Norton Moore (ed.), *Law and Civil War in the Modern World* (1974), p. 446, at p. 453.

39 Declaration on Principles of International Law Concerning Friendly Relations and Co-operation Among States in Accordance with the Charter of the United Nations, G. A. Res. 2625, art. 1, October 24, 1970.

40 G. A. Res. 2708, December 14, 1970.

41 Definition of Aggression, G. A. Res. 3314, art. 7, December 14, 1974.

42 Stone, *supra* note 26, pp. 66–86.

43 Tom J. Farer, "The Regulation of Foreign Intervention in Civil Armed Conflict," *Recueil des Cours*, vol. 142, p. 297, at p. 367 (1974, no. 2).

44 G. A. Res. 2787, art. 3, December 6, 1971.

45 G. A. Res. 34/44, paras. 2, 12, November 23, 1979.

46 "Resolution on the Palestinian Question," para. 1, Council of Ministers of the Organization of African Unity, Forty-Fourth Ordinary Session, Addis Ababa, Ethiopia, July 21–26, 1986, Doc. CM/Res.1061 (XLIV), in United Nations, Division of Palestinian Rights, *Bulletin*, vol. 9, nos. 9–10, September–October 1986, p. 20, at p. 22.

47 Nathan Feinberg, "The Legality of the Use of Force to Recover Occupied Territory," *Israel Law Review*, vol. 15, pp. 160–179 (1980).

48 Oscar Schachter, "In Defense of International Rules on the Use of Force," *University of Chicago Law Review*, vol. 53, p. 113, at p. 132 (1986).

49 Derek Bowett, *Self-Defence in International Law* (1959), p. 18.

50 R. Y. Jennings, *The Acquisition of Territory in International Law* (1963), p. 72.

51 S. C. Res. 338, October 22, 1973.

52 Hirst, *supra* note 3, pp. 303–304.

53 S. C. Res. 262, December 31, 1968.

54 Hirst, *supra* note 3, pp. 251, 306.

55 S. C. Res. 265, April 1, 1969.

56 S. C. Res. 270, August 26, 1969.

57 G. A. Res 40/61, December 9, 1985.

58 *Al-Fajr*, September 12, 1986, "Poll Results Supplement," p. C. *Jerusalem Post*, international edition, week ending September 20, 1986, p. 9.

59 David Shipler, *Arab and Jew: Wounded Spirits in the Promised Land* (1986), p. 108.

60 John Quigley, "Eliminating Terrorism: A Law and Justice Approach," *Connecticut Journal of International Law*, vol. 3, p. 47, at p. 59 (1987).

61 G. A. Res. 34/145, December 17, 1979. Vote: 118–0–22.

27 Guns and Stones: Resistance by the Palestine Arabs to Occupation

1 Barry Levenfeld, "Israel's Counter-*Fedayeen* Tactics in Lebanon: Self-Defense and Reprisal Under Modern International Law," *Columbia Journal of Transnational Law*, vol. 21, p. 1, at pp. 17–18 (1982).

2 S. C. Res. 279, May 12, 1970.

3 S. C. Res. 280, May 19, 1970.

4 S. C. Res. 285, September 5, 1970.

5 S. C. Res. 313, February 28, 1972.

6 S. C. Res. 316, June 26, 1972.

7 *New York Times*, May 31, 1972, p. A1.

8 *Id.*, September 6, 1972, p. A1.

9 *Id.*, September 9, 1972, p. A1. David Hirst, *The Gun and the Olive Branch: The Roots of Violence in the Middle East* (1984), p. 251.

10 Hirst, *supra* note 9, pp. 318–322.

11 S. C. Res. 337, August 15, 1973.

12 *New York Times*, April 12, 1974, p. A1.

13 *Id.*, May 16, 1974, p. A1. Hirst, *supra* note 9, pp. 328–331. ·

14 Cheryl Rubenberg, *Israel and the American National Interest* (1986), pp. 197, 227.

15 S. C. Res. 425, March 19, 1978.

16 Francis A. Boyle, "Israeli Invasion and UN Charter," *Chicago Daily Law Bulletin*, July 9, 1982. Uri Avnery, *My Friend, the Enemy* (1986), p. 234. Rubenberg, *supra* note 14, pp. 267, 276.

17 Michael Jansen, *The Battle of Beirut* (1982), p. 8.

18 Rubenberg, *supra* note 14, p. 281. Noam Chomsky, *The Fateful Triangle: the United States, Israel and the Palestinians* (1983), p. 221.

19 Rubenberg *supra* note 14, p. 278.

20 *Id.*

21 Harold Saunders, "An Israeli-Palestinian Peace," *Foreign Affairs*, vol. 61, p. 100, at p. 110 (1982).

22 S. C. Res. 509, June 6, 1982.

23 S. C. Res. 515, July 29, 1982.

24 "Excerpts from Report on Israelis' Responsibility in Massacre," *New York Times*, February 9, 1983, p. A18. Linda A. Malone, "The Kahan Report, Ariel Sharon and the Sabra-Shatilla Massacres in Lebanon: Responsibility Under International Law for Massacres of Civilian Populations," *Utah Law Review* (1985), p. 373.

25 S. C. Res. 521, September 19, 1982. G. A. Res. ES 7/9, September 24, 1982. G. A. Res. 37/123D, December 16, 1982.

26 S. C. Res. 573, October 4, 1985.

27 *State of Israel: Press Bulletin: Report of the Commission of Inquiry into the Methods of Interrogation of the General Security Service Regarding Hostile Terrorist Activity (communicated by the coordinator of the commission of inquiry),* November 1–8 1987, excerpted in *Jerusalem Post,* international edition, week ending November 7, 1987, p. 1, and in *Jerusalem Post,* November 1, 1987.

28 Bennie Morris, "A Strain on Credulity," *Jerusalem Post,* international edition, week ending November 14, 1987, p. 10.

29 Landau Commission findings, reported in *Jerusalem Post,* international edition, week ending November 7, 1987, p. 1. John Quigley, "International Limits on Use of Force to Elicit Confessions: A Critique of Israel's Policy on Interrogation," *Brooklyn Journal of International Law,* vol. 14, p. 485, at p. 488 (1988).

30 *Jerusalem Post,* international edition, week ending November 7, 1987, p. 2.

31 *Jerusalem Post,* international edition, week ending November 14, 1987, p. 1. Quigley, *supra* note 29, p. 487.

32 Ann Lesch, "Israeli Deportation of Palestinians from the West Bank and the Gaza Strip, 1967–1978," *Journal of Palestine Studies,* vol. 8, no. 2, p. 101, at p. 102 (1979) (1,151 individual expulsions 1967–1978). Article continues in *Journal of Palestine Studies,* vol. 8, no. 3, pp. 81–112 (1979). *New York Times,* April 13, 1988 p. A8. Joost Hiltermann, *Israel's Deportation Policy in the Occupied West Bank and Gaza* (1986), p. 1.

33 Rafik Halabi, *The West Bank Story* (1982), p. 38.

34 Noam Chomsky, *The Fateful Triangle: the United States, Israel and the Palestinians* (1983), p. 97. Amos Perlmutter, "Menachem Sharon? Well, No," *New York Times,* May 17, 1982, p. A15.

35 Halabi, *supra* note 33, p. 40.

36 *Treatment of Palestinians in Israeli-Occupied West Bank and Gaza: Report of the National Lawyers Guild 1977 Middle East Delegation* (1978), pp. 61–82.

37 Dani Tzidkoni, "Leftist in Gaza Put Before the Military Court," Davar, January 8, 1987, in Israel Shahak, *Collection: The Real Situation in the Occupied Territories, 1987* (1987), p. 11.

38 Ron Jourard, "No division between politics, crime in West Bank," *Jerusalem Post,* international edition, week ending May 10, 1986, p. 5.

39 Military Order No. 101, August 27, 1967, as amended by Military Order No. 718, in Raja Shehadeh and Jonathan Kuttab, *The West Bank and the Rule of Law* (1980), pp. 126–128.

40 Esther Cohen, "Justice for Occupied Territory? The Israeli High Court of Justice Paradigm," *Columbia Journal of Transnational Law,* vol. 24, p. 471, at p. 506 (1986). Esther Cohen, *Human Rights in the Israeli-Occupied Territories 1967–1982* (1985), p. 506.

41 Ruling of September 16, 1987, in *Al-Fajr,* October 18, 1987, p. 8.

42 Abu Awad v. IDF Commander of Judea and Samaria, High Court of Justice 97/79, *Piskei Din,* vol. 33, part 3, p. 309 (1979).

43 Joel Brinkley, "U.S. Criticism Sets Off a Furor in Israel," *New York Times,* August 25, 1988, p. A3.

44 Cohen, *Human Rights, supra* note 40, p. 110.

45 G. A. Res. 2535(B), December 10, 1969. G. A. Res. 2792(C), December 6, 1971.

46 National Lawyers Guild, *International Human Rights Law and Israel's Efforts to Suppress the Palestinian Uprising* (1989) pp. 5–6.

47 "Situation in Occupied Palestine," UN Commission on Human Rights, Resolution 1988/3, para. 3, February 22, 1988. Vote: 30–4–8.

48 S. C. Res. 605, December 22, 1987.

49 *New York Times*, January 22, 1988, p. A10.

50 *Id.*, January 23, 1988, p. A6.

51 *Jerusalem Post*, January 26, 1988, p. 1.

52 National Lawyers Guild, *supra* note 46, pp. 69–74.

53 U.S. Dept. of State, *Country Reports on Human Rights Practices for 1988* (1989), p. 1379.

54 "U.S. Criticizes Israeli Expulsion Policy," *Al-Fajr*, August 28, 1988, p. 4.

55 S. C. Res. 607, January 5, 1988, UN Doc. S/INF/607 (1988).

56 Security Council, *Provisional Verbatim Record*, January 5, 1988, p. 11, UN Doc. S/PV.2780 (1988), reprinted in UN *Law Reports*, vol. 22, p. 37 (1988).

57 U.S. Dept. of State, *Country Reports on Human Rights Practices for 1988* (1989), pp. 1376–1387.

58 UN Human Rights Commission, "Question of the Violation of Human Rights in Occupied Palestine," para. 3, February 17, 1989, UN Doc. E/CN.4/1989/L.4 (1989). Vote: 32–1–9.

28 Statehood in the Making: Palestine Declares Independence

1 Palestine National Covenant, art. 6, *New York University Journal of International Law and Politics*, vol. 3, p. 227 (1970).

2 Philip Mishalani, "The National Question and the PLO," in Fouzi El-Asmar, Uri Davis, and Naim Khader (eds.), *Debate on Palestine* (1981), p. 102, at pp. 106–107.

3 *Id.*, p. 107. David Hirst, *The Gun and the Olive Branch: The Roots of Violence in the Middle East* (1984), pp. 292–294. Helena Cobban, *The Palestinian Liberation Organisation: People, Power and Politics* (1984), p. 16.

4 Naim Khader, "An Initial Response to Dr. Emile Tuma and His Comments on the Socialist Republic of Palestine," in El-Asmar, Davis, and Khader, *supra* note 2, p. 83, at p. 93.

5 *Id.*, p. 93. Uri Avnery, *My Friend, the Enemy* (1986), p. 67.

6 Hirst, *supra* note 3, p. 299.

7 *Id.*, pp. 325–326. Sally Morphet, "The Palestinians and Their Right to Self-Determination," in R. J. Vincent (ed.), *Foreign Policy and Human Rights: Issues and Responses* (1986), p. 85, at p. 93. Norton Mezvinsky, "The Palestinian People and the Right to Self-Determination," in Hans Köchler (ed.), *The Legal Aspects of the Palestine Problem with Special Regard to the Question of Jerusalem* (1981), p. 34, at pp. 39–40.

8 Avnery, *supra* note 5, p. 190.

9 Mishalani, *supra* note 2, p. 121. Cobban, *supra* note 3, at p. 17.

10 Jacques Dehaussy, "La crise du Moyen-Orient et l'onu," *Journal du droit international*, vol. 95, pp. 853–888 (1968).

11 G. A. Res. 3237, November 22, 1974.

12 G. A. Res. 3236, art. 4, November 22, 1974.

13 G. A. Res. 3151 G, December 14, 1973.

14 G. A. Res. 3379, November 10, 1975.

15 Jeane Kirkpatrick, "Ten Years as an 'Outlaw State,'" *Chicago Tribune*, November 10, 1985, p. 3.

16 G. A. Res. 3376, November 10, 1975.

17 G. A. Res. 32/40, para. 1, December 2, 1977.

18 G. A. Res. 34/65D, para. 1, December 12, 1979.

19 G. A. Res. 38/58C, December 13, 1983.

20 "The 18th Palestine National Council Resolutions: The Political Report," para. 5, *Al-Fajr*, May 3, 1987, p. 13.

21 UN Doc. A/43/827, S/20278, p. 13 (1988).

22 Steve Lohr, "Arafat Says P.L.O. Accepted Israel," *New York Times*, December 8, 1988, p. A1. Paul Lewis, "'Right of All Parties' Accepted by Arafat," *New York Times*, December 15, 1988, p. A19. "Statement by Arafat on Peace in Mideast," *New York Times*, December 15, 1988, p. A19.

23 Celestine Bohlen, "U.S. Plan Faulty, a PLO Aide Says," *New York Times*, March 13, 1989, p. A6.

24 "Transcript of Shultz Remarks Outlining New U.S. Position toward P.L.O.," *New York Times*, December 15, 1988, p. A18.

25 "Excerpts from Hussein's Address on Abandoning Claims to the West Bank," *New York Times*, August 1, 1988, p. A4.

26 Jerome M. Segal, *Creating the Palestinian State: A Strategy for Peace* (1989), pp. 104–114.

27 Paul Lewis, "Arabs at U.N. Relax Stand on P.L.O.," *New York Times*, December 6, 1989, p. A3.

28 G. A. Res. 43/177, December 15, 1988.

29 "Editorial: The Battle for Jerusalem," *Jerusalem Post*, October 22, 1990, p. 4.

30 Joost R. Hiltermann, "Settling for War: Soviet Immigration and Israel's Settlement Policy in East Jerusalem," *Journal of Palestine Studies*, vol. 20, no. 2, p. 71, at pp. 77–78 (1991).

31 Cheryl A. Rubenberg, *The Palestinians in Search of a Just Peace* (2003), p. 27.

29 Oslo via Madrid: A Turn to Peace?

1 R. W. Apple Jr., "Mideast Foes List Demands and Trade Angry Charges across Conference Table," *New York Times*, October 31, 1991, p. A1.

2 "The Peace Conference," *Palestine Yearbook of International Law*, vol. 6, pp. 262–302 (1990–91).

3 U.S. Department of State, Letter of Assurances (to the Palestinian team), October 18, 1991, in *Palestine Yearbook of International Law*, vol. 6, pp. 281–282 (1990–91).

4 Paul Lewis, "U.N. Repeals Its '75 Resolution Equating Zionism with Racism," *New York Times*, December 17, 1991, p. A1.

5 G. A. Res. 46/86, December 16, 1991.

6 Raja Shehadeh, *From Occupation to Interim Accords: Israel and the Palestinian Territories* (1997), p. 115.

7 Jose Rosenfeld and Herb Keinon, "Ministry Changes List of Areas Receiving Housing Incentives," *Jerusalem Post*, July 6, 1993 (news section).

8 Awad Mansour, *Clever Concealment: Jewish Settlement in the Occupied Territories under the Rabin Government: August 1992–September 1993* (1994), pp. 1–2.

9 Evelyn Gordon, "Peace Now Petition against Settlement-Building Rejected," *Jerusalem Post*, August 26, 1993 (news section).

10 Cheryl A. Rubenberg, *The Palestinians In Search of a Just Peace* (2003), p. 325.

11 "Text of Declaration of Principles," *Jerusalem Post*, September 15, 1993, p. 4A.

12 *Palestine Yearbook of International Law*, vol. 7, pp. 230–231 (1992–94).

13 *Security Council Official Records*, 50th year, 3538th mtg., p. 7, UN Doc. S/PV/3538 (1995).

14 *Id.*, pp. 3, 4, 5, 8.

15 *Palestine and the* UN (Monthly Bulletin of Permanent Observer Mission of Palestine to the United Nations), vol. 1, issue 1, p. 4 (October 1996).

16 Vienna Convention on the Law of Treaties, art. 26, UN Treaty Series, vol. 1155, p. 331.

17 Patrick Cockburn, "Jews Given Swathe of Arab East Jerusalem for Homes," *Independent*, February 27, 1997, p. 13.

18 *Security Council Official Records*, 52nd year, 3747th mtg., p. 4, March 7, 1997, UN Doc. S/PV.3747 (1997). Paul Lewis, "U.S. Vetoes U.N. Criticism of Israel's Construction Plan," *New York Times*, March 8, 1997, p. A3.

19 G. A. Res. 51/223, March 13, 1997. Paul Lewis, "Israel's Plan for Jerusalem Is Condemned by Assembly," *New York Times*, March 14, 1997, p. A12.

20 *Security Council Official Records*, 52nd year, 3756th mtg., p. 6, March 21, 1997, UN Doc. S/PV.3756 (1997). Paul Lewis, "U.S. Again Vetoes a Move by U.N. Condemning Israel," *New York Times*, March 22, 1997, p. A4.

21 G.A. Res. ES-10/2, April 25, 1997. "Israel Warned to Halt New Housing for Jews," *New York Times*, April 26, 1997, p. A4.

22 G. A. Res. ES-10/3, July 15, 1997.

30 Talks Fail: The Sword Replaces the Pen

1 Eric Silver, "Netanyahu Hits First Crisis over Cabinet Line-up," *Independent*, June 19, 1996, p. 10.

2 Interim Agreement on Trade and Trade-Related Matters between the European Community and the European Coal and Steel Community, of the One Part and the State of Israel, of the Other Part, *Official Journal of the European Communities* (L71, March 20, 1996), vol. 39, p. 2.

3 "Israel Angered by EU Call to Boycott Settlers' Produce," BBC Summary of World Broadcasts, May 15, 1998, from Voice of Israel, Jerusalem, in English, 0400 GMT, May 14, 1998 (available on LEXIS, News Library).

4   "EU/Israel: Plan for Embargo on Exports from Jewish Settlements," European Report, May 16, 1998 (available on LEXIS, News Library).

5   *Id.* Mark Dennis, "Breaking Through: Has the EU Found How to Make Netanyahu Listen?," *Newsweek*, June 15, 1998, p. 18.

6   G. A. Res. 52/250, July 13, 1998.

7   Cheryl A. Rubenberg, *The Palestinians In Search of a Just Peace* (2003), p. 83.

8   S. C. Res. 1435, September 24, 2002.

9   "Report of the Special Rapporteur of the Commission on Human Rights, Mr. John Dugard on the Situation of Human Rights in the Palestinian Territories Occupied by Israel since 1967," December 17, 2002, UN Doc. E/CN.4.2003/30.

10 "Concluding Observations of the Committee on Economic, Social and Cultural Rights: Israel," para. 15, May 23, 2003, UN Doc. E/C.12/1/Add.90. "Concluding Observations of the Human Rights Committee: Israel," para. 11, August 21, 2003, UN Doc. CCPR/CO/78/ISR.

11 "Concluding Observations of the Human Rights Committee: Israel," paras. 15, 16, 18, 19, August 21, 2003, UN Doc. CCPR/CO/78/ISR.

12 "Concluding Observations of the Committee on the Rights of the Child," para. 4, October 9, 2002, UN Doc. CRC/C/15/Add.195.

13 "Concluding Observations of the Committee on Economic, Social and Cultural Rights: Israel," para. 16, May 23, 2003, UN Doc. E/C.12/1/Add.90.

31   Jerusalem and the Settlements: Who Should Stay?

1   Basic Law: Jerusalem, Capital of Israel, *Laws of the State of Israel*, vol. 34, p. 209 (1980).

2   Temple Mount Faithful Association v. Attorney General, High Court 4185/90, 47(5) Piskei Din 221 (1993), summarized in Asher Felix Landau, "Israel's Rights on Temple Mount Undisputed," *Jerusalem Post*, November 15, 1993, p. 7.

3   UN Doc. A/43/827, S/20278 (1988).

4   Henry Cattan, *Palestine and International Law* (1973), pp. 64–73.

5   G. A. Res. 181, part 3, November 29, 1947.

6   Emergency Regulations (Land Requisition—Accommodation of State Institutions in Jerusalem) (Continuance in Force of Orders) Law, *Laws of the State of Israel*, vol. 4, p. 106 (1950). "Jerusalem Named Capital of Israel," *New York Times*, January 24, 1950, p. A1.

7   Musa Mazzawi, *Palestine and the Law: Guidelines for the Resolution of the Arab-Israel Conflict* (1997), pp. 202–218.

8   S. C. Res. 252, May 21, 1968.

9   Basic Law: Jerusalem, Capital of Israel, *Laws of the State of Israel*, vol. 34, p. 209 (1980).

10 S. C. Res. 478, August 20, 1980. G. A. Res. 35/169E, December 15, 1980.

11 S. C. Res. 476, June 30, 1980.

12 G. A. Res. 37/123F, December 20, 1982.

13 S. C. Res. 672, October 12, 1990.

14 "Report Submitted to the Security Council by the Secretary-General in Accordance with Resolution 672," para. 3, UN Doc. S/21919 (1990).

15 S. C. Res. 673, October 24, 1990.

16 B'tselem, *A Policy of Discrimination: Land Expropriation, Planning and Building in East Jerusalem* (1995), p. 1.

17 "Israeli Ministry Says 1967 East Jerusalemites "Permanent Residents" of Israel: Text of Report by Israeli Government Press Office Communicated by Tova Elinson, Interior Ministry Spokeswoman," 6 February 1997, BBC Summary of World Broadcasts, February 8, 1997 (available on LEXIS, News Library).

18 Gesetz vom 10. Juli 1945 über die Überleitung in die österreichische Staatsbürgerschaft (Staatsbürgerschafts-Überleitungsgesetz—St-ÜG) §1, 1945 Staatsgesetzblatt für die Republik Österreich (no. 59), p. 81.

19 Treaty of Peace between the State of Israel and the Arab Republic of Egypt, March 26, 1979, Annex I: Protocol concerning Israeli Withdrawal and Security Arrangements, art. 1, *Israel Law Review*, vol. 15, p. 306 (1980).

20 International Covenant on Civil and Political Rights, art. 7, UN Treaty Series, vol. 999, p. 171.

21 David K. Shipler, "Israel Completes Pullout, Leaving Sinai to Egypt," *New York Times*, April 25, 1982, p. A1.

22 William Claiborne, "Israel, Settlers Fail to Agree on Sinai Payments," *Washington Post*, January 12, 1982, p. A1.

23 Herb Keinon, "Unsettled Settlers: Many Will Go if the Price Is Right," *Jerusalem Post*, December 10, 1993, p. 2B.

24 Susan Hattis Rolef, "Back to Green Line Israel," *Jerusalem Post*, January 15, 1996, p. 6.

25 Treaty of Peace between the Allied and Associated Powers and Italy, art. 19(1), February 10, 1947, UN Treaty Series, vol. 49, p. 3.

26 *Loizidou v. Turkey* (merits), Judgment of December 18, 1996.

32 The Displaced: Where Will They Go?

1 John Fischer Williams, "Denationalization," *British Year Book of International Law*, vol. 8, p. 45, at p. 56 (1927). P. Weis, *Nationality and Statelessness in International Law* (1979), p. 47.

2 Universal Declaration of Human Rights, G.A. Res. 217A, art. 13, para. 2, UN Doc. A/810, p. 71 (1948).

3 International Covenant on Civil and Political Rights, art. 12, para. 4, UN Treaty Series, vol. 999, p. 171.

4 Ruth Lapidoth, "The Right of Return in International Law, with Special Reference to the Palestinian Refugees," *Israel Year Book on Human Rights*, vol. 16, p. 103, at p. 114 (1986).

5 Nationality of Natural Persons in Relation to the Succession of States, art. 5, G. A. Res. 55/153, December 12, 2000.

6 Ian Brownlie, "The Relations of Nationality in Public International Law," *British Year Book of International Law*, vol. 39, p. 284, at p. 320 (1963).

7 Rudolf Graupner, "Nationality and State Succession: General Principles of the Effect of Territorial Changes on Individuals in International Law," *Transactions of the Grotius Society*, vol. 32, p. 87 (1947).

8 Research in International Law, Harvard Law School, "Nationality, Responsibility of States, Territorial Waters: Drafts of Conventions Prepared in Anticipation of the First Conference on the Codification of International Law, The Hague, 1930," The Law of Nationality, art. 18, *American Journal of International Law*, vol. 23, p. 13 (Supplement 1929).

9 *Id.*, p. 61 (comment to art. 18).

10 F. A. Mann, "The Effect of Changes of Sovereignty upon Nationality," *Modern Law Review*, vol. 5, p. 218, at p. 221 (1941–42).

11 Convention concerning the Exchange of Greek and Turkish Populations (Lausanne), January 30, 1923, art. 1, *League of Nations Treaty Series*, vol. 32, p. 75.

12 E. Reut-Nicolussi, "Displaced Persons and International Law," *Recueil des cours* (Hague Academy of International Law), 1948(2), p. 1, at p. 29.

13 Stephen P. Ladas, *The Exchange of Minorities: Bulgaria, Greece and Turkey* (1932), p. 341.

14 UN Doc. A/648 (1948).

15 G. A. Res. 194, para. 11, December 11, 1948.

16 The Ambassador in France (Bruce) to the Secretary of State, Top Secret, June 12, 1949, *Foreign Relations of the United States 1949*, vol. 6, pp. 1124–1125.

17 Lapidoth, *supra* note 4, p. 116.

18 *General Assembly Official Records*, 3d Sess., Part I, C.1, Summary Records of Meetings 21 September–8 December 1948, p. 686, UN Doc. A/C.1/SR.205 (1948).

19 *General Assembly Official Records*, 3d Sess., Part I, C.1, Summary Records of Meetings 21 September–8 December 1948, p. 724, UN Doc. A/C.1/SR.209 (1948).

20 G. A. Res 3236, November 22, 1974.

21 S. C. Res. 242, November 22, 1967.

22 Eyal Benvenisti and Eyal Zamir, "Private Claims to Property Rights in the Future Israeli-Palestinian Settlement," *American Journal of International Law*, vol. 89, p. 295, at p. 326 (1995).

23 W. Thomas Mallison and Sally V. Mallison, *The Palestine Problem in International Law and World Order* (1986), p. 188.

24 Sarah Honig and David Makovsky, "Religious Issues Delay Coalition Deal," *Jerusalem Post*, June 17, 1996, p. 1 (quoting aide to Netanyahu). Dilip Hiro, "Netanyahu Considers Pre-emptive Strike on Clinton," Interpress Service, July 8, 1996 (quoting Netanyahu).

25 S. C. Res. 779, October 6, 1992.

26 "Report of the United Nations High Commissioner for Refugees," *General Assembly Official Records*, 33rd Sess., Supp. (No. 12), p. 14, UN Doc. A/33/12 (1978).

27 *General Assembly Official Records*, 3d Sess., Part I, Annexes to the Summary Records of Meetings, p. 69, UN Doc. A/C.1/398.Rev.2 (1948).

28 *General Assembly Official Records*, 3d Sess., Part I, C.1, Summary Records of Meetings 21 September–8 December 1948, p. 910, UN Doc. A/C.1/SR.226 (1948).

29 *Id.*, p. 906.

30 *Id.*, p. 912.

31 *Id.*, p. 910.

32 *Id.*, p. 909.

33 "General Framework for Peace in Bosnia and Herzegovina: Annex 7: Refugees and Displaced Persons," art. 1, December 14, 1995 (Dayton agreement), *International Legal Materials*, vol. 35, p. 75 (1996).

34 "Neubauer Welcomes Estonian President's Call as Model for Czechs," Czech News Agency, CTI National News Wire, October 10, 1995 (available on LEXIS, News Library).

35 V.M. Broshevan, *Deportatsiia zhitelei Kryma* [The Deportation of the Residents of Crimea], in *Krims'ki Tatari: Istoriia i suchasnist' (do 50-richchia deportatsii Krims'kotatars'kogo narodu): materiali mizhnarodnoi naukovoi konferentsii, Kiiv, 13–14 travnia 1994 r.* [The Crimean Tatars: History and the Present Day (towards the 50th Anniversary of the Deportation of the Crimean Tatar People: Materials of the International Scholarly Conference, Kiev, May 13–14, 1994], p. 44 (I. Kuras ed. 1995).

Index

About the Author. John Quigley is Professor, College of Law, and Adjunct Professor, Department of Political Science, The Ohio State University. He is the coauthor of *Treatment of Palestinians in Israeli Occupied West Bank and Gaza*, as well as several books on Soviet law.

Library of Congress Cataloging-in-Publication Data
Quigley, John B.
The case for Palestine : an international law perspective.—2nd ed.
p. cm.
Rev. and expanded ed. of: Palestine and Israel. 1990.
Includes bibliographical references and index.
ISBN 0-8223-3527-1 (cloth : alk. paper)
ISBN 0-8223-3539-5 (pbk. : alk. paper)
1. Arab-Israeli conflict. 2. Israel—History. 3. Palestinian Arabs—Israel. 4. West Bank. 5. Gaza Strip.
I. Quigley, John B. Palestine and Israel. II. Title.
DS119.7.Q7219   2005
956.04—dc22   2004021263